Associationism
and the
Literary Imagination

For Linda

ASSOCIATIONISM AND THE LITERARY IMAGINATION

FROM THE PHANTASMAL CHAOS

Cairns Craig

Edinburgh University Press

Edinburgh University Press Ltd
22 George Square, Edinburgh

Typeset by the Research Institute of Irish and Scottish Studies,
University of Aberdeen
and printed and bound by
Biddles Ltd, King's Lynn, Norfolk

A CIP record for this book is available from the British Library

ISBN 978 0 7486 0912 3 (Hardback)

Contents

Acknowledgments

This book revisits some of the issues I raised in my *Yeats, Eliot, Pound and the Politics of Poetry* published in 1982. After that time, my energies, both practical and intellectual, were taken up by the demands of Scottish culture in the dark days after the failure of the devolution referendum on a Scottish parliament in 1979, and almost all of my work since then – from my *History of Scottish Literature* in 1987 to *The Modern Scottish Novel* in 1999 – was directly concerned with Scottish literature and culture. As a result, I did not expect to engage again with issues relating to associationist philosophy and psychology. My return to the aesthetic consequences of British empirical philosophy was inspired first by a conference in honour of George Davie, on the topic of 'Empiricism and its Legacy', organised by Alexander Bird in Edinburgh in 1996, and then by an invitation from Jeffrey Andrew Barash to contribute to a special issue of the *Revue de Métaphysique et de Morale* which he was editing on the topic of *Mémoire, histoire* in 1998. In working on these I discovered that not only were the implications of associationism more far-reaching than I had previously argued, but that the major criticism of my earlier book – that it was impossible to accept the influence of an eighteenth-century theory of taste on modernist poetry – deserved less credence than I had been prepared to allow it. I am extremely grateful, therefore, to Professors Bird and Barash for their stimulus to my continued exploration of the topic, and to my rediscovery of just how rooted these arguments were in a Scottish context.

Almost all of the research for the book was done in Edinburgh during my time as Head of the English Literature Department, and I hope that it adequately reflects the intellectual and professional support of my former colleagues – especially Randall Stevenson, Ian Campbell, Colin Nicholson, Penny Fielding, Susan Manning, Ken Millard and Aileen Christianson – who, though they may not have realised it, contributed substantially to my thinking on these matters. And to those colleagues and students in Edinburgh who were members of the 'Friday Reading Group' at the Centre for the History of Ideas in Scotland between 1997 and 2005, I am particularly indebted, since many of the issues that this book raises were drawn to my attention in our discussions of nineteenth- and twentieth-century Scottish philosophy and theology. Especially, I would like to thank David Fergusson, Donald Rutherford, Ronald Turnbull, John Gordon, Alex Thomson, Laurence Nicol and Gavin Miller for helping sustain the kind of intellectual community that is all too often impossible in contemporary university environments.

The writing of *Associationism and the Literary Imagination* was supported by sabbatical leave from the University of Edinburgh and by an award from the (then) Arts and Humanities Research Board, to both of whom I am extremely grateful. I am also deeply indebted (as ever) to Jackie Jones and her colleagues at Edinburgh University Press for their patience, as my return to the University of Aberdeen in 2005 disrupted completion of the manuscript. Equally, without the unstinting support of the staff of the National Library of Scotland, Edinburgh University Library and Aberdeen University Library the book – at least in this form – would have been impossible. And my special thanks to Jon Cameron of the AHRC Centre for Irish and Scottish Studies at the University of Aberdeen, both for helping create the space in a hectic schedule for getting the book finished and for assistance in completing its production.

The theme of the book is association, and its writing will, for me, always be associated with the person whose life has been entwined with its production – Conan Craig, now aged four. And with the person to whom it is dedicated, my wife Linda.

Abbreviations

AC: Northrop Frye, *Anatomy of Criticism: Four Essays* (Princeton: Princeton University Press, 1957).

AET: Archibald Alison, *Essays on the Nature and Principles of Taste,* 2 Vols (Edinburgh: Bell and Bradfute, 1811; 1790).

Au: John Stuart Mill, *Collected Works of John Stuart Mill,* 33 Vols, Vol. I, *Autobiography and Literary Essays,* ed. John M. Robson and Jack Sillinger (Toronto: University of Toronto Press, 1981).

BL: Samuel Taylor Coleridge, *Biographia Literaria or Biographical Sketches of My Literary Life and Opinions,* ed. James Engell and W. Jackson Bate, *Collected Works of Samuel Taylor Coleridge,* Vol. 7:1 (Princeton: Princeton University Press, 1983; 1817).

CI: I. A. Richards, *Coleridge on Imagination* (London: Kegan, Paul, Trench, Trubner, 1934).

DC: Charles Dickens, *The Personal History of David Copperfield,* ed. Trevor Blount (Harmondsworth: Penguin, 1966).

DR: Gilles Deleuze, *Difference and Repetition,* trans. Paul Patton (London: Continuum, 2004; 1968).

E: David Hume, *Essays Moral, Political and Literary,* ed. Eugene F. Miller (Indianapolis: Liberty Fund, 1985).

EHU: David Hume, *Enquiries Concerning the Human Understanding and Concerning the Principles of Morals,* ed. L. A. Selby-Bigge (Oxford: Clarendon Press, 1962; 1777).

ETEC: Leslie Stephen, *English Thought in the Eighteenth Century,* 2 Vols (London: Smith, Elder and Co., 1902; 1876).

GET: Alexander Gerard, *An Essay on Taste* (Menston, Yorkshire: Scolar Press, 1971; 1759).

HM: James Ward, *Heredity and Memory* (Cambridge: Cambridge University Press, 1913).

HPW: Francis Hutcheson, *Philosophical Writings*, ed. R. S. Downie (London: J. M. Dent, 1994).

ML: M. H. Abrams, *The Mirror and the Lamp: Romantic Theory and the Critical Tradition* (New York: W. W. Norton & Co., 1958; 1953).

O: David Hartley, *Observations on Man, his Frame, his Duty, and his Expectations* (London: S. Richardson, 1749).

OD: George Steiner, *On Difficulty and Other Essays* (Oxford: Oxford University Press, 1972).

PC: I. A. Richards, *Practical Criticism* (London: Kegan Paul, Trench, Trubner, 1929).

PLC: I. A. Richards, *Principles of Literary Criticism* (London: Routledge 1967; 1924).

PP: James Ward, *Psychological Principles* (Cambridge: Cambridge University Press, 1918).

PR: I. A. Richards, *The Philosophy of Rhetoric* (Oxford: Oxford University Press, 1936).

RN: Thomas Hardy, *Return of the Native* (London: Macmillan, 1974; 1878)

RX: John Livingston Lowes, *The Road to Xanadu: A Study in the Ways of the Imagination* (2nd edition, London: Constable, 1951; 1927).

T: David Hume, *A Treatise of Human Nature*, ed. L. A. Selby-Bigge (Oxford: Clarendon Press, 1888).

SR: Thomas Carlyle, *Sartor Resartus,* ed. Roger L. Tarr (Berkeley: University of California Press, 2000; 1833).

TL: Virginia Woolf, *To the Lighthouse* (Harmondsworth: Penguin, 1964; 1927).

TS: Laurence Sterne, *The Life and Opinions of Tristram Shandy,* ed. Graham Petrie (London: Penguin, 1967; 1760).

TW: Virginia Woolf, *The Waves*, ed. Gillian Beer (Oxford: Oxford University Press, 1992).

U: James Joyce, *Ulysses*, ed. Hans Walter Gabler (London: Penguin, 1986).

VI: W. K. Wimsatt, *The Verbal Icon: Studies in the Meaning of Poetry* (London: Methuen, 1970; 1954).

WIG: Sydney Owenson, Lady Morgan, *The Wild Irish Girl*, ed. Kathryn Kirkpatrick (Oxford: Oxford University Press, 1999; 1806).

WW: *William Wordsworth*, ed. Stephen Gill (Oxford: Oxford University Press, 1984).

Introduction:
A Chain of Associations

In his *Autobiography* John Stuart Mill recounts how, in the autumn of 1826, at the age of twenty, he suffered the onset of a depression – 'a dull state of nerves . . . unsusceptible to enjoyment or pleasurable excitement'[1] – which was to continue during the following two years. Thirty years later Mill thought that 'in all probability my case was by no means so peculiar as I fancied it' but the 'idiosyncracies of my education had given to the general phenomenon a special character, which made it seem the natural effect of causes that it was hardly possible for time to remove' (*Au*, 145). Those 'idiosyncracies' derived from the theories of his father, James Mill, Scottish psychologist and proponent of the Utilitarian social philosophy of Jeremy Bentham: the elder Mill undertook the education of his son himself, determined to prove that a child could acquire 'an amount of knowledge in what are considered the higher branches of education, which is seldom acquired (if acquired at all) until the age of manhood' (*Au*, 33). The younger Mill's prodigious knowledge of classics and of political economy when only in his teens was apparent testimony to the benefits of his father's educational practices, giving him what he himself described as the 'advantage of a quarter of a century over my contemporaries' – despite the fact that he rated himself in 'natural gifts' as 'rather below than above par' (*Au*, 33). His precocious emergence as a radical commentator in the *Westminster Review* in the early 1820s suggested someone whose career would be devoted to advancing the political implications of the principles of which

---

[1] John Stuart Mill, *Autobiography and Literary Essays, Collected Works of John Stuart Mill*, 33 Vols, Vol. I, ed. John M. Robson and Jack Sillinger (Toronto: University of Toronto Press, 1981), 137; hereafter cited in the text as *Au*.

he was himself such an outstanding example. Indeed, when he read Bentham's works in 1821, the younger Mill was convinced that he had discovered his 'object in life; to be a reformer of the world' (*Au*, 37), an object which, he believed, would assure his own happiness by identifying it with 'something durable and distant, in which some progress might be always making, while it could never be exhausted by complete attainment' (*Au*, 137). And yet, in that 'dry heavy dejection of the melancholy winter of 1826–7' (*Au*, 143), it appeared that 'the whole foundation on which my life was constructed fell down'. The 'happiness' that he had expected to find in his devotion to social reform disappeared: 'The end had ceased to charm, and how could there ever again be any interest in the means? I seemed to have nothing left to live for' (*Au*, 139).

Ironically, the years of John Stuart Mill's depression were the years when his father was writing the book that codifed the psychological principles on which the younger Mill's education had been based – *The Analysis of the Phenomena of the Human Mind*, eventually published in 1829. For James Mill, in his son's words, all experience can be reduced to 'sensations, ideas of sensation and association' and these between them 'generate and account for the principal complications of our mental nature'.[2] In its analytical reductionism, tracing all the phenomena of mind back to 'sensation' and the way these are associated together as ideas, Mill's psychology stands squarely in the tradition of British empiricism, and the younger Mill's crisis has been read as symptomatic of the flaws in empiricist accounts of the mind. Indeed, it was to the very process of 'analysis' as invoked in James Mill's title that the younger Mill attributed his illness, since analysis 'has a tendency to wear away the feelings' (*Au*, 141), in such a way that though it is 'favourable to prudence and clearsightedness', it is 'a perpetual worm at the root of both the passions and of the virtues' (*Au*, 142).

Mill's crisis has come to be read as more than merely personal. It has been taken to be symbolic of a general crisis in nineteenth-century culture: J. S. Mill was, as F. R. Leavis put it, 'a great representative figure in Victorian intellectual history',[3] and what he represents are the destructive consequences of utilitarianism's conception of the human mind and of the aims and purposes of

---

2 James Mill, *Analysis of the Phenomena of the Human Mind, A new edition with notes illustrative and critical by Alexander Bain, Andrew Findlater, and George Grote*; edited with additional notes by John Stuart Mill, 2 Vols (London: Longman, Green, Reader and Dyer, 1869; 1829), Vol. 1, x.

3 F. R. Leavis (ed.), *Mill on Bentham and Coleridge* (London: Chatto & Windus, 1950), 12.

education. At the very time that Mill was writing his *Autobiography* in the 1850s, utilitarian education was to be famously parodied by Charles Dickens in *Hard Times*: 'Herein lay the spring of the mechanical art and mystery of educating the reason without stooping to the cultivation of the sentiments and affections. Never wonder. By means of addition, subtraction, multiplication, and division, settle everything somehow, and never wonder'.[4] Dickens's Gradgrind, who gives voice to this philosophy of 'reason', was compared directly with James Mill by Leavis, who regarded John Stuart Mill's *Autobiography* as the account of a heroic survivor of utilitarianism's refusal to acknowledge the emotions: 'he worked indefatigably to correct and complete Utilitarianism by incorporating into it the measure of truth attained by the other side'.[5] In Mill's struggle towards recovery, in his growing recognition 'that the passive susceptibilities needed to be cultivated as well as the active capacities', and that, as a consequence, 'the cultivation of the feelings became one of the cardinal points in my ethical and philosophical creed' (*Au*, 147), Leavis saw a profound support to his own arguments about the importance of a literary education. For it was literature which was crucial to Mill's recovery: to convey the nature of his depression Mill quotes two lines from Coleridge – 'Work without hope draws nectar in a sieve,/And hope without an object cannot live' – and he records how this 'state of my thoughts and feelings made the fact of my reading Wordsworth for the first time (in the autumn of 1828) an important event in my life' (*Au*, 149). Wordsworth's poems provided 'a medicine for my state of mind' because 'they expressed, not mere outward beauty, but states of feeling, and of thought coloured by feeling, under the excitement of beauty. They seemed to be the very culture of the feelings, which I was then in quest of' (*Au*, 151). Push-pin may have been as good as poetry to Bentham, as long it generated the greatest happiness of the greatest number, but to John Stuart Mill, poetry was productive of a more specific and personal happiness: 'I long continued to value Wordsworth less according to his intrinsic merits, than by the measure of what he had done for me' (*Au*, 153).

The importance of Coleridge in defining for Mill the nature of his illness, and of Wordsworth in helping him recover from it, has been taken as proof of the superiority of the psychology and the aesthetics of the first generation of English romantics over those of Bentham and James Mill. In particular, it has

---

[4] Charles Dickens, *Hard Times*, ed. David Craig (Harmondsworth: Penguin, 1969; 1854), 89.

[5] Leavis, *Mill on Bentham and Coleridge*, 11–12.

been taken as proof that the 'associationism' on which James Mill's conception of the mind was based could not provide a sufficient foundation for the
kind of cultural wholeness towards which the younger Mill was struggling. In
The Cambridge Companion to Victorian Poetry, for instance, Joseph Bristow argues
that the elder Mill's insistence that 'all mental and moral feelings and qualities,
whether of a good or a bad kind, were the results of association'[6] is replaced
in the son's criticism by a belief that 'the object of poetry is confessedly to act
upon the emotions'[7] – as though the latter were entirely incompatible with the
former. As a consequence, James Mill's psychological associationism is generally treated as already outmoded by the time of the publication of the *Analysis*
in 1829 – it is, as it were, the last leftover of what is a fundamentally eighteenth-
century conception of the mind, one transcended by the developments of
the romantic movement. Even so well-founded a book as Alan Richardson's
British Romanticism and the Science of the Mind starts from the assumption that
associationism can be no more than a residual element in the development
of the new neural science – inaugurated 'by F. J. Gall in Austria, Pierre-Jean-
George Cabanis in France, and Erasmus Darwin and Charles Bell in England'
– which inspired romantic artists by emphasising that 'that the mind is an
active processor, rather than passive register, of experience'.[8] By the 1820s,
William Lawrence's famous lectures on physiology, reveal, for Richardson,
'how dated the mechanistic, sensationalist psychology of eighteenth-century
associationism has become within the London medical community'.[9] Yet, far
from discarding his father's psychology, John Stuart Mill reissued the *Analysis
of the Phenomena of the Human Mind* in 1869, with additional notes by himself and Alexander Bain, one of the key contributors to the development of
experimental psychology in mid-Victorian Britain. In his 'Introduction' to this
edition, Mill defended the integrity of his father's scientific methodology:

> Not only is the order in which the more complex mental phenomena fol-
> low or accompany one another, reducible, by an analysis similar in kind to

---

[6] Joseph Bristow (ed.), *The Cambridge Companion to Victorian Poetry* (Cambridge:
Cambridge University Press, 2000), 'Reforming Victorian Poetry: poetics
after 1832', 1–24, 12.

[7] John Stuart Mill, 'Thoughts on Poetry and its Varieties', *Autobiography and
Literary Essays*, 344.

[8] Alan Richardson, *British Romanticism and the Science of the Mind* (Cambridge:
Cambridge University Press, 2001), 5, 6.

[9] Ibid., 27.

the Newtonian, to a comparatively small number of laws of succession among simpler facts, connected as cause and effect; but the phenomena themselves can mostly be shown, by an analysis resembling those of chemistry, to be made up of simpler phenomena.[10]

And he went on to suggest that from his father's work stemmed the most important developments in contemporary psychology, 'especially the work of two distinguished thinkers in the present generation, Professor Bain and Mr Herbert Spencer; in the writings of both of whom, the Association Psychology has reached a still higher development'.[11] Rather than recovering from the debilitating effects of associationism through the influence of poetry, Mill explained both his own recovery, and poetry itself, by the workings of association as described by his father. Mill's admiration for Coleridge never tempted him to accept Coleridge's *a priori* conception of the mind, and in the essay in which he declared Coleridge to be one of the seminal figures of nineteenth-century thought Mill also declared that 'the truth on this much-debated question lies with the school of Locke and Bentham', since there is 'no ground for believing that anything can be the object of our knowledge except experience'.[12] In an appropriately unassertive footnote he also added (as though the author was someone to whom he had no relation) that 'the solution of the problems of the operation of the mind was best to be found in the *Analysis of the Human Mind* by the late Mr. Mill'.[13] Indeed, John Stuart Mill's *Logic*, which was published in 1843 and which was to become a foundational text for British philosophy and psychology for a generation, vigorously reasserts, as Christopher Turk has noted, 'the classic epistemology of associationsim, and even the organization of his argument follows his father's *Analysis*'.[14]

The construction of intellectual history which has read in John Stuart Mill's crisis of 1826 the overthrow of associationist psychology, as represented by his father's philosophy of the mind, have halted at only the introductory stages of Mill's autobiography: writing of his 'duty to philosophy and the memory of my father' which led to the reissue of the *Analysis*, Mill comments:

---

[10] Mill, *Analysis of the Phenomena of the Human Mind*, Vol. 1, viii.

[11] Ibid., xviii–xix.

[12] 'Coleridge', *Collected Works of John Stuart Mill*, Vol. X, *Essays on Ethics, Religion and Society* (Toronto: University of Toronto Presss, 1969), 128.

[13] Ibid., 130.

[14] Christopher Turk, *Coleridge and Mill: A Study of Influence* (Aldershot: Avebury, 1988), 74.

Having been originally published at a time when the current of meta-physical speculation ran in a quite opposite direction to the psychology of Experience and Association, the *Analysis* had not obtained the amount of immediate success which it deserved, though it had made a deep impression on many individual minds, and had largely contributed, through those minds, to create that more favourable atmosphere for the Association Psychology of which we now have the benefit. (*Au*, 287–8)

Whatever modifications Mill made to Utilitarianism, he remained committed to an associationist psychology, and committed to it as the one which provided the most scientific – and therefore also the most *modern* – account of the mind. Far from having been made redundant by developments in the first third of the nineteenth century, associationism was so much the *dominant* psychological theory of the last third of that century that it is against 'associationism' that the new psychologies of the early twentieth century – whether Henri Bergson's, William James's or even Sigmund Freud's – strove to distinguish themselves. To follow the development of nineteenth-century literature, to understand the emergence of modernism and modern literary criticism in the twentieth century, we have to restore to its proper place the dominant intellectual context of both early and late nineteenth-century British culture – an empiricist phi-losophy and an associationist psychology. And we have to recognise that these were neither eighteenth-century survivals nor, as Rick Rylance has implied, the 'tired, reluctant, or makeshift' remains coming at the 'end of this tradition',[15] but one of the most vigorous, influential and productive elements in British thought in the second half of the nineteenth century, one whose success in extending the scientific understanding of the mind exerted a profound influ-ence across the whole range of humanistic disciplines.

When John Stuart Mill came, thirty years later, to probe the nature of his depression of 1826, what he discovered was that it was *not* his father's associative version of the mind that was the problem, but that his analytic emphasis had put severe constraints precisely on the encouragement and development of his *associations*: 'Analytic habits may thus even strengthen the associations between causes and effects, means and ends, but tend altogether to

---

[15] Rick Rylance, *Victorian Psychology and British Culture, 1850–1880* (Oxford: Oxford University Press, 2000), 187. Rylance actually suggests that 'it would be wrong to suggest' such things of Bain's psychology, but leaves the impression that only Bain's personal enthusiasm – rather than the intellectual relevance of associationism – prevents their being true.

weaken those which are, to speak familiarly, a *mere* matter of feeling' (*Au*, 143). Such 'mere feelings' could not be enhanced by adopting a transcendentalist philosophy but could be developed only by encouraging certain elements in Mill's own associations in order to produce 'a due balance among the faculties' (*Au*, 147). Thus what is redemptive in Wordsworth's poetry for Mill is not that he learns *new* emotions from it but that it helps him recollect his pre-existing 'love of rural objects and natural scenery, to which I had been indebted . . . for much of the pleasure of my life' (*Au*, 151); rather than the poetry introducing him to nature, it is 'the power of rural beauty' that provided 'a foundation for taking pleasure in Wordsworth's poetry' (*Au*, 151). What poems and nature together prove, for Mill, is not the negation, or even the limitation of his previous intellectual life, but its underlying validity: 'the delight which these poems gave me, proved that with culture of this sort, there was nothing to dread from the most confirmed habit of analysis' (*Au*, 153). In the resolution of his crisis, poetry was not a replacement for Mill's previous beliefs but a justification of them: 'Whom, then, shall we call poets?' he asks in 'Thoughts on Poetry and Its Varieties', written in 1833, five years after his recovery from depression. The answer reveals how the associationist psychology of the father remains the foundation of the son's thinking: 'Those who are so constituted, that emotions are the links of association by which their ideas, both sensuous and spiritual, are connected together' (*Au*, 356). 'What constitutes the poet', Mill states later in the same essay, 'is not the imagery nor the thoughts, nor even the feelings, but the law according to which they are called up' (*Au*, 361–2) – the law of association by which 'the succession of his ideas is subordinate to the course of his emotions' (*Au*, 362).

Far from escaping his depression by overthrowing his father's association-ist psychology, Mill interpreted his depression *by means* of that associationist psychology. When he insists that there may have been 'greater poets than Wordsworth' in his own age, 'but poetry of deeper and loftier feeling could not have done for me at that time what his did', what he acknowledges is that the purpose of the poetry was to recall for him his own earlier memories, to re-activate and strengthen his healthy associations with the world of nature – his 'love of rural objects', his 'ideal of natural beauty' in mountains, learned from his 'early Pyrenean excursion', his 'interest in . . . the common feel-ings and common destiny of human beings' (*Au*, 152–3). In responding to Wordsworth in this way, Mill is enacting precisely what associationist theo-ries of art insisted on, that our aesthetic experiences are dependent not on the nature of the work of art itself, but on its ability to stimulate our powers of recollection – poetry 'is interesting only to those to whom it recals what they have felt' (*Au*, 345). What stimulates this associative recall in the reader, however, will have been produced by a mind which is poetic because in it 'thoughts and images will be linked together' not by reason or by logic but 'according to the similarity of feelings which cling to them. A thought will introduce a thought by first introducing a feeling which is allied with it' (*Au*, 357). The reader's mind strives to emulate the poet's mind, which exemplifies, for Mill, 'a well-known law of association, that the stronger a feeling is, the more quickly and strongly it associates itself with any other object or feeling' (*Au*, 357). Association is the fundamental law both of the mind and of poetry.

II

In his 'Introduction' to the *Analysis of the Phenomena of the Human Mind*, John Stuart Mill traced the intellectual lineage of his father's associationism to 'Hobbes and Locke, who are the real founders of that view of the Mind which regards the greater part of its intellectual structure as having been built up by Experience', and whose names are 'identified with the great fundamental law of Association of Ideas'.[16] James Mill's specific debt, however, was to David Hartley, who 'was the man of genius who first clearly discerned that this is the key to the explanation of the more complex mental phenomena',[17] though Hartley's theories were restricted in their influence by the fact that their 'publication so nearly coincided with the commencement of the reaction against the Experience psychology, provoked by the hardy scepticism of Hume'.[18] Hume's *A Treatise of Human Nature* had been published in 1739 (falling, in his own words, 'dead-born from the press'),[19] a decade before Hartley's *Observations on Man, his Frame, his Duty, and his Expectations* in 1749, and though Hartley does not acknowledge Hume's influence both were attempts to apply to the human mind – and, in Hartley's case, to the human brain – the methods that had proved so strikingly successful in Newtonian physics. Hume's *Treatise* is subtitled 'An attempt to introduce the experimental Method of Reasoning

---

[16] Mill, *Analysis of the Phenomena of the Human Mind*, Vol. I, x.

[17] Ibid., x–xi.

[18] Ibid., xii.

[19] David Hume, *Essays Moral, Political and Literary*, ed. Eugene F. Miller (Indianapolis: Liberty Fund, 1985), xxiv; hereafter cited in the text as *E*.

into Moral Subjects'[20] and Hartley acknowledges that his theory 'is taken from the hints concerning the performance of sensation and motion, which Sir *Isaac Newton* has given at the End of his *Principia*, and in the *Questions* annexed to his *Optics*'.[21] Both attribute the fundamental organisation of the mind to the 'association of ideas', since, as Hume puts it, 'all simple ideas may be separated by the imagination, and may be united again in what form it pleases, were it not guided by some universal principles, which render it, in some measure, uniform with itself' (*T*, 10). The three forms of those 'universal principles' by which the mind moves from one idea to another are 'resemblance, contiguity and cause and effect', and these provide 'a kind of ATTRACTION, which in the mental world will be found to have as extraordinary effects as in the natural, and to shew itself in as many and as various forms' (*T*, 12–13). The experimental methods and empirical aims of Newtonian physics can thus be transferred to the mental world, with the 'hope, therefore, that, by pursuing and perfecting the doctrine of associations, we may some time or other be enabled to analyse all that vast variety of complex ideas, which pass under the name of ideas of reflection, and intellectual ideas, into their simple compounding parts, *i.e.* into the simple ideas of sensation, of which they consist' (*O*, 75–6). 'Association' governs our emotions – our 'passions' – as effectually as it does our ideas; it provides the building blocks of mind and society: understanding its operations will explain the workings of both and provide the resources to shape and organise them better.

If a mid-eighteenth-century public took little notice of Hume's and Hartley's theories, the language of 'association' was to become, by the end of the century, a common component of philosophical and, indeed, political discourse, and to become central to the tradition that is now generally described as British Empiricism. In the work of the founder of that tradition, John Locke, 'association' had played only a minor role. Association was introduced by Locke in the fourth edition of his *Essay Concerning Human Understanding* (1700)[22] as a means of explaining 'something unreasonable in most men', something which substituted for the proper working of reason

---

[20] David Hume, *A Treatise of Human Nature*, ed. L. A. Selby-Bigge (Oxford: Clarendon Press, 1888); hereafter cited in the text as *T*.

[21] David Hartley, *Observations on Man, his Frame, his Duty, and his Expectations*, 2 Vols (London: James Leake and Wm. Frederick, 1749), 5; hereafter cited in the text as *O*.

[22] John Locke, *An Essay Concerning Human Understanding*, ed. Peter H. Nidditch (Oxford: Clarendon Press, 1975), Book II, Ch. xxxiii, 394.

a 'connexion of ideas wholly owing to *chance* or *custom*'.[23] For Locke, such connections were potentially dangerous, and the language of his description of them implies a kind of mental anarchy or terrorism: 'Ideas that in themselves are not at all of kin come to be so united in some men's minds that it is very hard to separate them; they always keep in company, and the one no sooner at any time comes into the understanding but its associate appears with it; and if they are more than two which are thus united, the whole gang, always inseparable, show themselves together'.[24] Such associations have none of the '*natural* correspondence and connexion with one another' which it is 'the office and excellency of our reason to trace',[25] and it is the business of the philosopher to help contain the contamination which they introduce into rational investigation. Hume and Hartley, however, reversed the relation between association and reason as presented by Locke, and instead of being disruptive of the efficient operation of reason, association is, for them, the foundation on which all mental activity, including reason, is built. The very tools of reason – language, number, symbolism and, indeed, relations of cause and effect – are simply the products of association, so that, for Hume, 'all our reasonings concerning causes and effects are deriv'd from nothing but custom' (*T*, 183), and for Hartley, 'rational assent then to any proposition may be defined a readiness to affirm it to be true, proceeding from a close association of the ideas suggested by the proposition, with the idea, or internal feeling, belonging to the word truth' (*O*, 324). Rather than a powerful reason imposing its order on 'gangs' of associations, reason is subservient to – or, indeed, the product of – those often uncontrollable gangs. For Hartley, 'a mathematical proposition, with the rational assent or dissent arising in the mind, as soon as it is presented to it, is nothing more than a group of ideas, united by association' (*O*, 328), and 'all reasoning, as well as affection, is the mere result of association' (*O*, 499). For Hume, the 'suppos'd pre-eminence of reason above passion' is based on the assumed 'eternity, invariableness, and divine origin of the former' as compared with the 'the blindness, unconstancy and deceitfulness of the latter' (*T*, 413); nonetheless, the power of association reveals 'the fallacy of all this philosophy', for 'Reason is, and ought only to be the slave of the passions, and can never pretend to any other office than to serve and obey them' (*T*, 415).

---

[23] Ibid., 394–5.
[24] Ibid., 395.
[25] Ibid.

The priority that association theory gave to the imagination – since association itself is nothing other than an operation of the imagination – as well as to the passions made it rapidly appealing in discussions of the origin and effects of art, and the contribution of associationism to the development of eighteenth-century theories of 'taste' has been well documented.[26] From early in the century, the Lockean notion of association was used as an explanation of the *failure* of individuals to have appropriate experiences of the beautiful. This is how Francis Hutcheson uses it in his *Inquiry Concerning Beauty, Order, Harmony, Design*, first published in 1725 and revised through four editions till 1738. For Hutcheson, beauty was the response of an 'internal sense' to 'complex ideas of objects',[27] characterised by 'uniformity amidst variety' (*HPW*, 15). The 'internal sense' theory provided the human mind with something like an organ fitted for the perception of beauty in exactly the same way that its other organs were fitted to receive sensations. This internal sense is 'natural to men' but clearly distinguishable from 'what we commonly call *reason*, or the external senses' (*HPW*, 5). It was, therefore, universally available to all normal human beings, even if subject to the same variations that occur in the other senses, where some have more acute hearing or more acute vision than others. In addition to such natural differences, however, which make some 'blind' to beauty, there are cases in which 'there is some accidental conjunction of a disagreeable idea which always recurs with that object, as in those wines to which men acquire an aversion after they have taken them in an emetic preparation' (*HPW*, 8). Such conjunctions deform the 'natural' response of the internal sense so that 'associations of ideas make objects pleasant or delightful which are not naturally apt to give any such pleasures; and in the same way, the casual conjunction of ideas may give a disgust where there is nothing disagreeable in the form itself' (*HPW*, 32). Thus, for Hutcheson, the improvement of an individual's 'taste' requires the casting off of all the unnatural (because accidental) conjunctions which the mind has acquired in the course of its experience, in

---

[26] See for instance, Walter Jackson Bate, *From Classic to Romantic* (Cambridge, MA: Harvard University Press, 1949); Martin Kallich, *The Association of Ideas and Critical Theory in Eighteenth-Century England* (The Hague: Mouton, 1970); Peter Kivy, *The Seventh Sense: A Study of Francis Hutcheson's Aesthetics and its Influence in Eighteenth-Century Britain* (Oxford: Clarendon Press, 2003; 1976); George Dickie, *The Century of Taste: The Philosophical Odyssey of Taste in the Eighteenth Century* (Oxford: Oxford University Press, 1996).

[27] Francis Hutcheson, *Philosophical Writings*, ed. R. S. Downie (London: J. M. Dent, 1994), 11; hereafter cited in the text as *HPW*.

order that the object of taste can be seen for what, in reality, it is. 'A Goth', he suggests, would be 'mistaken when from the effects of education he imagines the architecture of his country to be the most perfect; and a conjunction of some hostile ideas may make him have an aversion to Roman buildings' (*HPW*, 34), but the very fact that the Goth recognises the virtues of the architecture of his own country means that he is not without a sense of beauty; nor, indeed, is that achitecture without virtue, since there will still be discoverable in it some degree of the 'uniformity amidst variety' which underpins the Goth's response. In order to overcome his aversion to Roman architecture, however, and in order to recognise its superior combination of uniformity and diversity, the Goth will have to learn to uncouple his long-held 'unreasonable association' (*HPW*, 40), though the power of such unreasonable associations is such that 'there must be frequent reasoning with ourselves, or a long series of trials without any detriment, to remove the prejudice' (*HPW*, 40). In other words, the counterweight of accidental or environmental association is potentially much more powerful than the natural powers of the original inner sense, and would undermine the trustworthiness of anyone's sense of beauty were it not for the benevolence of a Creator who has so framed the world for mankind that 'all apparent beauty produced is an evidence of the execution of a benevolent design to give them the pleasures of beauty' (*HPW*, 30).

If Hume and Hartley's inversion of the value attributed to the elements of Locke's epistemology were correct, however, an equivalent inversion of Hutcheson's theory of beauty would reveal that the association of ideas could account not merely for *deficiencies* of taste but for all the aesthetic effects of nature and of art. Alexander Gerard's *Essay on Taste*, published in 1759, accepts the validity of Hutcheson's theory of the internal sense – 'Taste consists chiefly in the improvement of those principles, which are commonly called *the powers of imagination*, and are considered by modern philosophers as *internal* or *reflex senses*, supplying us with finer and more delicate perceptions, than any which can be properly referred to our external organs'[28] – but the workings of those 'powers of imagination' and the 'internal senses' are entirely governed by the force of association. Apparently 'wild and lawless as this faculty appears to be, it commonly observes certain general rules, associating chiefly ideas which *resemble*, or are *contrary*, or those that are conjoined, either merely by *custom*, or by the connection of their objects in *vicinity, coexistence,* or *causation*' (*GET*, 67–8).

---

[28] Alexander Gerard, *An Essay on Taste* (Menston, Yorkshire: Scolar Press, 1971; 1759), 1–2; hereafter cited in the text as *GET*.

Unlike Hutcheson, however, Gerard is interested not just in the *experience* of objects of taste but in their creation, and what characterises the artist is 'an extensive comprehensiveness of imagination, in a readiness of associating the remotest ideas, that are any way related. In a man of genius the uniting principles are so vigorous and quick, that whenever any idea is present to the mind, they bring into view at once all others, that have the least connection with it' (*GET*, 173). The diversity and distance of the associations which genius brings together will initially produce 'a rude and indigested chaos', as though all order has been undone and Locke's 'gangs' had taken control of the mental landscape. It is an image whose threat to social and mental stability will constantly recur in discussions of associationism but for Gerard the mind of genius 'designs a regular and well proportioned whole' (*GET*, 174) from the initial chaos of its associations, forming them to a single idea:

> Wherever fancy supposes, or perceives in ideas any of the uniting qualities just now mentioned, it readily, and with a kind of eagerness, passes from one idea to its associates; it bestows such a connection on them, that they become almost inseparable, and generally appear together. Their union is so strong, the transition from one to the other is so easy, that the mind takes in a long train of related ideas with no more labour than is required for viewing a single perception; and runs over the whole series with such quickness, as to be scarce sensible that it is shifting its objects. On this account, when a number of distinct ideas are firmly and intimately connected, it even combines them into a whole, and considers them as all together composing one perception. This is the origin of all our complex perceptions . . . All the objects that affect taste, and excite its sentiments, are certain forms or pictures made by fancy, certain parts or qualities of things, which it combines into complex modes. (*GET*, 168–9)

Rather than the objects of taste being characterised by Hutcheson's 'uniformity amidst variety', for Gerard they represent diversity *compounded into unity*: the artist, 'by compounding several distant ideas into one whole' (*GET*, 196), produces from an initially chaotic or random mass of associated material something which appears 'as all together composing one perception'.

Gerard's emphasis on 'compounded' in one of the earliest associationist accounts of art is of some importance because it is a regular complaint of opponents of associationism – one that we will encounter in later discussions – that it reduces experience to 'atomistic' and isolated units which are then linked together by a series of 'mechanical' connections that do not take account of the real complexity, and felt 'wholeness', of our inner experience. Though it is true that Hume and Hartley both believe that our experience can be *analysed* into constituent simple elements, and must originally derive from such simple elements, it is not these simple elements of which we are (most of the time) directly conscious. In the process of association, Hartley suggests, 'the simple ideas of sensation must run into clusters and combinations, by association; and that each of these will, at last, coalesce into one complex idea, by the approach and comixture of the several compounding parts' (*O*, 74). Indeed, as 'compounding' implies, the fundamental model is *chemical* rather than *mechanical*, an implication noted by John Stuart Mill: 'It was reserved for Hartley to show that mental phenomena, joined together by association, may form a still more intimate, and as it were chemical union – may merge into a compound, in which the separate elements are no more distinguishable as such, than hydrogen and oxygen in water; the compound having all the appearance of a phenomenon *sui generis*, as simple and elementary as the ingredients, and with properties different from any of them; a truth which, once ascertained, evidently opens a new and wider range of possibilities for the generation of mental phenomena by means of association'.[29] Mill may give priority to Hartley but for Hume too what we actually experience are 'compounds', which, like chemical compounds, can be analysed into their simpler components: 'When we analyze our thoughts or ideas' we will discover that 'however compounded or sublime, we always find that they resolve themselves into such simple ideas as were copied from a precedent feeling or sentiment'.[30] Thus the fact that 'among different languages, even where we cannot suspect the least connexion or communication, it is found, that the words, expressive of ideas, the most compounded, do yet nearly correspond to each other' is a 'certain proof that the simple ideas, comprehended in the compound ones, were bound together by some universal principle' (*EHU*, 23). Association does not simply thread ideas together like beads on a string: it *compounds* elementary sensations into complex unities which return to be further compounded in later associational contexts.

---

[29] John Stuart Mill, 'Bain's Psychology', in J. M. Robson (ed.), *Collected Works of John Stuart Mill*, Vol. XI, *Essays on Philosophy and the Classics*, 347. Originally published in the *Edinburgh Review*, October 1859.

[30] David Hume, *Enquiries Concerning the Human Understanding and Concerning the Principles of Morals*, ed. L. A. Selby-Bigge (Oxford: Clarendon Press, 1962; 1777), 19; hereafter cited in the text as *EHU*.

For both Hume and Hartley the ideas in trains of association may be either simple sensations or complex compounds, but their passage through the mind is more like the passage of a sentence, with all the requirements of connecting beginning to end, of understanding nuance and irony, than it is like the passage of a train under a bridge. The acquisition of written language is, for Hartley, not only 'a type of these associated combinations, but one part of the thing typified' (O, 320), and, in a comparison which will be used by many subsequent theorists, he links the development of the mind's associational framework to the development of the ability to read:

> Thus the reiterated impressions of the simple sensible pleasures and pains made upon the child, so as to leave their miniatures, or ideas, are denoted by his learning the alphabet; and his various associations of these ideas, and of the pleasures and pains themselves, by his putting letters and syl-lables together, in order to make words: and when association has so far cemented the component parts of any aggregate of ideas, pleasures and pains, together, as that they appear one indivisible idea, pleasure or pain, the child must be supposed by an analogous association to have learnt to read without spelling. (O, 319)

Language is formed by associations; associations form themselves into pat-terns with all the complexity of a language, and develop to maturity in the same way that our linguistic abilities develop.

> As the child's words become more and more polysyllabic by composition and decomposition, till at length whole clusters run together into phrases and sentences, all whose parts occur at once, as it were, to the memory, so his pleasures and pains become more and more complex by the combin-ing of combinations; and in many cases numerous combinations concur to form one apparently simple pleasure. (O, 319)

That associations are formed from elementary sensations is fundamental to an empiricist philosophy, but this does not mean that in the developed mind we are either conscious of or, indeed, able to discriminate, those elemen-tary particles, any more than we are able to perceive the atomic elements that constitute the objects of the natural world. What passes through the mind are complex combinations, having both vertical connections – like the connections of individual letters to sound, and sounds to meanings – and horizontal connections – like the connections of clauses in a sentence. Indeed, Hartley's conception of association involves a continuous reappropriation of past experience in which an association between two or more elements, once established, becomes a single experience, capable of being built into higher combinations in which the original elements are not only invisible, but have produced a level of meaning to which those original elements could not have aspired. Association, in other words, may operate in an apparently linear fashion – in trains or chains – but rather than uniform units passing steadily through the mind, calling up other units of a similar status, what we have are complex outcomes of previous associational connections – complex by the 'combining of combinations' – which produce an ever more richly *tex*tured experience, of whose underlying associational connections we are as unaware as the child is of the etymology of the words it acquires. Association may be the fundamental principle of the human mind but it does not remain the same in its operation through time: it is a self-enhancing, self-developing process which necessarily grows in complexity as long as the mind is able to recollect and reactivate past experiences in relation both to new external impressions and to new combinations of past experiences. Thus the 'sentences' of the mind's associational experiences become increasingly more dense, generating new combinations of an ever more complex layering of pasts in a present rich with anticipations of the future.

By taking the acquisition of language as the exemplary case of associa-tion-in-action and as a model of the growth of associational complexity, Hartley also challenges two other related criticisms of associationist psychol-ogy which we will regularly encounter in the following pages: first, that it is reductively mechanical and cannot account for the higher functions of the mind; second, that it presents the mind as a passive receiver of ideas and impressions over which it has no control, a passive receiver which could never rise to the complex condition of a 'self'. The 'mechanical' aspect of association theory, however, derives not directly from Hartley's account of association as such, but from his attempt to describe the ways in which mental events might have physical correlates. Being a medical practitioner, Hartley wanted to establish not just the ways in which ideas related to each other in the mind but the ways in which the mind was informed by the body. Since 'poisons, spiritous liquors, opiates, fever, blows upon the head, &c. all plainly affect the mind, by first disordering the medullary substance' (O, 9), it seemed reasonable to Hartley to suppose that associations were physical traces in the stuff of the brain, laid down by vibrations created when the body experiences any sensation. These traces would then be reactivated by memory, so 'that *vibrations* should infer *associations* as their effect, and *association* point to *vibrations* as its cause' (*O*, 6). This 'reduction' of the mental to the physical, of the spiritual to the mechanical was considered by many to involve a degradation of our conception of what it means to be a human being. Hartley, however, was well aware of how little the body's workings were understood, and accepted that 'if any other law can be made the foundation of association, or consistent with it, it may also be made consistent with the analysis of the intellectual pleasures and pains, which I shall here give' (*O*, 416). Indeed, his work was to achieve popularity largely through the efforts of Joseph Priestley, whose edition of the *Observations on Man*,[31] published in 1775, excises Hartley's mechanism of vibrations from the text, both because he thought more sophisticated scientific explanations were in the offing and in order better to promote the virtues of the principle of the association of ideas in its epistemological purity. Without the theory of 'vibrations', Hartley's associationism comes much closer to Hume's, which makes no assumption about the ultimate sources from which our ideas and impressions, and their patterns of association, derive.

Without the focus of the body, however, Hartley's theory, like Hume's, presents the self as 'nothing but a bundle or collection of different perceptions, which succeed each other with an inconceivable rapidity, and are in a perpetual flux and movement' (*T*, 252). This 'bundle' theory of the self is in turn often criticised as being as reductive as the physicalist conception of the mind, since it transforms an active person into a mere spectator of his or her own life. But for both Hume and for Hartley the 'self' is, as Richard C. Allen's has argued, an 'emergent'[32] category: the self comes into existence 'as a complex psychological structure of memories, thoughts, and especially dispositions', and 'arises out of a ground of purely physical responses to one's circumstances'.[33] The self is not a given: it is achieved through the increasing complexity that is generated as our emotions link diverse associational contexts and thereby create uniquely particular ways of responding to experience. The self comes into existence as the product of its compound associations, which

---

31 David Hartley, *Observations on Man*, ed. Joseph Priestley (London: J. Johnson, 1775).

32 Richard C. Allen, *David Hartley on Human Nature* (Albany: State University of New York Press, 1999): 'At the center of Hartley's *Observations* is a theory of the emergence and then transcendence of the self', 265.

33 Ibid., 265–6.

give it dispositions, expectations, and the 'readability' that allow us to predict how we and others will react in certain circumstances.

Allen's reading of Hartley follows the same trajectory as Norman Kemp Smith's radical re-reading of Hume, which first appeared as early as 1905 but was completed only with his major book, *The Philosophy of David Hume: A Critical Study of its Origins and Central Doctrines*, published in 1941. Kemp Smith argues that what is important in Hume's theory is,

> the doctrine that the determining influence in human, as in other forms of animal life, is feeling, not reason or understanding . . . 'Passion' is Hume's most general title for instincts, propensities, feelings, emotions and sentiments, as well as for the passions ordinarily so-called; and belief, he teaches, is a passion. Accordingly the maxim which is central to his ethics – 'Reason is and ought to be the slave of the passions' – is no less central to his theory of knowledge, being there the maxim: 'Reason is and ought to be subordinate to our natural beliefs'.[34]

The crisis of the *Treatise*, when Hume seems to despair of his own metaphysical speculations at the end of Book I, is not, therefore, the *reductio ad absurdam* of Hume's philosophy – as so many commentators have suggested – but Hume's dramatisation of the necessary failure of reason to surmount the challenges with which it is confronted. The isolated rational consciousness cannot make sense of the world because the sense of the world lies in human – and animal – passion, rather than in reason. The distressed philosopher must learn that 'since reason is incapable of dispelling these clouds' produced by metaphysical speculation, he must trust to nature and be determined not to 'seclude myself . . . from the commerce and society of men, which is so agreeable' (*T*, 269–70). It is in our interaction with other human creatures that our passions come into play, and reason, which 'alone can never produce any action or give rise to volition' (*T*, 414), mistakes its own role when it seeks to separate itself from that passional existence, when it reduces the self to a thinking thing instead of a social agent. The 'self' cannot be revealed by the introspection through which the philosopher inspects the workings of his own mind: it can only be discovered in the interactions of the social world.

---

[34] Norman Kemp Smith, *The Philosophy of David Hume: A Critical Study of its Origins and Central Doctrines* (London: Macmillan, 1966; 1941), 11.

It is an argument taken up by Gilles Deleuze in *Empiricism and Subjectivity* (1953), in which he argues for a distinction between the Humean mind in the process of introspection, when it is aware only of the flow of ideas and impressions, and the Humean *subject* which is generated out of the increasing complexity of its associational structures: 'The mind is not subject; it is subjected. When the subject is constituted in the mind under the effect of the principles [of association], the mind apprehends itself as a self, for it has been qualified'.[35] The self develops when impressions and ideas in the mind achieve a level of complexity which transforms the passive recipient of experience into a true subject, an active social being. As Constantin V. Boundas summarises it in his 'Introduction' to Deleuze's study, associations bring 'constancy to the mind' because 'they form habit, they establish belief, and they constitute the subject as an entity that anticipates'.[36] The inner associations of our psychological life are turned inside out to become the sociable associations of our public life.

For both Hartley and Hume, then, the self is the product of habits of association which, though fundamentally random in origin, emerge, like language itself, towards a level of relative stability, and as they do so allow the subject to engage actively with a world which shares in that relative stability. In this emergent world, however, boundaries are uncertain. Compound associations, like the words that are their models, are involved in a 'feedback loop' in which they are continually transformed by the contexts in which they participate, and the new connotations they thereby acquire.[37] The self is in continual transformation as its associations are recollected, re-experienced and re-ordered and since its associations are the products of the imagination, the self is, in essence, imaginary: 'the identity, which we ascribe to the mind of man, is only a fictitious one' (*T*, 259). To invoke the reliability of memory against this 'fictitious' identity can have no purchase in Hume's philosophy, since the boundaries between the remembered and the imagined are entirely porous: 'memory is known, neither by the order of its *complex* ideas, nor the nature of its *simple*

---

[35] Gilles Deleuze, *Empiricism and Subjectivity: An Essay on Hume's Theory of Human Nature*, trans. Constantin V. Boundas (New York: Columbia University Press, 1991; 1953), 31.

[36] Ibid., 'Introduction', 15.

[37] The word 'connotation' itself exemplifies this process, since it was invented by James Mill to identify the associations which cluster specifically around words, but gradually came to be used as an apparently more 'scientific' alternative to the language of association.

ones; it follows, that the difference betwixt it and the imagination lies in its superior force and vivacity' (*T*, 85). Memories can decay to the point where they will be believed to be imaginary; imagination can be sufficiently powerful to convince that it is memory, and our discussions of past events can proceed 'even supposing the impressions shou'd be entirely effac'd from memory' because 'the conviction they produc'd may remain' (*T*, 64). As a consequence, in Deleuze's reading of Hume, 'the world as such is essentially the Unique. It is a fiction of the imagination – never an object of the understanding'.[38] And precisely because the world can only ever be 'a fiction', association, despite the stabilities formed by habit, introduces a potentially disruptive uncertainty into our relations with the world, an uncertainty whose classic form is Hume's challenge to the 'necessary connexion' of cause and effect.

Having made cause and effect one of the three modes by which ideas are associated, because the mind moves easily in remembrance from a cause to its effect, Hume reverses the procedure by showing that there is no more connection between things in reality than there is between ideas as they arise in the mind. Cause and effect is simply the result of a constant conjunction between two events that leads us, by association, to expect one to follow on the other: there is no force or agency which we can discover that would *necessarily* link the cause and effect together. If it be the case that 'thought has evidently a very irregular motion in running along its objects, and may leap from the heavens to the earth, from one end of creation to the other, without any certain method or order' (*T*, 92), there can be no certainty that any particular idea or impression will call up the same train of association in the future that it produced in the past. Given the randomness of the imagination, 'we can at least conceive a change in the course of nature' (*T*, 89), so that 'there can be no *demonstrative* arguments to prove, *that those instances, of which we have had no experience, resemble those, of which we have had experience*' (*T*, 89). The self may be constituted by habit but it remains part of a world that is always potentially different from any of our expectations of it.

This dialectic in Hume between the power of habit, which establishes order and continuity, and the potential disruption of all known laws of nature, which generates uncertainty, has profound implications for art: it is the dynamic, transformative quality of association – Richard C. Allen describes Hartley's theory of the self as a 'dynamic system'[39] – which makes the question of

---

[38] Deleuze, *Empiricism and Subjectivity*, 75.
[39] Allen, *David Hartley on Human Nature*, 290.

'The Standard of Taste' such a key issue in eighteenth-century aesthetic theory. Written for a general rather than a 'philosophic' public, Hume's famous
essay on the topic does not deploy the details of an associationist conception
of art, but associationist theory lies behind its assertion that though 'every
voice is united in applauding elegance, propriety, simplicity, spirit in writing;
and blaming fustian, affectation, coldness, and a false brilliancy', the fixity of
these judgments rapidly dissolves 'when critics come to particulars', for then
'it is found that they had affixed a very different meaning to their expressions'
(E, 227). Personal associations interpose between the artwork and any general
judgment, as they interpose between our different usages of the same words,
and yet without those associations the artwork would not be experienced *as*
art at all, since, as Gerard had put it, '*Association* has a very great influence
on taste; and every philosopher, who examined the affections with tolerable
care, has remarked on the great dependence which they have on association'
(*GET*, 196–7). For Hume, cultural authority and shared education produce *a*
standard of taste, but it is one which can survive 'the different humours of particular men, the particular manners and opinions of our age and country'(*E*,
243) only because a cultural elite continues to ensure the effectiveness of a
shared classical culture and the common associations on which it draws. But
even within that elite 'it is almost impossible not to feel a predilection for that
which suits our particular turn and disposition' (*E*, 244). The only standard,
therefore, is a statistical one, the fact that, for 'a real genius, the longer his
works endure, and the more wide they are spread, the more is the admiration
which he meets with' (*E*, 233). The study of works that have lasted may help
improve our judgment but 'few are qualified to give judgment on any work
of art, or establish their own sentiment as the standard of beauty', because
'the organs of internal sensation are seldom so perfect as to allow the general
principles their full play' (*E*, 241). As a consequence, for Hume, 'Beauty is no
quality of things themselves. It exists merely in the mind which contemplates
them; and each mind perceives a different beauty' (*E*, 230). Beauty, as John
Stuart Mill recognised in his response to Wordsworth, is a function not of the
artwork itself but of the particular associations that are stimulated in the self
as it has been constituted by its previous habits of association.

    The relativism which Hume both acknowledges and resists in his account
of 'The Standard of Taste' was the logical conclusion of the transformation
of Hutcheson's 'internal sense' of beauty – with its universal experience of
'unity amidst diversity' merely obscured by individual association – to one in
which taste is *nothing other* than the effects of association, effects which can be

produced by any object in an appropriate observer. The cause of beauty and its effect are as unnecessary to one another as any other cause and effect: they are merely the product of an association of ideas which claims a constancy of conjunction that is even more fragile than the other constant conjunctions to which we attribute a necessary connection. Art is untethered: what it produces will be as different in each mind as those minds are different in their associational habits.

III

The rapid and decisive application of association theory to the understanding of art can be traced in two of the most influential discussions of aesthetic theory in the latter part of the eighteenth century, Joseph Priestley's *Oratory and Criticism* (1777), and Archibald Alison's *Essays on the Nature and Principles of Taste* (1790). Both explicitly base their accounts of aesthetic experience on an associationist psychology, and an exploration of the associationist theories set out in these texts will to help to reveal not only the immediate implications for art of the associationists' account of the mind but the limitations of many of the later characterisations of associationism by its critics.

Linking his work explicitly to Hartley's associationism, Priestley refuses to accept any internal sense of beauty and attributes all aesthetic effects to association. As already noted, many critics of associationism represent it as a *passive* conception of the mind, since it is entirely constrained on the one side by the 'impressions' addressed to it from the outside world and, on the other, by the laws of association which govern the ways in which ideas are generated in response to those impressions. Impressions and ideas 'arise' in the mind unbidden, not only beyond our control but beyond our understanding: in Hume's words, 'as to those *impressions*, which arise from the *senses*, their ultimate cause is, in my opinion, perfectly inexplicable by human reason' (*T*, 84). Priestley, however, was a political activist as well as a distinguished scientist (responsible for discovering 'oxygen') and his adoption of Hartleian associationism was not because of its passive virtues – though he did espouse its necessitarian consequences. For Priestley, aesthetic experience lies precisely in the *activity* of the mind, since the pleasure that the mind finds in the exercise of its own faculties is similar to the pleasure that we find in the exercise of our bodies. Works of literature which merely invite the reader to 'allow trains of ideas [to] pass before our minds', and in which 'no active powers of the soul are exerted' will be given over 'with disgust'.[40] The best works are those which most disturb our normal trains of association and force the mind into the active construction of new associative connections which are 'like its entering upon a new world'.[41] The power of a work of art lies in its ability to produce either unexpected ideas or familiar ideas in unexpected situations: where Hume's aesthetic assumes that association will work best where art develops familiar contexts of association – especially those of classical literature – Priestley argues that it is the *disruptive* effect of new associations which makes art interesting, precisely because it rouses the mind to a more intense state of activity in the attempt to organise the associations which are generated by novelty. Similarly, the sublime is effective because it demands that the mind try to match itself with 'great objects' and in doing so creates new experiences 'by the exercise they give to our faculties'.[42] This muscular associationism assumes that judgments of taste are, by and large, transpositions of bodily experience to intellectual activity, and that when our intellectual capacities are put to 'moderate exercise'[43] they give us a pleasure which cannot be produced by the indolence of passive association nor the pain of more demanding intellectual effort. It is an aesthetic which is thoroughly Hartleian, because it is founded on the fact that the mind is corporeal and experiences the same pleasure from the active exercise of its own capacities as does the body.[44]

Priestley's theory presumes that aesthetic experience is not in itself different from any other mental activity: it is the manner and the level of operation of the associations, rather than their nature, which it makes it pleasurable. It is therefore clear that the level of pleasure produced by works of art will depend as much on the constitution and experience of the recipient as it does on the elements of the work itself, and that even for a particular individual, the greater the fitness of the mind, the more pleasure it will take in demanding works and the less it will find in the easier ones which it might, at an earlier stage in its development, have enjoyed. Since the *work* of art is carried out as much in the

---

[40] Joseph Priestley, *A Course of Lectures on Oratory and Criticism* (Menston, Yorkshire: Scolar Press, 1970; 1777), 2.

[41] Ibid., 147.

[42] Ibid., 151.

[43] Ibid., 164.

[44] For an alternative view of Priestley's aesthetic, see Dabney Townsend, 'The Aesthetics of Joseph Priestley', *The Journal of Aesthetics and Art Criticism*, Vol. 51, No. 4 (Autumn 1993), 561–71. Townsend argues that Priestley's views are essentially Lockean and that the commitment to Hartley does not affect the Lockean construction of his conception of art.

reader as the artist, the artist will fail if he has 'left nothing to the exercise of the active faculties of his readers, [and] the whole excites nothing but a train of *passive perceptions*'.[45] Far from submitting to a passive conception of the self, associationist theories of art insist on the *activity* of the observer or recipient, an activity without which aesthetic experience would be impossible.

That active engagement of the reader in the production of the work of art is equally fundamental to Archibald Alison's account in his *Essays on Taste*, since 'the simple perception of the object, we frequently find, is insufficient to excite these emotions, unless it is accompanied with this operation of the mind, unless, according to common expression, our imagination is seized, and our fancy busied in pursuit of all those trains of thought, which are allied to this character or expression'.[46] It is the *busy-ness* of the mind which is crucial to the commencement of aesthetic experience. For Alison, however, that busyness is only possible as a result of the body's suspension from effort and the mind's from decision-making, thus allowing the associations 'to rise spontaneously in the mind, upon the prospect of any object to which they bear the slightest resemblance, and they lead it almost insensibly along, in a kind of bewitching reverie, through all its store of pleasing or interesting conceptions' (*AET*, 21). Suspension of the will allows the mind to discover the richness of its own associational potential, and it is the sheer quantity of associational material released in this suspension that constitutes aesthetic experience. Although the person is, therefore, passive, the mind itself is in a state of heightened activity and intensity, and, for Alison, as for Priestley, it is not the work of the artist to produce a completed or finished artefact but so to construct his work as to maximise this activity in the spectator or reader. As Francis Jeffrey summarised it in a review of the second edition of Alison's *Essays* in 1811 – a review which vastly increased the influence of Alison's theories, since it became the basis of the *Encyclopaedia Britannica*'s article on 'Taste' from 1824 till 1875 – 'the emotions which we experience from the contemplation of sublimity or of beauty, are not produced by any intrinsic quality in the objects we contemplate, but by the recollection or conception of other objects which are associated in our imaginations with those before us'.[47] In such a framework, *any* object is capable

---

45 Priestley, *Lectures on Oratory*, 141.

46 Archibald Alison, *Essays on the Nature and Principles of Taste*, 2 Vols (Edinburgh: Bell and Bradfute, 1811; 1790), Vol. 1, 2; hereafter cited in the text as *AET*.

47 Francis Jeffrey, *Edinburgh Review*, Vol. XVIII, No. XXXV (May 1811), 1–45, 3.

of being the focus of aesthetic experience for a mind sufficiently stimulated to produce those trains of associations which alone constitute the pleasure of 'taste' – an overturning of all 'essential' theories of art so radical that, as Samuel Monk noted as long ago as 1935, it represented 'the rise of a totally new attitude towards art',[48] one which was, in the words of Walter J. Hipple, to 'revolutionaize aesthetic speculation in Britain'.[49]

Alison does not acknowledge the influence of Hume – as a churchman, he could hardly attach his work to the notorious atheist. What he acknowledges is the influence of Thomas Reid, and Reid's analysis of 'active powers', which formed the basis of his argument against the representative theory of perception – 'the way of ideas' – of both Hume and Locke. But Reid's theories had been reshaped by his disciple Dugald Stewart into one which could also accommodate the pervasiveness of association in Hume's philosophy: 'When a train of thought takes its rise from an idea or conception, the first idea soon disappears, and a series of others succeeds, which are gradually less and less related to that with which the train commenced; but in the case of perception, the exciting cause remains steadily before us, and all the thoughts and feelings which have any relation to it, crowd into the mind in rapid succession, strengthening each other's effects, and all conspiring in the same general impression'.[50] For Stewart, it is to Hume that later thinkers are indebted for an understanding of the workings of the mind – 'the relations which connect all our thoughts together, and the laws which regulate their succession, were but little attended to before the publication of Mr Hume's writings'[51] – but Hume's theories have to be modified in the light of Reid's insistence that 'the mind by its nature was cognitively active and that, unlike matter, it was self-activating'.[52] As a result, associations allow us to understand the nature of the mind at work – the influence of 'the laws of Association', Stewart says, 'is so great that we may often form a pretty shrewd judgment concerning a man's prevailing turn of thought, from the transitions he makes in conversation or writing'[53]

[48] Samuel Monk, *The Sublime* (New York: Modern Language Association of America, 1935), 155.

[49] Walter J. Hipple, *The Beautiful, the Sublime and the Picturesque* (Carbondale: Southern Illinois University Press, 1957), 8.

[50] Sir William Hamilton (ed.), *The Collected Works of Dugald Stewart, Volume II, Elements of the Philosophy of the Human Mind*, Vol. I (Bristol: Thoemmes Press, 1994; 1854–60), 257.

[51] Ibid., 261.

[52] Ibid., Knud Haakonssen, 'Introduction', 9.

[53] Ibid., 267.

– but at the same time the mind is not passively constituted by its trains of associations: trains of associations can be *re-trained* in order that 'by means of habit, a particular associating principle may be strengthened to such a degree, as to give us a command of all the different ideas in our mind which have a certain relation to each other, so that when any one of the class occurs to us, we have almost a certainty that it will suggest the rest'.[54] Stewart was Alison's closest friend from their student days (at his family home in Ayrshire, Stewart introduced Alison to his near neighbour Robert Burns) and it is to Stewart's remodelling of Hume that Alison is indebted for a theory which insists that the operations of association represent 'a law of the human mind by which Nature plainly meant to put into the hands of every successive generation, the culture of the moral principles, and the formation of the moral habits of those to whom they have given existence'.[55] With this remodelling, in the words of George Dickie, 'a *fully* associationist theory of taste has come into being'.[56]

Despite widespread acknowledgment of the contribution that association-ist aesthetics made to the transformation of sensibility which accompanied the rise of romanticism – early 'romantic' works such as Samuel Rogers's *The Pleasures of Memory* (1792) are thoroughly associationist – associationism is regularly presented as a *prelude* to the emergence of a fully-formed romantic imagination, and of the modern conception of the nature and purpose of art, but one which ceased to be relevant on the arrival of the less 'mechanistic' conceptions of the psyche inspired by the philosophy of Immanuel Kant, and translated into British romanticism by Samuel Taylor Coleridge. Even before Mill's crisis of 1826, in other words, associationism is assumed to be of only historical interest – useful in understanding the eighteenth century's concern with 'taste' but irrelevant to the subsequent evolution of romantic or modernist literature.[57] In the 1830s, however, it was not only John Stuart Mill who continued to deploy an associationist framework. Arthur Hallam, the much lamented friend of Tennyson whose early death inspired *In Memoriam*, defended Tennyson's poetry from charges of obscurity in a review of *Poems, Chiefly Lyrical* which was published in *The Englishman's Magazine* of 1831. For Hallam, the problem in communication between poet and reader in mod-ern poetry – he is thinking primarily of the 'poets of sensation', like Shelley

---

[54] Ibid.

[55] Ibid., 522.

[56] Dickie, *Century of Taste*, 56.

[57] See, for instance, J. R. Watson, *English Poetry of the Romantic Period 1789–1830* (London: Longman, 1992), 13ff.

and Keats, whom he opposed to 'poets of reflection', such as Wordsworth – derives from the fact that the processes of association in poets' minds are far more subtle and complex than in the minds of most readers, 'producing a number of impressions too multiplied, too minute, and too diversified to allow of our tracing them to their causes, because just this was the effect, even so boundless, and so bewildering, produced on their imaginations by the real appearance of Nature'. To properly experience the work of such writers, the reader has to be able to replicate the process of association through which the poet composed the poem, and such a recapitulation is possible only because 'the emotions of the poet, during composition, follow a regular law of association'. As a consequence, with whatever difficulty, a diligent reader can follow the poet's associations 'up to the harmonious prospect of the whole, and to perceive the proper dependence of every step on that which preceded it', as long as that reader is able 'to clearly apprehend the leading sentiment in the poet's mind, by their conformity to which the host of suggestions are arranged'.[58] Reading becomes, for Hallam, the process of re-enacting the associative processes of the poet's mind in order to understand the unique associational connections by which all of the parts of the poem are linked, and the power of poetry lies in its ability to disrupt and reorganise the habitual associations by which the reader ordinarily experiences the world. Hallam's deployment of associationism is not merely incidental to his argument but foundational, for his surviving works are all deeply indebted to associationist thinking. His essay 'On Sympathy', for instance, begins by asking whether it is 'necessary to consider sympathy as an ultimate principle, or are there grounds for supposing it to be generated by association out of primary pleasures and pains'; the answer is that the latter supposition 'will perhaps give so clear an impression of the great powers of association, as to help very considerably the future investigation'.[59] As Isobel Armstrong has noted, Hallam's essay was rapidly repudiated by his own circle in favour of a more moralistic view of poetry but it was to become a key aesthetic document to later nineteenth-century

---

[58] A. H. Hallam, 'On Some Characteristics of Modern Poetry', *Englishman's Magazine* I (August 1831), 616–28; quoted from Isobel Armstrong (ed.), *Victorian Scrutinies* (London: Athlone Press, 1962), 88–9.

[59] *Remains in Verse and Prose of Arthur Henry Hallam* (London: John Murray, 1863), 97. Hallam concludes his essay by indicating how his argument would have been developed: 'I should then have detailed the gradual generation of the virtues from the primary feelings of sympathy, taking for my guide the principle of association' (110).

thinkers – 'the positions of Hallam's essay are taken up, fractured, developed and reappropriated by different formations in different and often contradictory ways throughout the century'.[60]

Opposed to Hallam's view of the poet's uniquely specialised associational processes, however, was an equally associationist aesthetic proposed by another reviewer of Tennyson's *Poems, Chiefly Lyrical* of 1830, W. J. Fox, who believed that 'a thought or an expression is poetical, exactly in proportion to its power of calling up . . . associations'.[61] He argued, however, for the poet's adoption of precisely those associations which would be most public and therefore most influential on the mass of the population. Poets, for Fox, can,

> Influence the associations of unnumbered minds; they can command the sympathies of unnumbered hearts; they disseminate principles; they can give those principles power over men's imaginations; they can excite in good cause the sustained enthusiasm that is sure to conquer; they can blast the laurels of the tyrants, and hallow the memories of the martyrs of patriotism; they can act with a force, the extent of which it is difficult to estimate, upon national feelings and character, and consequently upon national happiness.[62]

Whether poetry in the 1830s is conceived of as an aestheticist, elitist fortress which can only be entered by the few, or as a clarion call to political action and national assertion, the explanation of its power lies in its appeal to the reader's associational capacity.

Rather than being, therefore, a belated reiteration of David Hartley's guess, in 1749, at 'the influence of *association* over our opinions and affections, and its use in explaining those things in an accurate and precise way, which are commonly referred to the power of habit and custom' (*O*, 5–6), James Mill's *Analysis* of 1829 was, as his son correctly surmised, prophetic of a more scientific study of the mind on associationist principles, and, therefore, of a scientifically-based criticism to which those principles would be central. In Alexander Bain's studies of *The Senses and the Intellect* (1855) and *The Emotions*

---

[60] Isobel Armstrong, *Victorian Poetry: Poetry, Poetics and Politics* (London: Routledge, 1993), 67.

[61] Quoted, ibid., 130; *Monthly Repository*, N.S. vi (1832), 190; review of Ebenezer Elliott.

[62] Armstrong, *Victorian Scrutinies*, 83; *Westminster Review*, XIV (January 1831), 210–24.

and the Will (1859), John Stuart Mill saw the revival of 'the Lockian, or *a posteriori* school', which was 'giving signs that it is likely soon again to have its turn of ascendancy',[63] in part because it fitted much better with 'the science of Physiology' whose development, since the time of Hartley, was such that it had 'assumed almost a new aspect, from the important discoveries which had been made in all its branches, and especially in the functions of the nervous system'.[64] Bain's materialism, determinism and associationism were as thoroughgoing as Hartley's, but much more scientifically grounded. He believed that not only 'all thinking for an end, – be it practical or speculative, scientific or æsthetic, – consists in availing ourselves of the materials afforded by association',[65] but that 'the flow of representations in dreaming and madness offers the best field of observation for the study of associations as such'.[66] Mill believed Bain's work was 'sure to take its place in the very first rank of the order of philosophical speculation to which it belongs'[67] and that, when taken together with Herbert Spencer's *Principles of Psychology*, also published in 1855, proved that 'the sceptre of psychology has decidedly returned to this island'.[68]

Mill's own contribution to the advancement of associationist psychology was far from insignificant and, as Edward S. Reed has pointed out, it was from the suggestion in Mill's *Logic* that 'some nonconscious mental processes are identical with, or at least resemble, the process of drawing inferences and making judgments', that the analysis of the unconscious begins, being taken up in Germany in Helmholtz and Wundt's study of 'unconscious inference'.[69] From them it was of course developed by Freud, but Freud probably owed the development of another key aspect of his therapeutic techniques – that of 'free association' – to the British tradition, and specifically, as Freud's biographer Ronald W. Clark has suggested, to the work of the Victorian polymath and empirical psychologist, Francis Galton:

---

[63] John Stuart Mill, 'Bain's Psychology', *Collected Works of John Stuart Mill*, Vol. XI, 342–3.

[64] Ibid., 352.

[65] Alexander Bain, 'On "Association"-Controversies', *Mind*, Vol. 12, No. 46 (April 1887), 180.

[66] Ibid., 175.

[67] Mill, 'Bain's Psychology', *Collected Works*, Vol. XI, 372.

[68] Ibid., 341.

[69] Edward S. Reed, *From Soul to Mind: The Emergence of Psychology from Erasmus Darwin to William James* (New Haven and London: Yale University Press, 1997), 131.

As early as 1879 Francis Galton, the British anthropologist, devised a technique later known as the 'word association test'. After a long series of experiments he concluded that the mind was 'apparently always engaged in mumbling over its old stores, and if any one of these is wholly neglected for a while, it is apt to be forgotten, perhaps irrecoverably.' Later he concluded a paper in the July issue of *Brain*, with the statement: 'Perhaps the strongest of the impressions left by these experiments regards the multifariousness of the work done by the mind in a state of half-unconsciousness, and the valid reason they afford for believing in the existence of still deeper strata of mental operations, sunk wholly below the level of consciousness, which may account for such mental phenomena as cannot otherwise be explained.'[70]

Freud's technique of 'free association' invites the patient to do exactly what the associationist aesthetics of the empiricist tradition had always insisted readers do in experiencing a poem – in the words of Archibald Alison, to let our fancy be 'busied in pursuit of all those trains of thought, which are allied to this character or expression' (*AET*, 2). And the work of the analyst is like the work of the critic, attempting to find, in Hallam's words, 'the leading sentiment in the poet's mind, by their conformity to which the host of suggestions are arranged' – or, as Freud describes it,

> If one listens to these copious associations, one soon notices that they have more in common with the content of the dream than their starting-points alone. They throw a surprising light on all the different parts of the dream, fill in gaps between them, and make their strange juxtapositions intelligible. In the end one is bound to become clear about the relation between them and the dream's content. The dream is seen to be an abbreviated selection from the associations, a selection made, it is true, according to rules that we have not yet understood . . .[71]

Freudian psychology did not introduce ideas of the unconscious and of the effectiveness of 'free association' into British intellectual life in the early part

---

[70] Ronald W. Clark, *Freud: the Man and the Cause* (London: Jonathan Cape and Weidenfeld and Nicolson, 1980), 119.

[71] Sigmund Freud, 'Revision of the Theory of Dreams', Lecture 29, *New Introductory Lectures on Psychoanalysis*, trans. James Strachey, *The Pelican Freud Library*, Vol. 2 (Harmondsworth: Penguin, 1973), 40.

of the twentieth century: it derived them from the nineteenth-century efflo-
rescence of the associationist tradition.

IV

The enormous contribution of associationism to the development of scientific psychology in the second half of the nineteenth century, and, in the work
of thinkers like Bain, Spencer and Galton, in relating psychological processes
to new discoveries in physiology and neurology, established it once again as
the principal theory from which later psychological developments had to distinguish themselves. Despite Mill's defence of 'compound association', and
despite, equally, his support for Bain's physiological answers to the problem
of the 'active element, or spontaneity, in the mind itself',[72] it was associationism's 'atomism' and 'passivism' which continued to trouble its critics. William
James, for instance, in *The Principles of Psychology* (1890) insists on the falseness
of associationists' conception of the elements which enter into our associations because they assume that the 'same' idea can repeat itself in the mind
at a variety of points in time: such reccurrences, James argues, are impossible
because 'every sensation corresponds to some cerebral action. For an identical
sensation to recur it would have to occur the second time *in an unmodified brain*.
But as this, strictly speaking, is a physiological impossibility, so is an unmodified feeling an impossibility . . . whatever was true of the river of life, of the
river of elementary feeling, it would certainly be true to say, like Heraclitus,
that we never descend twice into the same stream'.[73] If an associated element
'returns', it returns to a new context by which it is necessarily 'modified', making it impossible for it to be recognised as identical with anything that has been
previously experienced. The same point is made at length by Henri Bergson
in *Matter and Memory*:

> Here we discover the radical vice of associationism. Given a present
> perception which forms by turns, with different recollections, several
> associations one after another, there are two ways . . . of conceiving
> the mechanism of this association. We may suppose that the perception

---

[72] Mill, 'Bain's Psychology', *Collected Works of John Stuart Mill*, Vol. XI, 354.
[73] William James, *The Principles of Psychology*, 2 Vols (Cambridge, MA: Harvard
University Press, 1981; 1890), Vol. 1, 227.

remains identical with itself, a true physical atom which gathers to itself others just as these happen to be passing by. This is the point of view of associationism. But there is also another – precisely the one which we have indicated in our theory of recognition. We have supposed that our entire personality, with the totality of our recollections, is present, undivided within our actual perception. Then, if this perception evokes in turn different memories, it is not by a mechanical adjunction of more and more numerous elements which, while remaining unmoved, it attracts around it, but rather by an expansion of the entire consciousness which, spreading out over a larger area, discovers the fuller detail of its wealth . . . In the first hypothesis (in favour of which there is little but its apparent simplicity and its analogy with a misunderstood physical atomism), each recollection is a fixed and independent being, of which we can neither say why it seeks to accrue to itself others, nor how it chooses, among a thousand memories which should have equal rights, those with which to associate itself in virtue of similarity or contiguity. We must suppose that ideas jostle each other at random, or that they exert among themselves mysterious forces, and, moreover, we have against us the witness of consciousness, which never shows us psychical facts floating as independent entities. From the second point of view, we merely state a fact, viz., that psychic facts are bound up with each other, and always given together to immediate consciousness as an undivided whole which reflection alone cuts up into distinct fragments.[74]

I have quoted the whole of this passage from Bergson because his description perfectly summarises the basis of opposition between the new psychologies of the late nineteenth century and what they considered to be associationism: it is an opposition between the 'atomistic' and the 'wholistic', between the 'fixed' and the 'fluid', between, in Bergson's terms, 'stiffened memory images' that act like 'ready-made things' and the 'natural return of the mind to the undivided unity of perception'.[75] They claim, in other words, to invert traditional associationism by giving priority to the whole rather than to its parts.

The very intensity of the ways in which these arguments are framed by both James and Bergson is testimony to the continuing hold that association-

---

[74] Henri Bergson, *Matter and Memory*, 5th edn, trans. Nancy Margaret Paul and W. Scott Palmer (New York: Zone Books, 1991; 1911), 165–6.

[75] Ibid., 164, 165.

ism had over theories of the psyche; the form in which they are put, however, is – as we have already seen – as reductive of the associationist position as they claim that associationists are of mental phenomena. They take no account of the fact that these are arguments which, far from being new, have already been made against associationism – arguments whose implications have already been addressed, if not answered, by associationists. A classic instance which formulates very similar arguments to those of James and Bergson is provided by Sir William Hamilton in a footnote to his edition of *The Works of Thomas Reid* (1863):

> The fact, – that the same one thought may, and commonly has, many connections, and consequently may suggest, and be suggested by, many different movements, shows, that the old and familiar simile of a Chain is inadequate to the phænomenon. For it implies, –1 Coexistence, to the exclusion of succession in consciousness; 2 equal and reciprocal suggestion. But these vices are common, the chain has others peculiar to itself. For, 3 it would lead us to suppose, that the mind could run only backwards and forwards, on one simple series; each consequent thought having, like the link of a simple chain, only a single determinate connection, before and after; whereas, the concatenations with every ring of the mental series, are indefinitely numerous. In this respect, instead of a mere chain, the simile of a hauberk, or *chain web*, would be better; and better still, *a sphere of chainwork*. But one defect there is in all of these similitudes, – any ring being moved, moves, and that *equally, all* the rings attached to it; which is not the case in the momenta of mental dependency.[76]

To overcome these perceived weaknesses, both of theory and of metaphor, Hamilton argued that what happened in association was not the return of isolated atoms but of the whole context in which the original association had been formed. This he called 'redintegration':

> Those thoughts suggest each other which had previously constituted parts of the same entire or total act of cognition. Now to the same entire or total act belong, as integral and constituent parts, in the first place,

---

[76] *The Works of Thomas Reid, D. D.*, Preface, Notes and Supplementary Dissertations by Sir William Hamilton, Bart (Edinburgh: Maclachlan and Stewart, 1863), 906.

thoughts which arose at the same time or in immediate consecution; and in the second, those thoughts which are bound up into one by their mutual affinity.[77]

Hamilton appeals, in other words, to the same need for totality that we see in Bergson, and even as he elaborates the metaphor of the 'chain' into 'chain web' he underlines the limitations of any metaphor based on such physical structures. Hamilton's arguments, however, did not go unanswered: they were countered by John Stuart Mill in his *Examination of Sir William Hamilton's Philosophy* (1865), in which he argued that it was precisely with 'wholes' that associationism had always been concerned, and that Hamilton had ignored,

> a very important part of the Laws of Association which may be termed the Laws of Obliviscence. If Sir W. Hamilton had sufficiently attended to those laws, he never would have maintained, that if we know the parts before the whole, we must continue to know the parts better than the whole. It is one of the principal Laws of Obliviscence, that when a number of ideas suggest one another by association with such certainty and rapidity as to coalesce together in a group, all those members of the group which remain long without being specially attended to, have a tendency to drop out of consciousness. Our consciousness of them becomes more and more faint and evanescent, until no effort of attention can recall it into distinctness, or at last recall it at all.[78]

For Mill, in other words, associationism has never been committed to what James believed was its 'one huge error – that of the construction of our thought out of the compounding of themselves together of immutable and incessantly recurring "simple ideas"';[79] or, indeed, that it supposed, as Bergson had insisted it did, that ideas and images were 'independent entities floating, like the atoms of Epicurus, in an inward space'.[80] What we *know* are wholes,

---

[77] Sir William Hamilton, *Lectures on Metaphysics and Logic*, ed. H. L Mansell and John Veitch, 2 Vols (Edinburgh: William Blackwood & Sons, 1865), Vol. II, 237.

[78] J. M. Robson (ed.), *The Works of John Stuart Mill*, Vol. IX, *An Examination of Sir William Hamilton's Philosophy* (Toronto: University of Toronto Press, 1979), 257.

[79] James, *Principles of Psychology*, Vol. I, 522.

[80] Bergson, *Matter and Memory*, 164.

wholes whose nature changes inevitably with the decay of memory and so are necessarily dynamic rather than fixed and static. To illustrate this process, Mill reverts to Hartley's comparison of the mind with the acquisition of language:

> After reading a chapter of a book, when we lay down the volume do we remember to have been individually conscious of the printed letters and syllables which have passed before us? Could we recall, by any effort of mind, the visible aspect presented by them, unless some unusual circumstances has fixed our attention upon it during the perusal? Yet each of these letters and syllables must have been present to us as a sensation for at least a passing moment, or the sense would not have been conveyed to us. But the sense being the only thing in which we are interested . . . we retain no impression of the separate letters and syllables. This instance is the more instructive, inasmuch as, the whole process taking place within our means of observation, we know that our knowledge began with the parts and not with the whole.[81]

The associated 'parts' disappear in a 'whole' which itself can never become a 'totality' because we can never recollect all of the individual elements of which it would have been constituted. Bergson's 'undivided unity of perception'[82] is a fiction, because many of our perceptions, Mill would argue, 'are important to us only as signs of something else, and which by repetition have come to do their work as signs with a rapidity to which our feelings is instantaneous, [and] cease altogether to be attended to; and through that inattention our consciousness of them ceases altogether, or becomes so fleeting and indistinct as to leave no revivable trace in the memory'.[83] Between the atomic fragment and an undivided totality, Mill postulates a world of 'wholes' to whose parts we have ceased to attend, even if we originally encountered them in terms of the individual parts: 'that this is consistent with having known the parts earlier than the wholes, is proved not only by the case of reading, but by that of playing on a musical instrument, and a hundred other familiar instances'.[84]

Ironically, and yet significantly, William James uses exactly the same example in *The Principles of Psychology*, where he records an attempt to calculate the number of associative acts involved in reading a page of prose, not count-

---

[81] Mill, *Examination of Sir William Hamilton's Philosophy*, 257–8.
[82] Bergson, *Matter and Memory*, 164.
[83] Mill, *Examination of Sir William Hamilton's Philosophy*, 257.
[84] Ibid., 258.

ing the faint contextual recollections with which, 'long as he may live, [the child] . . . will never hear the name without the faint arousal of the image of the object'[85] with which he first associated it. Having challenged association- ism for its failings, and having elaborated his alternatives, James is driven to 'admit that few principles of analysis, in any science, have proved more fertile' than the associationist one, 'however vaguely formulated it often may have been'. And James explicitly acknowledges that in relation to 'the phenomena which Hartley undertook to explain by cerebral physiology . . . he was, in many essential respects, on the right track'. As a consequence, James mod- estly viewed his own role as 'simply to revise his conclusions by the aid of distinctions which he [Hartley] did not make'.[86] Bergson, too, ends not by over- throwing associationism but by restoring it: 'The opponents of associationism have . . . followed it onto this ground. They combat the theory because it explains the higher operations of the mind by association, but not because it misunderstands the true nature of association itself'.[87] Far from overthrowing associationism, James and Bergson challenge what they describe as the tradi- tion of associationism – a tradition conceived in largely reductive form – in order to re-establish a new and enlarged associationism: the end of Bergson's argument is the beginning of Hume's, since Bergson has established *why* 'of all the associations which can be imagined, those of resemblance and contiguity are therefore at first the only associations that have a vital utility'.[88]

This ironic reversal, in which associationism is overthrown only in order that the 'true nature of association' can be discovered, finds its crucial trope in James's adoption, for the workings of the mind, of the metaphor of 'a sensi- bly continuous stream'.[89] This is often represented as a radical departure from 'traditional' associationist conceptions, and often assumed to be a product of Freudian psychology.[90] But the irony of James's adoption of the image of a 'stream of consciousness' is that it was precisely the *fluidity* of associationist theory by which Coleridge was appalled. As John Sutton has pointed out, it

---

[85] James, *Principles of Psychology*, Vol. 1, 525.
[86] Ibid., 522.
[87] Bergson, *Matter and Memory*, 241.
[88] Ibid., 242.
[89] James, *Principles of Psychology*, 230.
[90] See Erwin R. Steinberg, *The Stream-of-Consciousness Technique in the Modern Novel* (Port Washington: Kennikat Press, 1979), 6: 'the present-day *stream- of-consciousness novel* is a product of Freudian psychology with its structure of psychological levels'.

was the fact that assocationist theories modelled the mind as a 'stream' that Coleridge wanted to challenge:[91] 'I will at least make the attempt to explain to myself the Origin of moral Evil from the *streamy* Nature of Association', he wrote in a notebook in 1803.[92] The image returns in *Biographia Literaria*, when Coleridge tries to image the consequences of Hartley's theory:

> . . . the will, the reason, the judgment and the understanding, instead of being the determining causes of association, must needs be represented as its creatures, and among its mechanical effects. Conceive, for instance, a broad stream, winding through a mountainous country with an indefinite number of currents, varying and running into each other according as the gusts chance to blow from the opening of the mountains. The temporary union of several currents in one, so as to form the main current of the moment, would present an accurate image of Hartley's theory of the will. [93]

For Coleridge, it is the accidental *flows* of the associationist conception of the mind rather than its atomistic fragmentation that is destructive; for Bergson, as for James, it is the *lack* of fluidity, the *rigidity* of the elements to be associated, that is associationism's weakness. A later generation claims to overthrow associationism by adopting precisely those images of the mind which an earlier generation of opponents of associationist theory thought to be characteristic of associationism itself. As James disenchantedly acknowledges at the close of his *Principles of Psychology*,

> From this practical point of view it would be a true *ignoratio elenchi* to flatter one's self that one has dealt a heavy blow at the psychology of association, when one has exploded the theory of atomistic ideas, or shown that contiguity and similarity between ideas can only be there after association is done. The whole body of the associationist psychology

[91] See John Sutton, *Philosophy and Memory Traces: Descartes to Connectionism* (Cambridge: Cambridge University Press, 1998), 244ff.

[92] Kathleen Coburn (ed.), *The Notebooks of Samuel Taylor Coleridge*, 8 Vols (Princeton: Princeton University Press, 1957–62), Vol. 1, 1770.

[93] Samuel Taylor Coleridge, *Biographia Literaria or Biographical Sketches of My Literary Life and Opinions*, ed. James Engell and W. Jackson Bate, *Collected Works of Samuel Taylor Coleridge*, Vol. 7:1 (Princeton: Princeton University Press, 1983; 1817), 100; hereafter cited in the text as *BL*.

remains standing after you have translated 'ideas' into 'objects', on the one hand, and 'brain-processes' on the other . . .[94]

Whatever challenges were addressed to it in the nineteenth century, the 'whole body of the associationist psychology' stood its ground, providing one of the most effective ways in which the workings of the mind could be understood.

Recent developments in cognitive psychology have merely underlined this continuity. If, as Robert M. Young has suggested, the principles of neuropsychology have not changed fundamentally since 1749,[95] then recent theories of the mind proposed under labels such as 'connectionism' have had to acknowledge that their theories, while 'not a *return* to associationism', are sufficiently related that they have to be distinguished from '*mere* associationism' because their 'most obvious ancestor is indeed associationism'.[96] As a result, Young has argued that 'association' is not only 'the most basic, the most fecund, and the most pervasive explanatory principle in the human and, to a lesser extent, the biological sciences', but that 'the principle in its most general form has played the central role in attempts to apply the methods and assumptions of science to the study of man'.[97] The traditions of British empiricism have underwritten that effort at a scientific understanding of the mind but despite this, associationism has been largely written out of the intellectual context of the development of British literature since romanticism. While earlier critics such as Arthur Beatty, in *William Wordsworth: His Doctrines of Art in their Historical Relations* (1927), or James Ralston Caldwell in *John Keats's Fancy* (1945), took seriously their subjects' engagement with the British psychology of their day, the development of criticism of the Romantic period since the 1960s has been focused largely by the effort to 'read the English Romantic poets in the light of their German contemporaries, both poets and philosophers'.[98] As a consequence what were the most potent developments in psychology, and

---

[94] James, *Principles of Psychology*, 569.

[95] Robert Young, 'Scholarship and the History of the Behavioural Sciences', *History of Science*, 5 (1966), 1–51, 23.

[96] William Bechtel and Adele A. Abrahamsen, *Connectionism and the Mind: An Introduction to Parallel Processing in Networks* (Oxford: Basil Blackwell, 1991), 102.

[97] Robert M. Young, 'The Association of Ideas', Philip P. Wiener (ed.), *Dictionary of the History of Ideas* (New York: Scribner's, 1968), Vol. 1, 111–18, 111.

[98] J. Hillis Miller, 'Tradition and Difference', *Diacritics* 2 (1972), 6–13, review of M. H. Abrams, *Natural Supernaturalism* (New York: Norton, 1971).

what underpinned some of the most radical developments in aesthetics, have disappeared as the formative environment of British writing. The power of associationism in the thought of Hume and Hartley had, however, been so substantiated by the empirical psychologies of the nineteenth century that its operations had to be incorporated even into the thought of those who wanted to resist the philosophies that had given rise to it in the first place. Advising schoolteachers on how best to approach their task, William James explained to them that though 'consciousness is an ever-flowing stream' in which it might seem that in 'the fluidity of these successive waves, everything is indeterminate', nonetheless 'each wave has a constitution which can be to some degree explained by the constitution of the waves just passed away' by 'the two fundamental "laws of association"'.[99] As a consequence, he suggested that, 'it is astonishing how many mental operations we can explain when we have once grasped the principles of association' because 'those laws run the mind'.[100] James concludes by insisting that teachers have to think of their pupils not as flowing consciousnesses but, in a reversion to precisely the kind of analogy that he had sought to challenge in an earlier associationism, as associating machines:

> I cannot too strongly urge you to acquire a habit of thinking of your pupils in associative terms. All governors of mankind, from doctors and jail-wardens to demagogues and statesmen, instinctively come so to conceive their charges. If you do the same, thinking of them (however else you may think of them besides) as so many little systems of associating machinery, you will be astonished at the intimacy of insight into their operations and at the practicality of the results which you will gain.[101]

Writers would have been similarly advised to consider the nature of their readers, and readers the creative processes of their writers: like the symbols of which it was composed, the literary text consisted of 'so many little systems of associating machinery'.

---

[99] William James, *Talks to Teachers on Psychology* (Cambridge MA: Harvard University Press, 1983; 1899), 55.

[100] Ibid., 57.

[101] Ibid., 60.

1 'Kant has not answered Hume': Hume, Coleridge and the Romantic Imagination

'For my own part', Joseph Priestley wrote in *Institutes of Natural and Revealed Religion* (1772), 'I do not hesitate to rank Hartley's *Observations on Man* among the greatest efforts of human genius'. Indeed, considering 'the great importance' of its object, Priestley had come to the conclusion by the time of the second edition that *Observations* was 'without exception, the most valuable production of the mind of man'.[1] The young Samuel Taylor Coleridge agreed: he looked forward in 'Religious Musings' to a time when the soul, attracted and absorbed by 'perfect Love', would attain to an 'exclusive consciousness of God' – as 'demonstrated by Hartley'.[2] By 1794 he was able to assert that 'I am a compleat Necessitarian — and understand the subject well almost as Hartley himself — but I go farther than Hartley and believe the corporeality of *thought* — namely that it is motion'.[3] Hartley was, for Coleridge, the intellectual underpinning for the revolutionary and millenarian expectations of the early 1790s when he hoped to escape to America in order to create an 'experiment of human Perfectibility on the banks of the Susquahanna; where our little Society, in its second generation, was to have combined the innocence of the patriarchal Age with the knowledge

---

[1] Joseph Priestley, *Institutes of Natural and Revealed Religion,* 2nd edn, 2 Vols (Birmingham, 1782; 1772), Vol. II, 161.

[2] Samuel Taylor Coleridge, 'Religious Musings', *Collected Works of Samuel Taylor Coleridge*, Vol. 16, *Poetical Works*, I, ed. J.C.C. Mays (Princeton: Princeton University Press, 2001), 176. Coleridge's reference to Hartley is in *Poems* (1797) and refers to the 1791 edition of *Observations on Man.*

[3] Earl Leslie Griggs (ed.), *Collected Letters of Samuel Taylor Coleridge*, 6 Vols, (Oxford: Clarendon Press, 2000; 1956), Vol. I, 1785–1800, 137 (11 December 1794; to Robert Southey).

and genuine refinements of European culture'.[4] A year later, he is using Hartley's conception of 'vibrations' as the 'miniatures' of our experience to assert the moral superiority of country over town: 'The pleasures, which we receive from rural beauties, are of little Consequence compared with the Moral Effect of these pleasures – beholding constantly the Best possible, we at last become ourselves the best possible. In the country, all around us smile Good and Beauty – and the Images of this divine [benevolence] are miniatured on the mind of the beholder, as a Landscape on a Convex Mirror'.[5] In September 1796 Coleridge named his first child David Hartley after the 'great Master of Christian Philosophy'[6] and his biographer, Richard Holmes comments that 'Hartley was to remain his father's lifelong favourite, the source of great pleasure and great anxiety, and some of his best poetry'.[7] If he was 'the source of great pleasure and great anxiety' and, indeed, of 'some of his best poetry', Hartley the metaphysician was not to remain Coleridge's 'lifelong favourite'. Many versions of the development of romanticism in Britain take as its decisive turning point Coleridge's account, in *Biographia Literaria*, of how he put behind him the associationist psychology of Hartley, declaring it inadequate to explain the creative power of the mind. The discovery of Kant, Fichte and Schelling then provided a language – one in which he declares that 'I first found a genial coincidence with much that I had toiled out for myself' (*BL*, I, 160) – through which his opposition to Hartley could be framed and which would allow him to envisage a great work on 'the Productive Logos human and divine' (*BL*, I, 136).

There is, however, a strange undercurrent that runs through these chapters of *Biographia Literaria*: Hartley, the stated object of Coleridge's refutation, is insistently displaced by David Hume, who haunts the chapters like a ghost that cannot be laid nor yet directly confronted. In the crucial chapters in which Coleridge is accounting for the growth of his own thought, the emergence of the German influence is matched by a profound, but profoundly repressed, effort to marginalise the influence of the most significant British thinker of the eighteenth century and of the philosophical tradition that derives

---

[4] Samuel Taylor Coleridge, *The Collected Works of Samuel Taylor Coleridge*, Vol. 4, *The Friend*, ed. Barbara E. Rooke (London: Routledge and Kegan Paul, 1969), Vol. II, 146–7.

[5] Griggs, *Collected Letters*, Vol. I, 10 March 1795, 'To George Dyer', 154.

[6] Quoted Richard Holmes, *Coleridge: Early Visions* (London: Hodder and Stoughton, 1989), 124.

[7] Ibid.

from him. Hume's presence – or, rather, his absence – can first be sensed in Chapter V when Coleridge quotes Sir James Mackintosh as having asserted that Hartley stands 'in the same relation to Hobbes as Newton to Kepler; the law of association being that to the mind, which gravitation is to matter' (*BL*, I, 92). It was Hume, however, who had claimed in the *Treatise* that association represented 'a kind of ATTRACTION, which in the mental world will be found to have as extraordinary effects as in the natural' (*T*, 12–13), while Hartley himself characterises 'attraction' much more broadly as 'gravitation, electricity, magnetism, and cohesion, with the repulsions which attend upon the three last' (*O*, 28).

As a consequence, almost by a kind of gravitational effect of its own, Coleridge's chapter is drawn to conclude with Hume rather than Hartley. At this point, however, Coleridge is engaged not with the truth or falsity of Hume's arguments but about the fact that he believes Hume to have copied his theory of association from Thomas Aquinas – a belief confirmed by his discovery that a Mr Payne had once possessed volumes of Aquinas belonging to Hume which were 'swathed and swaddled' (*BL*, I, 104) in Hume's commentary. Coleridge, so desperate to defend *himself* against accusations of plagiarism, dismisses Hume's account not in terms of its intellectual coherence but as though Hume has become the real perpetrator of the crimes with which Coleridge himself was later to be charged.[8] Coleridge then presents his own intellectual development as reaching a crisis 'after I had successively studied in the schools of Locke, Berkeley, Leibnitz and Hartley, and could find in neither of them an abiding place for my reason' (*BL*, I, 140–1). The absence of Hume from this succession of philosophical engagements – given his earlier presence in Coleridge's narrative and his acknowledged importance to the Kant who would prove Coleridge's salvation – is striking, the more striking since, in 1801, the *Letters* record that after 'long wakeful nights' in which 'the subject of my meditations ha[s] been the Relations of Thoughts

---

[8] See Sir William Hamilton (ed.), *The Works of Thomas Reid, D.D.* (Edinburgh: Maclachlan and Stewart, 1863), 890 fn.: 'Among his other dreaming errors, Coleridge charges Hume with plagiarising from Aquinas (who, by the way herein only repeats Aristotle) his whole doctrine of association. But Coleridge charging plagiarism! 'Quis tulerit Gracchum, de seditione querentem?' – See my ingenious friend, Mr Burton's excellent biography of David Hume, lately published'. Hamilton also suggests that Coleridge's whole account of association is plagiarised from the 'Paralipomena' and 'Beytræge' of Maass (1787, 1792).

to Things, in the language of Hume, of Ideas to Impressions',[9] he proposed writing a book for Longman 'on the originality and merits of Locke, Hobbes, & Hume which work I mean as a *Pioneer* to my greater work, and as exhibiting a proof that I have not formed opinions without an attentive perusal of the works of my Predecessors from Aristotle to Kant'.[10]

Coleridge's perusal of Hume led him to believe that Hume might have correctly identified the key problems but that what he produced was 'so worthless and so untenable that it induced a more patient and dispassionate huntsman [Kant] to seek the scent again at the point from which his predecessor had flown off, and having again once more caught it on the breeze, he follows it undeterred by the steep and difficult uplands whither it leads him'.[11] Hume, indeed, is regularly cited by Coleridge when he wishes to indicate what is unacceptable to his notion of culture; thus, in envisaging the tradition of English letters, Coleridge requires that 'England be Sir P. Sidney, Shakespeare, Milton, Bacon, Harrington, Swift, Wordsworth, and never let the names of Darwin, Johnson, Hume *furr* it over!'[12] And in his account of his (unwritten) history of metaphysics in England he declares that he will 'confine myself to facts in every part of the work, excepting that which treats of Mr. Hume: – *him* I have assuredly besprinkled copiously from the fountains of Bitterness and Contempt'.[13]

Hume has been regarded as so irrelevant to Coleridge's intellectual history that he is not even mentioned in the first volume of Richard Holmes's biography, *Coleridge: Early Visions*, and appears in only one footnote in the second, *Coleridge: Darker Reflections*. The latter, however, is suggestive, since it points to Coleridge's use of the image of the 'waterboatman' insect as an analogy for the workings of the imagination and notes that this image, though 'marvellously original', nonetheless 'seems to expand on a simile from the philosopher David Hume', a simile in which Hume 'remarks on the intrinsic energy of the Imagination, which "is apt to continue, even when its object fails it, and like a galley put in motion by the oars, carries on its course without any new

---

[9] *Collected Letters of Samuel Taylor Coleridge*, ed. Earl Leslie Griggs (Oxford: Clarendon Press, 1956), Vol. II, 671.

[10] Ibid., 707.

[11] Alice D. Snyder, *Coleridge on Logic and Learning, with Selections from the Unpublished Manuscripts* (New Haven: Yale University Press, 1929), 96.

[12] *The Notebooks of Samuel Taylor Coleridge*, ed. Kathleen Coburn, 5 Vols (London: Routledge & Kegan Paul, 1962), Vol. 2, 2598.

[13] Coleridge, *Collected Letters*, Vol. II, 'To Samuel Purkis, Feb 17, 1803', 490–1.

impulse"'.[14] Coleridge, in other words, introduces the moment of his own discovery of the active power of the imagination, and of the inadequacy of Hartley's associationism, by an image which reflects back on his reading of Hume. It is significant that the imagination has no special role in Hartley's theory, so that Hartleian associationism represents no challenge to the innovation of Coleridge's foregrounding of IMAGINATION as 'the living Power and Prime agent of all human perception' (*BL*, I, 304), while in Hume, on the other hand, associationism is *nothing but* the operation of the imagination. Coleridge's repressed acknowledgment of Hume in the image of the waterboatman is a signal of how much of the intellectual ground that Coleridge wishes now to command by the concept of the imagination was already explicit in Hume, for whom, as the *Treatise* puts it, 'the memory, senses, and understanding are, therefore, all of them founded on the imagination' (*T*, 265).

It is as if, in other words, through the key chapters of *Biographia Literaria* dealing with his own intellectual growth, what Coleridge is in fact trying to achieve is the dismissal of the associationism of Hume, rather than of Hartley, with all of the aesthetic, political and religious consequences that it brought in its train, but trying to achieve it without confronting directly the challenge posed by Hume's radical conception of the imagination. The symptoms of Coleridge's concern with Hume can be seen in a series of images in which the associationist conception of the mind is compared with balls on a billiard table. This starts in Chapter IV when Coleridge attributes to Hobbes the notion of 'successive particles propagating motion like billiard balls' (*BL*, I, 101); the image, in fact, does not appear in Hobbes but the reference two pages later to 'Hume's essay on association' (*BL*, I, 104) points perhaps to its real source, and Coleridge's real objection. The billiard ball image then becomes the basis of Coleridge's attack on Hartley's associationism, focusing in particular on Hartley's conception of the mind as related by 'vibrations' to objects in the external world:

> It is a mere delusion of the fancy to conceive the pre-existence of the ideas in any chain of association as so many differently coloured billiard-balls in contact, so that when an object, the billiard-stick, strikes through the first or white ball, the same motion propagates itself through the red,

---

[14] Richard Holmes, *Coleridge: Darker Reflections* (London: HarperCollins, 1998), 70. The quotation from Hume is from *Treatise of Human Nature*, Book I, Part IV, Sect. II, 198.

green, blue, black etc., and sets the whole in motion. No! We must suppose the very same force which constitutes the white ball to constitute the red or black; or the idea of a circle to constitute the idea of a triangle, which is impossible. (*BL*, I, 108)

There are two problems with this as an argument against Hume's associationism. First, Hume's theory, unlike Hartley's, makes no assumptions about the origins of impressions in relation to the external world: associationism does not require the physicalist hypotheses of Hartley (as in the case, for instance, of Berkeley). By focusing on the already – by 1817 – long-outdated physiology of Hartley's theory, Coleridge allows himself to evade the more radical challenge of Hume's associationism. Second, Hume does indeed use the analogy of the billiard balls but he uses it in the *Enquiry Concerning Human Understanding*, not as an image of the associative process but as an example of the impossibility of predicting, before experience, how things in the world will act: 'We fancy, that were we brought on a sudden into this world, we could at first have inferred that one Billiard-ball would communicate motion to another upon impulse; and that we needed not to have waited for the event, in order to pronounce with certainty concerning it' (*EHU*, 28). Coleridge adopts Hume's image – an image for the impossibility of knowing *a priori* the nature of the world – and turns it into an argument for the fact that we cannot, on an associationist account, know the force that governs mental activity. This, however, is precisely the point that Hume himself is making: for Hume, the ultimate grounds of human experience can never be fully known because we can only ever have *empirical* knowledge of their causes. When Coleridge identifies that 'to bring in the will, or reason, as causes of their own cause, that is, as at once causes and effects' (*BL*, I, 112), is the fundamental flaw in associationist theory, he sidesteps the fact that it is precisely such a conception of 'cause' that Hume has set in doubt, 'cause' having been already revealed by Hume to be no more than 'constant conjunction' – in other words, a special case of association. Equally, one can only pose as a problem the issue of how the will, reason, judgment and understanding relate to the process of association by ignoring the fact that, for Hume, these are all derivations *from* association rather than possible determinants of it – they are ways of *describing* particular aspects of the associative process, not separate faculties derivable independently of association itself. It is not that these aspects of Hume's theory are inviolable to criticism: it is simply that Coleridge does not confront them, deflecting his criticism on to the much easier target of Hartley's physiological psychology, as though, in dismissing the latter he had, effectively, defeated the former.

Coleridge uses the same procedure when attacking the associationist account of the self. What he argues against is Hartley's world of necessary causes that determine all human actions:

> according to this hypothesis the disquisition, to which I am at present soliciting the reader's attention, may be as truly said to be written by Saint Paul's church, as by *me*: for it is the mere motion of muscles and nerves; and these again are set in motion from external causes equally passive, which external causes stand themselves in interdependent connection with every thing that exists or has existed. Thus the whole universe co-operates to produce the minutest stroke of every letter, save only that I myself, and I alone, have nothing to do with it, but merely the causeless and *effectless* beholding of it when it is done. (*BL*, I, 118–19)

Lurking behind this representation of Hartley's necessitarian world of physical forces, however, is the Humean reduction of the self from 'a real separable being' to something no more than an 'ens logicum' (*BL*, I, 117), the transformation of 'the real agent' to 'a *something-nothing-every-thing*, which does all of which we know, and knows nothing of all that itself does' (*BL*, I, 120). An atheism which would deny the eternity of the soul and the substantiality of the self is the direct consequence of associationism and must, therefore, be overthrown if the process by which 'Hume degraded the notion of cause and effect into a blind product of delusion and habit' is not to lead to 'the equal degradation of every *fundamental* idea in ethics or theology' (*BL*, I, 121). That Hume belatedly but explicitly enters the argument at this point as the object of Coleridge's philosophical ire is clear from the fact that he attempts to save Hartley – the 'excellent and pious Hartley' (*BL*, I, 121) – from any personal contamination by such outcomes, on the basis that 'no errors of the understanding can be morally arraigned unless they have proceeded from the heart' (*BL*, I, 122). Instead, Coleridge turns to condemn those in 'an unfortunate neighbour-nation at least, who have embraced this system with a full view of all its moral and religious consequences' and who 'need discipline, not argument; they must be made better men before they can become wiser' (*BL*, I, 122). The 'neighbour nation' might, from the context and Coleridge's quotation from his own poetry of 1796, be France, but it might equally be Scotland since, for Coleridge, what Hume writes the French imitate and send back to

England: 'But Hume wrote – and the French imitated him – and we the French – and the French us – and so philosophisms fly to and fro – in serieses of imitated Imitations – Shadows of shadows of shadows of a farthing Candle placed Between two Looking-glasses'.[15]

The historical and philosophical suppression involved in Coleridge's substitution of Hartley for Hume as preparation for the proclamation of the superiority of German idealism is one that has been regularly repeated by much modern criticism, ignoring the fact that Coleridge needed to engage in such a repression not because of the *failure* of those who followed Hume's associationist theories but, as the previous chapter illustrated, precisely because of their success. Equally, it is assumed that Coleridge was, at the very least, going with the tide of philosophical development in adopting the Kantian response to Hume, since German idealism is evidently more advanced than the 'mechanical' philosophies of the empiricists. As J. Hutchison Stirling, who first introduced Hegelian philosophy to the British public in 1861 in his *Secret of Hegel*, ruminated:

> I suppose there is no one in Germany at present, and scarcely anyone anywhere else, it may be, to whom, even on slight acquaintance with the subject, it is not *understood* that Kant has answered Hume: rather indeed that this, so to speak, is the least of it, and that Kant has not only answered but passed Hume; with simply a word, moreover, in the bygoing to intimate: 'I take your back, David Hume, merely as a starting ground to a leap – a leap into a new world – a new world of hitherto undiscovered metaphysic, of heretofore despaired-of philosophy.'[16]

Romanticism itself is identified with this 'leap into a new world', the achievement of a 'heretofore despaired-of philosophy' which surpasses all previous thought. That leap, it is assumed, is the same as the leap made by the British romantics, producing the identification of Wordsworth and Coleridge with Kantian and post-Kantian developments in German thought which has been the burden of much Anglo-American literary criticism since the Second World War. Cynthia Chase's introduction to *Romanticism* notes, for instance, that 'the connection between English Romantic poetry and German Idealist philoso-

---

[15] Coleridge, *Collected Letters*, Vol. I, 'To Robert Southey', October 15, 1799, 538.

[16] J. Hutchison Stirling, 'Kant has not answered Hume', *Mind,* Vol. 9, Issue 36 (October 1884), 531.

phy, established through the mediation of Coleridge, has long been a truism of literary scholarship', with the consequence that 'some of Wordsworth's philosophical ideas can be traced to Coleridge's reading of Kant and Schelling'.[17] The assumption is that the Kantian answer to Hume provides a philosophy not only superior to empiricism, especially in the realm of aesthetic thought, but also fundamentally more encouraging of creativity, more *productive* for literature, than anything in the empiricist tradition.

Against such universal expectations, however, Stirling declared himself in 1884 'greatly disposed to doubt . . . the success of the start, the success of Kant in opposition to Hume'.[18] If Kant has failed to answer the empiricist problematic posed by Hume, then critical perspectives that assume idealism's necessary transcendence of empiricism lose their sense of historical inevitability. For Stirling, Hume's work was not simply the 'spark' that helped Kant wake from his 'dogmatic slumber';[19] rather, 'Kant's whole work (and what alone led to all the others, Fichte, Schelling, Hegel) rose out of one consideration only: 'What was – whence was – that very strange and peculiar species of necessity to which Hume has drawn attention in the phenomena of cause and effect'.[20] As a consequence, the whole edifice of the '*Kritik of Pure Reason*, nay, German philosophy as a whole, has absolute foundation in the *whence* or *why* of *necessary connexion*',[21] and on this crux of the issue Stirling finds Kant not only to have failed to answer Hume but to have realised, belatedly, the significance of his own failure.

The problem that Kant could not resolve – according to Hutchison Stirling – was how the operation of the categories accounted for the 'necessity' that Hume could not find in our experience of causality. According to Stirling, Kant's category of cause could not be effectively imposed on the world by the mind without the phenomena having already suggested to the categories the ways in which 'real' cases of causation are to be distinguished from mere regular succession. Two different kinds of constant conjunction – the causal kind and that which is simply a matter of regular contiguity – could never be distinguished from one another if the categories themselves *impose* the order

[17] Cynthia Chase (ed.), *Romanticism* (London: Routledge, 1993), 8.
[18] *Mind,* Vol. 9, Issue 36 (October 1884), 'Kant has not answered Hume, I', 531–47, 531.
[19] *Mind,* Vol. 10, Issue 37 (January 1885), 'Kant has not answered Hume, II', 45–72, 47.
[20] Ibid., 48.
[21] Ibid.

of causality on the world, because in order to impose the category of cause on some but not all of these cases there must already be something *in* the phenomena that directs the categories to establish one as properly causal and the other as not. That which is supposed to be supplied only by the categories in constructing the 'world' must already be evidenced in the phenomena by the very necessity which only the categories are supposed to provide:

> Kant is found to be suspended here between his two perceptions of the state of the case. He perceives, first, that sense as sense is always contingent. But then he perceives, second, that if a sensation A and another sensation B are to be subsumed under the category and converted into an antecedent and a consequent, they must of themselves have already given us reason to assume for them precisely that quality – precisely that relation! This latter perception we suppose to have come late to Kant; and it is precisely in consequence of this perception that we attribute the cold sweats to him which attend that endless tangle of the Second Analogy where we see only bewildered attempts to renew courage in himself by the constant *refrain*, Necessity of synthesis cannot be due to sense, and must be due to understanding! But the renewed courage must ever fail again . . .[22]

The only way out of this quandary would be 'to conceive that each category, quite unknown to me, without any consciousness on my part, might unerringly scent a case of its own'[23] but then the whole purpose of the categories would be defeated: 'the single purpose they are there for, what they are alone to do, is to give necessity; and this necessity, which they alone are to give, which they alone are to explain, *already exists!*'[24] Stirling can see no conclusion but that 'the vast transcendental machinery is a signal failure'[25] and that Kant's 'position is no more and no better than that of Reid, Beattie, Oswald, and all the rest'[26] who had tried to resist Hume's analysis. The superiority of the Kantian position is entirely undermined, leaving the debate between Humean empiricism and its Scottish opponents of the Common Sense school as intact as ever it had been before the rise of German philosophy.

---

[22] Ibid., 59.
[23] Ibid., 60.
[24] Ibid., 65.
[25] Ibid., 70.
[26] Ibid., 71.

Hutchison Stirling's argument casts in doubt that transcendence of the empiricist tradition on which the Kantian-Coleridgean position, both in the philosophers' own works and the modern criticism that derives from them, depends: it underlines that those who rejected the Kantian transcendental were not simply attempting to resist the inevitable tide of modern thought. If Kant has not answered Hume, there is no intellectual justification for abandoning either a Humean empiricism or, indeed, the philosophy of common sense which had opposed it. The supposed superiority with which, retrospectively, the transcendental argument has been endowed may not be justified and those who, like Dugald Stewart, believed that 'Mr Hume's own countrymen' had provided 'far more luminous refutations of scepticism than the *Critique of Pure Reason*',[27] were not simply refusing to enter the world of modernity when he felt under no compulsion to reject Scottish philosophical traditions in favour of German ones. And this should lead us to reflect on the assumption that Coleridge's conception of the imagination represents a better account of the creative mind than is provided for in the associationism which he abandoned. Many accounts of romanticism are built on this presupposition. Frank Kermode, for instance, in *Romantic Image*, surveyed the territory that linked the romantic movement to modernism as a series of rejections of scientific mechanism:

Whether the objects of one's hatred are Bacon, Locke and Newton or Darwin, Huxley and Lepage, or other monsters chosen by nineteenth century Frenchmen, one is going, whenever one uses language about art, to be involved in some organicist challenge to the basic eighteenth-century mechanistic treatment of the subject. The most famous statement of this challenge in English is in *Biographia Literaria*, where Coleridge refutes Hartley's mechanistic psychology . . . Before this there had been a prolonged effort by eighteenth century aestheticians and psychologists in the tradition of Hartley (notably Hazlitt's favourite Tucker and, to a lesser extent, Alison, to whom Wordsworth listened) to develop within the Locke-Hartley tradition a certain freedom from pure determinism, without abandoning that uniformity of impulse which made the imagination as much as the memory dependent upon the nervous reorganization of

---

[27] Sir William Hamilton (ed.), with a new Introduction by Knud Haakonssen, *Collected Works of Dugald Stewart, Volume I, Dissertation: Exhibiting the Progress of Metaphysical, Ethical and Political Philosophy, since the Revival of Letters in Europe* (Bristol: Thoemmes Press, 1994; 1854), 445.

sense-impressions. But however ingenious such attempts might be, they could never have led to an organicist theory of art, because they could only conceive of extremely complicated *mechanical* processes performed upon material supplied by the 'vegetative' world. [28]

Kermode invokes a series of assumptions in this passage which are, I believe, unwarranted. First, the idea that eighteenth-century associationism is reductively 'mechanistic' and that this is inevitably a weakness, can be challenged from two directions. Hartley was a medical practitioner: his concern was precisely with 'organs' and their operation, in ways which might much more appropriately be described as 'organicist' than the speculative 'organicism' of his romantic critics. Hartley's concern, like Hume's, was also with how a child could acquire knowledge that was clearly pre-rational in terms of its intellectual development: their concern was with the organism as a developing being, and with the ways in which this organic development was related to development in animals as well as humans. For Hume, for instance, the crucial question is framed as follows:

> When a child has felt the sensation of pain from touching the flame of a candle, he will be careful not to put his hand near any candle; but will expect a similar effect from a cause which is similar in its sensible qualities and appearance. If you assert, therefore, that the understanding of the child is led into this conclusion by any process of argument or ratiocination, I may justly require you to produce that argument; nor have you any pretence to refuse so equitable a demand. You cannot say that the argument is abstruse, and may possibly escape your enquiry; since you confess that it is obvious to the capacity of a mere infant. (*EHU*, 39)

The infant is a test of philosophy because our knowledge is the result of our *organic* experience as a developing creature. Similarly, for Hartley, 'the laws of vibrations and association may be as universal in respect of the nervous systems of animals of all kinds, as the law of circulation is with respect to the system of the heart and blood-vessels; and their powers of sensation and motion be the result of these three laws, *viz.* circulation, vibrations and association, taken together' (*O*, 404). Hartley's theory is 'organic' in the sense

---

[28] Frank Kermode, *Romantic Image* (London: Routledge and Kegan Paul, 1957), 92–3.

that he assumes all organisms are based on the same principles – something which is not true of the idealist philosophy which is supposed to represent an irreversible development beyond the empiricists' 'mechanisms'. There are ways in which, in other words, eighteenth-century 'mechanists' may be more *modern* than nineteenth-century organicists, and to assume that histori-cal succession is equivalent to philosophical superiority is simply to allow nineteenth-century organicist conceptions of history to define their own transcendence of their predecessors. Kermode's discussion is a rhetorical sleight-of-hand which adopts romantic tropes as truths and assumes that history itself is an organic development in which each stage is necessarily a growth beyond its predecessors. Recent work on cognitive theory, on the other hand, suggests the possibility that Hartley's conception of traces laid down in the brain may be more accurate than Coleridge's assertion that the human mind is 'a repetition in the finite mind of the eternal act of creation in the infinite I AM' (*BL*, I, 304).

Kermode also accepts the radical distinction between 'imagination' – which has 'a certain freedom from pure determinism' – and 'memory' – 'dependent upon the nervous reorganization of sense-impressions' – as characteristic not just of *some* nineteenth-century philosophies but of the development of thought itself. The imagination's 'freedom' is, of course, its release from the 'mechanism' of 'association': in Coleridge's terms, the operation of the fancy, which is a function of memory and 'must receive all its materials ready made from the law of association', has to be absolutely distinguished from the real nature of the creative imagination which 'dissolves, diffuses, dissipates, in order to recreate' (*BL*, I, 304). Even James Engell's *The Creative Imagination*, which traces in abundance the eighteenth-century and empiricist sources of Coleridge's ideas, assumes that although 'in forming his concept of the imagination, Coleridge draws on nearly every other writer who discussed the subject', his work 'states more about the imagination' than others' because he 'distills, connects, and adds to the background with which he was so familiar'.[29] Coleridge's version of the 'imagination', in other words, does for the concept exactly what he says the imagination itself does when it 'dissolves, diffuses, dissipates, in order to re-create': it transforms all past insights into a new reality, requiring not only that we recognise 'Coleridge as at once a culminating and an original figure' but as the creator of a conception of the

---

[29] James Engell, *The Creative Imagination: Enlightenment to Romanticism* (Cambridge, MA: Harvard University Press, 1981), 328.

imagination so radically different from all its predecessors that 'we are still somewhere in the mid-course of discovering all that this idea truly means'.[30] The associationist theories that Coleridge transcends with the same leap that the imagination itself transcends the fancy are thus consigned to irrelevance, despite the fact that the distinction between imagination and fancy was one that had already regularly been made by those who accepted associationist accounts of art. Dugald Stewart, for instance, in his *Elements of the Philosophy of the Human Mind*, argued that in the 'poetical imagination, it is the association of ideas that supplies the materials out of which its combinations are formed' and that 'the association of ideas, therefore, although perfectly distinct from the power of imagination, is immediately and essentially subservient to all its exertions';[31] as a consequence, 'to fancy, we apply the epithets of rich or luxuriant, – to imagination, those of beautiful or sublime'.[32] Rather than being a distinctive criterion of a superior conception of the imagination, the imagination-fancy distinction is one that had already been accommodated *within* an associationist account of art. Equally, the insistence on the importance of imagination itself in Coleridge's thought ignores the fact that it is, as we have seen and as Engell himself notes, in David Hume's philosophy, and within Hume's entirely associationist conception of the mind, that the imagination comes first to play an absolutely central role. In this sense, as Douglas Hedley has pointed out, M. H. Abrams' famous distinction between the mirror (representing the mimetic principle) and the lamp (representing expressivism) as indicative of the paradigm shift from an eighteenth-century to a romantic aesthetic is deeply misleading: 'Considered as philosophers Hume is the philosopher of the lamp (the projectionist) and Coleridge as the platonic idealist, is the philosopher of the mirror'.[33]

Neither on the grounds of the centrality of the imagination nor on the basis of the imagination-fancy distinction can Coleridge's theories be distinguished from empiricist and associationist accounts of the mind. The distinction between the two traditions rests not on such structural issues but on their very different conceptions of the *ends* of imaginative activity. In the

---

[30] Ibid., 366.

[31] Sir William Hamilton (ed.), *The Collected Works of Dugald Stewart, Volume II: Elements of the Philosophy of the Human Mind* (Bristol: Thoemmes Press, 1994; 1854), I, 259.

[32] Ibid., 260–1.

[33] Douglas Hedley, *Coleridge, Philosophy and Religion: Aids to Reflection and the Mirror of the Spirit* (Cambridge: Cambridge University Press, 2000), 208.

Kantian-Coleridgean conception, the imagination is the means by which we can gain insight into those transcendental truths that lie beyond the limits of our ordinary experience, what Coleridge describes in relation to the symbol as 'the translucence of the Eternal through and in the Temporal'.[34] For Coleridge, imagination and memory have to be rigorously distinguished – even if they work, in practice, together – because only imagination can escape the 'fixities' of the temporal order to reveal the transcendental truths of eternity. Within Hume's theory, however, imagination and memory are only quantitatively and not qualitatively different.[35] Memory is simply the imagination in operation when it retains the apparent order and sequence in which ideas or emotions previously occurred, rather than producing a new order out of alternative forms of associative connection. For Hume, the imagination does not provide us with a higher order of truth. Rather, the lack of 'truth' which is typical of Hume's conception of cause, in which we can only ever know the fact of 'constant conjunction' rather than 'necessity', affects all the products of the imagination. Only through the workings of the imagination can we discover a stable world – 'I am naturally led to regard the world, as something real and durable, and as preserving its existence, even when it is no longer present to my perception' (T, 197) – but that stable world is, in the end, a 'fiction': 'The smooth passage of the imagination along the ideas of the resembling perceptions makes us ascribe to them a perfect identity. The interrupted manner of their appearance makes us consider them as so many resembling, but still distinct beings, which appear after certain intervals. The perplexity arising from this contradiction produces a propension to unite these broken appearance by the fiction of a continu'd existence' (T, 205). The real that can only be discovered in and through the imagination is, in exactly the same constructive act, dissolved into what we know can only be a 'fiction', a series of associations held together, like the mind, in 'a heap or collection of different perceptions, and supposed, tho' falsely, to be endow'd with a perfect simplicity and identity' (T, 205). 'This deficiency in our ideas,' Hume notes, 'is not, indeed, perceiv'd in common life, nor are we sensible, that in the most usual conjunctions of cause and effect we are as ignorant of the ultimate principle, which binds them together, as in the most unusual and extraordinary. But this proceeds merely

---

[34] Samuel Taylor Coleridge, *Lay Sermons, The Collected Works of Samuel Taylor Coleridge*, Vol. VI, ed. R. J. White (Princeton: Princeton University Press, 1972), 30.

[35] See Jan Wilbanks, *Hume's Theory Of Imagination* (The Hague: Martinus Nijhoff, 1968), 63.

from an illusion of the imagination; and the question is, how far we ought to yield to these illusions' (*T*, 267). The imagination, for Hume, is both absolutely central to our experience of the world – there would, indeed, be no sense of a world as opposed to mere subjective sensations without its operations – and, at the same time, it subverts all our certainties about the world: even 'if the consideration of these instances makes us take a resolution to reject all the trivial suggestions of the fancy, and adhere to the understanding, that is, to the general and more establish'd properties of the imagination; even this resolution, if steadily executed, wou'd be dangerous, and attended with the most fatal consequences' because 'the understanding, when it acts alone, and according to its most general principles, entirely subverts itself, and leaves not the lowest degree of evidence in any proposition' (*T*, 267). Far from providing us with ontological security, what the Humean imagination shows us is that 'we have, therefore, no choice left but betwixt false reason and none at all' (*T*, 268).

Applied to aesthetics, this Humean conception of the imagination produces a profound sense of contingency, of the random and the accidental – of the fragility by which we are bound to the objects of our aesthetic contemplation: as Alison puts it, 'we are conscious of a variety of images in our minds, very different from those which the objects themselves can present to the eye. Trains of pleasing or of solemn thought arise spontaneously within our minds; our hearts swell with emotions, of which the objects before us seem to afford no adequate cause' (*AET*, 5–6). That the art object is 'no adequate cause' for the experience it produces and that it will therefore produce very different experiences in different spectators or readers, undermines any notion of the 'authority' of the artist or, indeed, of the ultimate significance of his or her imagination. Associationist aesthetics treats the art object as the stimulus to what is a fundamentally private experience: as Francis Jeffrey put it in his account of Alison's theories in 1811: 'if it be true, that the emotions which we receive from beauty are thus various in themselves, and that they partake thus largely of the character of other emotions, why should we not conclude, that they are but modifications of these more familiar affections, – and that the beauty which we impute to external objects, is nothing more than their power of reflecting these several inward affections?'[36] Art, in effect, invites us to explore a narrative that is organised by the laws of association and constructed from the recollected materials of our own past experiences. It is this contingency that Coleridge needs to resist, because it undermines

---

[36] Francis Jeffrey, *Edinburgh Review*, Vol. XVIII, No. XXXV (May 1811), 7.

both the hierarchy of meaning, and the hierarchy of being, whose summit is God, for if all thinking and all language is only the workings of association, then,

> The existence of an infinite spirit, of an intelligent and holy will, must on this system be mere articulated motions of the air. For as the function of the human understanding is no other than merely (to appear to itself) to combine and to apply the phaenomena of the association; and as these derive all their reality from the primary sensations; and as the sensations again all their reality from the impressions *ab extra*; a God not visible, audible or tangible can exist only in the sounds and letters that form his name and attributes. (*BL*, I, 120–1)

As David Adam Kaiser puts it, 'For Coleridge, the worldview of empiricism is an "idea-less philosophy" because it cannot comprehend the real nature of "Ideas". In contrast, a worldview informed by the faculty of Reason is able to see that "Ideas" are forces that constitute and guide the material world'.[37] Humean associationism deprives us, Coleridge believes, of those 'powers whose function it is to controul, determine and modify the phantasmal chaos of association' (*BL*, I, 116). It returns us, in other words, to a world before creation, before the 'repetition in the finite mind of the eternal act of creation in the infinite I AM' (*BL*, I, 304), and makes impossible the identification of those symbols that reveal the 'translucence of the Eternal through and in the Temporal'.[38] The contingencies of associationism's subjective narratives negate the higher meaning of which Biblical narrative is the type:

> In the Bible every agent appears and acts as a self-subsisting individual: each has a life of its own, and yet all are one life. The elements of necessity and free-will are reconciled in the higher power of an omnipresent Providence, that predestinates the whole in the moral freedom of the integral parts. Of this the Bible never suffers us to lose sight. The root is never detached from the ground.[39]

---

[37] David Aram Kaiser, *Romanticism, Aesthetics and Nationalism* (Cambridge: Cambridge University Press, 1999), 31.

[38] Samuel Taylor Coleridge, *The Statesman's Manual*, *The Collected Works of Samuel Taylor Coleridge* Vol. VI, ed. R. J. White (London: Routledge and Kegan Paul, 1972), 30.

[39] Ibid., 31–2.

Events in the Biblical narrative are not part of the 'phantasmal chaos'; in their 'translucence' they reveal the reconciliation of individuality with totality, freedom with predestination. They are the model for an art that will construct or reveal the symbols through which human beings can discern the outlines of the Eternal. Hume is Coleridge's ultimate adversary because Hume's version of the imagination offers no such consolation: it is purely social, entirely contingent; generating associations without end, it is always detached from any ground and never capable of reaching an ultimate conclusion.

II

'It was a misfortune to any man of talent,' William Hazlitt wrote in his essay on Coleridge in *The Spirit of the Age*, 'to be born in the latter end of the last century':

> Genius stopped the way of Legitimacy, and therefore it was to be abated, crushed, or set aside as a nuisance. The spirit of the monarchy was at variance with the spirit of the age. The flame of liberty, the light of intellect, was to be extinguished with the sword – or with slander, whose edge is sharper than the sword. The war between power and reason was carried on by the first of these abroad, by the last at home.[40]

In the battle between 'the spirit of monarchy' and 'the flame of liberty', Coleridge, like Wordsworth and Southey, had followed Edmund Burke, and become in Hazlitt's eyes a 'great apostate from liberty and betrayer of his species into the hands of those who claimed it as their property by divine right'.[41] The young Coleridge had been both a literary and a political inspiration to Hazlitt: he 'had nerved his heart and filled his eyes with tears, as he hailed the rising orb of liberty, since quenched in darkness and in blood, and had kindled his affections at the blaze of the French Revolution, and sang for joy, when the towers of the Bastille and the proud palaces of the insolent and the oppressor

---

[40] P. P. Howe (ed.), *The Complete Works of William Hazlitt in Twenty-One Volumes*, Vol. XI, *The Spirit of the Age* (London and Toronto: Routledge, 1930–4), 'Mr. Coleridge', 37.

[41] Ibid., 'Sir James Mackintosh', 100.

fell',[42] but the older Coleridge ends by 'concluding his career where the Allies have concluded theirs, with the doctrine of Divine Right; which he does not however establish quite so successfully with the pen, as they have done with the sword'.[43]

For Hazlitt, this is not simply a matter of political backsliding on the part of once republican poets – it sets in doubt the very sources of poetry and the political inclination of the imagination itself: 'Poverty invites a sort of pity, a miserable dole of assistance; necessity, neglect and scorn; wealth attracts and allures to itself more wealth by natural association of ideas or by that innate love of inequality and injustice which is the favourite principle of the imagination'.[44] The imagination is attracted to where associations accumulate, it favours power, and poets, it seems, are themselves transformed by the power of the imagination that they seek. Hazlitt therefore cannot recognise in the later Coleridge the young preacher whom he 'got up one morning before day-light to walk 10 miles in the mud' to hear, and 'could not have been more delighted if I had heard the music of the spheres. Poetry and Philosophy had met together, Truth and Genius had embraced under the eye and with the sanction of Religion'.[45] The Coleridge who supports the Divine Right of Kings is as much changed as the Burke in whose footsteps he follows: 'Mr. Burke, the opponent of the American war, and Mr. Burke, the opponent of the French Revolution, are not the same person, but opposite persons – not opposite persons only, but deadly enemies'.[46] Burke, whose 'eloquence was that of the poet; of the man of high and unbounded fancy',[47] has been transformed by courting the power of the imagination, which is also the imagination of power: 'In the one, he insulted kings personally, as among the lowest and worst of mankind; in the other, he held them up to the imagination of his readers, as sacred abstractions'.[48] Burke 'constructed his theory of government, in short, not on rational, but on picturesque and fanciful principles',[49] and Coleridge now inhabits this world of fabrication: 'if we can once get rid of the restraints of common sense and honesty we

---

[42] Ibid., 'Mr. Coleridge', 34.
[43] Hazlitt, *Complete Works*, Vol. 7, 'Mr Coleridge's Statesman's Manual', 121.
[44] Hazlitt, *Complete Works*, Vol. 8, *Table Talk*, 'On Will-Making', 115.
[45] Hazlitt, *Complete Works*, Vol. 7, 'Mr. Coleridge's Lay-Sermon', 128, 129.
[46] Ibid., 'The Character of Mr. Burke', 226.
[47] Ibid., 302.
[48] Ibid., 226–7.
[49] Ibid., 228.

may easily prove, by plausible words, that liberty and slavery, peace and war, plenty and famine, are matters of perfect indifference. This is the school of politics, of which Mr. Burke was at the head; and it is perhaps to his example, in this respect, that we owe the prevailing tone of many of those newspaper paragraphs, which Mr. Coleridge thinks so invaluable an accession to our political philosophy'.[50]

In one of his earliest publications when he still had philosophical ambitions – *An Essay on the Principles of Human Action*, published in 1805 – Hazlitt had set out to challenge those philosophies – principal among which was Hartley's associationism – whose passive conception of the psyche compromised belief in the natural 'disinterestedness' of the human mind and therefore undermined political radicalism: 'It has been said that this principle [association] is of itself sufficient to account for all the phenomena of the human mind, and is the foundation of every rule of morality. My design is to shew that both these assertions are absolutely false, or that it is an absurdity, and an express contradiction to suppose that association is either the only mode of operation of the human mind, or that it is the primary and most general principle of thought and action'.[51] In the critical essays of later years, however, it is to the principle of association that Hazlitt regularly appeals to explain the workings of art: in 'Genius and Common Sense', for instance, he defines 'common sense' as 'tacit reason',[52] and illustrates 'tacit reason' by the story of a radical escaping from London to Wales in 1794, whose discomfort over breakfast is suddenly explained by the second appearance of a face which he had not, on its first appearance, taken any conscious notice of, but who turns out to be a well-known spy:

> To the flitting, shadowy, half-distinguished profile that had glided by his window was linked unconsciously and mysteriously, but inseparably, the impression of the trains that had been laid for him by this person; – in this brief moment, in this dim, illegible short-hand of the mind he had just escaped the speeches of the Attorney and Solicitor-General over again; the gaunt figure of Mr. Pitt glared by him; the walls of a prison enclosed him; and he felt the hands of the executioner near him, without knowing it till the tremor and disorder of his nerves gave information to

---

[50] Ibid., 229.

[51] Hazlitt, *Complete Works*, Vol. 1, *Remarks on the Systems of Hartley and Helvetius*, 51.

[52] Hazlitt, *Complete Works*, Vol. 8, 'On Genius and Common Sense', 33.

his reasoning faculties that all was not well within. That is, the same state of mind was recalled by one circumstance in the series of association that had been produced by the whole set of circumstances at the time, though the manner in which this was done was not immediately perceptible.[53]

This example Hazlitt takes to be 'one case of what the learned understand by the *association of ideas*', a concept which Hazlitt defines in materialist terms as the condition under which,

as laid down by physiologists, any impression in a series can recal any other impression in that series without going through the whole in order: so that the mind drops the intermediate links, and passes on rapidly and by stealth to the more striking effects of pleasure or pain which have naturally taken the strongest hold of it. By doing this habitually and skilfully with respect to the various impressions and circumstances with which our experience makes us acquainted, it forms a series of unpremeditated conclusions on almost all subjects that can be brought before it, as just as they are of ready application to human life; and common sense is the name of this body of unassuming but practical wisdom.[54]

On this associational foundation of common sense reason depends – 'reason, not employed to interpret nature, and to improve and perfect common sense and experience, is, for the most part, a building without a foundation'[55] – and the same is true of aesthetic creation and experience: 'There is no rule for expression. It is got at solely by *feeling*, that is, on the principle of the association of ideas'. That is why our responses to art are governed 'not by pre-established rules, but by the instinct of analogy, by the principle of association, which is subtle and sure in proportion as it is variable and indefinite'.[56] As David Bromwich has pointed out,[57] Hazlitt's aesthetic theories run in parallel with Archibald Alison's, and Hazlitt's account of his favourite critical term, 'gusto', recapitulates Alison's insistence that the

---

[53] Ibid., 34.
[54] Ibid., 35.
[55] Ibid., 36.
[56] Ibid., 38.
[57] David Bromwich, *Hazlitt: The Mind of a Critic* (Oxford: Oxford University Press, 1983), 228.

objects of our aesthetic experiences can be so only because they are *expressive* of our own feelings:

> There is hardly any object entirely devoid of expression, without some character of power belonging to it, some precise association with pleasure or pain: and it is in giving this truth of character from the truth of feeling, whether in the highest or the lowest degree, but always in the highest degree of which the subject is capable, that gusto consists.[58]

For Hazlitt, Hartley may have been wrong in trying to make association the single determining element of psychological experience – 'if association were every thing, and the cause of every thing, there could be no comparison of one idea with another, no reasoning, no abstraction, no regular contrivance, no general sense of right and wrong, no sympathy'[59] – but association nonetheless accurately describes much of what takes place in the psyche, and especially what takes place in the workings of art:

> the more ethereal, evanescent, more refined and sublime part of art is the seeing nature through the medium of sentiment and passion, as each object is a symbol of the affections and a link in the chain of our endless being. But the unravelling this mysterious web of thought and feeling is alone in the Muse's gift, namely in the power of that trembling sensibility which is awake to every change and every modification of its ever-varying impressions.[60]

Imagination, for Hazlitt, is not the transcendence of association, but its most intense apprehension.

Hazlitt's prime example of a purely associational artist is Wordsworth, whose 'genius is the effect of his individual character' and he stamps that character, that deep individual interest, on whatever he meets'. To Wordsworth, an 'object is nothing but as it furnishes food for internal meditation, for old associations'.[61] It is because of this associational preoccupation that in Wordsworth's poetry 'a subject or a story [are] merely pegs or loops to hang

---

[58] Hazlitt, *Complete Works*, Vol. 4, 'On *Gusto*', 77.
[59] Hazlitt, *Complete Works*, Vol. 1, *Remarks on the Systems of Hartley and Helvetius*, 67.
[60] Hazlitt, *Complete Works*, Vol. 8, 'The Indian Jugglers', 82–3.
[61] Ibid., 'On Genius and Common Sense', 44.

thought and feeling on';[62] 'Mr. Wordsworth has passed his life in solitary musing or in daily converse with the face of nature. He exemplifies in an eminent degree the power of *association*; for his poetry has no other source or character'.[63] This associational poetry exemplifies 'the spirit of the age':

> It is one of the innovations of the time. It partakes of, and is carried along with, the revolutionary movement of our age: the political changes of the day were the model on which he formed and conducted his poetical experiments. His Muse (it cannot be denied, and without this we cannot explain its character at all) is a levelling one.[64]

This *levelling* poetry overthrows art's aristocratic pretensions: 'It takes the commonest events and objects, as a test to prove that nature is always interesting from its inherent truth and beauty, without any of the ornaments of dress or pomp of circumstances to set it off'; it 'has discarded all the tinsel pageantry of verse'.[65] Such a *levelling* effect is implicit in Alison's undermining of Edmund Burke's hierarchy of the sublime and beautiful, for instead of two separate principles of aesthetic experience, one mighty and one diminutive, both are simply aspects of the effects of association: 'When any object, either of sublimity or beauty is presented to the mind,' Alison writes, 'I believe every man is conscious of a train of thought being immediately awakened in his imagination, analogous to the character or expression of the original object' (*AET*, 2). For Coleridge it was precisely the levelling effects of association which had to be overcome by a conception of the imagination – surmounting as it does the workings of fancy – which would reintroduce a psychological and aesthetic hierarchy that mirrored the social hierarchy to which his later politics were committed. As Gerald McNiece has suggested, Coleridge's

> new perspective required a re-assessment of the French Revolution as a product of mechanical associationism and social atomism. Empiricism and sensationism produce a *French* nature not a *human* nature . . . . The passion for atomistic tinkering with conventions, constitutions and

---

[62] Hazlitt, *Complete Works*, Vol. 11, *The Spirit of the Age*, 87.
[63] Hazlitt, *Complete Works*, Vol. 11, 'Mr. Wordsworth', 89.
[64] Ibid., 87.
[65] Ibid., 87, 88.

contracts must give way to the insight of organicism that 'the whole is prior to the parts'.[66]

Hazlitt might continue to insist, as he did in his 'Letter to William Gifford', that 'the spirit of poetry is . . . favourable to liberty and humanity', but in his own times that belief had to be severely qualified: 'but not when its aid is most wanted, in encountering the shocks and disappointments of the world . . . Standing on its feet, jostling with the crowd, it is liable to be overthrown, trampled on and defaced'.[67]

Hazlitt is caught between an associationist and democratic conception of poetry which lacks power – 'The force, the originality, the absolute truth and identity with which he feels some things, makes him indifferent to so many others', he says of Wordsworth[68] – and a poetry whose assertion of power is at one with reaction and repression. In his account of Shakespeare's *Henry V*, Hazlitt takes the opportunity to use Henry as a symbol of 'kingly power from the beginning to the end of the world'; it is a power which can only be 'triumphant when it is opposed to the will of others, because the pride of power is only then shewn, not when it consults the rights and interests of others, but when it insults and tramples on all justice and all humanity'.[69] Why should such a character appeal to us? 'We like him in the play', Hazlitt answers because,

There he is a very amiable monster, a very splendid pageant. As we like to gaze at a panther or a young lion in their cages in the Tower, and catch a pleasing horror from their glistening eyes, their velvet paws, and dreadless roar, so we take a very romantic, heroic, patriotic, and poetical delight in the boasts and feats of our younger Harry, as they appear on the stage and are confined to lines of ten syllables; where no blood follows the stroke that wounds our ears, where no harvest bends beneath horses' hoofs, no city flames, no little child is butchered, no dead men's bodies are found piled on heaps and festering the next morning – in the orchestra![70]

---

[66] Gerald McNeice, *The Knowledge that Endures: Coleridge, German Philosophy and the Logic of Romantic Thought* (Basingstoke: Macmillan, 1992), 145.

[67] Hazlitt, *Complete Works*, Vol. 9, 50.

[68] Hazlitt, *Complete Works*, Vol. 11, 'Mr. Wordsworth', 94.

[69] Hazlitt, *Complete Works*, Vol. 4, 'Henry V', 285–6.

[70] Ibid., 286.

The pleasures of this aestheticised violence, violence apparently contained in its effects within the walls of the theatre and within the boundaries of the aesthetic, is undermined by the irony of Hazlitt's prose, for the contemporary invasion of France has produced exactly these outcomes in the effort to reinstate Henry's kind of kingly power: 'the object of war formerly, when the people adhered to their allegiance, was to depose kings; the object latterly, since the people swerved from their allegiance, has been to restore kings, and to make common cause against mankind'.[71] Because the imagination is moved by power, and not by sympathy, and because power commands more associations, both social and psychological, poetry in the modern age favours the opponents of the 'people' and of the revolution which might release them from their suffering:

> The cause of the people is indeed but little calculated as a subject for poetry: it admits of rhetoric, which goes into argument and explanation, but it presents no immediate or distinct images to the mind, 'no jutting frieze, buttress, or coigne of vantage' for poetry 'to make its pendant bed and procreant cradle in'. The language of poetry naturally falls in with the language of power. The imagination is an exaggerating and exclusive faculty: it takes from one thing to add to another: it accumulates circumstances together to give the greatest possible effect to a favourite object. The understanding is a dividing and measuring faculty: it judges of things, not according to their immediate impression on the mind, but according to their relations to one another. The one is a monopolizing faculty, which seeks the greatest quantity of present excitement by inequality and disproportion; the other is a distributive faculty, which seeks the greatest quantity of ultimate good, by justice and proportion. The one is an aristocratical, the other a republican faculty. The principle of poetry is a very anti-levelling principle.[72]

This disenchanted conception of the imagination is the outcome of Burke's and Coleridge's hijacking of the revolutionary potential Hazlitt thought he had glimpsed in the speech of the young Coleridge – a potential still visible in the associationist art of Wordsworth's early poetry. Now, however, he knows that the imagination 'has its altars and its victims, sacrifices,

---

[71] Ibid.

[72] Ibid., 'Coriolanus', 214.

human sacrifice. Kings, priests, nobles, are its train-bearers, tyrants and slaves its executioners. – "Carnage is its daughter." – Poetry is right royal. It puts the individual for the species, the one above the infinite many, might before right'.[73] As Tom Paulin has noted,[74] 'Carnage is thy daughter' is an ironic quotation from Wordsworth's 'Thanksgiving Ode' of January 1816, celebrating the defeat of Napoleon at Waterloo: Hazlitt turns the language of apostasy back against itself to reveal the real nature of its politics. Such unacknowledged allusion is typical of Hazlitt's style, which is embedded with quotations and what Paulin describes as 'associative clusters':[75] 'these interconnections are applications of the concept of association', Paulin comments, 'a concept which functions as a shaping critical principle for Hazlitt'.[76] It is as though Hazlitt's prose is designed to embody the 'level-ling principle' of Wordsworth's poetry and to resist the reactionary power of the imagination; as though Hazlitt's criticism encloses and surrounds transcendental conceptions of imagination with an alternative associationist aesthetic that can neutralise its 'anti-levelling principle'.

Hazlitt's sustained associationist criticism underlines the extent to which the literature we identify as 'Romantic' is not only compatible with associationism, but provides it with some of its key resources for new literary experiments. The profound influence of Hazlitt's writing on Keats, for instance – who regarded Hazlitt as 'almost an embodiment of the modern idea of genius'[77] – is indicative of how associationism could continue to inspire new developments in Romantic poetry: 'by helping Keats to revise his own idea of the imagination', David Bromwich suggests, 'Hazlitt altered the course of modern poetry'.[78] Far from being relegated by romanticism as irrelevant to modern poetics, associationism continues in the work of Hazlitt and Keats to be the inspiration of some of its major developments.

---

[73] Ibid., 214–15.

[74] Tom Paulin, *The Day-Star of Liberty: William Hazlitt's Radical Style* (London: Faber and Faber, 1998), 40.

[75] 'Deep in Hazlitt's critical imagination there appears to be an associative clus-ter – *plodding petrific prose Locke English Dutch decomposition* – which makes the elements of prose look very like the flat aggregated soil of hell or the level plains of the Dutch state (Crabbe is associated with 'Dutch interiors, hovels, and pig-styes')', *Day-Star of Liberty*, 93.

[76] Paulin, *Day-Star of Liberty*, 260.

[77] Bromwich, *Hazlitt: The Mind of a Critic*, 365.

[78] Ibid., 401. Bromwich also suggests that Keats's famous 'Beauty is truth, truth beauty' is based on 'Hazlitt's writings on associationism'; ibid., 399.

III

Because of his central place in modern criticism, it is easy to forget that Coleridge's contemporary influence as a thinker was much less than the importance accorded to him in our retrospective construction of literary history. James Engell's *The Creative Imagination* may make Coleridge the fulcrum on which the development of the concept of the imagination turns, but as J. H. Muirhead pointedly demonstrated by excluding Coleridge from his study of *The Platonic Tradition in Anglo-Saxon Philosophy*,[79] Coleridge's influence on British thought was extremely slow to develop, and Muirhead's own, highly influential study of *Coleridge as Philosopher*[80] was designed, in 1930, to recuperate from Coleridge's incomplete presentation the outlines of a philosophy which would be prescient of late-nineteenth-century British Idealism, though it had had little actual influence on its development. Muirhead's explanation of the ineffectuality of Coleridge's thinking on his immediate successors is a 'certain unripeness of the time for the acceptance by philosophers'[81] of his ideas. The consequence is that Coleridge's contribution to nineteenth-century thought can, for Muirhead, only be *retrospectively* important, since it 'bears witness to the vitality and inherent attractiveness of the voluntaristic form of idealist philosophy' that Muirhead believes 'marks the present time'.[82]

Muirhead believed that the crucial element in Coleridge's transformation of associationist theories of taste lay in the fact that for Coleridge 'association depends in a much greater degree on the recurrence of resembling states of feeling than trains of ideas' and that, as he wrote to Southey in 1803, 'I almost think that ideas never recall ideas, as far as they are ideas, any more than leaves in a forest create each other's motion. The breeze it is that runs thro' them – it is the soul, the state of feeling'.[83] In fact, however, Coleridge is here only repeating something that is quite explicit in Hume's account of associations, in which he argues that the association of *ideas* 'operates in so silent and imperceptible a manner, that we are scarce sensible of it', because in itself it 'produces no emotion'. For Hume, the 'relation of ideas' works

---

[79] J. H. Muirhead, *The Platonic Tradition in Anglo-Saxon Philosophy* (London: George Allen & Unwin, 1931).

[80] J. H. Muirhead, *Coleridge as Philosopher* (London: George Allen & Unwin, 1930).

[81] Ibid., 259.

[82] Ibid., 117.

[83] Ibid., 199, *Collected Letters*, Vol. II, 961, 7 August 1803.

together with 'a relation of the affections', each feeding and supporting the other and leading to 'the transition of affections along the relation of ideas' (*T*, 305–6). It is a point emphasised by Thomas Brown, Dugald Stewart's successor at the University of Edinburgh, who replaces 'association' with 'suggestion' precisely in order to escape the notion that ideas are connected simply and directly to other ideas: trains of such suggestions 'take place, not directly as a sequence of mere conceptions, but by the intervention of some emotion or other common feeling, which the analogous objects have each a tendency to excite, and have before separately excited'.[84] This is particularly important for poetry, because

> Our similes and metaphors are all founded on some agreement of this kind, of the feelings that have attended the separate contemplation of the analogous objects: and he in whom the most lively emotions are excited by objects, or who is accustomed to give his mind most freely to their sway, so as to indulge the longest in the contemplation of the objects that excite them, will, in consequence of this greater liveliness and frequency of and permanence of the resulting feelings, have a greater variety of conceptions that have co-existed with them on different occasions, and that admit, accordingly, of reciprocal suggestions. When the corresponding emotion, therefore, has been excited by any new object, it is not wonderful, that some one of the objects which before excited it should rise to the mind, as if suggested directly by the common analogy in this respect. It thus happens, that the suggestions of analogy, which constitute poetic invention, are most abundant in minds of the liveliest feelings . . .[85]

While J. S. Mill's account of the poet in 1833 – 'Those who are so constituted, that emotions are the links of association by which their ideas, both sensuous and spiritual, are connected together' (*Au*, 356) – clearly echoes Brown, one of the students who listened to Brown's lectures, and who was close to Mill in the 1830s, was Thomas Carlyle. Carlyle, however, utterly rejected Brown's associationism. In 'Signs of the Times' (1829), he castigated 'our "Theories of Taste", as they are called, wherein the deep, infinite, unspeakable Love of Wisdom and Beauty, which dwells in all men, is "explained",

---

[84] Thomas Brown, *Observations on the Nature and Tendency of the Doctrine of Mr Hume concerning the relation of Cause and Effect* (Edinburgh: Mundell and Son, 1806), 204–5.

[85] Ibid., 205–6.

made mechanically visible, from "Association" and the like'.[86] And it was Carlyle who became the standard-bearer for Germanic transcendentalism from the 1830s: Edward Caird, one of the leading figures of the British Idealist movement which Muirhead saw Coleridge as foreshadowing, looked back to Carlyle as 'the first in this country who discovered the full significance of the great revival of German literature, and the enormous reinforcement which its poetic and philosophic idealism had brought to the failing faith of man'. For Caird, Carlyle spoke 'from what was recognisably a higher point of view than that of the ordinary sects and parties which divided opinion in this country, a higher point of view than any of the prevailing orthodoxies and heterodoxies', and his impact was all the greater because he was 'the first from whom we heard the great words of Goethe and Fichte, of Schiller and Richter and Novalis'.[87] For Carlyle, as for Coleridge, it is the 'Pyrrhonism of Hume and the Materialism of Diderot' which associationism underpins, and from which we can only escape with the help of German transcendentalism: we now know 'that Pyrrhonism and Materialism, themselves necessary phenomena in European culture, have disappeared; and a Faith in Religion has again become possible and inevitable for the scientific mind'.[88]

Central to Carlyle's as well as to Coleridge's transcendentalism was the theory of the symbol, but it was Carlyle's which was to be the inspiration for major developments in nineteenth-century literature:

> In the Symbol proper, what we can call a Symbol, there is ever, more or less distinctly and directly, some embodiment and revelation of the Infinite; the Infinite is made to blend itself with the Finite, to stand visible, and, as it were, attainable there.[89]

Carlyle's definition was appealed to by the French symbolists[90] and Arthur Symons' *The Symbolist Movement in Literature* (1890) not only quoted the above definition in the text but drew its epigraph from another passage

---

[86] Thomas Carlyle, 'Signs of the Times', *Works*, ed. H. D. Traill, 30 Vols (London: Chapman and Hall, 1896–9), Vol. 27, 76.

[87] Edward Caird, *Essays on Literature and Philosophy* (Glasgow: James Maclehose and Sons, 1892), 232.

[88] 'Characteristics', *Works*, Vol. 28, 40–1.

[89] Thomas Carlyle, *Sartor Resartus*, ed. Roger L. Tarr (Berkeley: University of California Press, 2000; 1833); hereafter cited in the text as *SR*.

[90] See Roger L. Tarr, 'Introduction', *Sartor Resartus*, xxvii.

in *Sartor Resartus*: 'It is in and through Symbols that man, consciously or unconsciously, lives, works, and has his being: those ages, moreover, are accounted the noblest, which can best recognize symbolical worth, and prize it highest'.[91] Despite its influence, however, Carlyle's account of the symbol is fraught with difficulties and his justification of it is constantly undermined by the very associationism that it is intended to transcend. An instance from his early essay 'Characteristics', in which Carlyle takes 'white light' as a symbol of the perfection of the unselfconscious life of the child, will illustrate the problem: childhood, Carlyle writes, is 'a pure, perpetual, unregarded music; a beam of perfect white light, rendering all things visible, but itself unseen, even because it was of that perfect whiteness, and no irregular obstruction had yet broken it into colours'.[92] The breaking of 'perfect whiteness' into its components colours is, for Carlyle, equivalent to the moment when the body becomes 'the prison-house of the soul';[93] it is the shattering of the spiritual by the mechanical: 'what [man] can altogether know and comprehend, is essentially the mechanical, small; the great is ever, in one sense or the other, the vital; it is essentially the mysterious, and only the surface of it can be understood'.[94] The relationship of white light to its component colours was, however, precisely what John Stuart Mill identified in his father's discussion as confirming the power of association to transform apparently discrete psychic elements into higher unities, and thereby to create new 'wholes' from fundamentally mechanical processes:

> When two or more ideas have often been repeated together, and the association has become very strong, they sometimes spring up in such close combination as not to be distinguishable. Some cases of sensation are analogous. For example, when a wheel, on the seven parts of which the seven prismatic colours are respectively painted, is made to revolve rapidly, it appears not of seven colours, but of one uniform colour white . . . Ideas, also, which have been so conjoined that whenever one exists in the mind, the others immediately exist along with it, seem to run into one another, to coalesce as it were, and out many for one idea; which

---

[91] Arthur Symons, *The Symbolist Movement in Literature* (New York: E. P. Dutton and Co., 1958; 1899), 1.

[92] Thomas Carlyle, 'Characteristics', *Works*, Vol. 28, 2–3.

[93] Ibid.

[94] Ibid.

idea, however in reality complex, appears to be no less simple, than any one of those of which it is compounded.[95]

What Carlyle reads as a case of the mechanical breaking of unity and wholeness, Mill uses as proof of the possibility of the production of unity and wholeness by 'mechanical' means. The symbol which, for transcendentalists, is 'vital' and therefore 'mysterious', is, like white light, perfectly reproducible or explainable in associationst terms which negate the transcendence claimed for it.

Carlyle's description of the symbol begins with the power of 'silence', which, unlike white light, cannot be broken down into its component parts: 'In a symbol there is concealment and yet revelation: hence, therefore, by Silence and by Speech acting together, comes a doubled significance' (SR, 162). It is because 'Speech is of time, Silence of Eternity' that the symbol can be made a gateway to higher truths: 'by Symbols, accordingly, is man guided and commanded, made happy, made wretched. He everywhere finds himself encompassed with Symbols, recognized as such or not recognized: the Universe is but one vast Symbol of God' (SR, 162–3). This all-encompassing and apparently indissoluble Symbol is, however, rapidly resolved by Carlyle into two different types of symbols, whose value is either 'extrinsic' or 'intrinsic' (SR, 164). Thus the 'clouted Shoe, which the Peasants bore aloft with them as ensign in their *Bauernkriek* (Peasants' War)' had no intrinsic significance, 'only extrinsic: as the accidental Standards of multitudes more or less sacredly uniting together' (SR, 164). The 'accidental' is the associational: it is a symbol arbitrarily associated with a particular cause. In this sense, even the Cross of Christianity is nothing but an extrinsic symbol, the effect of the accumulation of associations with which the symbol is imbued in the minds of its perceivers.

Defining the intrinsic symbol, however, proves to be extraordinarily difficult for Carlyle. The difficulty may have some justification in *Sartor Resartus* because it is the Editor rather than Carlyle who is providing this commentary, an editor with a British empiricist background who is struggling to understand a German philosophical text. But the very dialectical structure of the work is indicative of the difficulties from which the real author was distancing himself. 'Another matter it is', we are told, 'when your symbol has intrinsic meaning,

---

[95] Mill, *Collected Works*, Vol. 9, *Examination of Sir William Hamilton's Philosophy*, 252.

and is of itself *fit* that men should unite round it'. But finding such a fit symbol leads us first to 'all true Works of Art: in them (if thou know a Work of Art from a Daub of Artifice) wilt thou discern Eternity looking through Time; the Godlike rendered visible' (*SR*, 165). The parenthesis, however, effectively dissolves the certainty which the symbol is supposed to provide: how do we know if we really know a 'Work of Art from a Daub of Artifice'? How do we know that this is truly an intrinsic symbol and that we are not simply responding to extrinsic associations in our own minds? The problem is then compounded by the fact that intrinsic symbols eventually begin to inherit extrinsic qualities: 'Here too may an extrinsic value gradually superadd itself: thus certain *Iliads*, and the like, have in three-thousand years, attained quite new significance'. Silence unravels into Speech with such insistence that the Silence is unheard: it is implied only 'in the Lives of heroic god-inspired Men: for what other Work of Art is so divine?' (*SR*, 165). The explication of the nature of the symbol ends on a rhetorical question which is self-defeating: is the work of art divine if the god-inspired men were *falsely* inspired? Is this an intrinsic symbol if their symbols were, after all, only of extrinsic significance to anyone who encountered them?

At each instance, Carlyle's text presents the intrinsic, the true symbol dissolving into the extrinsic, the merely associative symbol, contingently linked in the memory and therefore subject to decay: 'But, on the whole, as Time adds much to the sacredness of Symbols, so likewise in his progress he at length defaces, or even desecrates them; and Symbols, like all terrestrial Garments, wax old' (*SR*, 165). In this moment of disintegration, a Prophet arrives 'who Prometheus-like, can shape new symbols, and bring new Fire from Heaven to fix it there' (*SR*, 165), but these too will eventually decay, or become shrouded in extrinsic significances. Carlyle's white light is constantly being decomposed into its colours; his Silence overrun with speech: the ultimate entry into the Infinite continually barred by a symbol of whose intrinsic value we can never be certain. The dialectical structure of *Sartor Resartus*, in which a German philosophy of the symbolic is being interpreted by a sceptical British editor, is a dramatization of the philosophical impasse in which Carlyle is caught. The transcendental symbol is never safe from being re-read as a case of secular association. It is a possibility that also haunts Carlyle's histories, which convey the frustration of a world busily creating symbols of Infinity that prove to be nothing but accidental psychological connections. In *The French Revolution*, Carlyle asserts 'that of man's whole terrestrial possessions and attainments, unspeakably the noblest are his Symbols, divine or divine-seeming; under which he marches and fights, with victorious assurance, in this life-battle'.[96] But how do we tell the difference between 'divine' and 'divine-seeming'? Uncertainty is again compounded by Carlyle's rhetorical strategies, for he appeals as confirmation for the value of the symbol to his own definition of it in *Sartor Resartus*, so that his philosophy of history is founded on an unresolved argument presented in a work of fiction.

John Stuart Mill's analysis of the symbol precisely reverses Carlyle's. For Mill, what was called by Leibniz 'symbolical' thinking[97] is a particular application of 'signs', in which 'class names' are used to allow us to think conceptually: however, conceptual thinking cannot be separated from the fact that 'we think by means of ideas of concrete phenomena, such as are presented in experience or represented in imagination, and by means of names, which being in a peculiar manner associated with certain elements of the concrete images, arrest our attention on those elements'.[98] A concept is used 'to *de*note the objects and *con*note the attributes' of a particular class: so, '*white* denotes chalk and other white substances, and connotes the particular colour which is common to them'.[99] Since the totality of what a concept involves can never enter into our mental state in any particular train of thought, because we think only with ideas which have been 'presented in experience or represented in imagination', concepts are effectively empty containers: 'in our processes of thought, seldom more than a part, and sometimes a very small part, of what is comprehended in the concept, is attended to, or comes into play'.[100] For Carlyle, the 'silence' of the symbol is the evidence of its fullness, of its excess over any meaning that we can fix or define: it is meaningful beyond any meaning we can assign. For Mill, on the other hand, the symbol is effective precisely because of its emptiness, its lack of significance:

> The word does not always serve the purpose of fixing our attention on the whole of the attributes which it connotes; some of them may be only recalled to mind faintly, others possibly not at all: a phaenomenon easily to be accounted for by the laws of Obliviscence. But the part of the attributes signified which the word does recal, may be all that it is

---

[96] Carlyle, *Works*, Vol. 2, 8.
[97] Mill, *Collected Works*, Vol. 9, *Examination of Sir William Hamilton's Philosophy*, 319.
[98] Ibid., 315.
[99] Ibid., 318.
[100] Ibid., 318.

necessary for us to think of, at the time and for the purposes in hand; it may be a sufficient part to set going all the associations by means of which we proceed through that thought to ulterior thoughts. Indeed, it is because part of the attributes have generally sufficed for that purpose, that the habit is acquired of not attending to remainder. When the attributes not attended to are really of no importance for the end in view, and if attended to would not have altered the results of the mental process, there is no harm done: much of our valid thinking is carried on in this manner, and it is to this that our thinking processes owe, in great measure, their proverbial rapidity.[101]

The effectiveness of the symbol is that we do not attend to all of its attributes: it represents, in Hazlitt's terms, the 'short-hand of the mind', and works, like shorthand, by reduction. From Mill's point of view, Carlyle mistakes the symbol's lack of content for a plenitude of content; he takes its radical exclusion of possible meaning for an endless enlargement of meaning. For Mill, a symbol allows us to speed up the process of thought by reducing the number of associations involved; for Carlyle the 'intrinsic' symbol transcends association by opening on to an infinite meaning which has no connection with the contingent and accidental formation of 'extrinsic' symbols. Of Carlyle's symbol, John Stuart Mill might well have said what he was to say of Ruskin, who regarded himself as having finally exploded associationist aesthetics:

> Mr Ruskin would probably be much astonished were he to find himself held up as one of the principal apostles of the Association Philosophy in Art. Yet, in one of the most remarkable of his writings, the second volume of *Modern Painters*, he aims at establishing, by a large induction and searching analysis, that all things are beautiful (or sublime) which powerfully recall, and none but those which recall, one or more of the certain series of elevating or delightful thoughts.[102]

Associationists thus translated the 'transcendence' of idealist thinkers back into the psychological workings of association, revealing how easily the intrinsic became the extrinsic, how easily the access to the Infinite could

---

[101] Ibid., 319.
[102] Mill, *Collected Works*, Vol. 11, 'Bain's Psychology', 363–4.

be seen simply as the infinite complexity of the human mind's associational workings.

IV

In his biography of Coleridge, Richard Holmes recounts that on 10 September 1802 Coleridge wrote to Southey to offer an account of the experiences which had led to a poem he was about to publish, and why he had chosen to set them in Switzerland rather than in England:

> I involuntarily poured forth a Hymn in the manner of the *Psalms*, tho' afterwards I thought the Ideas etc disproportionate to our humble mountains – & accidentally lighting on a short Note in some Swiss Poems, concerning the Vale of Chamouny, & its Mountain, I transferred myself thither, in the Spirit, & adapted my former feelings to these grander external objects. You will soon see it in the Morning Post.[103]

This 'involuntary' expression of the sublime, this transport of the 'Spirit', this direct effusion of the imagination, turned out to be, substantially, an unacknowledged translation of a German poem by Frederike Brun – a carefully repressed memory trace which Coleridge had 'associated' with his own experience. Some lines from the poem, addressed to those 'grander external objects', might be read as turning back in an implied question to their supposed author:

> And you, ye five wild torrents fiercely glad!
> Who called you forth from night and utter death,
> From dark and icy cavern called you forth,
> Down those precipitous, black, jagged rocks,
> For ever shattered and the same for ever?
> Who gave you your invulnerable life,
> Your strength, your speed, your fury, and your joy,
> Unceasing thunder and eternal foam.[104]

---

[103] Coleridge, *Collected Letters*, Vol. II, 864–5.
[104] Samuel Taylor Coleridge, *Poetical Works*, ed. E. H. Coleridge (Oxford: Clarendon Press, 1912), 378–9.

Of the 'torrents' of *this* imagination, it is only too appropriate to ask 'Who gave you your invulnerable life,/Your strength, your speed, your fury, and your joy?'. The answer is certainly not Coleridge alone. The power of the imagination that 'dissolves, diffuses, dissipates in order to re-create', in order 'to idealize and to unify', that rises to a transcendent totality, is reversed in an image of a 'streamy' torrent which, though 'the same for ever', is also 'for ever shattered'. The 'eternal' is 'foam' on the surface of the stream of life.

Coleridge's 'forged' association between his own emotion and Brun's expression was not uncovered till 1842,[105] but the possibility that Coleridge's imagination, even when not actually stealing, worked by associative recall from his past reading was to lead to one of the most famous pieces of literary detection of the twentieth century – John Livingston Lowes's *The Road to Xanadu: A Study in the Ways of the Imagination* (1927) – which charts how fragments from Coleridge's reading had been *forged* into 'two of the most remarkable poems in English',[106] 'The Rime of the Ancient Mariner' and 'Kubla Khan'. Lowes decomposes the imaginative unity of Coleridge's poem to uncover, from clues in Coleridge's *Notebooks*, the origins of words, images and scenes in texts that Coleridge had been reading, because 'at moments of high imaginative tension associations, not merely in pairs but in battalions, are apt in similar fashion to stream together and coalesce' (*RX*, 44). Lowes's aim, in other words, is to prove the truth of Coleridge's own theory of the imagination, and to show how the normal processes of association which operate in memory can be transformed by the imagination into a higher unity; to show how, in Coleridge's words, the imagination, 'out of the chaos of elements or shattered fragments of memory, *puts together some form to fit it*';[107] or, in Lowes's words, to show how 'there emerges from chaotic multiplicity a unified and ordered world' (*RX*, 429). Lowes tracks down the associational materials that were incorporated into Coleridge's poetry but Coleridge's theory of the imagination is invoked to prove that the associations do not *constitute* the poetry because they have to be re-formed into a higher order of significance: 'in a chaos of teeming reminiscences the shaping spirit saw and seized a hint

---

[105] In an article by Thomas De Quincy, *Tait's Magazine*, 1834: see fn. 1, *Collected Letters of Samuel Taylor Coleridge*, Vol. 2, 865.

[106] John Livingston Lowes' *The Road to Xanadu: A Study in the Ways of the Imagination* (2nd edition, London: Constable, 1951; 1927), 3; hereafter cited in the text as *RX*.

[107] Ernest Hartley Coleridge (ed.), *Anima Poetae: From the Unpublished Notebooks of Samuel Taylor Coleridge* (London: William Heinemann, 1845), 244.

of Form, and, through a miracle of conscious art, out of chaos itself has been moulded a radiant and ordered whole' (*RX*, 71).

Association, in other words, is the handmaiden of imagination, providing the mechanical materials which it will transform into an organic order. Lowes envisages the process as one in which materials are stored in an 'unconscious' where 'images and impressions converge and blend', but where, in the 'wonder-working depths' of a 'genius', 'the fragments which sink incessantly below the surface fuse and assimilate and coalesce' (*RX*, 59, 60). Indeed, a quasi-mechanical explanation of the process is suggested in which, in a phrase from Epicurus quoted by Henri Poincaré, the associations are described as 'hooked atoms' which are released to 'plough through space in all directions, like a swarm of gnats, for instance, or, . . . like the gaseous molecules in the kinetic theory of gases. Their mutual collisions may then produce new combinations . . .' (*RX*, 62). What is striking about Lowes's account is that it is based on a thoroughly assocationist account of the workings of memory – and this in the 1920s – even though he insists that we have to 'recognize that one office of the imagination is to curb and rudder the clustering associations which throng up from the nether depths of consciousness, until out of the thick of the huddle springs beauty' (*RX*, 73). Ironically, however, in illustration of the effects of 'imagination', Lowes appeals to exactly the model that James Mill had used to illustrate why such higher order unities could be explained in purely associationist terms: 'the unity that has somehow come about', he comments, 'is as integral as the union of the seven colours which blend in a beam of white light. You may break up the beam into its spectrum, as we have resolved our shapes of light into their elements' but 'the result in either case is the same: the enhancement of the miracle of their unity' (*RX*, 54). The very image which the associationists had used to prove that 'mechanical' interactions could produce a higher unity without the intervention of any other faculty is reproduced by Lowes in order to prove its opposite – that we need a *higher* theory of the imagination to explain how associations can be fused together into 'the new whole which has been wrought from them' (*RX*, 48).

The crux of Lowes's argument is also the crux of Coleridge's – that association by itself operates without the intervention of the will and that it is the *will* which transforms mere associational material into art: for Coleridge, the imagination is 'first put in action by the will and the understanding' (*BL*, II, 16), and for Lowes, the difference between the 'Ancient Mariner' and 'Kubla Khan' is that the former is art, shaped by the will, while the latter is simply the record of an associational reverie in which the will has never been involved, and which was therefore incapable of having been shaped into completed poem:

> in Kubla Khan the complicating factor – the will as a consciously constructive agency – was in abeyance. 'All the images rose up before him as *things*, with a parallel production of the correspondent expressions, without any sensation or consciousness of effort.' The dream, it is evident, was the unchecked subliminal flow of blending images, and the dreamer merely the detached and unsolicitous spectator. And so the sole factor that determined the form and sequence which the dissolving phantasmagoria assumed, was the subtle potency of associative links. There was this time no intervention of a waking intelligence intent upon a plan . . . (RX, 401)

The elements of 'Kubla Khan' are the result of a 'streaming vision of *passive* association' (RX, 411), and while 'to the making of both poems went the ceaseless vivid flow of the linked images', the difference between them lies in the fact that in '"The Ancient Mariner" "thinking" was imperially present; in "Kubla Khan" it had abdicated its control' (RX, 413). Given, however, that Lowes wants to claim 'Kubla Khan' as one of the glories of English poetry, it is clear that, from his perspective, 'mere' association can indeed be effectively *creative*, since by its power alone Coleridge has managed to produce a poem of the very highest value.

This is obviously a troubling conclusion if only the *imagination* can be truly creative, and Lowes acknowledges it in a footnote in which he asks, 'What is one to say of the paradox of a seemingly conscious control of sheer metrical technique in the marvelous rhythms of "Kubla Khan"?' (RX, 413). The associative vision that Coleridge experienced was a series of 'images' that 'rose up before him as *things*': the language of the poem was not part of that vision but a later elaboration of it. Lowes argues in a further footnote even more removed from his main argument that Coleridge's mastery of rhythm led to 'the effortless utterance of a genius to whom rhythmical expression was as simple as breathing, and as natural' (RX, 598), and that therefore it was as *unconscious* in its production as the associations themselves, despite the fact that 'few poems bear more palpable marks of finished, even cunning, craftsmanship' (RX, 597). The contradiction has to be displaced to an on-page footnote and then to an end note because if rhythm is 'as simple as breathing, and a natural', then why shouldn't the narrative design of 'The Ancient Mariner' be similarly the unconscious product of a genius who does not need to *will* the effects of 'cunning craftsmanship'? The distinction between the *willed* creations of the imagination and the mere flow of associations disappears, and 'The Ancient Mariner' could be the outcome of the 'effortless utterance' of association just as easily as 'Kubla Khan'. Coleridge's theory of the imagination dissolves in a distinction that cannot be sustained even in the analysis of his own poetry. If association works in the unconscious 'well' of the mind, as Lowes describes it, that unconscious 'well' could be as responsible for narrative structure as he believes it to be of rhythmic structure, could be as responsible for the totality of the poem as it is, in his analysis, for the individual images.

The distinction that Lowes wants to make between 'The Ancient Mariner' and 'Kubla Khan' is fundamental to the idealist refutation of associationism, because it assumes that the 'will' is something outside or above the mere *passive* flow of associations: association may give rise to the flow of images that is 'Kubla Khan', but in its very incompleteness 'Kubla Khan' reveals that association by itself could not have produced the *finished* work of art that is 'The Ancient Mariner'. Lowes attempts to illustrate this difference with a personal anecdote about a train of associations set off by the arrival of a letter 'from an English friend' – an illustration which neatly reverses Coleridge's anecdote of how his writing down of the vision of 'Kubla Khan' was interrupted by the arrival of a man from Porlock, after which 'all the rest had passed away like the images on the surface of a stream into which a stone had been cast, but, alas! without the restoration of the latter!'[108] Lowes's letter sets off a train of associations that he takes to be 'an instance, normal enough, of "the streamy nature of association"' (RX, 430), which

> was set in motion and unrolled without my will. For the moment I simply allowed the images to stream. Then I deliberately assumed control. For when, an hour later, I came back to write, I saw that here, like manna from heaven, was grist to my mill. The sentence about the world of images at the centre of which we live stood already on the page, and the skeleton of a plan was in my head. And with the play of free associations fresh in my mind, a new agency was interposed. For I have now consciously selected and rejected among the crowding elements of the phantasmagoria, and

---

[108] Coleridge, *Collected Works*, Vol. 16, *Poems*, I, 512.

> the elements accepted have been fitted into my design. The streamy nature
> of association has been curbed and ruddered . . . (RX, 431)

Association is the passive phase that provides the creative material; the
will edits that material to produce the final outcome as matter 'consciously
selected'. But if, in 'Kubla Khan', there was conscious selection, and rhythmic
organisation, *without* the operation of the will, then the fundamental distinction on which Lowes builds his whole opposition disappears. Even more so,
however, if what Lowes takes to be the 'will' is itself a function of the process of association. Recall what Hartley says about the relationship between
association and the learning of a language: writing is the outcome of a whole
series of associations which have become invisible to us because they are so
habitual:

> As the child's words become more and more polysyllabic by composi-
> tion and decomposition, till at length whole clusters run together into
> phrases and sentences, all whose parts occur at once, as it were, to the
> memory, so his pleasures and pains become more and more complex by
> the combining of combinations; and in many cases numerous combina-
> tions concur to form one apparently simple pleasure. (O, 319)

The ability to write sentences, in other words, is the outcome of associations
which have apparently disappeared through mastery: they are so automatic that
we do not even acknowledge them in the performance of a task which seems
to be under our own direction. In fact, however, what we are performing is a
complex series of habitual associations which *make possible* the construction of
something which has never before existed. For associationists, the will is not
an independent entity: it is the product of associations so naturalised as to be
invisible to consciousness – they are the equivalent of the beating of the heart
or the workings of the stomach, all essential to human life but of which we
are 'unconscious' until they cease to function effectively. The *will*, assumed by
Lowes to be the opposite of association, is – for associationists – the *product* of
association. As Alexander Bain puts it,

> Spontaneous movements occurring in a fresh and vigorous system give
> pleasure; and with the pleasure there is an increased vitality extending to
> the movement, which are thereby sustained and increased; the pleasure
> as it were feeding itself. Out of the primitive force of self-conservation,

we have the very effect that characterizes the will, namely, movement or action for the attainment of pleasure . . . When this experience is repeated several times, an association will be formed between the state of constraint and the definite movements that lead to a release; so that the proper course shall be taken at once, and without the writhings and uncertainties attending the first attempts. As soon as this association is complete, we have a step in the career of voluntary acquirement.[109]

Rather than standing outside the associational process and intervening in it, the will is in fact the *outcome* of accidents which turn into habits: repeated conjunctions gradually accumulate into a purposive sense of control in which the movement of our limbs, like every letter that we read, is the product of an association so automatic as to be *unconscious* to ordinary awareness. When Lowes describes how his mind works – 'For the moment I simply allowed the images to stream' but, subsequently, 'I deliberately assumed control' – he misconstrues the process of association (at least, according to the associationists), because the *normal* process of association is operating precisely when he 'deliberately assumed control' – it is then that he is invoking those unconscious associations that allow him to write sentences without thinking of the letters he uses, that allow him to *foresee* outcomes – like narrative structures – on the basis of past experience. It is the case of 'free association' that is abnormal, because it deliberately suspends the purposive associations by which our life is structured in order to allow *chance* associations to form: it returns us, as it were, to the primitive state in which we have not yet learned from constant conjunction.

Lowes's use of 'Kubla Khan' as exemplary of 'association' rather than 'imagination' therefore rebounds: its rhythmic complexity reveals that association is capable of producing precisely the effects which are attributed to the imagination, and that there is no way of telling the difference between imagination and association except by assuming in advance that 'good', or 'well constructed' works of literature are the products of imagination and that less good, less orderly works of literature are the products of association. 'Imagination', in other words, is a term invoked after the event to describe the qualitative difference between works of literature – it is simply a commenda-

---

[109] Alexander Bain, *Mental and Moral Science* (London: Longmans, Green and Co., 1884), 326

tion – while the actual processes attributed to the imagination can be fully accounted for by the workings of 'association'.

Lowes' discussion of Coleridge returns us to the fundamental issue by which 'Kant has not answered Hume'. Lowes strives to show that Coleridge's processes of association, once we have tracked them down, are 'inevitable': 'Coleridge being Coleridge, with that prehensile associative faculty of his, it was really the inevitable which happened' (RX, 372); 'it would be next to impossible for Coleridge to read of either [image of subterranean caverns] without some reminiscence of the other' (RX, 391). In *inevitability* lies the superiority of genius over mundane perception, though it is still the case that 'without the co-operant Will, obedient to the Vision' it will not be possible to realise 'the pattern perceived in the huddle' and so obtain 'objective reality' (RX, 432). Lowes's account of the Will, however, repeats the problem that Hutchison Stirling analyses in Kant's account of necessity:

> if a sensation A and another sensation B are to be subsumed under the category and converted into an antecedent and a consequent, they must of themselves have already given us reason to have assumed for them precisely that quality – precisely that relation![110]

The quality of 'imagination' in Lowes's analysis stands in exactly the same quandary as Kant's conception of 'cause': it is applied to certain works as a quality of their structure, but this quality is in fact a product of a certain operation of the mind – 'imagination' – which cannot be distinguished except by presupposing the necessary connection between its causal operation and the effect which it produces. From the effect – order, coherence, unity – the cause is inferred – the power of the imagination to create new unities – but the *necessary* connection of the cause and the effect can never be observed – so that 'mere' association may be just as likely to produce order, coherence and unity as the imagination. The products of the imagination are not only always capable of being 'decomposed' into their associative components – as Lowes does in tracking the origins of Coleridge's imagery – but those associative components may be capable of generating the final product without the need for any higher order faculty – imagination – to explain the 'necessity' which binds the work of art together. As Hutchison Stirling said of Kant's categories, 'The single purpose they are there for, what they are alone to do, is

---

[110] 'Kant has not answered Hume', *Mind*, Vol. 10, Issue 37 (January 1885), 59.

to give necessity; and this necessity, which they alone are to give, which they alone are to explain, *already exists!*'[111] Association is assumed to be equivalent to *succession*; imagination to *causation*; but the necessity which distinguishes one from the other is invisible, except by 'constant conjunction', so that if a case of succession (like 'Kubla Khan') can achieve the qualities typical of a case of *causation*, or, indeed, if a case of *causation*, like 'The Ancient Mariner', can be decomposed into a case of mere *succession*, then the distinction between the two is dissolved. The aesthetic 'necessity' that differentiates imagination from fancy, active control from passive association, is just as unattainable as the 'necessity' which Kant could not discover binding cause to effect. In effect, Lowes's work becomes a testimony to the continuing power of association to explain what its opponents – and Lowes himself – claim it incapable of explaining. Through his own analyses of the workings of Coleridge's poems, the need for a conception of the creative imagination that can transcend 'mere' association is made irrelevant.

---

[111] Ibid., 65.

2 Signs of Mind and the Return of the Native: Wordsworth to Yeats

'The historical importance of Coleridge's imagination', M. H. Abrams wrote in *The Mirror and the Lamp* (1953), 'has not been overrated'.[1] It is a curious sentence, suspended between referring to Coleridge's *theory* of the imagination and Coleridge's own imaginative faculty, and its immediately succeeding sentence maintains the confusion: 'It was the first important channel for the flow of organicism into the hitherto clear, if perhaps not very deep, stream of English aesthetics'. The confusion is a significant one, since the story that Abrams has to tell is that, 'as in his philosophy, so in his criticism, Coleridge roots his theory in the constitution and activity of the creative mind', thus focusing the discussion of poetry on 'the mental processes of the poet' (*ML*, 115). It is almost as though Abrams allows his own syntax to accept and support the fundamental truth of Coleridge's theory: it is not so much *about* the creative mind but rather is 'rooted' *in* it, thus justifying his presentation of Coleridge's *imagination* – both in theory and in practice – as the crucial turning point of English literary thought. Beyond that point, the expressivism of romantic notions of creativity (the 'lamp') can be distinguished from traditional Aristotelian theories of imitation (the 'mirror'), and organicism replaces the mechanical or mechanistic theories of the eighteenth century.

The centrality that Abrams gives to Coleridge's imagination, however, produces an odd outcome in his discussion of William Wordsworth's contribution to the development of romantic aesthetics. On the one hand, Wordsworth is

---

[1] M. H. Abrams, *The Mirror and the Lamp: Romantic Theory and the Critical Tradition* (New York: W. W. Norton, 1958; 1953), 168; hereafter cited in the text as *ML*.

hailed as 'the critic whose highly influential writings, by making the feelings of the poet the center of critical reference, mark a turning-point in English literary theory' (*ML*, 103); on the other, 'in his critical writings, Wordsworth retained to a notable degree the terminology and modes of thinking of eighteenth-century associationism' (*ML*, 182). The consequence is that 'only in his poetry, not in his criticism, does Wordsworth make the transition from the eighteenth-century view of man and nature to the concept that the mind is creative in perception, and an integral part of an organically inter-related universe' (104). Abrams' assumption that Coleridge's theories represent a necessary progression beyond the merely mechanical and atomistic associationism of the eighteenth century produces a schizophrenic Wordsworth – the poet marching on into the nineteenth century while his critical alter ego is impaled on the date 1800.

That outcome, however, is the inevitable product of Abrams' reading of Wordsworth's 'Preface' to *Lyrical Ballads* as a document in the rise of expressivism, with its emphasis on the mind and the emotions of the poet. For Abrams, the only alternative to expressivism is some form of imitative theory of literature, whether based on the empirical observation of the real (Aristotle) or the transcendental depiction of the ideal (Plato). Despite the familiarity of Wordsworth's dictum in the 'Preface' that 'all good poetry is the spontaneous overflow of powerful feelings' (*WW*, 598) – which Abrams quotes as foretelling theories of literature that involve 'the elimination, for all practical purposes, of the conditions of the given world, the requirements of the audience, and the control by conscious purpose and art as important determinants of the poem' (*ML*, 48) – Wordsworth's argument in the 'Preface' to *Lyrical Ballads* actually invokes a very different conception of both poetry and the poetic mind, one based, as Coleridge recognised in his critique of Wordsworth in *Biographia Literaria*, on the *elaboration* rather than the overturning of associationism. Wordsworth's statement about the 'spontaneous overflow of powerful feelings' needs to be set in its full – and necessarily rather extensive – context in order to bring out that Wordsworth is committed neither to an expressivist nor to a mimetic conception of literature:

> For all good poetry is the spontaneous overflow of powerful feelings: but though this be true, Poems to which any value can be attached, were never produced on any variety of subjects by a man, who being possessed of more than usual organic sensibility, had also thought long and deeply. For our continued influxes of feeling are modified and

directed by our thoughts, which are indeed the representatives of all our past feelings; and, as by contemplating the relation of these general representatives to each other we discover what is really important to men, so, by the repetition and continuance of this act, our feelings will be connected with important subjects, till at length, if we be originally possessed of much sensibility, such habits of mind will be produced, that, by obeying blindly and mechanically the impulses of those habits, we shall describe objects, and utter sentiments, of such a nature and in such connection with each other, that the understanding of the being to whom we address ourselves, if he be in a healthful state of association, must necessarily be in some degree enlightened, and his affections ameliorated. (*WW*, 598)

The very length of this concluding sentence, and its complexity, underlines the *but* – of 'but though this be true' – which severely qualifies the 'spontaneous overflow'. What Wordsworth is asserting is precisely *not* an emotivist conception of poetry: the poet's 'feelings' are directed by thoughts which are 'the representatives of all our past feelings' – that is, by memories shaped by association; these in turn produce 'habits of mind' which, because of their efficiency, act as though 'blindly and mechanically' but in fact are of 'such a nature and in such connection with each other' that they will be similar to the feelings of the reader, 'if he be in a healthful state of association'; with the result that the poet's associations will connect with and help improve the state of mind of the reader by adding to the stock of those 'habits' which constitute the mind's 'healthful state of association'. Wordsworth's theory of poetry, in other words, challenges the emotivist emphasis which Abrams wishes to ascribe to it by insisting on a theory which interlinks the workings of the poet's mind with the workings of the reader's mind, and these two poles of the poetic experience will be co-ordinated with each other only as long as both are in a 'healthful state of association'.

What is truly radical in Wordsworth's theory of poetry and what is taken up by his successors is not the emphasis on 'expression', to which Abrams gives priority, but his working out of the implications of association, which Abrams takes to be a historical regression. Wordsworth is certainly much more concerned than his predecessors, like Archibald Alison, with how the work of art is created – with the associative processes of the poet – but he remains as deeply concerned as they were with the *reception* of the work of art, with its interaction with the associations of its readers. Wordsworth's interest in the activities of the artist's mind does not produce an artist-centred theory of poetry because he remains equally concerned with how associations are transferred effectively to the minds of the audience. The poet, Wordsworth insists, 'makes a formal engagement that he will gratify certain known habits of association' (*WW*, 596) in his readers and much of his concern in the 'Preface' is that readers may accuse him of having reneged on this commitment. That is why he underlines that the content of his poetry involves the representation of the 'primary laws of our nature: chiefly, as far as regards the manner in which we associate ideas in a state of excitement' (*WW*, 597); no matter how unusual the poetry may seem, its content is universal – shaped by the 'primary laws of our nature' – and appropriate to that state of aesthetic receptiveness which is itself a matter of how 'we associate ideas in a state of excitement'.

Significantly, Wordsworth acknowledges that the poet may fail to fulfil this 'formal engagement' between poet and reader if he does not avoid associative connections which are either peculiar to himself or the consequence of arbitrary connections attached to the words he uses: 'I am sensible that my associations must have sometimes been particular instead of general, and that, consequently, giving to things a false importance, sometimes from diseased impulses I may have written upon unworthy subjects, . . . [or] my language may frequently have suffered from those arbitrary connections of feeling and ideas with particular words and phrases, from which no man can altogether protect himself' (*WW*, 612). There is no certain guide to the universality of associations, either in the poet or in the reader, and, having acknowledged the fallibility of his own associative connections, Wordsworth cautions his Reader 'never to forget that he is himself exposed to the same errors as the Poet, and perhaps in a much greater degree' because 'it is not probable that he will be so well acquainted with the various stages of meaning through which words have passed, or the fickleness or stability of the relations of particular ideas to each other' (*WW*, 612). It is this intertwining of author's and reader's associations with which Wordsworth is concerned; it is the overcoming of the arbitrary nature of those associations that he seeks; and it is on the foundation of communication of a common basis of association that he asserts both the influence and the importance of poetry: 'the poet writes under one restriction only, namely, that of the necessity of giving immediate pleasure to a human Being possessed of that information which may be expected from him, not as a lawyer, a physician, a mariner, an astronomer or a natural philosopher, but as a Man' (*WW*, 605).

In his insistence in putting Coleridge at the centre of a new aesthetic – 'it was above all in his exploitation of this new aesthetics of organism that Coleridge, more thoroughly than Wordsworth, was the innovative English critic of his time' (*ML*, 124) – Abrams not only seriously misconstrues Wordsworth's theories, but misunderstands both how Wordsworth's 'Preface' derives from those of his predecessors, and how it influences subsequent developments of modern poetry and literary theory. The challenge of the associationist conception of art is that it is focused not only on the origin of art in the particular associational formation of the artist but, equally, on the reception of the work of art in the associations of the reader, and, in this crucial period of its development from an eighteenth- into a nineteenth-century philosophy, it sought to find a common ground between them in 'nature' – whether in human nature or in the natural world. Neither 'mirror' nor 'lamp' is an appropriate metaphor for this theory (which is why it escapes from Abrams' categorisation): it is, rather – to use the metaphor often invoked to describe the process of association itself – a chain, which links author and world, work and reader, in a fragile interconnection that is constantly threatened with breakdown between any of its various elements, because it is a chain anchored only in the contingencies and accidents of individual experience.

Wordsworth's defence of the poems of *Lyrical Ballads* is based on presenting them as the fulfilment of – or logical outcome of – an associationist aesthetic. The emphasis on the avoidance of poetic diction is governed not by rhetorical distaste but by the fact 'many expressions, in themselves proper and beautiful, . . . have been foolishly repeated by bad Poets, till such feelings of disgust are connected with them as it is scarcely possible by any art of association to overpower' (*WW*, 601); the effects of metre arise from 'the blind association of pleasure which has been previously received from works of rhyme or metre of the same or similar construction' (*WW*, 611); and the significance of a poem lies in its ability 'to excite thought or feeling in the Reader' (*WW*, 613), to produce that 'unusual and irregular state of mind' in which 'ideas and feelings do not in that state succeed each other in accustomed order' but without 'such deviation' that 'more will be lost from the shock which will be thereby given to the Reader's associations' (*WW*, 609). Wordsworth's constant concern, in other words, is with how the chain of associations linking poet to reader via the vehicle of the poem can be kept intact, corrupted neither by 'those arbitrary connections of feelings and ideas with particular words and phrases' nor by the loss of a 'healthful state of association'. That this associationist foundation of Wordsworth's aesthetic was neither simply tactical – adopted to suit an audience which itself was still accustomed to associationist theory – nor a phase which he would outgrow, is clear from the challenge he offered to Coleridge in the 'Preface to *Poems 1815*': where, for Coleridge, association is the characteristic which allows us to distinguish between fancy and imagination, for Wordsworth, 'to aggregate and associate, to evoke and to combine, belong as well to the Imagination as to the Fancy' (*WW*, 635). For Abrams, this confirms that though thinkers such as A. N. Whitehead have taken Wordsworth's work as a 'conscious reaction against the mentality of the eighteenth century' and 'a protest on behalf of the organic view of nature' (*ML*, 117–18), Wordsworth failed to transcend a supposedly mechanical conception of his art: 'from Coleridge's point of view', Abrams insists, 'Wordsworth's vocabulary showed a regressive tendency to conflate the organic imagination with mechanical fancy, by describing it once again in terms of the subtraction, addition, and association of the elements of sensory images; and in doing this, Wordsworth had incautiously given the key to their position away to the enemy' (*ML*, 182). Abrams reads Wordsworth's refusal to follow Coleridge's theory of the imagination as conspiring with the 'degeneration of Coleridge's distinction' (*ML*, 182), but looked at from the perspective of the successful developments in associationist psychology in the nineteenth century, it should be seen rather as a contribution to the *regeneration* of associationism as the truly modern and appropriate aesthetic for the age, as a refusal to allow Coleridge's ideology of the imagination to dominate the 'spirit of the age'.

It is symptomatic, therefore, of Abrams' reading of the developments in the period that he mentions only once, in a footnote, the most radical associationist theory of art of the period and Wordsworth's most influential predecessor – Archibald Alison's *Essays on Taste* (1790). Unlike previous theorists such as Gerard and Burke, Alison developed a theory of taste which relied on no foundation except that of association. Burke, for instance, had acknowledged the role of association in art but provided it with a basis in non-associative experiences:

> But as it must be allowed that many things affect us after a certain manner, not by any natural powers they have for that purpose, but by association; so it would be absurd, on the other hand, to say that all things affect us by association only; since some things must have been originally and naturally agreeable or disagreeable, from which the others derive their associated powers; and it would be, I fancy, to little purpose to look for

the cause of our passions in association, until we fail of it in the natural properties of things.[2]

Alison, however, finds 'no natural properties of things' separable from our associations, which is why,

> every man of sensibility will be conscious of a variety of great or pleasing images passing with rapidity in his imagination, beyond what the scene of description immediately before him can of themselves excite. They seem often, indeed, to have but a very distant relation to the object that at first excited them; and the object itself appears only to serve as a hint, to awaken the imagination, and to lead it through every analogous idea that has a place in the memory. It is then, indeed, in this powerless state of reverie, when we are carried on by our conceptions, not guiding them, that the deepest emotions of beauty and sublimity are felt; that our hearts swell with feelings which language is too weak to express; and that, in the depth of silence and astonishment, we pay to the charm that enthralls us, the most flattering mark of our applause. (*AET*, 58–9)

Alison's description of the spectator, for whose experience the aesthetic object 'appears only to serve as a hint' to the opening up of the resources of memory, is mirror image to Wordsworth's creator, whose poetry 'takes its origin from emotion recollected in tranquillity: the emotion is contemplated till by a species of reaction the tranquillity disappears, and an emotion, kindred to that which was before the subject of contemplation, is gradually produced, and does actually exist in the mind' (*WW*, 611). For both, the immediate object of contemplation is only the beginning of a process in which recollection leads to the creation of emotion and emotion to the experience of or the creation of art. But because the beautiful and the sublime are produced purely by association, no objects are ruled out as possible sources of aesthetic experience. Wordsworth's insistence on his right to 'chuse incidents and situations of common life, and to relate or describe them, throughout, as far as was possible, in a selection of language really used by men' (*WW*, 596–7), derives directly from his associationism, which

---

[2] Edmund Burke, *A Philosophical Enquiry into the Origins of our Ideas of the Sublime and the Beautiful*, *The Works of the Right Honourable Edmund Burke*, 16 Vols (London: C. and J. Rivington, 1826), Vol. I, Part IV, Sect. ii, 258.

allows the most unprepossessing of objects to be used by the writer who can 'throw over them a certain colouring of imagination, whereby ordinary things should be presented to the mind in an unusual way' (*WW*, 597). And because aesthetic experience is not rooted in a special class of objects but in the associational flow it produces, the most ordinary of scenes can acquire, in an appropriate mind, a powerful associational significance that renders it beautiful:

> There is no man, who has not some interesting associations with particular scenes, or airs, or books, and who does not feel their beauty or sublimity enhanced to him, by such connections. The view of the house where one was born, of the school where one was educated, and where the gay years of infancy were passed, is indifferent to no man. They recall so many images of past happiness and past affections, they are connected with so many strong or valued emotions, and lead altogether to so long a train of feelings and recollections, that there is hardly any scene which one ever beholds with so much rapture. (*AET*, 23–4).

The autobiographical ordinariness of Wordsworth's poetry is founded in this associational recollection which turns even the most banal of environments into a potential contributor to the experience of beauty:

> The earth
> And common face of Nature spake to me
> Rememberable things: sometimes, 'tis true,
> By chance collisions and quaint accidents
> Like those ill-sorted unions, work supposed
> Of evil-minded fairies, yet not vain,
> Nor profitless, if haply they impressed
> Collateral objects and appearances,
> Albeit lifeless then, and doomed to sleep
> Until maturer seasons called them forth
> To impregnate and to elevate the mind
> ('Prelude', 614–24; *WW*, 390).

What unites the ordinary and the extraordinary in our experience is, for Alison, 'that the beauty and sublimity of such objects are to be ascribed, not

to the material qualities themselves, but to the qualities they signify; and, consequently, that the qualities of matter are not to be considered sublime or
beautiful in themselves, but as the SIGNS or EXPRESSIONS of such qualities as,
by the constitution of our nature, are fitted to produce pleasing or interesting
emotion' (*AET*, 416). The *expressivism* that Abrams takes to be characteristic
of romantic conceptions of the artist is reversed in Alison's theory to become
the *expressions* that objects offer us as a result of the associations that have accumulated around them: '*the beauty and sublimity which are felt in the various appearances*
of matter are finally to be ascribed to their expression of mind' (*AET*, 423). It is such
associations that allow Wordsworth to assert that,

> To every natural form, rock, fruit or flower,
> Even the loose stones that cover the high-way,
> I gave a moral life, I saw them feel,
> Or linked them to some feeling: the great mass
> Lay bedded in a quickening soul, and all
> That I beheld respired with inward meaning.
>   ('Prelude', III, 214–19; *WW*, 407)

And it is because of the effect of such associations that Alison is able to
attribute to natural objects a moral influence which is, in fact, the reflection of
those moral meanings with which we have invested them:

> There is not one of these features of scenery which is not fitted to
> awaken us to moral emotion – to lead us, when once the key of our
> imagination is struck, to trains of fascination and of endless imagery;
> and in the indulgence of them to make our bosoms either glow with
> conceptions of mental excellence, or melt in the dreams of moral
> good. Even upon the man of the most uncultivated taste, the scenes of
> Nature have some inexplicable charm: there is not a chord, perhaps,
> of the human heart which may not be awakened by their influence; and
> I believe there is no man of genuine taste who has not often felt, in the
> lone majesty of nature, some unseen spirit to dwell, which in his hap-
> pier hours touched, as if with magic hand, all the springs of his moral
> sensibility, and rekindled in his heart those original conceptions of the
> moral or intellectual excellence of his nature, which it is the melancholy
> tendency of the vulgar pursuits of life to diminish, if not altogether to
> destroy. (*AET*, 437–8)

The sublime and the beautiful in nature force us to recollect those 'original conceptions of the moral or intellectual excellence' which are degraded by the ordinary course of experience: they connect us with 'some unseen spirit' and thus justify our sense that in the natural world we encounter not merely signs created by us, but signs created for us, revealing 'the power, the wisdom, and the beneficence of the Divine Artist' (*AET*, 418).

In Alison's *Essays*, as in Hartley's philosophy, associationism is the foundation not of Coleridge's 'philosophy of mechanism, which, in everything that is most worthy of the human intellect, strikes Death'[3] but of a spiritual universe. Since 'matter is not beautiful in itself, but derives its beauty from the expression of MIND', Alison aligns his theory with what he regards as the 'DOCTRINE that appears very early to have distinguished the PLATONIC school' (*AET*, 416), and concludes that it is 'by means of the expression of which it is every where significant, that the material universe around us becomes a scene of moral discipline, and that in the hours when we are most unconscious of it, an influence is perpetually operating, by which our moral feelings are awakened, and our moral sensibility exercised' (*AET*, 440). Theorists committed to associationism are not proponents of a dead universe of mechanical interactions without colour, without spirit, without purpose: our associations transform the world into a place not only rich in meaning, but subjective rather than objective in its metaphysical implication:

> Our minds, instead of being governed by the character of external objects, are enabled to bestow upon them a character which does not belong to them; and even with the rudest, or the most common appearances of Nature, to connect feelings of a nobler and more interesting kind than any that mere influences of matter can ever convey. (*AET*, 428)

Wordsworth's conception of a spiritual universe in which

> The unfettered clouds and region of the heavens,
> Tumult and peace, the darkness and the light,
> Were all like workings of one mind, the features
> Of the same face, blossoms upon one tree,

---

[3] Coleridge to Wordsworth, 30 May 1815, *Collected Letters of Samuel Taylor Coleridge*, ed. Earl Leslie Griggs, 6 Vols (Oxford: Oxford University Press, 1959), Vol. IV, 969.

Characters of the great Apocalypse,
The types and symbols of Eternity,
Of first and last, and midst, and without end.
                    ('Prelude', VI, 566–72; *WW*, 464)

is not the product of an organicist poet overcoming the mechanistic incli-
nations of an associationist critic: it is the transfer into poetry of precisely
that world of natural signs that Alison takes to be the expressive outcome of
associationism.

Indeed, at the very time that Wordsworth was resisting Coleridge's account
of the imagination and restating the associationist basis of his art, Dugald
Stewart's successor at the University of Edinburgh, Thomas Brown, returned
to David Hume's associationism to modernise it in terms of new developments
in physiology. Hume's 'impressions' and 'ideas' become, in Brown's terminology, 'external affections of the mind' and 'internal affections of the mind', the
latter being subdivided into 'intellectual states of the mind' and 'emotions'.
Like his predecessors, however, Brown insists that these must not be conceived
as independent and free-standing entities: 'When I say . . . that they are sufficiently distinct in their own nature, I do not mean to say, that they are not often
mingled in one complex state of mind; – in the same way as when I call separately and distinctly sights and sounds, I do not mean that we are incapable of
perceiving visually the instrument of the music, and the musician, to whom we
may at the same time be listening'.[4] The analysis of this mingled and complex
state is compared with the work of the chemist, since, 'we never suppose, that
when a chemist has demonstrated to us the similarity of the elementary atoms
which form the beautiful products of our gardens, he objects on that account
to the very convenient names, by which we distinguish one flower or fruit
from another: – and what we do not suppose of the chemist, whose inquiries
are directed to matter, we should as little suppose of the analytical inquirer in
to the beautiful combinations which diversify the field of our thought'.[5] The
analytical 'atomism' of associationism does not imply that the actual events in
the mind are atomistic: our experience is of 'organic' wholes.

In applying his associationism to aesthetics, Brown argues that the superiority of genius depends upon the subtlety and range of the artist's associational

---

[4] Thomas Brown, *Sketch of a System of the Philosophy of the Human Mind: Part
First, comprehending the Physiology of the Mind* (Edinburgh: Bell & Bradfute,
Manners and Miller and Waugh and Innes, 1820), 42–3.

[5] Ibid., 258.

capacity: 'in [such] minds, there is a very powerful tendency to suggestions of *analogy*: the events which they relate become, therefore, a source of immediate illustration, by resemblances that had never been traced before, or even suspected; and in their sprightly sallies of original wit, image after image is poured upon us in dazzling profusion, as from a source that is inexhaustible'.[6] The 'inexhaustible' resources of genius are translated to the reader or spectator as a feeling of the same inexhaustible inner resources, because 'we see our common nature reflected, and reflected with a beauty of which we were not sensible before; and while thought succeeds thought, and image rises upon image, according to the laws of succession which we have been accustomed to recognize in the trains of our own fancy, these thoughts and images are, as it were, for the moment ours; and we have only the delightful impression that we are of a race of nobler beings than we conceived'.[7] The inexhaustibility of this inner world brings us close not only to a sense of infinity but to the Infinite, so that Brown is able to attribute to the associating mind not merely the constant infusion of its own emotions into the objects of sense, giving them a colour unique to each individual, but a repetition of God's original act of creation: 'in the creation of this internal world of thought, the Divine Author of our being has known how to combine infinity itself with that which may almost be considered as the most finite of things: and has repeated, as it were, in every mind, by the almost creative sensibilities with which he has endowed it, that simple but majestic act of omnipotence, by which, originally, he called from the rude elements of chaos, or rather from nothing, all the splendid glories of the universe'.[8] The associationist tradition can, in effect, match Coleridge's claims for the God-like creative potential of the individual mind, without needing to resort to anything except association itself to explain how chaos is transformed into order – indeed, association *is* the very mechanism by which God has ensured chaos *can* be transformed into order.

II

At the end of Chapter VII of *Biographia Literaria*, Coleridge dismisses what he describes as the 'Arts of Memory' (*BL*, 128). Wordsworth's 'Prelude', on

---

[6] Ibid., 201.

[7] Thomas Brown, *Lectures on the Philosophy of the Human Mind*, 4 Vols (Edinburgh: Tait, 1820), Vol. II, 259–60.

[8] Ibid., Vol. I, 462.

the other hand, is devoted to the power of memory: 'And yet the morning gladness is not gone/ Which then was in my mind' ('Prelude' VII, 3–4;
WW, 452). The nature of the poet's memory is of crucial significance to
the art produced, and 'The Prelude' is a prelude precisely to the extent that
it explains and justifies the sources of the memory to which the poet has
access for the creation of his poetry – which is why, ironically, it could not
be published until his poetic career was over. It is not so much a part of
Wordsworth's poetry but, anterior and exterior to it, a justification of the
associational habits on which his poetry is based. It is a meta-poetic commentary on the resources which make Wordsworth's personal memories more
than personally significant. When he insists in Book XI of *The Prelude* that
'There are in our existence spots of time/Which with distinct pre-eminence
retain/A renovating Virtue' ('Prelude' XI, 258–60; *WW* 565), Wordsworth's
generalisation ('our existence') is laden with particular significance for the
poet, for the poet is someone who, 'As far as memory can look back, is
full/Of this beneficent influence' ('Prelude' XI, 278–9; *WW*, 566), a phrase
poised between referring to the beneficent influence of *what* is recollected
– 'moments worthy of all gratitude' ('Prelude' XI, 274; *WW*, 565) – and the
power that makes recollection possible. The poet is both capable of recollection and capable of recollecting things of value – not one, like Coleridge,
trapped in the 'self-created sustenance of a mind/Debarred from Nature's
living images' ('Prelude', VI, 312–13; *WW*, 458), but one whose past experience has produced a power of recollection which is itself a mirror to the
powers of nature, and which

>   exists by interchange
> Of peace and excitation, finds in her
> His best and purest Friend, from her receives
> That energy by which he seeks the truth,
> Is rouzed, aspires, grasps, struggles, wishes, craves,
> From her that happy stillness of the mind
> Which fits him to receive it, when unsought.
>   ('Prelude', XII, 7–14; WW, 569)

The poet is fitted to receive the message of nature by having been a child of
nature: it is the nature of a poet to be a poet of nature, because, for him, nature
has become a language, its characters responding to his character, its signs
signalling his feelings:

Ye Presences of Nature, in the sky
Or on the earth! Ye Visions of the hills!
And Souls of lonely places! can I think
A vulgar hope was yours when Ye employed
Such ministry, when Ye through many a year,
Haunting me thus among my boyish sports,
On caves and trees, upon the woods and hills,
Impressed upon all forms the characters
Of danger and desire . . .

('Prelude', I, 490–500; *WW*, 387)

The superiority of the nature poet's memory is the fact that it 'Holds up before the mind, intoxicate/With present objects and the busy dance/Of things that pass away, a temperate shew/Of objects that endure' ('Prelude', XII, 33–6; *WW*, 569). His business will be to resist, as 'Preface' to Lyrical Ballads puts it, 'transitory and accidental ornaments' (*WW*, 607) and 'arbitrary and capricious habits of expression' (*WW*, 597) in order to give expression to what is 'more durable' – the condition in which 'the passions of men are incorporated with the beautiful and permanent forms of nature' (*WW*, 597). The poet who *associates* with 'low and rustic life' (*WW*, 597) acquires associations which are 'permanent' rather than 'transitory', allowing his poetry to escape the threat of associations which are 'particular instead of general', as well as from 'those arbitrary connections of feelings and ideas with particular words and phrases' (*WW*, 612).

The irony of Wordsworth's 'Preface' is, of course, that it claims this permanent and universal foundation for his personal associations in the context of defending his poetry from having been misunderstood – the permanence and universality of its associations made ineffective by the deficiencies of an audience all too 'intoxicate' with 'things that pass away'. These deficiencies are even more carefully analysed in the 'Essay, Supplementary to the Preface' of 1815 which argues that because it is poetry's duty 'to treat of things not as they *are*, but as they *appear*' (*WW*, 641), it is only too easy for inexperienced readers to be lured into a 'world of delusion' (*WW*, 641). The memories which the poet invokes, therefore, not only have to connect with the associations of his readers but have to have 'a renovating Virtue' to those readers by equipping them with memories like his own – rendering their feelings, as Wordsworth put it in his letter to John Wilson, 'more sane pure and permanent, in short, more consonant to nature, that is, to eternal nature, and the great moving spirit of

things'.[9] It is the failure of the reader's associations to match with the author's
– even when they are derived from the permanent and universal – that means
'that every Author, as far as he is great and at the same time *original*, has had
the task of *creating* the taste by which he is to be enjoyed' (*WW*, 657). In order
that poetry can succeed, its audience must already have acquired the memories which it is the business of the poetry to invoke. Given the absence of
those memories, the poetry itself must correct and re-educate the memories
through which it will be experienced. Associationist theories of art can never
escape this paradox: poetry must either be subservient to an already existing
body of memory in its audience (threatening, if not cliché, then at least mere
imitation of previous forms of poetry); or it must use the poem itself to *create* the memories by which the poem can be experienced; or it must provide
at least the context of those memories by a 'Preface' or a 'Prelude', without
which 'originality' will simply be, for the audience, absence.

It is a paradox that Wordsworth explored in two of the most famous
poems in *Lyrical Ballads*, 'Tintern Abbey' and 'Michael', poems which, despite
their very different modes, address the same central issues of associationist
aesthetics, and which create models for many subsequent poems that depend
on an associationist aesthetic. The issue which both address is the continuity of memory. In 'Tintern Abbey', the return of the poet to the scene that
he had visited five years before is the occasion for celebrating the virtue of
memory by measuring the difference between his immediate sensations in
the present, his sensations in the past, and the memories of those sensations which bridge the gap between. Then, five years before, he had been
a mere sensationalist, who 'had no need of a remoter charm,/By thought
supplied, or any interest/Unborrowed from the eye' (82–3; *WW*, 133). Now,
those earlier feelings have been the subject of repeated recollection – 'These
forms of beauty have not been to me,/As is a landscape to a blind man's eye'
(24–5; *WW*, 132) – and in so doing have been transformed: the *sensation* of
the scene, its immediate presence to the eye – 'The day is come when I again
repose/Here, under this dark sycamore' (9–10; *WW*, 131–2) – is now one
in which sensation and recollection are combined, in which the landscape
has become 'the language of the sense' (109; *WW*, 134) because it is a sign
not only of the mind which perceived it (five years before), and of the mind

---

[9] Ernest de Selincourt (ed.), *The Letters of William and Dorothy Wordsworth,
Second Edition, Vol. I, The Early Years 1787–1805* (Oxford: Clarendon
Press, 1967), 355.

currently perceiving it, but because it will be the sign by virtue of which, in the future, the poet will recollect his present self – 'in this moment there is life and food/For future years' (65–6; *WW* 133) – and by which he will be remembered when he is no longer able to perceive it:

> Nor, perchance,
> If I should be, where I no more can hear
> Thy voice, nor catch from thy wild eyes these gleams
> Of past existence, wilt thou then forget
> That on the banks of this delightful stream
> We stood together.
>
> (147–52; *WW*, 135)

The poem establishes a chain of memory – between his past self and his present self, between his sister's present self and her future self – which guarantees that the landscape as a recollection of his own earlier self will continue to function as a mnemonic sign beyond even the extinction of his own memory. What, at the beginning of the poem, appears to be a purely personal signature of the self upon the landscape becomes, at the end, an impersonal signature of the landscape upon any self capable of responding to it. A chain of associations is established which the poem at once records – by inscribing Wordsworth's experience on the landscape – and guarantees – by making the landscape the sign of that experience. At the same time, the poem enacts the gathering of associations which make the landscape signifi-cant. In his earlier, sensationalist phase, Wordsworth was 'like a man/Flying from something that he dreads' (71–2; *WW*, 133), a dread whose source was the fact that immediacy was all to him; now, the poem is a gathering place for past and present, for himself and his sister, associates whose associations are in harmony with each other in such a way as to make them not only com-municants in the same religion – 'worshipper of Nature . . . unwearied in that service' (153–4; *WW*, 135) – but communicators between present, past and future. They form, as it were, the perfect union of poet and audience for the poem of which they are a part, since their associations, though separated in time, are identical, and have developed by passing through the same stages and transcending the same difficulties. The poem thus records the 'signs of mind' in the landscape and bears witness to the possibility of the recovery of those signs in the return of one for whom such signs are inherently mean-ingful – landscape, poem, and audience re-enact the poet's experience not simply as a return to nature but as a return to the signs that confirm that one is native to this landscape.

'Michael', on the other hand, is a poem apparently much more bleakly tragic than 'Tintern Abbey' but it in fact enacts – objectively rather than subjectively – the same construction of an associational unity. The poem's opening, requesting the reader to turn aside 'from the public way' (1; *WW*, 224), marks the very private nature of the associations on which it is based: their physical sign, 'a straggling heap of unhewn stones' (17; *WW*, 225), is one which one 'Might see and notice not' (16; *WW*, 225), and the story itself is important only because 'It was the first,/The earliest of those tales that spake to me/Of Shepherds' (21–3; *WW*, 225), though they too were significant not in themselves 'but for the fields and hills/Where was their occupation and abode' (25–6; *WW*, 225). The lengthening trail of trivial associations is apparently the opposite of that intense harmony of mind and nature with which we are presented in 'Tintern Abbey', but 'Michael', just as much as 'Tintern Abbey', is about the passing on of shared associations. To the shepherd, the landscape has 'impressed/So many incidents upon his mind' that it is 'like a book' which 'preserved the memory' (67–8, 70; *WW*, 226) of his past; to his son, who is about to leave for the city, he passes on his own memories – 'I still/Remember them who loved me in my youth' (373–4; *W*, 234) – before getting him to lay the corner-stone of the sheep-fold; and the sheep-fold in turn becomes the corner-stone of people's memories of Michael after his son's disgrace in the city – ' 'Tis not forgotten yet . . . /That many and many a day he thither went/And never lifted up a single stone' (471–5; *W*, 236). Michael's memories of his parents; the community's memory of him, for there are 'no few/Whose memories will bear witness to my tale' (134–5; *W*, 228); the poet's memories of them and of him, form a chain which defeats the forgetfulness that would reduce the sheep-fold to a mere 'straggling heap of unhewn stones', and unites the oral memory of a traditional society with the written memory of a modern one.

The stones are hewn by memory from their apparent chaos to be significant signs of a human community of which the poet is an integral part: 'Not with a waste of words, but for the sake/Of pleasure, which I know that I shall give/To many living now, I of this Lamp/Speak thus minutely' (131–4; *WW*, 227). That Lamp stands as refutation of Abrams' conception of the 'lamp of art' since its existence in the poem depends, not on the poet, but on the community of which he is a part. The emotion whose spontaneous overflow the poem records is theirs as well as his, and by reading the poem, the reader acquires the same memories as the community and becomes, as it were, an equal participant, one who would not fail to see in the stones the signs understood by those native to the place. By the telling of its story, 'Michael' enacts the creation of an associational community which is a chain uniting past, present and future and which is the model of the community of readers required by the associationist poet – readers of the landscape, readers of the poem, natives of a place in which landscape and poem are each the familiar sign of the other.

III

The envisioning of such an 'associated' community in the late 1790s was a heroic ideal threatened on every side – by war, by government oppression, by mass education which eradicated folk memories and by industrialisation, which inured the habitants of towns and cities to a world of signs that had no continuity either with the communal past or with the natural world. When Francis Jeffrey wrote an extensive review of the second edition of Alison's *Essays on Taste* in the *Edinburgh Review* in 1811, it was not the possibility of a community of associates that he emphasised but the fact that Alison's associationism necessarily separates people into discrete groups defined by their social status and by the particular stock of memories which professional role or personal experience imposed on them. Having shown how 'the grand mistake . . . which seems to have misled almost all inquirers into this curious subject, consists in their taking it for granted, that beauty, in whatever variety of objects it might be found, was always itself one and the same',[10] Jeffrey goes on to assert, on the basis of Alison's analysis, that aesthetic experiences 'are not original emotions, nor produced by any qualities in the objects which excite them; but are reflections, or images, of the more radical and familiar emotions . . . and are occasioned, not by any inherent virtue in the objects before us, but by the accidents, if we may so express ourselves, by which they have been enabled to suggest or recal to us our own past sensations and sympathies'.[11] The associations on which aesthetic experience depend are, for Jeffrey, 'accidents': some of them may be founded on 'natural signs' which are the 'perpetual concomitants of happiness or of suffering', but

---

[10] Francis Jeffrey, *Edinburgh Review*, Vol. XVIII, No. XXXV (May 1811), 1–45, 6.

[11] Ibid., 8.

these will have no inherent justification; they will simply be stable versions of 'the arbitrary or accidental concomitants of such feelings'.[12] Thus Jeffrey gives the example of the 'noise of a cart rattling over the stones, [which] is often mistaken for thunder; and as long as the mistake lasts, this very vulgar and insignificant noise is actually felt to be prodigiously sublime. It is so felt, because it is then associated with ideas of prodigious power and undefined danger;— and the sublimity is destroyed, the moment the association is dissolved, though the sound itself, and its effects on the organ, continue exactly the same'.[13] What the example proves is not that the cart represents an accidental association and the thunder a natural one, but that the connection of thunder with sublimity is an equally accidental association – one that might be dissolved, for instance, by a scientific understanding of its origin that undermined 'its necessary connexion with that vast and uncontrouled Power which is the natural object of awe and veneration'.[14] In this world of entirely accidental associations the language of Wordsworthian nature has no universal import:

> . . . let us now take a Welch or a Highland scene . . . Here we shall have lofty mountains, and rocky and lonely recesses, – tufted woods hung over precipices, – lakes intersected with castled promontories, – ample solitudes of unploughed and untrodden valleys, – nameless and gigantic ruins, – and mountain echoes repeating the scream of the eagle and the roar of the cataract. This, too, is beautiful; – and to those who can interpret the language it speaks, far more beautiful than the prosperous [English] scene with which we have contrasted it. Yet, lonely as it is, it is to the recollection of man and of human feelings that its beauty is also owing. The mere forms and colours that compose its visible appearance, are no more capable of exciting any emotion in the mind, than the forms and colours of a Turkey carpet. It is sympathy with the present or the past, or the imaginary *inhabitants* of such a region, that alone gives it either interest or beauty; and the delight of those who behold it, will always be found to be in exact proportion to the force of their imaginations, and the warmth of their social affections.[15]

---

[12] Ibid., 9.
[13] Ibid., 10.
[14] Ibid., 10.
[15] Ibid., 14.

The sublime imagination is no longer, as it was for Wordsworth, based on 'a sense of the truth of the likeness, from the moment that it is perceived, [which] grows – and continues to grow – upon the mind'; its purpose is not 'to incite and to support the eternal' (*WW*, 636); it is the product of the *social affections*, of 'the recollection of man and of human feelings'. It is not the return of memories founded in universal truths but the return of memories that are the accidents of social circumstance. For Jeffrey the power of accidental associations is such that his advice to the artist, as indeed to the person of taste, is to adopt a pragmatic division between the common associations of the public world and the private and accidental – but *effective* – associations of our subjective experience:

> As all men must have some peculiar associations, all men must have some peculiar notions of beauty, and, of course, to a certain extent, a taste that the public would be entitled to consider as false or vitiated. For those who make no demands on public admiration, however, it is hard to be obliged to sacrifice this source of enjoyment; and, even for those who harbour for applause, the wisest course, perhaps, if it were only practicable, would be to have two tastes, – one to enjoy, and one to work by, – one founded upon universal associations, according to which they finished those performances for which they challenged universal praise, – and another guided by all casual and individual associations, through which they looked fondly upon nature, and upon the objects of their secret admiration.[16]

Rather than the source of our *common* associations, nature is the object of our 'casual and individual associations', an aesthetic experience to be cherished only in 'secret admiration', as the outcome of our 'peculiar associations' and their concomitant 'peculiar notions of beauty'.

The secret, peculiar, casual and individual nature of the poet's associations, characteristics that Wordsworth had sought to avoid – or, perhaps, to evade – and which Jeffrey's account of Alison had all too conscientiously revealed, established a context in which the *peculiarity* of the poets' associational habits were both the source and strength of their originality and, at the same time, the reason why they were so incomprehensible to the general public. It was on this division that Arthur Hallam was to base his defence of Tennyson's poetry

---

[16] Ibid., 45.

in 1831, turning Wordsworth against himself by insisting that the sensation-alist recollected in 'Tintern Abbey' was the true poet, and that the meditative expositor of the consequences of sensation was the betrayer of his better poetic self. For Hallam, Shelley and Keats are the truly modern poets because, 'they are both poets of sensation rather than reflection. Susceptible of the slightest impulse from external nature, their fine organs trembled into emo-tion at colours, and sounds, and movements, unperceived or unregarded by duller temperaments'.[17] As a consequence, beauty is for them something which is 'constantly passing before "that inward eye, which is the bliss of soli-tude"',[18] and in this isolation, this 'secret' and 'peculiar' world of their personal associations,

> Poetry is a sort of magic, producing a number of impressions too mul-tiplied, too minute, and too diversified to allow our tracing them to their causes, because just such was the effect, even so boundless, and so bewildering, produced on their imaginations by the real appearance of Nature.[19]

Nature no longer offers a common language for the poet: it is the stimulus to a private language. Confronted by such peculiarity and such privacy of response, however, the question is – and it is a question which Hallam him-self immediately raises – does not this 'prove that there is barrier between these poets and all other persons, so strong and immovable, that, as has been said of the Supreme Essence, we must be themselves before we can understand them in the least?'[20] Hallam's answer, despite his excoriation of Wordsworth's 'reflective' poetry, echoes Wordsworth's challenge to the notion of 'taste' in the 'Essay, Supplementary to the Preface (1815)'. Wordsworth argues that theories of 'taste' are based on a *passive* conception of the reader, whereas what he requires is 'the exertion of a co-operating *power* in the mind of the Reader', because without such 'there can be no adequate sympathy with either of these emotions' (i.e. the pathetic and the sublime). This active power in the reader, without which 'auxiliar impulse elevated or profound passion cannot exist', transforms the reader from the likeness of 'an Indian Prince or General – stretched on his Palanquin, and borne by his slaves' into

---

[17] Armstrong, *Victorian Scrutinies*, 87.
[18] Ibid., 87.
[19] Ibid., 88.
[20] Ibid., 89.

a dutiful foot-soldier, 'invigorated and inspired by his Leader, in order that he may exert himself, for he cannot proceed in quiescence, he cannot be carried like a dead weight' (*WW*, 659–60). Such an active readership is also the basis of Hallam's answer to the peculiar and private nature of the poet's sensations:

> Every bosom contains the elements of those complex emotions which the artist feels, and every head can, to a certain extent, go over in itself the process of their combination, so as to understand his expressions and sympathize with his state. But this requires exertion; more or less, indeed, according to the difference of occasion, but always some degree of exertion. For since the emotions of the poet, during composition, follow a regular law of association, it follows that to accompany their progress up to the harmonious prospect of the whole, and to perceive the proper dependence of every step on that which preceded, it is absolutely necessary *to start from the same point*, i.e. clearly to apprehend the leading sentiment in the poet's mind, by their conformity to which the host of suggestions are arranged.[21]

The reader has to actively situate himself in the psychological position from which the poet's associations derive and thereby to follow the linkages by 'which the host of suggestions are arranged'. Since such activity is difficult – the reader would rather 'peruse his author in a luxurious passiveness'[22] – it is not surprising that the poets of 'sensation' should be so little approved of by the reading public.

What Hallam proposes to readers of Tennyson's poems is a method of reading garnered from what he takes to be Tennyson's own practice in constructing his dramatic monologues, 'a new species of poetry, a graft of the lyric on the dramatic', for which 'Tennyson deserves the laurel of an inventor, an enlarger of our modes of knowledge and power'. In these 'he collects the most striking phenomena of individual minds, until he arrives at some leading fact, which allows him to lay down an axiom, or law, and then, working on the law thus attained, he clearly discerns the tendency of what new particulars his inventions suggests, and is enabled to impress an individual freshness and unity on ideal combinations'. They are, Hallam suggests, 'like

---

[21] Armstrong, *Victorian Scrutinies*, 89.
[22] Ibid.

summaries of mighty dramas',[23] the only ones possible to modern poets, since 'the age in which we live comes late in our national progress'[24] and it is no longer possible for poets to 'speak to the hearts of all' as the Elizabethans had done, 'and by the magnetic force of their conceptions elevate inferior intellects into a higher and purer atmosphere'.[25] The dramatic monologue provides the model for the reading of a poetry which celebrates the 'return of the mind upon itself, and the habit of seeking relief in idiosyncracies rather than community of interest'.[26] To read such poetry requires an act of ventriloquism on the part of readers by which, through sympathetic *exertion*, they take up the position of the speaker, and, by following the associational logic of that position, are enabled to follow the progress of the poem in spite of the 'peculiarity' of its processes of association.

Tennyson's 'Maud' (1855) might then stand as exemplary of the crisis into which the breakdown of associational connection between poet and reader casts the Victorian poet. Instead of the Wordsworthian poet who reveals the coherent narrative that makes order out of the disorder of that 'straggling heap of unhewn stones', we are presented with a character who cannot explain the rock that still lies in 'the dreadful hollow behind the little wood' (I, 1), 'the rock that fell with him when he fell' (I, 8); instead of a poet who compensates for the failure of inheritance from father to son by taking up and continuing the memory the son has cast aside, we are presented with a son disinherited by the death of his father, seeking to escape from the burden of memory that is his inheritance:

What! am I raging alone as my father raged in his mood?
Must *I* too creep to the hollow and dash myself down and die
Rather than hold by the law that I made, nevermore to brood
On a horror of shatter'd limbs and a wretched swindler's lie?

(I, 53–6)

As readers we are given the disorderly trains of association that constitute the mind of the protagonist, a mind which seems to flicker into self-consciousness only intermittently, leaving us to fill in the gaps in the narrative. There may be, behind these transitions 'a regular law of association' but the work is designed

---

[23] Ibid., 99.
[24] Ibid., 91.
[25] Ibid., 90.
[26] Ibid., 91.

to ensure that we can never be certain that we know how 'to apprehend the leading sentiment in the poet's mind, by their conformity to which the host of suggestions are arranged'. Take for instance, the transition between the first and second poems of Part II:

> Arise, my God, and strike, for we hold Thee just,
> Strike dead the whole weak race of venomous worms,
> That sting each other here in the dust;
> We are not worthy to live.

II

> See what a lovely shell,
> Small and pure as a pearl,
> Lying close to my foot,
> Frail, but a work divine,
> Made so fairly well
> With delicate spire and whorl,
> How exquisitely minute,
> A miracle of design!
>   (I, 45–9; II, 1–8)

Is the shell a symbol of divine design – 'Let him name it who can,/ The beauty would be the same' (11–12) – and a sign of a meaningful universe as compared with the 'race of venomous worms' against whom the God of wrath is invoked in the previous poem? Or is the significant fact about the shell that it is empty?

> The tiny shell is forlorn,
> Void of the little living will
> That made it stir on the shore.
>   (II, 12–14)

Is it simply a sign of death, and insignificant death at that? Tennyson has created a poem – as its many competing interpretations prove – in which it is impossible to fulfil Hallam's dictum that 'it is absolutely necessary *to start from the same point*' as the poet. The poet, concealed behind the associations of the character – associations which in themselves give us no secure starting point

– provides us with a poem which generates an *excess of association*, an excess
which cannot be reduced to order but which can only be escaped from as the
character himself escapes, by ceasing to indulge in aesthetic reverie – 'And
it was but a dream, yet it yielded a dear delight' (III, VI, 15) – and turning to
action – in his case, the action of war:

> Let it flame or fade, and the war roll down like a wind,
> We have proved we have hearts in a cause, we are noble still,
> And myself have awaked, as it seems, to the better mind;
> It is better to fight for the good than to rail at the ill;
> I have felt with my native land, I am one with my kind,
> I embrace the purpose of God, and the doom assign'd.
>
> (III, VI, 54–9)

There can be no resolution of the associations except by turning away from
them, by returning to to commitment to the 'native land' which the poem
began by excoriating. In the excess of signs the 'better mind' is one which acts
and in acting casts aside the mind's multiplying associations – leaving them to
the readers of the poem and to the realm of literature in which the multiplication of associations has a value – an aesthetic value – which is incompatible
with the demands of life.

'Maud' is thus a dramatisation of the theory of reading that Hallam proposed for Tennyson's earlier monologues, and in taking the theory to its extreme
it can be read either as glorying in its own multiplicity or as providing an ironic
commentary on that multiplicity – the poet guiltily indulges in an excess of
associational reverie and then cuts it off to proclaim the needs of national
duty. But Hallam's early death was, of course, the subject of Tennyson's *In
Memoriam*, which presents the opposite case: a world denuded of association and therefore unavailable to aesthetic experience. The famous section in
which Tennyson confronts the emptiness of Hallam's home concludes on a
line which reveals the nature of the world when the mind is incapable of rous-
ing its associative past:

> Dark house, by which once more I stand
>   Here in the long unlovely street,
>   Doors, where my heart was used to beat
> So quickly, waiting for a hand,

A hand that can be clasped no more—
Behold me, for I cannot sleep,
And like a guilty thing I creep
At earliest morning to the door.

He is not here: but far away
The noise of life begins again,
And ghastly through the drizzling rain
On the bald street breaks the blank day.
(VII)

Memory, stricken by loss and incapable of any relationship with the world, sees only vacancy: the '*bald* street', the '*blank* day' are emblems of a world that has lost all its associations since Tennyson lost his closest associate. The poem's progress is the progressive recovery of a memory which can make the world rich again in association even though it recognises that those associations have nothing but a personal significance, unsustained by anything in the external world. In sections C and CI the move towards recovery – 'I find no place that does not breathe/Some gracious memory of my friend' (3, 4) – is balanced against the fact that the landscape in which these memories inhere will itself be transformed in time, no longer signs of the poet's but some other native's mind:

Till from the garden and the wild
A fresh association blow,
And year by year the landscape grow
Familiar to the stranger's child;

As year by year the labourer tills
His wonted glebe, or lops the glades;
And year by year our memory fades
From all the circle of the hills.
(CI, 17–24)

The landscape whose associations return Tennyson's former associate to him becomes the image of the ultimate obliteration of memory: 'The hills are shadows, and they flow/From form to form, and nothing stands' (CXXIII, 4, 5). Evanescent signs in a world whose real meanings will become available only in a future evolutionary development when some 'crowning race' (CXXXI, 128), 'No longer half-akin to brute' (133), will be able to encounter Nature 'like an open book' (132). For the modern poet and his or her audience, however, the chain of mutually assuring associations on which Wordsworth had founded his poetry is impossible: the natural world will not sustain the signs of the poet's mind such that they will be intelligible to any future community of readers.

Associationism's insistence that the world was necessarily invested with our personal meanings, together with its equal insistence that there could be no guarantee that those meanings would ever be shared by anyone else, made it the appropriate medium by which late-Victorian culture could dramatise the insignificance of human events in the vastly expanded horizons revealed by geology and by Darwinian theories of evolution. Thomas Hardy, for instance, for whom 'the beauty of association is entirely superior to the beauty of aspect, and a beloved relative's old battered tankard to the finest Greek vase',[27] presents Clym Yeobright in *The Return of the Native* (1878)[28] as the ironic inversion of the Wordsworth who returns to find at Tintern Abbey a nature still inscribed with his own memories. Clym and the landscape of Egdon Heath are so associated, both in Clym's own mind and in the minds of his community, that each becomes a sign of the other:

> If any one knew the heath well it was Clym. He was permeated with its scenes, with its substance, and with its odours. He might be said to be its product. His eyes had first opened thereon; with its appearance all the first images of his memory were mingled; his estimate of life had been coloured by it; his toys had been the flint knives and arrowheads which he found there, wondering why stones should 'grow' to such odd shapes. (197)

Clym's character is a product of the heath but, equally, the heath has come to be represented by Clym: 'Clym had been so inwoven with the heath in his boyhood that hardly anybody could look upon it without thinking of him' (RN, 192). The ultimate significance of this mutual inscription of mind and landscape is, however, undermined by the very nature of the landscape with which Clym is identified, because it is a landscape that is utterly resistant to

---

[27] Florence Emily Hardy, *The Life of Thomas Hardy 1840–1928* (London: Macmillan, 1962), 120–1.

[28] Thomas Hardy, *Return of the Native* (London: Macmillan, 1974; 1878), hereafter cited in the text as *RN*.

human meanings: 'The untameable, Ishmaelitish thing that Egdon now was it always had been. Civilization was its enemy' (*RN*, 35). Egdon is a place where 'everything around and underneath had been from prehistoric times as unaltered as the stars overhead' (*RN*, 36) but far from representing the security of an unchanging nature its form appeals to the associations of 'a more recently learned emotion, than that which responds to the sort of beauty called charming and fair', an emotion in which 'the chastened sublimity of a moor, a sea, or a mountain will be all of nature that is absolutely in keeping with the moods of the more thinking among mankind' (*RN*, 34). Egdon appeals associatively to modern humanity precisely because it images nature's unconsciousness of human needs or purposes; any signs to be found on it 'were not caused by pickaxe, plough, or spade, but remained as the very finger-touches of the last geological change' (*RN*, 36). The associations which make the heath significant to Clym are such as return only to mock his search for significance:

> He frequently walked the heath alone, when the past seized upon him with its shadowy hand, and held him there to listen to its tale. His imagination would then people the spot with its ancient inhabitants: forgotten Celtic tribes trod their tracks about him, and he could almost live among them, look in their faces, and see them standing beside the barrows which swelled around, untouched and perfect as at the time of their erection. Those of the dyed barbarians who had chosen the cultivable tracts were, in comparison with those who had left their marks here, as writers on paper beside writers on parchment. Their records had perished long ago by the plough, while the work of these remained. Yet they all had lived and died, unconscious of the different fates awaiting their relics. It reminded him that unforeseen factors operate in the evolution of immortality. (*RN*, 399)

The signs of mind on the landscape are accidental, their apparent 'immortality' only an ironic commentary on the 'unforeseen' in the processes of evolution, their ability to recall the past evidence only of how 'forgotten' that past actually is.

Hardy – amongst whose most powerful influences was Leslie Stephen, father of Virginia Woolf and, in *English Thought in the Eighteenth Century*, defender of the tradition of the British empiricists – is in the direct line from Alison when he insisted that 'the poetry of a scene varies with the minds of the perceivers. Indeed, it does not lie in the scene at all'.[29] But by the latter part of the nineteenth century associationism's 'arts of memory' have to operate in an environment which reduces memory itself to insignificance, its recollections purely personal signs unsustained by the landscape with which they are associated:

> It filled but a minute. But was there ever
>   A time of such quality, since or before,
> In that hill's story? To one mind never,
>   Though it has been climbed, foot-swift, foot-sore
>   By thousands more.

> Primaeval rocks form the road's steep border,
>   And much have faced there, first and last,
> Of the transitory in Earth's long order;
>   But what they record in colour and cast
>   Is – that we two passed.

'At Castle Boterel' is poem which celebrates the power of association to recall from the landscape a moment of the past only in order to acknowledge the fragility on which such association is based: in defiance of the vast expanse of geological time, the associating eye retains the past as permanence – gestured to by that assertive 'Is' – only for the ear to hear its negation, as 'we two passed' doubles into 'we too passed':

> I look and see it there, shrinking, shrinking,
>   I look back at it amid the rain
> For the very last time; for my sand is sinking
>   And I shall traverse old love's domain
>   Never again.

Our personal associations leave no signs on the landscape. The world is a canvas which memory paints only to have its visions erased, reduced forever to that blank from which Tennyson was fleeing in *In Memoriam*:

---

[29] Florence Emily Hardy, *Life of Thomas Hardy*, 50. Tom Paulin, in *Thomas Hardy: The Poetry of Perception* (London: Macmillan, 1975), notes that Hardy listed Hume along with Darwin, Huxley, Spencer and Mill as the major influences on his work.

> The railway bore him through
> An earthen cutting out from a city:
>   There was no scope for view,
> Though the frail light shed by a slim young moon
>   Fell like a friendly tune.
>
>   Fell like a liquid ditty,
> And the blank lack of any charm
>   Of landscape did no harm.
> The bald steep cutting, rigid, rough,
>   And moon-lit, was enough
> For poetry of place: its weathered face
> Formed a convenient sheet whereon
> The visions of his mind were drawn.

'After a Romantic Day', Hardy's poem is titled: the modern mind travels through places whose 'blank lack of any charm' will never recall its visions, whose visions will never inscribe themselves on a significant place.

IV

In *The Century of Taste*, James Dickie takes Archibald Alison to task for proposing that any scene which is connected with a significant memory – whether the home of a famous person or the landscape of some famous historical incident – will become a place of beauty to its observers. Alison suggests that,

> The scenes which have been distinguished by the residence of any person, whose memory we admire, produce a similar effect . . . The scenes themselves may be little beautiful; but the delight with which we recollect the traces of their lives, blends itself insensibly with the motions which the scenery itself, excites; and the admiration which these recollections afford, seems to give a kind of sanctity to the place where they dwelt, and converts everything into beauty which appears to have been connected with them. (*AET*, 16)

Dickie insists that such places are capable of producing experiences neither of beauty nor of sublimity:

the idea of the residences [of persons we admire] that are of little or no
beauty coalesces with an idea of something of beauty to make the residences beautiful . . . there is not only the mystery of how two distinct
ideas can coalesce but also the mystery of where the beauty is supposed
to come from. The answer is that it does not come from anywhere and the
situation Alison describes is not one in which beauty is present. Alison is
right that being in such places . . . produces in us feelings of a kind of
sanctity . . . Nevertheless, the undoubted pleasure we take in the experience of such objects does not convert them into objects of beauty. Many
of these objects are just ordinary looking, and some may even be ugly. Of
course, some of the objects may be beautiful, but not because of their
associations.[30]

Alison, however, was not only attempting to unify an aesthetic world divided
between the beautiful and the sublime, the natural and the artificial, but to
provide an account that could explain how new forms of aesthetic pleasure can develop. Dickie's 'mystery of how two distinct ideas can coalesce'
is no mystery: compound or complex associations are fundamental to the
associationist account of the mind, as we have seen, but, in any case, 'coales-
cence' is unnecessary in this case: all that Alison needs is that the object – the
residence of the person we admire – should provoke an unmotivated train
of associations that sustains the *reverie* characteristic of all aesthetic experience. What Dickie's attempted criticisms reveal is precisely the strength of
Alison's theory, which is that it makes no presuppositions about what can
be aesthetically interesting (and therefore 'beautiful', 'sublime' or any other
term that may emerge to designate such objects). Since the aesthetic experience is not *in* the object – as Dickie wishes to believe – but in a particular
mode of perception *of* the object, the contribution of historical memory to
the production of that mode of perception is as valid as any other memories
which an aesthetic object brings into play. 'There are scenes,' Alison tells us,
'undoubtedly, more beautiful than Runnymede, yet to those who recollect the
great event which passed there, there is no scene, perhaps, which so strongly
seizes upon the imagination' (*AET*, 16). To those who know the history of
a place, its objects develop an aesthetic potential that is invisible to those
without such memories; history increases the resources of memory and so

---

[30] George Dickie, *The Century of Taste: The Philosophical Odyssey of Taste in the
Eighteenth Century* (Oxford: Oxford University Press, 1996), 79–80.

provides an increase in the associative material that can be brought into play in aesthetic experience.

Such an aestheticisation of history – or aestheticisation by history – is one of the consequences of the associationist theory of art. Walter Scott records in his 'Autobiography' how in his youth – at the very time when Alison was composing his *Essays on Taste* – his passion for the historical was regarded as an eccentricity:

> My principal object in these excursions was the pleasure of seeing romantic scenery, or what afforded me at least an equal pleasure, the places which had been distinguished by remarkable historical events. The delight with which I regarded the former, of course had general approbation, but I often found it difficult to procure sympathy with the interest I felt in the latter. Yet to me, the wandering over the field of Bannockburn was the source of more exquisite pleasure than gazing on the celebrated landscape from the battlements of Stirling castle.[31]

The historical scene as an aesthetic object is necessarily a construction of the memory and in *Waverley* (1814), his first and usually considered the world's first historical novel, Scott draws attention precisely to the associational effects on which his historical fiction depends:

> With a mind more at ease, Waverley could not have failed to admire the mixture of romance and beauty which renders interesting the scene through which he was now passing – the field which had been the scene of tournaments of old – the rock from which the ladies beheld the contest, while each made vows for the success of some favourite knight – the towers of the Gothic church, where those vows might be paid – and, surmounting all, the fortress itself, at once a castle and a palace, where valour received the prize from royalty, and knights and dames closed the evening amid the revelry of the dance, the song, and the feast. All these were objects fitted to arouse and interest a romantic imagination.
>
> But Waverley had other objects of meditation . . .[32]

---

[31] J. G. Lockhart, *Memoirs of Sir Walter Scott*, 10 Vols (Edinburgh: Adam and Charles Black, 1869; 1836), Vol. I, 'Autobiography', 70.

[32] Walter Scott, *Waverley*, ed. Andrew Hook (Harmondsworth: Penguin, 1972), 289–90.

Waverley misses the beauty of Stirling Castle; the reader, thanks to Scott's construction of a chain of appropriate associations, does not. Scott's novel, in other words, not only transcribes a historical event from fact into fiction, it also transforms the landscape across which the fiction moves by making it the sign of those historical events. The author draws on historical memories to generate associations that will make the landscape aesthetically interesting but thereby *adds* to the associational resources of the landscape, increasing its potential for future aesthetic experience. Literature and landscape thus become involved in a mutually reinforcing process of recollection: to view the landscape is to recall the literature; to read the literature is to re-view the landscape and reinscribe it with memories which make it worth recalling or revisiting. Each enhances the other's associative intensity and aesthetic potency. Scott's poems and novels created a tourist industry in Scotland by so enriching the landscape with his own art that it became, to his readers, as full of associations as it had been to him:

> The romantic feelings which I have described as predominating in my mind, naturally rested upon and associated themselves with these grand features of the landscape around me; and the historical incidents, or traditional legends connected with many of them, gave to my admiration a sort of intense impression of reverence, which at times made my heart feel too big for its bosom. From this time the love of natural beauty, more especially as combined with ancient ruins, or remains of our fathers' piety and splendour, became with me an insatiable passion . . .[33]

Literature thus writes itself on to the landscape, making it a sign both of the historical past and of the mind which retains – or creates – that past.

This double movement had already been revealed in one of the earliest novels about British tourism (and one of Scott's major influences), Tobias Smollett's *The Expedition of Humphry Clinker* (1771), in which the furthest destination of the Welsh tourists who are surveying the territory of the only recently United Kingdom – a territory whose political unity had been cast in doubt by Jacobite Rebellion of 1745 and the Wilkes' riots in London in the 1760s – is the Scottish Highlands, where the 'country is amazingly wild, especially towards the mountains, which are heaped upon the backs of one another, making a most stupendous appearance of savage nature, with hardly

---

[33] J. G. Lockhart, *Memoirs of Sir Walter Scott*, Vol. I, 'Autobiography', 55.

any signs of cultivation, or even of population. All is sublimity, silence, and solitude'.[34] The sublimity of the natural landscape, however, is enhanced by another sublimity:

> We have had princely sport in hunting the stag on these mountains – These are the lonely hills of Morven, where Fingal and his heroes enjoyed the same pastime; I feel an enthusiastic pleasure when I survey the brown heath that Ossian wont to tread; and hear the wind whistle through the bending grass – When I enter our landlord's hall, I look for the suspended harp of that divine bard, and listen in hopes of hearing the aerial sound of his respected spirit – The poems of Ossian are in every mouth.[35]

The tourists retrace the actions of ancient heroes, view the landscape through their recollection, listen for the spirit of the poet and repeat his compositions. The apparently 'natural' sublime to which Burke had appealed is in fact produced in and through the literary sublime: the recollection of the literary text infuses the landscape with memory, and that memory generates the landscape's aesthetic significance.

For the majority of human beings, Alison argues, the perspectives of the natural world have no aesthetic import, and 'are regarded by them with no other sentiments, than as being useful for the purposes of human life'. This, he believes, was originally 'the state of our own minds', a condition in which 'we' would have continued but for the cultivation of new associative potentialities in the course of education and in the experience of classical literature:

> it is probable that most men will recollect, that the time when nature began to appear to them in another view, was, when they were engaged in the study of classical literature. In most men, at least, the first appearance of poetical imagination is at school, when their imaginations begin to be warmed by the descriptions of ancient poetry, and when they have acquired a new sense, as it were, with which they can behold the face of nature. (*AET*, 48–9)

---

[34] Tobias Smollett, *The Expedition of Humphry Clinker*, ed. Angus Ross (London: Penguin, 1965), 290.

[35] Ibid., 277.

Associations derived from literature add what is effectively 'a new sense' to the experience of the natural world: Hutcheson's universal 'internal sense' of beauty has been transformed into the entirely relative – and largely accidental – acquisition of certain kinds of memories:

> How different, from this period, become the sentiments with which the scenery of nature is contemplated, by those who have any imagination! The beautiful forms of ancient mythology, with which the fancy of poets peopled every element, are now ready to appear to their minds, upon the prospect of every scene. The description of ancient authors, so long admired, and so deserving of admiration, occur to them at every moment, and with them, all those enthusiastic ideas of ancient genius and glory, which the study of so many years of youth so naturally leads them to form. Or, if the study of modern poetry has succeeded to that of the ancient, a thousand other beautiful associations are acquired, which, instead of destroying, serve easily to unite with the former, and to afford a new source of delight. (*AET*, 49)

Without such memories, the process of association cannot start and the experience of beauty, even of the natural world, becomes impossible: 'With such images in their minds, it is not common nature that appears to surround them. It is nature embellished and made sacred by the memory of Theocritus and Virgil, and Milton and Tasso; their genius seems still to linger among the scenes which inspired it, and to irradiate every object where it dwells; and the creation of their fancy seem the fit inhabitants of that nature, which their descriptions have clothed with beauty' (*AET*, 49–50). The landscape that Smollett's travellers encountered was not sublime because the 'country is amazingly wild', or because it had 'a most stupendous appearance of savage nature', full of 'silence, and solitude', but because their reading of Ossian had provided them with the textual memories by which such aspects of the landscape could be identified and responded to. To become the object of aesthetic experience, the landscape has to be clothed by literary memories.[36] The discovery that Macpherson's Ossianic poetry was, if not fictional, then certainly not historical, did not immediately diminish its effect: landscape, as Macpherson's

---

[36] This was a debate which shaped the emergence of American literature in the 1810s and 20s; see Robert E. Streeter, 'Association Psychology and Literary Nationalism in the North American Review, 1815–1825', *American Literature*, Vol. 17, No. 3 (November 1945), 243–54.

imitators across Europe were to prove, is as powerfully transfigured by a fictional history as by a real history.

Smollett's account of his tourists' experiences underlines the extent to which the rage for Macpherson's poetry and associationist aesthetics were profoundly intertwined. Hugh Blair's 'A Critical Dissertation on the Poems of Ossian', which first appeared in 1763, was extended in 1765 at the instigation of David Hume and shows the marked influence of Hume's theories both of the psyche and of history. Blair's defence of the authenticity of the Ossianic epics was based partly on 'conjectural history', on the assumption – common to Hume, Smith and Ferguson – that in the early stages of civilisation, 'imagination' and 'sentiment' dominate over the first steps of reason and that art, therefore, is '*The Poetry of the Heart*': 'It is a heart penetrated with noble sentiments, and with sublime and tender passions; a heart that glows, and kindles the fancy; a heart that is full, and pours itself forth'.[37] Despite his dismissive attitude to Macpherson, Wordsworth's 'spontaneous overflow of powerful feelings' (*WW*, 598) is, in fact, an echo of Blair's defence of Ossian, and Wordsworth's celebration of the imagination and the language of 'low and rustic life', where 'the essential passions of the heart find a better soil in which they can attain their maturity' (*WW*, 597), is a modernisation of Blair's defence of the powers of imagination in primitive society:

> As the world advances, the understanding gains ground upon the imagination; the understanding is more exercised; the imagination, less. Fewer objects occur that are new or surprising. Men apply themselves to trace the causes of things; they correct and refine one another; they subdue or disguise their passions; they form their exterior manners upon one uniform standard of politeness and civility . . . Hence, poetry, which is the child of imagination, is frequently most glowing and animated in the first stages of society.[38]

For Blair, the authenticity of Ossian is proved not just by the sociological evidence of the primitive society which the poems record – the 'total absence', for instance, 'of religious ideas from this work'[39] – but because of the nature of the poem's imagery and the ways in which it provokes associations: 'Very

---

[37] Howard Gaskill (ed.), *The Poems of Ossian and Related Works* (Edinburgh: Edinburgh University Press, 1996), 356.
[38] *Poems of Ossian*, 346.
[39] Ibid., 355.

often two objects are brought together in a simile, though they resemble one another, strictly speaking, in nothing, only because they raise in the mind a train of similar, and what may be called concordant ideas; so that the remembrance of the one, when recalled, serves to quicken and heighten the impression made by the other'.[40] The strangeness of the combinations of imagery in the Ossianic poetry derives, in other words, from a reversal of the normal work-ings of simile: instead of objects being brought together because they have some basis of likeness, they are brought together as a result of suggesting similar trains of association: 'Such analogies and associations of ideas as these, are highly pleasing to the fancy . . . They diversify the scene; they aggrandize the subject; they keep the imagination awake and sprightly'.[41] In the Ossianic narratives can be discerned the fundamental premises which will be invoked and evolved by succeeding generations of artists in the associationist tradition: 'a style always rapid and vehement; in narration concise even to abruptness; and leaving several circumstances to be supplied by the reader's imagination'.[42] The work is necessarily *incomplete* because the artwork only becomes complete when surrounded by and filled in by a reader's memories, and from the outflow of its associations finally to experience the text as fulfilled art.

In Macpherson's Ossianic poetry the 'return of the native' also has a very different significance from what it was to have for a Wordsworth or a Hardy: an art native to the landscape returns after a long amnesia and reinscribes it with nearly – or, indeed, entirely – forgotten but now recollected – and usually, quite literally, *collected* – memories. By means of a recovered literary artefact, an old memory is resurrected and made available again to a new audience, one for whom these original memories are necessarily acquired at second hand and by means of editorial revision or actual translation. Instead of the landscape providing signs for the literary imagination, the literary imagination endows the landscape with its significance and creates signs which would be invisible except to a readerly observer. It is a relationship which Macpherson dramatised in two related ways. First, his characters are hyper-conscious of the importance of memory, not simply in terms of the fact that 'the bard shall preserve their names, and repeat them to future times',[43] but that their memory will be inscribed on the landscape itself: 'And some hunter may say, when he leans on a mossy tomb, here Fingal and Swaran fought, the heroes

---

[40] Ibid., 382.
[41] Ibid., 383.
[42] Ibid., 354.
[43] Ibid., 'Fingal', Book I, 62.

of other years. Thus hereafter shall he say, and our fame shall last for ever'.[44] Secondly, however, since Ossian is aged, blind and childless, he is the last remaining link of memory to the nobility of the past: 'Such, Fingal! Were thy words; but thy words I hear no more. Sightless I sit by thy tomb. I hear the wind in the wood; but no more I hear my friends. The cry of the hunter is over. The voice of war is ceased'.[45] The anguish of the poetry is not simply in the tragedies that it recounts – the deaths of Fingal and of Oscur – but in the fact that the memory of those events is about to disappear. Ossian, the last guardian of an ancient memory, is redeemed by Macpherson, who preserves his voice from destruction – 'excepting the present poem, those pieces are in a great measure lost, and there only remain a few fragments of them';[46] Macpherson, however, was the representative of a culture itself threatened with destruction in the aftermath of the 1745 Jacobite rising, a culture for which Ossian can be made to speak:

> How hast thou fallen like an oak, with all thy branches round thee! Where is Fingal the King? Where is Oscur my son? Where are all my race? Alas! In the earth they lie. I feel their tombs with my hands. I hear the river below murmuring hoarsely over the stones. What dost thou, O river, to me? Thou bringest back the memory of the past.[47]

The memory which infuses the landscape with significance is inherently fragile: threatened with destruction, it knows that forgetfulness may reduce its world of signs again to a mere blank. The contingency of memory has to be constantly resisted, the power of recollection continually renewed, if an all-engulfing oblivion is to be prevented.

Macpherson's Ossianic poetry thus reflects in its content, as well as in its form, the threat of an amnesia which will strip the work of its associative potential and thereby render it dumb. Overcoming that amnesia required Macpherson's successors in Scotland – including Burns and Scott – to repeat both his efforts at collecting and assembling the fragments of a nearly forgotten poetry and the self-conscious dramatisation of its extinction. In the very year when *The Report of the Highland Society of Scotland, appointed to inquire*

---

[44] Ibid., 'Fingal' Book VI, 101.
[45] Ibid., 'Fragments of Ancient Poetry', 8.
[46] Ibid., 'A Dissertation Concerning the Antiquity, &c. of the Poems of Ossian the Son of Fingal', 51.
[47] Ibid., 'Fragments of Ancient Poetry', VIII, 18.

into the Nature and Authenticity of the Poems of Ossian was published, 1805, that 'second Macpherson' (as he described himself in the preface to *Ivanhoe*),[48] Sir Walter Scott, published 'The Lay of the Last Minstrel', which transferred the associative resources of the Scottish past from the Highlands to the Borders. The threat of cultural extinction which Macpherson-Ossian resisted by the *re*-collection of the deeds of Celtic heroes, is repeated by Scott's Minstrel who, Ossian-like, provides the last frail link to the memories of a past society:

> The harp, his sole remaining joy,
> Was carried by an orphan boy.
> The last of all the Bards was he,
> Who sung of Border chivalry;
> For, welladay! Their date was fled,
> His tuneful brethren all were dead;
> And he, neglected and oppress'd,
> Wish'd to be with them, and at rest.
> ('Introduction', 5–12)

Inspired 'with all a poet's ecstasy', however, the potential blank of memory is resisted once again:

> Cold diffidence, and age's frost,
> In the full tide of song were lost;
> Each blank in faithless memory void,
> The poet's glowing thought supplied;
> And while his harp responsive rung,
> 'Twas thus the LATEST MINSTREL sung.
> ('Introduction', 95–100)

It is a gesture which was to be regularly repeated as the smaller nations of the newly United Kingdom – Ireland having been added by the Union of 1801 – strove to maintain the memories without which their cultural distinction – in both its senses – would be obliterated. Lady Morgan's 'The Lay of the Irish Harp', for instance, begins with an epigraph from Ossian – "Voice of the days of old, let me hear you. – Awake the soul of song' before launching into what,

---

48 Walter Scott, 'Dedicatory Epistle', *Ivanhoe*, ed. Ian Duncan (Oxford: Oxford University Press, 1996; 1819), 14.

according to Fiona Stafford, 'appeared to rally nationalistic spirit' but 'was really an elegy':[49]

> Why sleeps the Harp of Erin's pride?
> Why with'ring droops its Shamrock wreath?
> Why has that song of sweetness died
> Which Erin's harp alone can breathe?

Such an elegiac recollection of the past appeared to justify Arnold's famous analysis of the Celts as 'this colossal, impetuous, adventurous wanderer, the Titan of the early world' who 'dwindles and dwindles as history goes on' because, quoting Ossian, 'They went forth to the war but they always fell'.[50] Stafford, however, misconstrues the irony of elegy in an associatonist context: by apparently laying to rest the elements of the national past, the elegy in fact reinvests that past with new associations for contemporary readers, and by so doing effectively reverses the decline which is being elegised. Instead of being laid to rest, the past emerges, like Ossianic ghosts, to haunt the present in voices that refuse to fall silent. It is a strategy which links revivalists of national memory in the early nineteenth century with those at the beginning of the twentieth, since it is precisely the strategy of W. B. Yeats's 'September 1913':[51]

> Was it for this the wild geese spread
> The grey wing upon every tide;
> For this that all that blood was shed,
> For this Edward Fitzgerald died,
> And Robert Emmet and Wolfe Tone,
> All that delirium of the brave?
> Romantic Ireland's dead and gone,
> It's with O'Leary in the grave.[52]

---

[49] Fiona J. Stafford, '"Dangerous Success": Ossian, Wordsworth, and English Romantic Literature', in Howard Gaskill (ed.), *Ossian Revisited* (Edinburgh: Edinburgh University Press, 1991), 65.

[50] Matthew Arnold, *On the Study of Celtic Literature* (London: Smith, Elder & Co., 1867), 106–7.

[51] W. B. Yeats, *The Collected Poems of W. B. Yeats* (London: Macmillan, 1950), 120.

[52] Ibid.

The elegy dismisses 'Romantic Ireland' as 'dead and gone', its memory having been erased with the death of Yeats's mentor in nationalism, John O'Leary, whose politics have been overtaken by the rise of a new, memoryless middle class:

> What need you, being come to sense,
> But fumble in a greasy till
> And add the halfpence to the pence
> And prayer to shivering prayer, until
> You have dried the marrow from the bone?

But by the very intensity with which it lists the names of Ireland's heroic eighteenth-century leaders, it recreates the associative context which it claims to have abandoned, a paradox syntactically enacted in the poem's final lines:

> But let them be, they're dead and gone,
> They're with O'Leary in the grave.

'Let them be' is poised on radically different possibilities: 'let them be', that is, forget them; or 'let them be', let them continue to haunt the memory of modern Ireland. The poem gestures to the first while enacting the second. 'Easter 1916' performs the same double gesture with the dead of the Easter Rising. To Yeats the ordinary man, the question is one of motivation: 'And what if excess of love/Bewildered them till they died'; but to Yeats the poet, who depends on the associative recollection of a national community, there is no choice but commitment to what is powerful in memory:

> I write it out in a verse –
> MacDonagh and MacBride
> And Connolly and Pearse
> Now and in time to be,
> Wherever green is worn,
> Are changed, changed utterly:
> A terrible beauty is born.

A poetry based on memory is committed to relentless acts of defiance of forgetfulness, and to the celebration of those acts of defiance which, because memorable, will continue to be associatively effective.

In Yeats's poetry, Lady Morgan's Irish harp still sounds in defiance of the elegy by which it was consigned to the past. The connection is not accidental: Lady Morgan's *The Wild Irish Girl* (1806) is a novel both associational and Ossianic, which at one and the same time documents the demise of ancient Irish culture – represented by the Prince of Inismore whose ancient castle, because 'fallen into decay', is also 'the fairy vision of poetic dreams, a combination of images more poetically fine, more strikingly picturesque' than 'Fancy, in her boldest flight'[53] – and the transferral of its memories – through the marriage of the Prince's daughter, Glorvina, to the son of an English Earl – into both the English language and the modern world. The process of this transferral is one in which the Englishman, who recognises that his views of the Irish can 'be traced to some fatal association of ideas received and formed in early life' (*WIG*, 13), gradually acquires a new set of associations that link the object of his immediate affection to ancient Celtic literature: 'Would you know the images now most buoyant in my cheered bosom: they are Ossian and Glorvina: it is for *him* to describe, for *her* to feel, the renovating charms of this interesting moment' (*WIG*, 206). He also thereby learns to associate his *literary* experience of Ossian with Ireland rather than with Scotland, thus transforming the Irish from 'rude people' associated with 'scenes appropriately barbarous' (*WIG*, 13) to a people with a classical culture: 'The ancient Irish, like the Greeks', he learns, 'were religiously attached to the consecrated fountain, the *Vel expiatoria*' (*WIG*, 153). Indeed, 'thus closely associated' (*WIG*, 119) with Glorvina, he discovers that 'no nation under Heaven was ever more enthusiastically attached to poetry and music than the Irish' (*WIG*, 138), even though the conditions under which they now labour mean that Glorvina's family is 'obliged to have recourse to our own memories' (*WIG*, 118) rather than the communal memory once sustained by the bardic tradition. Those memories, however, have been sustained by Macpherson's poetry, because of the 'superior merits' of his 'poems, as compositions, over those wild effusions of our Irish bards when he compiled them' (*WIG*, 115), and will be further enhanced when Englishmen like himself take the trouble to learn the Irish language, and 'to listen to the language of Ossian with the same respect a Hindoo would to the Shanscrit of the Bramins' (*WIG*, 161). In one of the strangest forays of the novel, the English protagonist and an Irish priest travel

---

[53] Sydney Owenson, Lady Morgan, *The Wild Irish Girl*, ed. Kathryn Kirkpatrick (Oxford: Oxford University Press, 1999; 1806), 46; hereafter cited in the text as *WIG*.

to Ulster where they encounter one of the last of the bards, who is described, in the Scots dialect of Northern Ireland, as the '*mon wi the twa heads*' because of 'an immense wen [lump or growth] on the back of his head' (*WIG*, 199). This 'hydra' bard, Irish but living in Scots-speaking Ireland and performing for an English tourist who recollects lines from Ossian on listening to him, represents a poetry whose associations now flow into many different memories, as they flow from many different heads. The many-headed culture of the United Kingdom is united in – because it was founded on – the ancient Celtic literature of the British Isles.

This 'unionist' construction of the significance of Ossianic poetry as the foundation on which the real unity of British culture rested was to pass into the formative accounts of English literature, not only Arnold's famous assertion that the achievements of English literature depended on its Celtic imagination – 'The Celts, with their vehement reaction against the despotism of fact, with their sensuous nature, their manifold striving, their adverse destiny, their immense calamities, the Celts are the prime authors of this vein of piercing regret and passion, – of this Titanism in poetry. A famous book, Macpherson's Ossian, carried in the last century this vein like a flood of lava through Europe'[54] – but influential histories of English literature, such as Henry Morley's *English Writers* (1887), which insists that without its Celtic substratum 'Germanic England would not have produced a Shakespeare'.[55] By the time that W. B. Yeats came to write his early poetry in the late 1880s, this Celticist version of the history of English literature was being supplanted by one based on Anglo-Saxon roots, one that was to be enshrined in the *Cambridge History of English Literature* (1907–16), which declared in its opening volume that '*Beowulf* – romance, history and epic – is the oldest poem on a great scale, and in the grand manner, that exists in any Teutonic language. It is full of incident and good fights, simple in aim and clear in execution; its characters bear comparison with those of the *Odyssey* and, like them, linger in the memory; its style is dignified and heroic'.[56] Though the first complete edition of *Beowulf*, edited by the Icelandic scholar Grim J. Thorkelin, had only been published in

---

[54] Matthew Arnold, *On the Study of Celtic Literature*, 152. Arnold acknowledges his own indebtedness to Morley's account of English writers before Chaucer, 96.

[55] Henry Morley, *English Writers: An Attempt towards a History of English Literature*, 11 Vols (London: Cassell, 1887), Vol. I, 189–90.

[56] A. W. Ward and A. R. Waller (eds), *The Cambridge History of English Literature*, 15 Vols (Cambridge: Cambridge University Press, 1907), Vol. I, 4.

1815, its construction as a Germanic origin for English literature had, by the end of the century, left Ossian to the Irish as representative of a different kind of unionism, the union of all the peoples – Catholic and Protestant; Celtic, Anglo-Irish and Scoto-Irish – resident on the island of Ireland. One of Yeats's first published poems is 'The Wanderings of Oisin' (1889) and it was his hope that in their shared association with Ossianic poetry the people of Ireland could find in the landscape of their country the signs of a single national mind, one inscribed for them by the literary works of those – like Yeats and Lady Gregory – who re-collect and re-present their past:

> When I asked the little boy who had shown me the pathway up the hill of Allen if he knew stories of Finn and Oisin, he said he did not, but that he had often heard his grandfather telling them to his mother in Irish. He did not know Irish, but he was learning it at school, and all the little boys he knew were learning it. In a little while he will know enough stories of Finn and Oisin to tell them to his children some day. It is the owners of the land whose children might never have known what would give them so much happiness. But now they can read Lady Gregory's book to their children, and it will make Slieve-na-man, Allen and Ben Bulben, the great mountain that showed itself before me every day through all my childhood and yet was unpeopled . . . as populous with memories as her Cuchulain of Muirthemne will have made Dundealgan . . .[57]

That route from an 'unpeopled' Ireland to one that would be again 'populous with memories' had, according to Yeats, been charted by the mid-nineteenth century Ulster poet, Sir Samuel Ferguson, whose work, like another Macpherson,

> went back to the Irish cycle, finding it, in truth, a fountain that, in the passage of centuries, was overgrown with weeds and grass, so that the very way to it was forgotten of the poets; but now that his feet have worn the pathway, many others will follow, and bring thence living waters for the healing of our nation, helping us to live the larger life of the Spirit, and lifting our souls away from their selfish joys and sorrows

---

[57] W. B. Yeats, 'Of Gods and Fighting Men', *Explorations* (London: Macmillan, 1962), 28–9.

to be the companions of those who lived greatly among the woods and hills when the world was young.[58]

By the return of the native, landscape becomes the sign of an emergent and yet ancient national mind, one that is thoroughly imbued with Irish associations even though it is expressed in the English language. Like Lady Morgan, Yeats found in associationism an aesthetic which could overcome the divisions of the Irish past by making a modern literature in English the superstructure of an ancient Irish memory, which not only provided the poetry with an associational richness lost to modern cultures but in the return to the sources of the 'native' helped recover poetry's function as the sign of the deepest forces of the natural world:

> Irish literature may prolong its first inspiration without renouncing the complexity of ideas and emotions which is the inheritance of cultivated men, for it will have learned from the discoveries of modern learning that the common people, wherever civilization has not driven its plough too deep, keep a watch over the roots of religion and all romance. Their poetry trembles on the verge of incoherence with a passion all but unknown among modern poets, and their sense of beauty exhausts itself in the countless legends and metaphors that seem to mirror the energies of nature.[59]

V

Arthur Symons's *The Symbolist Movement in Literature* (1899) is dedicated to W. B. Yeats, 'whose Irish literary movement is one of its expressions'.[60] Yeats's conception of the symbol, however, repeats the collusion of symbolism with association that we saw in Carlyle. For, like Carlyle, Yeats tried to draw a

---

58 W. B. Yeats, 'Poetry of Sir Samuel Ferguson – I' (*Irish Fireside*, 9 October 1886), *Uncollected Prose*, ed. John P. Frayne, 2 Vols (London: Macmillan, 1970), Vol. 1, 82.

59 W. B. Yeats, 'The Literary Movement in Ireland' (*North American Review*, December 1899), *Uncollected Prose*, ed. John P. Frayne and Colton Johnson, 2 Vols (London: Macmillan, 1975), Vol. 2, 118.

60 Arthur Symons, *The Symbolist Movement in Literature* (New York: E. P. Dutton and Co., 1958; rev. edn, 1919), xix.

distinction between 'inherent symbols and arbitrary symbols'[61] – Carlyle's 'intrinsic' and 'extrinsic' – but found the distinction rapidly breaking down, 'for everything in heaven or earth has its association' and 'one never knows what forgotten events may have plunged it, like the toadstool and the rag-weed, into the great passions'.[62] Yeats's associationism derived from Hallam's essay on Tennyson – 'I alone loved criticism of Arthur Hallam's sort'[63] – but sought to escape the isolation of Hallam's conception of the poet by acquir-ing associations that would link him to his native land: 'I filled my imagination with the popular beliefs of Ireland, gathering them up among forgotten nov-elists in the British Museum or in Sligo cottages. I sought some symbolic language reaching far into the past and associated with familiar names and conspicuous hills that I might not be alone amid the obscure impressions of the senses'.[64] Such communal associations, however, are themselves the after-echo of previous literature: the world of our ordinary perception is nothing but the outcome of an associational chain that recapitulates the whole his-tory of humanity:

> Yet works of art are always begotten by previous works of art, and every masterpiece becomes the Abraham of a chosen people. When we delight in a spring day there mixes, perhaps, with our personal emotion an emo-tion Chaucer found in Guillaume de Lorris, who had it from the poetry of Provence; we celebrate our draughty May with an enthusiasm made ripe by more meridian suns; and all our art has its image in the Mass that would lack authority were it not descended from savage ceremo-nies taught amid what perils and by what spirits to naked savages. The old images, the old emotions, awakened again to overwhelming life, like the gods Heine tells of, by the belief and passion of some new soul, are the only masterpieces.[65]

It was for this reason that Yeats believed that art called up not the memory of individual human beings, or even some local communal memory, but a transhistorical memory. In his essay on 'The Philosophy of Shelley's Poetry' he suggests that Shelley 'seems in his speculation to have lit on that memory of

---

[61] W. B. Yeats, *Essays and Introductions*, 'Magic', 49.
[62] Ibid., 50.
[63] W. B. Yeats, 'Art and Ideas', *Essays and Introductions*, 349.
[64] Ibid.
[65] Ibid., 353–3.

Nature the visionaries claim for the foundation of their knowledge; but I do not know whether he thought, as they do, that all things good and evil remain for ever, "thinking the thought and doing the deed", though not, it may be, self-conscious; or only thought that "love and beauty and delight remain for ever"'.[66] Shelley's writings, Yeats suggests, reveal that he might have found 'in some old book or on some old monument, a strange and intricate image that had floated up before him, and to grow perhaps dizzy with the sudden conviction that our little memories are but a part of some great Memory that renews the world and men's thought age after age, and that our thoughts are not, as we suppose, the deep, but a little foam upon the deep'.[67]

The Great Memory becomes the metaphysical resource which under-pins an associationist art, ensuring the artist's escape from his merely local associations, since 'it is only by ancient symbols, by symbols that have num-berless meanings besides the one or two the writer lays emphasis upon, or the half-score he knows of, that any highly subjective art can escape from the bar-renness and shallowness of a too conscious arrangement, into the abundance and depth of Nature'.[68] Though it may be through the local memory that the artist finds a gateway to the Great Memory, in the Great Memory the universe is revealed as nothing more than an associating mind, with the consequence that associationism has been transformed from an account of the minds of human beings to an account of the very being of the universe – what Yeats called the *Anima Mundi*:

> Shelley was of the opinion that the 'thoughts which are called real or external objects' differed but in regularity of occurrence from 'hallucina-tions, dreams and ideas of madmen', and noticed that he had dreamed, therefore lessening the difference, 'three several times between intervals of two or more years the same precise dream'. If all our mental images no less than apparitions (and I see no reason to distinguish) are forms exist-ing in the general vehicle of *Anima Mundi*, and mirrored in our particular vehicle, many crooked things are made straight.[69]

For Yeats, Shelley's account of this phantasmagoric universe revealed an accidental recovery of the power of an ancient symbolism. Shelley's account,

[66] Ibid., 'The Philosophy of Shelley's Poetry', 74.

[67] Ibid., 79.

[68] Ibid., 87.

[69] W. B. Yeats, *Essays* (London: Macmillan, 1924), 518.

however, was attributed to much more modern sources by Walter Bagehot, who suggested in an essay of 1853, that Shelley had derived it from his reading of Hume, who taught him that 'there was no substantial thing, either matter or mind; but only "sensations and impressions" flying about the universe, inhering in nothing and going nowhere'. Shelley, according to Bagehot, accepted Hume's philosophy because 'it was a better description of his universe than of most people's; his mind was filled with a swarm of ideas, fancies, thoughts, streaming on without his volition, without plan or order'.[70] By way of Shelley, Hume's philosophy of the human mind as built on the principles of association becomes the foundation of Yeats's metaphysics of a universe of associations in the *Anima Mundi*.

When Yeats challenged 'English empirical genius' for its inability to recognise this spiritual universe, it was to Locke's separation of 'primary and secondary qualities' that he attributed the source of English acceptance of 'certain great constructions that were only in relation to the will':[71]

> Locke sank into a swoon;
> The Garden died;
> God took the spinning-jenny
> Out of his side[72]

In doing so, however, he was separating Locke from his successors in the so-called 'British Empiricist tradition', for it was on precisely this that Berkeley had challenged Locke – Locke, according to Yeats, had been 'indicted by Berkeley as Burke was to indict Warren Hastings fifty years later'.[73] To Yeats, an anecdote about Locke's French translator was proof of the falsity of Lockean philosophy:

> When Locke's French translator Coste asked him how, if there were no 'innate ideas', he could explain the skill shown by a bird in making its nest, Locke replied, 'I did not write to explain the actions of dumb creatures', and his translator thought the answer 'very good, seeing that he had named his book *A Philosophical Essay upon Human Understanding*.' Henry

---

[70] Norman St John-Stevas (ed.), *The Collected Works of Walter Bagehot*, 7 Vols, (London: The Economist, 1965), Vol. I, *The Literary Essays*, 451.

[71] W. B. Yeats, 'Bishop Berkeley', *Essays and Introductions*, 400–1.

[72] W. B. Yeats, 'Fragments', *Collected Poems*, 240

[73] W. B. Yeats, 'Bishop Berkeley', *Essays and Introductions*, 401.

More, upon the other hand, considered that the bird's instinct proved the existence of the Anima Mundi, with its ideas and memories. Did modern enlightenment think with Coste that Locke had the better logic, because it was not free to think otherwise?[74]

It was the point on which Hume also separated himself from Locke when he insisted 'that beasts are endow'd with thought and reason as well as men' (T, 176). Overturning Locke's use of the association of ideas as an explanation for the *failures* of reason, Hume turned reason into 'nothing but a wonderful and unintelligible instinct in our souls, which carries us along a certain train of ideas' (T, 179). In this he had followed Berkeley, whose associational conception of the relation of ideas – 'where there is no such relation of similitude or causality, nor any necessary connexion whatsoever, two things, by their mere coexistence, or two ideas, merely by being perceived together, may suggest or signify one the other, their connexion being all the while arbitrary'[75] – was the starting point of Hume's analysis of the mind.[76] Yeats's recovery of Berkeley – the return of an alternative conception of what was native to Ireland – provided him with an Irish foundation for a conception of the world in which reality consisted not of extension 'without colour, sound, taste, tangibility'[77] but of the intertwining of associations between the individual mind and the Great Memory: 'I know now that revelation is from the self, but from that age-long memoried self, that shapes the elaborate shell of the mollusc and the child in the womb, that teaches the birds to make their nest; and that genius is a crisis that joins that buried self for certain moments to our trivial daily mind'.[78] Yeats, a better historian both of literature and of ideas than those who see in the associationist tradition nothing but mechanism, found in associationism the justification of his nationalism, which makes associates of those who might otherwise be simply a crowd: 'Was not the a nation, as distinguished from a crowd of chance comers, bound together by this interchange among streams or shadows; that Unity of Image, which I sought in national literature, being

[74] W. B. Yeats, *Autobiographies*, 265.

[75] A. A. Luce (ed.), *The Works of George Berkeley*, 9 Vols (London: Nelson, 1948), Vol. I, 'The Theory of Vision Vindicated', 264.

[76] See *Treatise*, 17, for Hume's acknowledgment of the influence of Berkeley's theory of 'abstract or general ideas'.

[77] W. B. Yeats, *Essays and Introductions*, 'Bishop Berkeley', 401.

[78] W. B. Yeats, *Autobiographies* (London: Macmillan, 1955), 272.

but an originating symbol?'[79] The promulgation in our individual memories of the associations of some 'Unity of Image' makes the nation itself a sign of the mind, and every work of art a return of the native by the resurrection of a forgotten past that reconnects our 'trivial daily mind' to more profound associations that reach back through the whole history of the nation to the ancient sources of our communal memory.

---

[79] Ibid., 263.

3 Strange Attractors and the Conversible World: Hume, Sterne, Dickens

When Wordsworth declared, in the 'Preface' to *Lyrical Ballads*, that 'the principal object' of his poems was to make 'incidents and situations from common life' of interest to his readers by 'tracing in them, truly though not ostentatiously, the primary laws of our nature: chiefly as far as regards the manner in which we associate ideas in a state of excitement' (*WW*, 597), he articulated an agenda that was to dominate much of literature from the early nineteenth century to the early part of the twentieth. The 'truth' of literature, from John Gibson Lockhart's insistence in 1817 'that the world of thought is the proper theatre of man'[1] to Virginia Woolf's effort in the 1920s to describe the 'atoms as they fall upon the mind, the pattern . . . which each sight or incident scores upon the consciousness',[2] would increasingly depend on the adequacy with which it could represent and the delicacy with which it could analyse ever more fugitive origins and ever more complex consequences of 'the manner in which we associate ideas in a state of excitement'. Wordsworth had been, briefly, in the 1790s, a follower of William Godwin and, as William D. Brewer has argued, one of the key innovations in the novels produced by Godwin and his circle is the way in which they 'display the main character's inner self by recounting the "'series of thoughts . . . linked together" that

---

[1] John Gibson Lockhart, 'Remarks on Godwin's New Novel, *Mandeville*', *Blackwood's Edinburgh Magazine*, 2 (December 1817), 26.

[2] Virginia Woolf, *Essays of Virginia Woolf Volume 4 1925–1928*, ed. Andrew McNeillie (London: Hogarth, 1994), 160.

form the protagonist's "personal identity" '.[3] Godwin was directly influenced by Hume – the second edition of *Political Justice* (1796) was largely rewritten to take account of Hume's philosophy – and in the novels of Godwin and his followers, 'character' comes to be described in terms of associational habit: 'identity' is nothing other than the ways in which new experiences evoke and are interpreted by means of the associational clusters laid down in the course of a character's growth to maturity. Or, as William James was to put it a century later in *Principles of Psychology*, 'each present brain-state is a record in which the eye of Omniscience might read all the foregone history of its owner'.[4] If such omniscience was a practical impossibility for the psychologist, psychology nonetheless provided tools by which a novelist could construct the pseudo-omniscience of the God-like narrator who was to become typical of realist fiction in the latter part of the nineteenth century. 'With memory set smarting like a reopened wound', George Eliot tells us in *Middlemarch*, 'a man's past is not simply a dead history, an outworn preparation of the present: it is not a repented error shaken loose from the life: it is a still quivering part of himself';[5] and increasingly the business of novelistic omniscience was to retrace those relations of past and present in order to reveal how a character's identity confirmed those 'primary laws of our nature'.

Such aspirations to omniscience, however, rested on the assumption that the orderly world as revealed in Newtonian physics was identical with the understanding that God would have of it – 'Nature, and Nature's Laws lay hid in Night./God said, Let Newton be! and All was Light'.[6] The scientific confidence with which Hartley could develop his theory of 'vibrations' from the 'Hints concerning the Performance of Sensation and Motion, which Sir Isaac Newton has given at the End of his *Principia*' (*OM*, 5) continued to underpin British empiricist psychology through to the late nineteenth century. Alexander Bain's compendium of 1868 is confidently titled *Mental and Moral Science*, and John Stuart Mill declared, in his *Examination of Sir William Hamilton's*

[3] William D. Brewer, *The Mental Anatomies of William Godwin and Mary Shelley* (London: Associated University Presses, 2001), 21–2.

[4] Williams James, *Principles of Psychology*, 2 Vols (Cambridge, MA: Harvard University Press, 1981), Vol. 1, 228.

[5] George Eliot, *Middlemarch*, ed. W. J. Harvey (London: Penguin, 1965; 1871–2), 663.

[6] Alexander Pope, 'Epigraph. Intended for Sir Isaac Newton, in Westminster-Abbey', *The Poems of Alexander Pope*, ed. John Butt (London: Methuen, 1963), 808.

Philosophy of 1865, 'hardly anything universal can be affirmed in psychology except the laws of association', because 'almost all general propositions which can be laid down respecting Mind, are consequences of these laws'.[7] However, despite the fact that in Hume's work can be found the beginnings of the science of psychology, there is something disquieting about Hume's initial claim in the *Treatise* to be a kind of Newton of the social sciences since, as J. A. Passmore has suggested, though Hume's thought has an 'admirable simplicity and clarity in each individual sentence', what we find in its overall structure is an 'intricacy of logical architecture and involved argument which often baffles and exasperates. . . just as much in its own way as does the writing of Hegel or Kant'.[8] Much of the philosophical debate about Hume's works, therefore, begins by reformulating his accounts of particular arguments in order to resolve what is seen to be a confusion in Hume's writings between 'an empirical law of psychology, the merits of which might today seem dubious' and 'the philosophical task of analyzing and clarifying certain concepts'.[9] An alternative, one adopted by John Richetti, is to see Hume as a *writer,* one whose work parodies rather than engages with the processes of philosophical debate. For Richetti, 'the speaker of the *Treatise* loves to pretend he is discovering difficulties as he writes, and the book is sometimes a comically overt record of the process of thought rather than simply the systematic exposition of the results of thought'. As a consequence, the *Treatise* is 'disrupted by a series of mock-serious surprises when the speaker seems overcome for a moment, trapped as he pretends to be within the inherently comic limitations of a philosophy that claims to be scrupulous but is simply impervious to new or, better, to a scandalously neglected truth'.[10] From this perspective, Hume's *Treatise* demands to be read as literary performance rather than as philosophical exposition or scientific analysis.

These conflicting approaches to the *Treatise* underline a fundamental conflict between the Newtonian methods that Hume asserts to be his model and the outcome that his philosophy actually produces. In the 1860s Bain can assert the discovered 'laws' governing our subjective world to be the 'law of

---

[7] Mill, *Collected Works*, Vol. 9, *Examination of Sir William Hamilton's Philosophy*, 315.

[8] Ibid.

[9] J. A. Robinson, 'Hume's Two Definitions of "Cause"', in V. C. Chappell (ed.), *Hume* (London: Macmillan, 1968), 129.

[10] John J. Richetti, *Philosophical Writing: Locke, Berkeley, Hume* (Cambridge, MA: Harvard University Press, 1983), 42.

contiguity' and the 'law of similarity', intereacting under a 'general law' of 'compound association', by which 'past actions, sensations, thoughts, or emotions, are recalled more easily, when associated either through contiguity or similarity, with more than one present object or impression'.[11] The finality of Bain's 'laws' is impossible, however, for Hume, because our inner world is one in which 'any thing may produce anything' (T, 173) and the general principles of 'resemblance, contiguity, and causation' (T, 92–3) have only a very limited applicability, since 'thought has evidently a very irregular motion in running along its objects, and may leap from the heavens to the earth, from one end of creation to the other, without any certain method or order' (T, 93). For Hartley, a divinely ordered world ensured that association led back to God; for Hume, on the other hand, association retained the potential for explaining that 'degree of madness'[12] which, for Locke, afflicted many human beings. Hume's project may begin in an apparently scientific search for the Newtonian laws that govern the mind, but it ends in the discovery that such laws are projections of the imagination. There is a profound instability in Hume's version of the associative mind that is quite the reverse of the stability projected by Newtonian physics. The observer of the material world may never 'see' gravity, but will be able to make effective predictions about the future positions of the various bodies in the solar system. The observer of our inner world, however, is confronted with 'a much greater complication of circumstances', one 'where those views and sentiments, which are essential to any action of the mind, are so implicit and obscure, that they often escape our strictest attention, and are not only unaccountable in their causes, but even unknown in their existence' (T, 175). What the analyst discovers is that 'human nature is too inconstant to admit of any such regularity. Changeableness is essential to it' (T, 283). In such a context, 'all knowledge', for Hume, 'degenerates into probability' (T, 180), dissolving the certainties to which Newtonian science apparently points us. 'While Newton seemed to draw off the veil from some of the mysteries of nature', Hume commented in The History of England, 'he showed at the same time the imperfections of the mechanical philosophy, and thereby restored her ultimate secrets to that obscurity in which they ever did and ever will remain'.[13]

Hume's emphasis on probability and uncertainty as the basis of scientific knowledge was to re-emerge in the nineteenth century when the science

---

[11] Bain, Mental and Moral Science, 151.

[12] Locke, An Essay Concerning Human Understanding, Bk II, Ch. xxxiii, 250.

[13] Hume, History of England from the Invasion of Julius Caesar to the Abdication of James the Second, 8 Vols (London: A. Millar, 1763), Vol. VIII, 323.

of thermodynamics began to reshape the Newtonian certainties of dynamics. In 1867 William Thomson and P. G. Tait's *Treatise on Natural Philosophy* (1867) set out to replace 'Newton's Principia of force with a new Principia of energy and extrema', exemplifying 'the ONE GREAT LAW of Physical Science, known as the Conservation of Energy'.[14] While Newtonian dynamics defined a world of balanced forces – for every action an equal and opposite reaction – Thomson's thermodynamics entailed a world of disequilibrium, dominated by the dissipation of energy as it is consumed by work, and, as his close collaborator, James Clerk Maxwell was to prove, by 'laws' which were not absolute determinants but only statistical probabilities. Thomson and Maxwell demonstrated, in the words of Ilya Prigogine, that 'classical dynamics [was] the science of eternal reversible trajectories' while, for thermodynamics, time is irreversible because of the entropic dissipation of energy, implying 'degradation and death'.[15] It is to Clerk Maxwell's work that much of contemporary 'chaos theory' – or the theory of complex systems – traces its beginnings, because Clerk Maxwell's work reveals that Newtonian science – in a manner which Michel Serres has argued to be typical of the whole history of Western rationalist thought[16] – had not abolished chaos but, rather, had repressed it. The success of Newtonian physics depended on its deliberate limitation of the range of phenomena to which it could be applied, a fact which would lead, in 1890, to Henri Poincaré's revelation that the so-called 'three body problem' – that is, the calculation of the mutual gravitational effects of the sun, the moon and the earth – was not resolvable by the use of Newtonian equations. The fact that complex systems cannot be understood on Newtonian principles has taken science towards a Humean emphasis on statistical probability rather than the certainty of determinate 'laws'. While Hume's belief, as Donald W. Livingston has argued, was 'that there are ultimate causal principles' but that no 'significant progress has been or ever will be made'[17] to discovering them, so-called 'chaos theory' assumes

---

[14] Quoted Crosbie Smith and M. Norton Wise, *Energy and Empire: A biographical study of Lord Kelvin* (Cambridge: Cambridge University Press, 1989), 352, 353.

[15] Ilya Prigogine and Isabelle Stengers, *Order out of Chaos: Man's New Dialogue with Nature* (London: Heinemann, 1984), 129.

[16] Michel Serres, *Hermes: Literature, Science, Philosophy*, ed. Josué V. Harari and David F. Bell (Baltimore: Johns Hopkins University Press, 1982).

[17] Donald W. Livingston, *Hume's Philosophy of Common Life* (Chicago: University of Chicago Press, 1984), 162.

that fundamental causes can be discovered but that they are governed by conditions of such complexity that knowledge of causes provides us with no basis for future prediction – in other words, is incapable of providing us with even the degree of 'constant conjunction' to which Hume reduced the notion of cause. In place of predictable causes, chaos theory posits what have come to be known as 'strange attractors' – statistical clusterings that reveal an underlying order to which even the most apparently chaotic and random systems inevitably tend. Rather than being the opposite of order, 'chaos', it is implied, may be the very foundation of order: the 'strange attractors' of a probabilistic conception of how complex systems evolve may be much more fundamental than the 'attraction' which Newtonian physics allows us to explain. Thus Prigogine suggests that chaos generates order through a process of 'spontaneous self-organisation'[18] which was inconceivable within the parameters of Newtonian physics. The 'phantasmal chaos' to which associationism reduced mental life indicated, to Coleridge, its inability to explain creativity, growth, development, purpose: to chaos theorists like Prigogine, however, it is precisely from the 'self-organisation' of chaotic systems that all of these teleological possibilities are generated.

The divergence between Hume and Coleridge on whether the flow of impressions and their associated ideas could ever give rise to all the capacities of the human mind has been echoed in recent times in debates over 'connectionism', a theory of the mind often described as – or accused of being – a modernised version of associationism. Jerry Fodor, for instance, has denigrated all associationist conceptions of the mind, and commended Kant's arguments, on the basis that associationism cannot account for the mind's ability to engage in rational argument: 'exactly what was wrong with Associationism, for example, was that there proved to be no way to get a rational mental life to emerge from the sorts of causal relations among thoughts that the "laws of association" recognized'.[19] As a consequence, Fodor believes that 'Conan Doyle was a far deeper psychologist – far closer to what is essential about mental life – than, say, James Joyce (or William James, for that matter)', because Holmes's deductions recognise what is distinctive about mind, and about the self – its systematic connection of thoughts in a logical sequence;

---

[18] For a discussion of Prigogine and Stengers' contribution to chaos theory, see *Chaos and Order: Complex Dynamics in Literature and Science*, ed. N. Katharine Hayles (Chicago: University of Chicago Press, 1991), 13 ff.

[19] Jerry A. Fodor, *Psychosemantics: The Problem of Meaning in the Philosophy of Mind* (Cambridge, MA: MIT Press, 1987), 18.

as a consequence, Fodor takes 'the concluding pages of Joyce's *Ulysses* for a – presumably inadvertent – parody of the contrary view'. Connectionists, on the other hand, follow associationists and chaos theorists in believing that complexity is capable of 'spontaneous self-organisation'. John Sutton has suggested, for instance, that 'rationalists and moralists',

> insist on external intervention in the linking and shuffling of ideas, impressed by hard, logical, brittle cognitive processes, which we some-times feel as effort in conscious calculation. Associationists privilege soft, defeasible, fluid transitions which are less accessible to consciousness, and must show how the mere statistical and causal play of a haphazard world on the mind can produce the faint degree of order that remember-ing sometimes retains.[20]

Out of the 'causal play of a haphazard world', order emerges, and with order the possibility of logic. In identifying associationism with chaos, Coleridge intended rebuttal: in terms of contemporary chaos theory he may, in fact, have gestured to the very grounds of associationism's strength, which is its insistence on the fact that all human cognition develops probabilistically as a result of what are now understood as 'mathematical, statistical explanations of the emergence at a higher level of a phenomenon which is not built up piecemeal from operations at the next lower level'.[21]

In going from Newtonian expectations of order to the discovery of complex patterns emerging out of apparent disorder, Hume was, in effect, revealing the limitations of Newtonianism long before those limitations could be scientifically demonstrated. Adam Smith, however, was clear about the implications of Hume's theories for Newtonian physics: in his 'Essay on Astronomy' he described the force of Newton's conception of the universe:

> And even we, while we have been endeavouring to represent all philosophical systems as mere inventions of the imagination, to connect together the otherwise disjointed and discordant phaenomena of nature, have insensibly been drawn in, to make use of language expressing

---

[20] John Sutton, *Philosophy and Memory Traces: Descartes to Connectionism* (Cambridge: Cambridge University Press, 1998), 226.

[21] William Bechtel, 'Connectionism and the Philosophy of Mind: An Overview', in Terence Horgan and John Tienson (eds), *Connectionism and the Philosophy of Mind* (Dordrecht: Kluwer, 1991), 30–59, 33.

the connecting principles of this one [Newton's], as if they were the real chains which Nature makes use of to bind together her several operations. [22]

The most powerful, the most convincing account of the phenomena of the universe that we have ever devised is only an 'as if', deceiving us into believing it to be a description of the 'real chains' of Nature, rather than simply the chains of the associating power of the imagination. Instead of producing a world of order, the equivalent of gravitational attraction in the psychological realm reveals a world of strange and often chaotic interactions between the contents of our minds and events in the world, and long before the development of the mathematics of stochastic processes – sequences of events determined by the influence of chance – Hume's theories revealed the mind – and therefore the world – to be nothing less than a scene of 'strange attractors'.

The power of strange attraction is most evident in Hume's analysis of causality: for Hume, as we have seen, there is no certain way of distinguishing between events in the world, organised by external forces, and our subjective associations and the expectations to which they give rise. Since the notion of cause and effect only arises from our associations, any particular coupling of events may always prove to be no more than a psychological association: 'even after experience has inform'd us of their constant conjunction, 'tis impossible for us to satisfy ourselves by our reason, why we shou'd extend that experience beyond those particular instances, which have fallen under our observation . . . When the mind, therefore, passes from the idea or impression of one object to the idea or belief of another, it is not determin'd by reason, but by certain principles, which associate together the ideas of these objects, and unite them in the imagination' (T, 91–2). It is the order of the psyche, not the order of nature, by which things are connected in the world: Hume's philosophy reshapes the external on the model of the internal, so that conjunctions in the world are only special cases of the associations that structure the elements of mind. It is the imagination, not the force of cause and effect, that binds the world together for human beings. Hume's description of the mind as 'a kind of theatre, where several perceptions successively make their appearance; pass, re-pass, glide away, and mingle in an infinite variety of postures and situations' (T, 253) underlines

---

[22] Adam Smith, *Essays on Philosophical Subjects*, ed. W. P. Wightman and J. C. Bryce (Indianapolis: Liberty Fund, 1982), 39.

the fusion of fiction and reality, of memory and imagination which his associationism encourages.

The strangeness of the world that Hume's philosophy uncovers leads to that crisis at the end of Part I of the *Treatise* in which the secure and composed language of philosophical argument is suddenly displaced by anguished autobiography, as the writer wrestles with the consequences of his philosophical arguments:

> The intense view of these manifold contradictions and imperfections in human reason has so wrought upon me, and heated my brain, that I am ready to reject all belief and reasoning, and can look upon no opinion even as more probably or likely than another. Where am I, or what? From what causes do I derive my existence, and to what condition shall I return? Whose favour shall I court, and whose anger must I dread? What beings surround me? And on whom have I any influence, or have influence on me? I am confounded with all these questions, and begin to fancy myself in the most deplorable condition imaginable, inviron'd with the deepest darkness, and utterly depriv'd of the use of every member and faculty. (*T*, 268–9)

The self that has just been revealed to be a fiction by the philosopher – 'the identity, which we ascribe to the mind of man, is only a fictitious one' (*T*, 259) – suddenly turns aside to voice a dramatic monologue to his readers in despair at his condition. The scientific enquirer who looks upon the human mind as an astronomer might look on the stars is transformed into a suffering individual, suddenly destitute of all the consolations that have made existence tolerable. We switch from the order of argument, whose temporality is that of the reader progressing through the text, to the time of writing – 'Here then I find myself absolutely and necessarily determin'd to live' (*T*, 269) – when the author is in actual process of composition. The disjunction forces us into seeing the text not as a timeless, logical construction but as the act of a mind in a particular historical setting.

It is a crisis that was to be repeated, some eighty years later, in Thomas Carlyle's *Sartor Resartus*, when Teufelsdröckh's philosophy thrusts him into the domain of 'The Everlasting No': 'What then was our professor's possession? We see him, for the present, quite shut out from Hope; looking not into the golden orient, but vaguely all round into a dim copper firmament, pregnant with earthquake and tornado' (*SR*, 123). Hume's answer to this crisis, however, is not the leap to a higher reality – Carlyle's 'Everlasting Yea' – or to a more secure version of the self – like Kant's – which will guarantee all that the associational self sets in doubt; it is that 'nature herself suffices' by 'some avocation, and lively impression of my senses, which obliterates all these chimeras'. Nature's answer to the philosopher's dilemma is the celebration of social life rather than individual ratiocination: 'I dine, I play a game of back-gammon, I converse, and am merry with my friends' (*T*, 69). It is not argument which overcomes the failures of reason to provide answers: it is a return to the world of sense, of sensation and, most of all, of conversation. The inner dissolution of the self from which reason can provide no escape is defeated not by logic but by merry conversation. The dissolution of the self which Hume's associationism seems to portend is diverted by a different, but deeply related kind of association – association with other human beings, commitment to a common experience in which the self is 'determin'd to live, and talk, and act like other people in the common affairs of life' (*T*, 269). It is a point that Hume was to reinforce in an essay entitled 'Of Essay-Writing', which was included in his first collection of *Essays, Moral and Political* in 1742 but excluded from later editions – presumably because its proposal had, in fact, been achieved by the success of Hume's essays. In it, Hume outlines for himself a future in which he will act as 'a Kind of Resident Ambassador from the Dominions of Learning to those of Conversation', promoting 'a good Correspondence betwixt these two States, which have so great a Dependence on each other'(*E*, 535). The world of philosophical analysis – of the resolution of all our experience into the internal workings of association – must be counterpointed with the world of active engagement in the social world: there must be conversation not only within the realm of Conversation but between the worlds of the 'learned' and the 'conversible' (*E*, 533).

The conversible provides us with an alternative way of conceiving the nature of association from that which drives us ever inward into the dissolution of the self. This is why, in *The Enquiry Concerning Human Understanding*, first published in 1748, the prime example of how association works is transferred from its inner effects on the self-reflecting mind to the sociable workings of conversation: 'Were the loosest and freest conversation to be transcribed, there would immediately be observed something which connected all its transitions. Or where this is wanting, the person who broke the thread of discourse might still inform you, that there had secretly revolved in his mind a succession of thought, which gradually led him from the subject of conversation' (*EHU*, 3).

Hume's model of association has switched from association as an entirely solitary principle of the self to a principle of the relatedness of selves in the social world: as Annette C. Baier puts it, 'Persons among persons are the liveliest objects of our mental attention, in part because we depend in so many ways upon those persons. The associations and relations between persons give us, in a parallel way, the liveliest of all our conceptions of relations'.[23] The 'social' contained within the word 'association' – and at the root of its origin in French – re-asserts itself as the primary context of our understanding: we know how association works not by the introspection of our solitary consciousnesses but by the vigorous interchange with others that we experience as the conversible world.

This shift is significant to how we read associationist theory in relation to works of literature: it is easy to see associationism inspiring the increasing interiority and subjectivity of the late nineteenth- and early twentieth-century novel (where, as we shall see, it undoubtedly plays a key role) but that interiority, as in the crisis of Hume's philosophy at the conclusion of Part I of the *Treatise*, has to be balanced against the fact that associations are not simply contained within the isolated monad of the self-reflecting individual: associations form the very structure of a conversible world. Novels that derive their strategies from associationist models of the psyche will engage not just with the interiority of subjective trains of association but with the transfer of associations between those engaged in that conversible world, and with an external world that is not the neutral object of depersonalised investigation but one necessarily shaped by the workings of associative and associated minds.

II

No novel might better fulfil – however parodically – Hume's desire to be 'a Kind of Resident Ambassador from the Dominions of Learning to those of Conversation' than Laurence Sterne's *Tristram Shandy* (1760). The novel is a ceaseless explication of abstruse learning delivered in a conversational setting – whether it is Walter Shandy's idiosyncratic reading in the history of noses or of curses, or Toby's study of fortifications, or Tristram's description of his narrative as a 'cyclopaedia of arts and sciences, where the instrumental

---

[23] Annette C. Baier, *A Progress of Sentiments: Reflections on Hume's Treatise* (Cambridge, MA: Harvard University Press, 1991), 47.

parts of the eloquence of the senate, the pulpit, the bar, the coffee-house, the bed-chamber, and fire-side, fall under consideration'.[24] But these deliveries by ironic 'ambassadors of learning' also take place in the context of an ongoing conversation with the novel's readers: '—We'll not stop two moments, my dear Sir, – only, as we have got through these five volumes, (do, Sir, sit down upon a set – they are better than nothing) let us look back upon the country we have passed through' (*TS*, 397; VI, 1). Hume himself thought *Tristram Shandy* 'the best book that has been writ by an Englishman these thirty years' – though the estimate was somewhat undercut by his view that England was 'so sunk in Stupidity and Barbarism and Faction that you may as well think of Lapland for an Author'.[25] Hume's judgment was perhaps biased by the fact that no novel of the eighteenth century makes more use of associationist principles than Sterne's. Characters in *Tristram Shandy*, as critics have regularly pointed out, are driven to their eccentricities by being the victims of 'an unhappy association of ideas which have no connection in nature' (*TS*, 39; I, 4), and therefore illustrate Locke's account of associations in his *Essay Concerning Human Understanding*, which, according to Tristram himself, is a 'history-book . . . of what passes in a man's own mind' (*TS*, 107; II, 2); or, as James Work expressed it in the introduction to his edition of the novel, 'the most important structural device is the principle of the association of ideas upon which the whole progression of the book is based'.[26] The Lockean provenance of Sterne's use of the association of ideas has both been taken for granted by generations of critics impressed by Sterne's acknowledgment that 'Locke's philosophy everywhere had tempered his thought and manner of procedure in *Tristram Shandy*'[27] and, just as regularly, challenged on the basis that Sterne is much more radically associationist, and much less of a rationalist in his conception of the human mind, than Locke. As John Traugott suggested in a groundbreaking study of *Tristram Shandy* in 1955, Sterne's 'history of

---

[24] Laurence Sterne, *The Life and Opinions of Tristram Shandy*, ed. Graham Petrie (London: Penguin, 1967; 1760), 138, II, 17; hereafter cited in the text as *TS*.

[25] Letter to William Strahan, 30 January 1773, *Letters of David Hume*, ed. J. Y. T. Greig, 2 Vols (Oxford: Clarendon Press, 1932), Vol. II, 269.

[26] James Aiken Work, 'Introduction', *Tristram Shandy* (New York: Odyssey Press, 1940), xlix.

[27] Arthur H. Cash, 'The Lockean Psychology of Tristram Shandy', *ELH*, Vol. 22, No. 2 (June 1955), 125–35 at 128, citing Wilbur Cross, *The Life and Times of Laurence Sterne* (New Haven: Yale University Press, 1922), Vol. 1, 277.

the mind is not Locke's history, but it is one informed by the contemporary development of Locke's notion of association-of-ideas madness into an epistemology such as Hume's'.[28] Traugott's suggestion directed later critics towards a Humean context for understanding Sterne's novel,[29] culminating in Jonathan Lamb's closely argued account of how Sterne's narrative illustrates both Humean and Hartleian conceptions of association, in which 'all parts of a Shandean narrative fall into patterns of indefinite mutual commentary, comparable to Hartley's world of endlessly involved analogies and Hume's of reversible sequences'.[30]

What these accounts have in common, however, is their concentration on the psychology of association – the theme of Book I of Hume's *Treatise* – rather than its sociology – the theme of Books II and III. Hume's description of association as taking place within conversation and between conversationalists throws into relief the fact that *Tristram Shandy* is associationist not because it prefigures the subjectivity of the 'stream of consciousness' novel – or what Denis Donoghue describes as the implication that 'every object of experience is translated into the diverse terms of its perceiving subject', so that 'of the object itself, independent of the perceiving consciousness, nothing remains'[31] – but because it is a novel of a conversible world, what we might describe as a 'stream of conversation' novel. For it is in *Tristam Shandy*'s conversations that we find much of its comic deployment of association, as when Walter is translating a treatise on noses for Toby's benefit:

> Now it happened then, as indeed it had often done before, that my uncle Toby's fancy, during the time of my father's explanation of Prignitz to him,——having nothing to stay it there, had taken a short flight to the bowling-green; —— his body might as well have taken a turn there too, — so that with all the semblance of a deep school-man intent upon the *medius terminus*, — my uncle Toby was in fact as ignorant of the whole

[28] John Traugott, *Tristram Shandy's World: Sterne's Philosophical Rhetoric* (Berkeley: University of California Press, 1954), 48.

[29] See, for instance, Francis Doherty, 'Sterne and Hume: A Bicentenary Essay', *Essays and Studies* XII (1969), 71–88, and Stuart Sim, 'Sterne. Chaos. Complexity', *Eighteenth Century Novel*, I (2001), 201–15.

[30] Jonathan Lamb, *Sterne's Fiction and the Double Principle* (Cambridge: Cambridge University Press, 1990), 81.

[31] Denis Donoghue, 'Sterne, Our Contemporary', in Arthur H. Cash and John M. Stedmond (eds), *The Winged Skull: Papers from the Laurence Sterne Bicentenary Conference* (London: Methuen, 1971), 45.

lecture, and all its pros and cons, as if my father had been translating
Hafen Slawkenbergius from the Latin tongue into the Cherokee. But the
word *siege*, like a talismanic power, in my father's metaphor, wafting back
my uncle Toby's fancy, quick as a note could follow the touch, —he
opened his ears, —and my father observing that he took his pipe out
of his mouth, and shuffled his chair nearer the table, as with a desire
to profit, —my father with great pleasure began his sentence again,
—changing only the plan, and dropping the metaphor of the siege of
it, to keep clear of some dangers my father apprehended from it. (*TS*,
243; III, 40)

Walter's and Toby's conversations are invariably disrupted by the very different
associations that words have for each of them. The irony of Toby's submission
to the 'talismanic power' of the word 'siege' is that the lecture from which he is
in flight is intended as an example of 'the great and principal act or ratiocination
in man' (*TS*, 242; III, 40) but is, in fact, a consequence of associations that
have made 'noses' as irrationally obsessive to Walter as sieges are to Toby. As
in Hume's example of conversation in the *Enquiry*, conversations between
the characters of *Tristram Shandy* force us to search for the 'something which
connected all its transitions', or to guess at what had 'secretly revolved' in the
mind that had 'gradually led him from the subject of conversation'.

The narrator of *Tristram Shandy* is, of course, mostly absent from the
conversations he 'records' – since he was not yet, or only just born when they
took place – and given his distance from them in time, as well as the vast bulk
of digressive material which intervenes between conversations, one would
expect the narrative voice itself to be distant from the voices it 'overhears'.
In fact, however, the narrative voice acts as though it is not only imaginatively
present at the conversations but as though it is linguistically present as well.
So, for instance, when Walter retreats to his bedroom after Tristram's nose
is crushed by Dr Slop's forceps, a brief passage of real time is stretched into
twelve chapters and over fifty pages of narrative time (including, in a kind of
structural pun, the 'bridge' from Book III to Book IV). This narrative trajectory
opens an enormous gap between what are, in fact, closely successive events,
and also explains much of the associational gap between Walter and Toby
which will culminate in their failed conversation when the narrative resumes:

did ever a poor unfortunate man, brother Toby, cried my father, receive
so many lashes?

—The most I ever saw given, quoth my uncle Toby, (ringing the bell at the bed's head for Trim) was to a grenadier, I think in Mackay's regiment.

—Had my uncle Toby shot a bullet through my father's heart, he could not have fallen down with his nose upon the quilt more suddenly. (TS, 276; IV, 3)

Walter's dead metaphor – 'so many lashes' – is turned back into reality by Toby – 'The most I ever saw' – but the narrator's description then adopts Toby's associational context – Walter is apparently 'shot' by Toby's wartime memories – in order to describe metaphorically Walter's response. Nothing in the typography alerts us that the final sentence is Tristram's narrative voice rather than another spoken contribution to the conversation, and it adopts the associative context of the previous speaker as though it were simply a continuation of that conversation. The narrator may have been absent from the scene but his voice participates in its conversible world as though he were immediately present. The associative connections leap between the time of the events and the time of writing, and infect each other as though everyone – characters and author – were present in the same room at the same time. Contiguous text, in other words, even when belonging to very different ontological levels of the fiction, or to very different narrative times, operates as if it were the next speaker in a continuous conversation. To Humean association by contiguity in space or time, Sterne has added association by contiguity in text, and it is this textual contiguity which continually disrupts the narrative action of the novel by distracting author and reader from the actual 'events' of the story.

The world of *Tristram Shandy* is thus like the model sieges that Toby constructs on his bowling-green. First, things that are in fact identical are transformed by contiguity:

The common men, who know very little of fortification, confound the ravelin and the half-moon together, —though they are very different things; —not in their figure or construction, for we make them exactly alike in all points . . . —Where then lies the difference? (quoth my father, a little testily.) —In their situations, answered my uncle Toby: —For when a ravelin, brother, stands before the curtin, it is a ravelin; and when a ravelin stands before a bastion, then the ravelin is not a ravelin; —it is a half-moon. (TS, 129; II, 12)

The 'ravelin is not a ravelin' depending on what it is contiguous to. Equally, things that are not identical are made so by the power of association, and remain so as long as Toby's and Trim's conversation maintains the associational context which gives their fictions coherence: '— then we'll demolish the mole, — next fill up the harbour, — then retire to the citadel, and blow it up into the air; and having done that, corporal, we'll embark for England. — We are there, quoth the corporal, recollecting himself' (*TS*, 447; VI, 35). The associative web which their conversations weave is so intense that the external world is transformed by it, until some accidental statement, such as 'embark for England', disrupts it and reveals another world than the one they have been living in. The disruption, however, is always only temporary because they live in a conversible world where events do not lead to action but turn to talk, whether it is Walter's oratorical response to the death of his son or the account of the battle of Steenkirk which follows on Tristram's accidental circumcision, or Toby's conclusion to Trim's tale of his passion for 'the fair Beguine', whose hand he had seized: '— And then thou clapped'st it to thy lips, Trim, said my Uncle Toby,— and madest a speech' (*TS*, 549; VIII, 22). Their conversations release into the public world the flow of their individual modes of associations and those associations interact to produce further associative digressions by their listeners which endlessly extend their conversation; at the same time, in a double meaning which Hume invokes when he notes 'that people associate together according to their particular tempers and dispositions' (*T*, 354), their very participation in conversation confirms their mutual association with, and profound involvement with, one another.

It is into this associative, conversible world, that Tristram is born, where 'whatever motion, debate, harangue, dialogue, project or dissertation, was going forwards in the parlour, there was generally another at the same time, and upon the same subject, running parallel along with it in the kitchen' (*TS*, 353; V, 6). Since our earliest associates provide us with out most intimate associations, Tristram's failure to provide us with the 'life and opinions' that the title of the novel promises is ironically reversed by his account of his conversational environment. From the moment of his 'conception', spoiled by 'an unhappy association of ideas which have no connection in nature' (*TS*, 39; I, 4), those conversing voices have shaped the associations which define his psychic structure, so that when Tristram's own story is displaced by the story of his Uncle Toby it is not, as some critics have suggested, because the inspiration with which Sterne had launched on Tristram's narrative had run dry, but because Tristram *is* his relations. In relating his family past he is also providing his readers with the relations which form his personality; as in his memory, for instance, of the time when his Uncle Toby caught and released a fly, because 'this world surely is wide enough to hold both thee and me':

> I was but ten years old when this happened; . . . but whether it was, that the action itself was more in unison to my nerves at that age of pity, which instantly set my whole frame into one vibration of pleasurable sensation; — or how far the manner and expression of it might go towards it; — or in what degree, and by what secret magic, — a tone of voice and harmony of movement, attuned to mercy, might find a passage to my heart, I know not; — this I know, that the lesson of universal good-will then taught and imprinted by my Uncle Toby, has never since worn out of my mind . . . — yet I often think that I owe one half of my philanthropy to that one accidental impression. (*TS*, 131; II, 12)

His associates accidentally inscribe the associations by which he will himself be defined. Thus when Tristram announces, after his brother Bobby's death, that 'from this moment I am to be considered as heir-apparent to the Shandy family' (*TS*, 332; Iv, 32), his relations with his family may have legally changed but his new status simply acknowledges his existing psychological status: he is heir to the characters – and, especially, of the voices – of the Shandy family, to those relations who were his most intimate associates and who, therefore, quite literally, people his associations.

As readers, we are not simply overhearers of Sterne's conversible world. 'Writing', Tristram insists, 'when properly managed, (as you may be sure I think mine is) is but a different name for conversation' (*TS*, 127; II, 1). Writing – when *im*properly managed – leads to isolation, to Hume's 'strange uncouth monster, who not being able to mingle and unite in society, has been expell'd all human commerce, and left utterly abandon'd and disconsolate' (*T*, 264). Such would be Tristram, 'sitting, this 12th day of August, 1766, in a purple jerkin and yellow pair of slippers, without either wig or cap on' (*TS*, 572; IX, 1), if it were not that his readers supply an alternative to the conversible world that he can now recall only in memory:

> ——How could you, Madam, be so inattentive in reading the last chapter? I told you in it, *That my mother was not a papist.* — Papist! You told me no such thing, Sir. Madam, I beg leave to repeat it over again, That I told you

> as plain, at least, as words, by direct inference, could tell you such a thing. — Then, Sir, I must have missed a page. — No, Madam, — you have not missed a word. —— Then I was asleep, Sir, — My pride, Madam, cannot allow you that refuge. (*TS*, 82; I, 20)

Associationism provides Sterne not only with the mechanisms by which he can construct his characters, and by which he can shape the 'strange attractors' that form the unpredictable links between the chapters of Tristram's narration – 'the first chapter of my next volume, if I live, shall be my chapter upon WHISKERS, in order to keep up some sort of connection in my works' (*TS*, 332; IV, 32) – but an awareness of the unpredictability of the associative context in which his work will be received. Tristram's uncertainty about what associations readers will bring to his text is made the occasion for ironic dialogues in which he seeks to delimit in advance the meanings his words will generate:

> I define a nose as follows — entreating only beforehand, and beseeching my readers, both male and female, of what age, complexion, and condition soever, for the love of God and their own souls, to guard against the temptations and suggestions of the devil, and suffer him by no art or wile to put any other ideas into their minds, than what I put into my definition. — For by the word *Nose*, throughout all this long chapter of noses, and in every other part of my work, where the word *Nose* occurs, — I declare, by that word I mean a Nose, and nothing more, or less. (*TS*, 225; III, 31)

Tristram's insistence, of course, unleashes the associative potential of 'nose' in the very act of trying to subdue it. The author, like his characters, has to be constantly aware that the reader may be nosing out an alternative meaning to his words, since 'the excellency of the nose is in a direct arithmetical proportion to the excellency of the wearer's fancy' – or, alternatively, that 'the nose begat the fancy' (*TS*, 238; III, 38). If the word 'siege' leads Toby to an alternative circuit of associations from those of Walter's account of the 'solutions of noses' (*TS*, 243; III, 41), the reader is under siege from all those 'temptations and suggestions of the devil' that would, precisely because the novel has raised their possibility, surround the word 'nose' with quite other associations than those provided in the dictionary definition. And if Walter's obsession with noses is one of those notions which 'at first entered upon the footing of mere whims' but then became fixed by association, then Tristram offers it as a 'warning to the learned reader against the indiscreet reception of such guests' because they can 'at length claim a kind of settlement there' (*TS*, 79, I, 19). Sterne, meanwhile, is engaging the reader in exactly the kind of 'indiscreet reception' that will create in the readerly mind a set of associations as inescapable as those that define the characters:

> ———Fair and softly, gentle reader! ———Where is thy fancy carrying thee? ———If there is truth in man, by my greatgrandfather's nose, I mean the external organ of smelling, and that part of man which stands prominent in his face, ———and which painters say, in good jolly noses and well-proportioned faces, should comprehend a full third, ———that is, measuring downwards from the setting on of the hair.———
> ———What a life of it has an author, at this pass! (*TS*, 228; III, 33)

The narrator is defeated – or so, at least, the author pretends – by the very associations which he has set running in the readers' minds, associations which make them as Hobby-Horsical as the characters, participants in a conversation which invites them, at one moment, freely to follow their own associations – 'The truest respect which you can pay to the reader's understanding, is to halve this matter amicably, and leave him something to imagine, in his turn, as well as yourself' (*TS*, 127; II, 11) – and at another to be the coach-horses of the narrator's associational travels: 'I would go fifty miles on foot, for I have not a horse worth riding on, to kiss the hand of that man whose generous heart will give up the reins of his imagination into his author's hands' (*TS*, 193; III, 12).

Sterne's ironic exploitation of the uncontrollability of associative responses to his work mirrors the equally unpredictable working of association in the lives of his characters. That unfortunate connection in Mrs Shandy's mind, by which 'it so fell out at length, that my poor mother could never hear the said clock wound up,——but the thoughts of some other things unavoidably popped into her head — & *vice versa*' (*TS*, 39; I, 4) illustrates not only the 'sagacious Locke' on 'strange combination' (*TS*, 39; I, 4) but illustrates, too, Hume's view that 'The fancy is by its very nature wavering and inconstant; and considers always two objects as more strongly related together, where it finds the passage equally easy both in going and returning, than where the transition is easy only in one of these motions. The double motion is a kind of double tie, and binds the objects together in the closest and most intimate manner' (*T*, 356). While causation in the world is unidirectional – cause is cause because it precedes that with which it forms a constant conjunction – the associative connection between conjoined elements is bi-directional: 'in order to produce a perfect relation betwixt two objects, 'tis requisite, not only that the imagination be convey'd from one to the other by resemblance, contiguity and causation, but also that it return back from the second to first with the same ease and facility' (*T*, 355). Since the imagination is the foundation of our knowledge of cause in the first place, this reversibility of causal sequence in the imagination makes it even more difficult for us to disentangle relations of cause from mere conjunctions. Such reversals of causal sequence constitute one of the typical disordering elements in the structure of *Tristram Shandy* – 'when a man is telling a story in the strange way I do mine, he is obliged continually to be going backwards and forwards to keep all tight together in the reader's fancy' (*TS*, 444; VI, 33) – but they also themselves cause many of the calamities to which Tristram is subject.

Thus Walter Shandy's belief that 'there was a strange kind of magic bias, which good or bad names, as he called them, irresistibly impressed on our characters and conduct' (*TS*, 77; I, 19) makes a *cause* out of one of the most arbitrary of connections between language and its object. The associations which have enveloped particular names because of events connected to persons of that name are then assumed to predict the consequence for any bearer of the name: 'would you, for the world, have called him Judas?' (*TS*, 78; I, 19). In Walter's case, however, this double motion of the relation of cause and effect reverses his efforts to escape it, resulting in the very outcome he tries to avert. By invoking the danger of that 'strange kind of magic' in names, and seeking to prevent the relations of cause and effect which he believes it to entail, he in fact attracts the very outcome he fears: his wish to have his child named by the fabulous name of Trismegistus, in order to compensate for the inadvertent and dissipated nature of his 'conception', leads directly to his being christened Tristram, the name for which 'he had the most unconquerable aversion' (*TS*, 81; I, 19).

Walter's hypothesis of the causal relation of names to character – his belief in the psychological efficacy of names as causes – provokes a series of causal connections – Susannah's incapability of remembering the name, the curate's pride in his own name – which attract upon the infant the very name from which Walter seeks to defend him. The arbitrary associations which disrupt the moment of Tristram's conception – the clock whose winding punningly 'wounds' him, because 'it scattered and dispersed the animal spirits' (*TS*, 36; I, 2) – are reversed in his naming, which seemingly attracts, as though as a matter of necessity, the name whose associations – at least for his father – will have the most dangerous effects on his character. It is as if the fear of the effects of the name produces such a close psychological relationship between the name and the infant that it induces the chain of causes which will result in the infant acquiring that very name. In precisely the same way, Walter's obsession with the symbolic consequences of the family 'nose' – a short nose portends the decline of the family's fortunes – seems to attract Dr Slop's forceps into breaking the bridge of Tristram's nose during his delivery, as though fear of the possible effect (the danger of the family's foreshortened nose) inevitably drew into existence its unpredictable cause (a nose actually broken at birth). The relationship of cause and effect in the world is reversed: instead of a train of causes and effects which culminate in a particular conjunction, the psychological expectation of a future conjunction induces, as it were retrospectively, an unforeseeable train of causes and events which produces the very conjunction that the character sought to avoid.

Associations thus come to work as 'strange attractors' in Tristram Shandy – though 'it seems to run opposite to the natural workings of cause and effects' (TS, 519; VIII, 5) – effectively invoking events into existence by the very power of the psychological connections which they establish. So it is 'Bridget's prenotification' of Toby's love for Mrs Wadman, 'and Susannah's repeated manifestoes thereupon to all the world' (TS, 518; VIII, 4), that produce the love they announce. These loops might be likened to the feedback loops which are characteristic features of contemporary chaos theory, producing non-linear systems entirely at odds with the linearity of Newtonian physics. In Chapter 40 of Book VI of Tristram Shandy, Sterne draws a series of distorted lines which he claims to be 'the four lines I moved through' in his previous volumes, and announces that he intends 'at the excellency of going on even thus', and draws an absolutely straight line across the page. The Chapter concludes with a question:

> Pray can you tell me, — that is, without anger, before I write my chapter upon straight lines — by what mistake — who told them so — or how has it come to pass, that your men of wit and genius have all along confounded this line, with the line of GRAVITATION? (TS, 454–5; VI, 40)

The 'strange attractors' that draw Sterne's associated events into each others' orbits defy, in their unpredictable interconnections, the unilinear relations of cause and effect projected by Newtonian physics. The 'chaos' of association produces a model of 'attraction' which is more like the 'flourish' of Trim's stick – an irregular upward spiral, defying gravitational fall (TS, 576; IX, 4)

– than like the 'straight line' of Newtonian physics, making of the novel an 'anti-gravity' machine that can, by 'Amusement' and 'Diversion' (*TS*, 569, 570; dedication to Vol. IX), distract us from, if not defy, a Newtonian world in which everything is doomed to fall, in all the associated senses of that word.

It is that falling world of gravity which Sterne invokes when Tristram comes to relate the circumstances of his accidental circumcision by the window sash: 'It is in vain', Sterne warns us, 'to leave this to the Reader's imagination: — to form any kind of hypothesis that will render these propositions feasible, he must cudgel his brains sore, — and to do it without, — he must have such brains as no reader ever had before him' (*TS*, 370; V, 18). The window sash and the child's organ of reproduction come together in a collision which is apparently the outcome of Newtonian forces – the result of the removal of gravity's 'counterweight' by Trim, 'who had taken the two leaden weights from the nursery window' to make model 'battering canons' for Toby's fortifications, 'and as the sash pullies, when the lead was gone, were of no kind of use, he had taken them away also, to make a couple of wheels for one of their carriages' (*TS*, 371; V, 19). The unpredictability of this event, however – 'Susannah did not consider that nothing was well hung in our family, – so slap came the sash down like lightning upon us' (*TS*, 368; V, 17) – reveals how limited is Newtonian explanation to human experience. In the early days of complexity theory, James Clerk Maxwell pointed to the fact that 'the match is responsible for the forest fire, but reference to a match does not suffice to understand the fire',[32] and it is the limitations of such monocausal explanations that are revealed by Sterne in the twenty-six chapters of associative chains of conjecture which follow the accident and which take up the remainder of the volume. The 'cause' of Tristram's wound lies neither in Susannah's lack of alertness as to how 'well hung' anything is in the Shandy household, nor in Trim's removal of the lead weights – 'you obeyed your orders' (*TS*, 372; V, 20). It may lie in Toby's effort to gain psychological control over the 'chance' that resulted in his own wounding 'from a stone, broke off by a ball from the parapet of a horn-work at the siege of Namur, which struck full upon my uncle Toby's groin' (*TS*, 91; I, 21), since Toby's theatrical re-enactment of the war on the bowling green introduces the chaos of war into the Shandys' domestic world. In that case, however, his own 'fall' on the field of battle is responsible for the 'accidental' fall that is Tristram's 'wounding', the latter attracted into existence by the 'necessity' not

---

[32] Quoted in Prigogine and Stengers, *Order out of Chaos*, 206.

of Newtonian causation but by the psychological and artistic necessity that Tristram should be heir to Toby's 'fall' as well as to his 'philanthropy'.

In Tristram's wound, we have an effect in search of an adequate cause, forcing us to acknowledge that cause and effect in a work of art are very different from cause and effect in the Newtonian world – and, in consequence, to consider that cause and effect in the world may be much more like cause and effect in a work of art than we realise. Thus,

> The Fates, who certainly all foreknew of these amours of widow Wadman and my uncle Toby, had, from the first creation of matter and motion (and with more courtesy than they usually do things of this kind) established such a chain of causes and effects hanging so fast to one another, that it was scarce possible for my uncle Toby to have dwelt in any other house in the world, or to have occupied any other garden in Christendom, but the very house and garden which joined and laid parallel to Mrs Wadman's. (TS, 527; VIII, 14)

The contiguity of Toby and Mrs Wadman is the outcome of a series of causes and effects of enormous – not to say, chaotic – complexity at the level of the realistic novel; but at the level of the novel as artifice it is the outcome of a very simple causality – the arbitrary 'intention' of the author. Causality in *Tristram Shandy* constantly shifts between alternative levels of explanation, at one moment seeking resolution on the level of the 'realistic' events of the novel; in the next, pointing to the psychological processes which operate in defiance of our normal expectations of causality, but then revealing the 'divine intervention' of the author in the construction of the chain of events which we are experiencing, and unveiling a very different order of causality to that of the 'real' world in which we (may) have assumed the characters to be living.

For Hume, the effectiveness of a narrative in convincing us of its connection with reality – he is thinking of a historical narrative – depended on the similarity of its parts, 'so that the mind runs easily along them, jumps from one part to another with facility': 'by this means a long chain of argument, has as little effect in diminishing the original vivacity, as a much shorter wou'd have, if compose'd of parts, which were different from each other, and of which each requir'd a distinct consideration' (T, 146). In a move which is typical of how writers exploited the potentialities of associationism, Sterne reverses this process, increasing the difficulty with which the mind can find connections between the parts of his narrative. Tristram describes his narrative method as one in which 'two contrary motions are introduced into it, and reconciled, which were thought to be at variance with each other' so that the work 'is digressive, and it is progressive too, — and at the same time' (*TS*, 95; I, 22). This not only mimics the workings of the associating mind, which is constantly juxtaposing present with past impressions, and is regularly diverted into chains of unexpected connections; it also forces the reader into continually generating more associative material in order to try to *find* from his or her own associations the connections which relate the parts of the narrative. Like the process of association itself, neither Tristram's narrative nor the reader's understanding of it can advance without retreating, and the fact that it will end at a time that precedes Tristram's own birth underlines how much of our apparently private associative material is dependent on our most intimate associates, on their memories and associations, and on our relations with the conversible world into which we are born. We would have an appropriate description of the associational plenitude to which Sterne's novel, like all associationist art, aspires if, in his description of his characters' relation to their Hobby-Horses, we replaced the word 'rider' with the word 'reader': 'by long journeys and much friction, it so happens that the body of the rider is at length filled as full of Hobby-Horsical matter as it can hold' (*TS*, 99; I, 24).

III

Famously, Sterne's experiments in the novel form were dismissed by Dr Johnson – 'Nothing odd will do long. *Tristram Shandy* did not last'[33] – and standard accounts of the development of the novel in English, though acknowledging that Sterne's work has lasted, regard it as untypical of the social realism which provided the foundations of the English novel in the eighteenth century, and which went on to dominate the development of the nineteenth-century novel.[34] Indeed, *Tristram Shandy* is regularly read as

---

[33] Quoted, Alan B. Howes, *Sterne: The Critical Heritage* (London: Routledge & Kegan Paul, 1974), 219.

[34] Ian Watt, for instance, set the direction for much later criticism when, in *The Rise of the Novel* (Berkeley: University of California Press, 1957), he suggested that 'so assured, indeed, is this mastery of realistic presentation [in *Tristram Shandy*] that, had it been applied to the usual purposes of the novel, Sterne would probably have been the supreme figure among eighteenth-century novelists. But, of course, *Tristram Shandy* is not so much

a novel prescient of modernity rather than integral to its historical period: 'here, miraculously, in an eighteenth-century artist, who ignores nature's simple plan, with its springs and cogs, to discover fragmentary and solipsistic life, we discover a kind of fellow spirit'.[35] No novel, it might seem, could be as unlike the fragmented and digressive structure of *Tristram Shandy* as a classic nineteenth-century *bildungsroman* such as Charles Dickens's *David Copperfield*, with its coherently progressive development and its narratorial 'retrospects' carefully placed at intervals through the text, with its tale of sustained growth to maturity and the achievement of a panoramic overview not only of an individual life but a whole society. But no less than Sterne, Dickens was indebted to associationism in constructing this pivotal work of his career. His knowledge of associationist theories of the psyche was sufficiently extensive – as Michael S. Kearns has pointed out, he was not only influenced by mesmerism, which had many connections with associationism, but owned copies both of Hume's *Treatise* and Dugald Stewart's *Elements of the Philosophy of the Human Mind*[36] – and the analysis of the workings of David's mind is imprinted throughout with associationist terminology: 'Here, as I sat looking at the parcels, packages, and books, and inhaling the smell of stables (ever since associated with that morning), a procession of most tremendous considerations began to march through my mind'.[37] This might be taken to contribute to the novel's realism, to the fact, as G. K. Chesterton put it in 1911, that Dickens creates 'creatures who cling to us and tyrannize over us, creatures whom we would not forget if we could, creatures who are more actual than the man who made them'.[38] But when David escapes from the

---

a novel as a parody of a novel' (291). As Jonathan Lamb has noted, 'the common method of assimilating [Sterne's] work to the new province of novel writing is to assume that the digressions, apostrophes, typographical outrages and zany time scheme that make it so unaccountable are the result of a thoroughgoing parody of the conventions of realism established during the previous decade by Richardson and Fielding'; 'Sterne and Irregular Oratory', in John Richetti (ed.), *The Cambridge Companion to the Eighteenth-Century Novel* (Cambridge: Cambridge University Press, 1996), 153.

[35] John Traugott, 'Sternian Realities', in Cash and Stedmond (eds), *The Winged Skull*, 77.

[36] Michael S. Kearns, 'Associationism, the Heart, and the Life of the Mind in Dickens' Novels', *Dickens Studies*, 15 (1986), 111–44.

[37] Charles Dickens, *The Personal History of David Copperfield*, ed. Trevor Blount (Harmondsworth: Penguin, 1966), 123; hereafter cited in the text as *DC*.

[38] Quoted, Trevor Blount, 'Introduction', ibid., 14.

power of the Murdstones, who have been responsible for the death of his mother, and arrives at his Aunt Betsey's house, he might indeed have arrived at a nineteenth-century version of Shandy Hall, where Aunt Betsey pursues donkeys – 'a donkey turned the current of her ideas in a moment' (DC, 251) – with all the vitality with which Toby is diverted by his Hobby-Horse, and where Mr Dick's 'memorial' advances even more slowly than Walter Shandy's *Tristra-paedia*. In Mr Dick's 'strange attraction' to the English revolution – 'he connects his illness with great disturbance and agitation, naturally, and that's the figure, or the simile, or whatever it's called, which he chooses to use' (DC, 261) – we have an instance not only of 'an unhappy association of ideas which have no connection in nature' (TS, 39; I, 4), but a case of associational obsession as profound as Uncle Toby's with his wounding. We also, of course, have a self-reflexive reference to that other King Charles – Dickens himself – whose head cannot help, any more than can Sterne's, introducing its own obsessions – and, therefore, its own associations – into the text. The attack, for instance, on the legal system in Chapter 26 gives Dickens's own views as David's and interrupts itself in properly Shandean fashion with, 'This is a digression' (DC, 448). The double time scheme of *Tristram Shandy*, in which we are aware both of the time of the narrated events and the actual time of their composition, is also replicated by *David Copperfield*: 'I fell at once into a solitary condition, – apart from all friendly notice, apart from the society of all other boys of my own age, apart from all companionship but my own spiritless thoughts, – which seems to cast its gloom upon this paper as I write' (DC, 204).

Dickens included Sterne 'in the list of things he said he had never outgrown (the others being Defoe, Cervantes and Le Sage)'[39] and the Shandean elements in *David Copperfield* suggest that this is a novel which may be much closer to the anti-realist tradition of *Tristram Shandy* than is often recognised. Indeed, so apparently antithetical is *David Copperfield* to the modernist literature which *Tristram Shandy* is assumed to prefigure that Alexander Welsh, in a list of the influence of Dickens's work on later novelists, notes that 'the book had also an extraordinary effect on Kafka, though one might think that of all of Dickens's novels this would have the least interest for a modernist'.[40] Kafka's interest, however, is not as unlikely as Welsh implies because one of the things

[39] John Forster, *Life of Charles Dickens*, 2 Vols (London: Dent, 1927), Vol. I, 166.

[40] Alexander Welsh, *From Copyright to Copperfield: The Identity of Dickens* (Cambridge, MA: Harvard University Press, 1987), 173.

that Dickens takes over from Sterne is the reversal of the relation between external causation and psychological attraction – a reversal which prefigures the reshaping of reality by psychological forces in Kafka's writings. Hume recognised that the reversal of causal and psychological determinations in his philosophy represented a profound challenge to common sense –

> What! The efficacy of causes lie in the determination of the mind! As if causes did not operate entirely independent of the mind, and wou'd not continue their operation, even tho' there was no mind existent to contemplate them, or reason concerning them. Thought may well depend on causes for its operation, but not causes on thought. This is to reverse the order of nature, and make that secondary, which is really primary. (*T*, 167)

– but Dickens's narrative procedure in *David Copperfield* will follow this path, reversing the order of nature so that reality will come to imitate fiction rather than fiction reality: 'I set down this remembrance here, because it is an instance to myself of the manner in which I fitted my old books to my altered life, and made stories for myself, out of the streets, and out of men and women' (*DC*, 224). If one's earliest association are with one's earliest associates, then David's are with the characters of the novels who were his only playmates in the oppressive regime that the Murdstones imposed on himself and his mother: 'It is curious to me how I could ever have consoled myself under my small troubles (which were great troubles to me), by impersonating my favourite characters in them – as I did – and by putting Mr and Miss Murdstone into all the bad ones – which I did too' (*DC*, 105–6). The consequence is that 'every barn in the neighbourhood, every stone in the church, and every foot of the churchyard, had some association of its own, in my mind, connected with these books, and stood for some locality made famous in them' (*DC*, 106), so that subsequent events in his life will suddenly give way to the remembrances of fiction: 'and when at last I did see a turnkey (poor little fellow that I was!), and thought how, when Roderick Random was in a debtors' prison, there was a man there with nothing on him but an old rug, the turnkey swam before my dimmed eyes and my beating heart' (*DC*, 221).

This confusion of fiction and reality is matched by the confusion of past and present at crucial moments in David's life, such as his marriage to Dora, which takes place 'through a mist of half-seen people, pulpits, monuments, pews, fonts, organs, and church windows, in which there flutter faint airs of association with my childish church at home, so long ago' (*DC*, 699). The motivation of David's choice of bride is turned not toward the future but towards the past, and the associations of childhood that suffuse the marriage ceremony prefigure the ways in which the marriage itself will turn its back upon a future of adult companionship as Dora is transformed into David's 'child wife' (*DC*, 711). The apparent mimesis of the progressive movement of time that begins with David's birth and ends in his still writing, 'far into the night' as a mature man at the novel's conclusion (*DC*, 950), is regularly interrupted not only by those moments when the past invades the time of writing – 'I tingle again from head to foot as my recollection turns that corner, and my pen shakes in my hand' (*DC*, 454) – but by the fact that the time of events in the novel is constantly being dissolved into or measured against the memories of previous events: 'When I found myself on the familiar Highgate road, pursuing such a different errand from that old one of pleasure, with which it was associated, it seemed as if a complete change had come on my whole life' (*DC*, 582).

It is appropriate then that a clock plays as important a role in David's birth as it did in Tristram Shandy's conception. The latter was spoiled by associations with the clock, as though physical conception and mental conception were one and the same, and David is similarly unlucky, since he was born at midnight on a Friday: 'the clock began to strike, and I began to cry, simultaneously' (*DC*, 49). Like Tristram, David is able to give his readers a detailed account of a time of which he has no memory, and like the forecast of the consequences of Tristram's name, the circumstances of David's birth prophesied 'first, that I was destined to be unlucky in life; and secondly, that I was privileged to see ghosts and spirits' (*DC*, 49). Of the latter part of this prophecy he declares 'that unless I ran through that part of my inheritance while I was still a baby, I have not come into it yet' (*DC*, 49). And yet, as many critics have pointed out, there is much that is ghostly or spiritualistic in David's progress through life, and much apparent destiny in his defiance of the first of these prophecies. As a writer about his own past he is continually engaged in calling up 'ghosts' – 'I now approach a period of my life, which I can never lose the remembrance of, while I remember anything: and the recollection of which has often, without my invocation, come before me like a ghost and haunted happier times' (*DC*, 205) – in order to make them present again both to himself and to the reader. David claims that as 'a child of close observation' and 'a man of strong memory of my childhood' *(DC,*61) his narrative is founded on veridical memory – on a memory so powerful that it can make the past real again:

> As I laid down my pen, a moment since, to think of it, the sea air came blowing in again, mixed with the perfume of the flowers; and I saw the old-fashioned furniture brightly rubbed and polished, my aunt's inviolable chair and table by the round green fan in the bow-window . . . *(DC,*250)

What calls all of this into existence, however, is the association of ideas:

> I seemed to be sustained and led on by my fanciful picture of my mother in her youth, before I came into the world. It always kept me company . . . I have associated it, ever since, with the sunny street of Canterbury, dozing as it were in the hot light. *(DC,* 244)

In moments such as this there is a double haunting – the young David is haunted by the ghost of his mother that travels before him (quite literally, since it is the image of his mother before he was born), while the older David is haunted by the streets of Canterbury where her image is now fixed in the past. The associations formed by the child's experience become the basis of the adult's ability to reconstruct his past. As the associations flow back and forth between the time of the narrative and the time of narrating, the veridical memory that keeps events locked into their temporal sequence slips into the associative memory that reconstructs that past from the point of view of the present. When David writes of his earliest memories, for instance, that 'There is nothing half so green that I know anywhere, as the grass of that churchyard; nothing half so shady as its trees; nothing half so quiet as its tombstones' *(DC,* 62), it is uncertain which 'I' is speaking. Is it the adult whose memory brings back these images suffused with later meaning or do they return as the authentic memory of 'my first childish associations'? *(DC,* 50). As narrator, David can recount only those memories which have not 'floated from me to the shore where all forgotten things will reappear' *(DC,* 185), but the memories which survive do so because of their associative linkages: 'I don't know why one slight set of impressions should be more particularly associated with a place than another, though I believe this obtains with most people, in reference especially to the associations of their childhood' *(DC,* 91). The events recalled, therefore, are subject to two different orders of organisation: on the one hand, they are connected together by the progressive and determinate succession in time that is constituted by memory; on the other, they are connected together by the digressive and disruptive effects of associations which cut across the order of succession like the disorderly progress of a conversation:

> 'I wonder,' said Peggotty, who was sometimes seized with a fit of wondering on some most unexpected topic, 'what's become of Davy's great-aunt?'
>
> 'Lor, Peggotty!' observed my mother, rousing herself from a reverie, 'what nonsense you talk!'
>
> 'Well, but I really do wonder, ma'am,' said Peggotty.
>
> 'What can have put such a person in your head?' inquired my mother. 'Is there nobody else in the world to come there?'
>
> 'I don't know how it is,' said Peggotty, 'unless it's on account of being stupid, but my head can never pick and choose its people. They come and they go, and they don't come and they don't go, just as they like. I wonder what's become of her?' (DC, 165)

Peggotty's mind forms a commentary on David's, whose head, equally, is full of people who come and go in the most irregular of fashions: 'It may have been in consequence of Mrs Crupp's advice, and, perhaps, for no better reason than because there was a certain similarity in the sound of the word skittles and Traddles, that it came into my head, the next day, to go and look after Traddles' (DC, 461). The apparently linear and progressive order of the events that David is relating is continually disrupted by encounters that have all the irregularity with which an association can inexplicably 'put such a person in your head'.

Recounting his earlier experiences, David the writer is surrounded by the ghostly presences whom his writing invokes – 'Let me remember how it used to be, and bring one morning back again' (DC, 103) – and by the associations with which they are connected: 'There were two great aloes, in tubs, on the turf, outside the windows; the broad hard leaves of which plant (looking as if they were made of painted tin) have ever since, by association, been symbolical to me of silence and retirement' (DC, 284). As a character in that past, however, he is haunted by the people whom he has previously encountered and who suddenly and unexpectedly reappear not as though their and David's paths have accidentally crossed as a result of the interaction of causal trajectories in the material world but as though the necessity of causality in the external world has been replaced some inner necessity of David's thought:

> As I passed the steps of the portico, I encountered, at the corner, a woman's face. It looked in mine, passed across the narrow lane, and disappeared. I knew it. I had seen it somewhere. But I could not remember where. I had some association with it, that struck upon my heart directly; but I was thinking of anything else when it came upon me, and was confused.
>
> On the steps of the church, there the stooping figure of a man, who had put down some burden on the smooth snow, to adjust it; my seeing the face, and my seeing him were simultaneous. I don't think I had stopped in my surprise; but, in any case, as I went on, he rose, turned, and came down towards me. I stood face to face with Mr Peggotty! (*DC*, 646)

The face which suddenly appears from the past but cannot be recalled (in both senses, because it disappears so quickly) evokes instantaneously the person with whom that face is associated from the time of Emily's disappearance. Is this an event governed by the accidental intersections of a populous world or is it an event governed by the reconstruction of David (the writer's) associative recollection of the events? The world in which David moves is full of such 'strange attractors' which link him to his old associates as if they gravitate towards him by his own powers of associational recall.

Take, for instance, the scene in Chapter 17 in which David, for the first time, visits the home of Uriah Heep. As a result of a conversational assault by Uriah and his mother, David finds himself 'perpetually letting out something or other that I had no business to let out and seeing the effect of it in the twinkling of Uriah's dinted nostrils' (*DC*, 314). As mother and son pump his past out of him, we are suddenly informed of something that had gone unacknowledged throughout the scene – that the door 'stood open to air the room, which was warm, the weather being close for the time of year'. In this open door appears unexpectedly the figure of Mr Micawber, who 'looked in, and walked in, exclaiming loudly, "Copperfield! Is it possible?"' (*DC*, 314–15). The question reflects back on Dickens's narrative technique – is it possible to allow, in a realistic novel, such an improbable conjunction of circumstances and characters, one to which Micawber himself draws attention: 'this is indeed a meeting which is calculated to impress the mind with a sense of the instability and uncertainty of all human – in short, it is a most extraordinary meeting' (*DC*, 315)? 'Instability and uncertainty of all human' what? – associations, both psychological and social. Mr Micawber, as a part of that portion of his past that David most desperately wants to conceal, has therefore been in his mind, and in his appearance at that moment it as though the memories that David is trying to repress call him into existence. As if, indeed, the associational chain of David's recollection passes from mind into reality, or as if David's memories are so potent that they attract into his present environment the repressed associate of his past. The same structure is repeated in Chapter 27, when David goes to visit Traddles in a street which 'reminded me forcibly of the days when I lived with Mr and Mrs Micawber' (*DC*, 461), only to discover that Traddles is, in fact, lodging with the Micawbers: "'Good heavens, Mr Traddles!" said Mr Micawber, "to think that I should find you acquainted with the friend of my youth, the companion of my earlier days!"' (*DC*, 468). In *David Copperfield* intimate associates of David's past can turn up in the causal connections of reality with the same ease and on the basis of the same suggestions as they turn up in a psychological chain of associations: the associations by which the older David recalls the events of his youth in the act of rewriting it operate as the context in which the younger David actually lives his life, so that his associations predict the appearance of the associates of his own earlier experience. The events of the novel thus hover indeterminately between the operation of psychological laws – the constant conjunctions governing the mind of the author in his recollection of his own past – and the apparently random conjunctions of a 'real' world. The division between the novel's realism, on the one hand, and its fantasy elements on the other – its invocation, for instance, of fairy tale motifs – is actually a tension between psychological and material modes of causation, in which 'the efficacy of causes' seems to lie not in the material world but 'in the determination of the mind'.

As the retrospective associations of the writer thus become intertwined with the associations of his earlier self – 'happening to arrive at the door as it was opened to the afternoon milkman, I was reminded of Mr and Mrs Micawber more forcibly yet (*DC*, 461) – they form what can only be described as *prospective* associations – a train of associations that leaps from memory into reality to produce an apparently 'chance' encounter with the characters whom both Davids have been associatively recalling. Attending his first play in London, for instance, David experiences the event through precisely that personal reverie which associationist theories of art argue to be central to aesthetic enjoyment: 'I was so filled with the play, and with the past — for it was, in a manner, like a shining transparency, through which I saw my earlier life moving along'. That reverie, however, switches from recollection of the past to evocation in the present when 'the figure of a handsome well-formed young man dressed with a tasteful easy negligence which I have reason to remember very well, became a real presence to me' (DC, 345). Steerforth steps out of the recollected past back into the immediate present as if he were the necessary conclusion of David's train of associations. The retrospective associations of the narrator with the 'figure . . . which I have reason to remember very well' discover themselves mirrored in the prospective associations of his own earlier self, whose memories do not pass along a chain of associated experiences until some new impression interrupts them but whose reverie ends by encountering in reality the very figure to which its associations have led it. The same interaction between mind and reality is repeated later when David as narrator, recalling the walks which took him past Steerforth's house, notes that,

> my mind could not go by it and leave it, as my body did; and it usually awakened a long train of meditations. Coming before me, on this particular evening that I mention, mingled with the childish recollections and later fancies, the ghosts of half-formed hopes, the broken shadows of disappointments dimly seen and understood, the blending of experience and imagination, incidental to the occupation with which my thoughts had been busy, it was more than commonly suggestive. I fell into a brown study as I walked on, and a voice at my side made me start. (DC, 734)

The voice invites him to 'walk in' to the house that has been the subject of his 'train of meditations', as though the train of memories itself has had the direct causal consequence of calling him into the house.

The transfer of the retrospective associations of the writer into the prospective associations of the character is governed, of course, by the fact that the writer is reconstructing a narrative whose outcomes he already knows. The character who struggles to achieve progress in time is dominated by a future in which his actions, directed towards an as yet unknown future, have already become links in an associative chain recalled from the known past. The associations by which David the writer structures his narrative thus become the 'reality' in which David the character is entangled, a reality whose 'necessity' is not the progressive order of history (or memory) but the psychological order by which the older David's associations have been determined. This prospective power of association comes to a climax when David returns to Yarmouth during the storm whose physical intensity is mirror-image to his psychological state, one which 'tossed up the depths of my memory and made a tumult in them' (*DC*, 860). The immediate 'disorder' of the character, however, reflects an equivalent disorder in the writer, who acknowledges at the beginning of Chapter 55 that the event it will contain is one 'so indelible, so awful, so bound by an infinite variety of ties to all that has preceded it, in these pages, that, from the beginning of my narrative, I have seen it growing larger and larger as I advanced, like a great tower in a plain, and throwing its forecast shadow even on the incidents of my childish days' (*DC*, 854). It is to this 'strange attractor' that the narrative has all along been prospectively drawn, one so dominating that its associative power can turn past into present:

> For years after it occurred, I dreamed it often. I have started up so vividly impressed by it, that its fury has yet seemed raging in my quiet room, in the still night. I dream of it sometimes, though at lengthened and uncertain intervals, to this hour. I have an association between it and a stormy wind, or the lightest mention of a sea-shore, as strong as any of which my mind is conscious. (*DC*, 854)

The disordered mind of David (the writer) in which memory becomes reality is matched by the disorder in which David (the character) anticipates the very reversal of the causal and psychological trains of events – 'the wild moon seemed to plunge headlong, as if, in a dread disturbance of the laws of nature, she had lost her way and were frightened' (*DC*, 857) – by which his life (as narrated by David the writer) has actually been structured: 'There was that jumble in my thoughts and recollections, that I had lost the clear arrangement of time and distance. Thus, if I had gone out into the town, I should not have been surprised, I think, to encounter someone who I knew must be then in London' (*DC*, 859–60). Such crossing of the psychological into the real is nothing less than the subliminal acknowledgment of the actual order by which David's life has been lived, so that, as he watches the doomed sailor on the shipwreck he notes how 'his action brought an old remembrance to my mind of a once dear friend' (*DC*, 865). The association calls Steerforth back from the ocean of memory just as, on the following morning, his body 'lying with his head upon his arm, as I had often seen him lie at school' (*DC*, 866) will form itself to the shape of David's memories. The world through which David (the character) travels is a world already organised according to the principles of association by which the mind of David (the writer) is governed: his associates form links in a chain of association organised not by the progressive movement of the character through time but by the retrospective recollection of the narrator looking back into the past. To the writer, it is Steerforth's posture in death that has made his sleeping position in school significant, but in the earlier part of the novel that relationship, already known to the narrator and organising the associations by which the past is recalled, has been concealed from us as readers, so that this seems, like David's other encounters, an accident veridically recorded by memory rather than an association reshaping the reality it recalls. While Sterne's progressive-regressive narrative method is designed to open up as many associational linkages as possible, Dickens's is designed to turn the past into a series of closed loops in which prospective and retrospective associations match each other exactly, producing, instead of the causal uncertainty of *Tristram Shandy*, a sense of organised finality from which everything accidental has been expunged.[41]

Such finality, however, reduces David (the character) to being a spectator of the unfolding of a life which is as if already lived – as if, in fact, his consciousness is the consciousness of David (the narrator) inhabiting the body of the character and unable to influence events which have already been lived through: 'We have all some experience of a feeling, that comes over us occasionally, of what we are saying and doing having been said and done before, in a remote time' (*DC*, 630). That the self is reduced to a spectator of its own experience is an argument often made against Hume's philosophy and David's passive witnessing of Steerforth's shipwreck echoes a passage in Hume, in which he uses the sight of a shipwreck close to shore – 'so near me, that I can perceive distinctly the horror, painted on the countenance of the seaman and passengers, hear their lamentable cries, see the dearest friends give their last adieu, or embrace with a resolution to perish in each others arms' (*T*, 594) – as the focus of his discussion of the operation of 'sympathy': 'No man has so savage a heart as to reap any pleasure from such a spectacle, or withstand the motions of the tenderest compassion and sympathy' (*T*, 594). If *David Copperfield* enacts Hume's claim that 'the efficacy of causes lie in the determination of the mind', it does so by regularly reducing David himself to a spectatorial role, depriving him of the will by which he could 'determine'

---

[41] This is a point made by J. Hillis Miller in *Charles Dickens: The World of his Novels* (Cambridge, MA: Harvard University Press, 1958), 155: 'The spiritual presence of the hero organises all these recollected events, through the powerful operation of association, into a single unified pattern which forms his destiny'. He does not, however, note the relevance of *associationism* to Dickens's ability to so structure the novel.

events rather than merely be witness to them. Most significantly, perhaps, at the moment when he and Steerforth arrive at Peggoty's boat in Chapter 21 and the narrative pauses to present in detail a family tableau: 'Mr Peggotty, his face lighted up with uncommon satisfaction, and laughing with all his might, held his rough arms wide open, as if for little Em'ly to run into them; Ham, with a mixed expression in his face of admiration, exultation, and a lumbering sort of bashfulness that sat upon him very well, held little Em'ly by the hand, as if he were presenting her to Mr Peggotty' (*DC*, 369). With the arrival of David and Steerforth, however, 'the little picture was so instantaneously dissolved . . . that one might have doubted whether it had ever been' (*DC*, 369) but the news that it betokens – Ham and Em'ly's engagement – traps David in his past associations: 'How far my emotions were influenced by the recollection of my childhood, I don't know. Whether I had come there with any lingering fancy that I was still to love little Em'ly, I don't know. I know that I was filled with pleasure by all this; but, at first, with an indescribably sensitive pleasure, that a very little would have changed to pain' (*DC*, 374). Unable to act, or, indeed, to speak, David is reduced to a spectator as Steerforth re-establishes the family's harmony by his own conversational skills: 'how gently and respectfully Steerforth spoke to her; how skilfully he avoided anything that would embarrass her; how he talked to Mr Peggotty of boats . . . how lightly and easily he carried on, until he brought us, by degrees, into a charmed circle, and we were all talking away without any reserve' (*DC*, 375). Steerforth creates a 'conversible world' into which everyone is drawn until it becomes reality itself: 'Steerforth told a story of a dismal shipwreck (which arose out of his talk with Mr Peggotty), as if he saw it all before him – and little Em'ly's eyes were fastened on him all the time, as if she saw it too' (*DC*, 375). The shipwreck is, of course, only too truly 'before him': conversation in this novel turns past associations – David's with Em'ly and Steerforth – into prospective associations – Steerforth's with Em'ly – and leads directly to the shipwreck of their lives. The shipwreck which will be such an associatively potent memory to David (the writer) is an equally potent prospective association in the conversible world which Steerforth dominates and in which David (the character) has no voice.

The scene is a microcosm of the structure of *David Copperfield*, in which David's role is to shuttle back and forth between different conversational groups, associating one with another by, quite literally, introducing his associates to each other: 'Mrs Micawber and myself cannot disguise from our minds that we part, it may be for years and it may be forever, with an individual linked by strong associations to the altar of our domestic life' (*DC*, 592). As insistently as *Tristram Shandy* digresses between topics, David digresses from one conversational group to another – his whole life, from his early encounter with Agnes, one long digression from his most intimate associate, and real purpose of his most intimate associations: 'I cannot call to mind where or when, in my childhood, I had seen a stained glass window in a church. Nor do I recollect its subject. But I know that when I saw her turn round, in the grave light of the old staircase, and wait for us, above, I thought of that window; and I associated something of its tranquil brightness with Agnes Wickfield ever afterwards' (*DC*, 280). This is why David's name is changed by each of the conversational groups he enters; he becomes, for each of them, a different person, one who is simply the vehicle – as when Mrs Crupp 'called me Copperful . . . in some indistinct association with washing day' (*DC*, 459) – of their own associational connections.

David is not only full of associations, he is an associating medium, turning his associations into associates and his associates into associations for one another, thereby producing 'such well-associated friends' (*DC*, 632). He introduces Steerforth into Peggotty's world just as he introduces Mr Dick into Dr Strong's or Mr Micawber into Uriah Heep's. The linkages he makes, however, like trains of association, are never under his control. Subject to 'the wandering ardour and unsettled purpose within me' (*DC*, 581), the forward purposes of David's life are continually defeated by his unsteady associations and his unsteady associates. Thus in Chapter 22, immediately following his introduction of Steerforth to the Peggotty household, he disappears into reveries over his childhood – 'my occupation in my solitary pilgrimages was to recall every yard of the old road as I went along it' (*DC*, 378) – while Steerforth is in the 'Willing Mind', the inn where Mr Peggotty's fisher community meet, becoming a parasite upon the 'will' which neither he nor David have of their own, and that will lead to his flight with Em'ly. David brings the other characters together with a strange power of attraction but the attractions which they forge with one another quite literally run away from him. He is the passive spectator of the consequences of association, just as he is spectator to Micawber's conning of Traddles of his savings, or Uriah Heep's influence over Agnes's father, or Rosa Dartle's confrontation with Em'ly. Indeed, in the latter case, he is so incapable of action that he watches as Rosa strikes Em'ly and does not attempt to intervene, but waits for the arrival of Peggotty's 'willing mind' in a terrified suspense which is more concerned with the effects on himself of what he witnesses than its effect on either of the two women who have become associated with each other through him:

'Would he never, never come? How long was I to bear this? How long could I bear it?' (*DC*, 790).

In the end, David will be redeemed by his power of writing, but writing in this case too, is but 'a different name for conversation' (*TS*, 127; II, 11), since the evocation of the past as again immediately present, which it is the aim of his writing to convey, is possible only because of the conversations he participates in, from Peggotty's recollections of the events of his birth to Mr Peggoty's account of Em'ly's escape from Steerforth:

> He saw everything he related. It passed before him, as he spoke, so vividly, that in the intensity of his earnestness, he presented what he described to me, with greater distinctness than I can express. I can hardly believe, writing now long afterwards, but that I was actually present in these scenes; they are impressed upon me with such an astonishing air of fidelity. (*DC*, 793) .

Indeed, if *David Copperfield* consists of David's associated memories, those memories consist largely of conversations, reconstructed with a detail which defies the ordinary powers of memory: rather than a 'Kind of Resident Ambassador from the Dominions of Learning to those of Conversation', David is an ambassador from the dominions of conversation to those of memory, saving in permanent form the transitory exchanges which have informed his most intimate associations. Dickens's exploration of the implications of associationism reveals how thoroughly it had permeated his thought, and, as so often, David's situation is parodically mirrored by Micawber who, like a Humean philosopher, turns the solitude of writing to despair:

> 'The die is cast – all is over. Hiding the ravages of care with a sickly mask of mirth, I have not informed you, this evening, that there is no hope of remittance! . . .
>
> 'Let the wretched man who now addresses you, my dear Copperfield, be a beacon to you through life. He writes with that intention, and in that hope. If he could think himself of so much use, one gleam of day might, by possibility, penetrate into the cheerless dungeon of his remaining existence . . . (*DC*, 321)

Yet Micawber, true to Humean philosophy, returns to the world by the support of being able to dine and converse and be merry with friends. Hurrying to give consolation to the Micawbers the morning after his receipt of one of these despairing epistles, David spies them on the London coach, 'Mr Micawber, the very picture of tranquil enjoyment, smiling at Mrs Micawber's conversation, eating walnuts out of a paper bag, with a bottle sticking out of his breast pocket' (*DC*, 322).

David, equally, will be thrust into 'the cheerless dungeon of his remaining existence' after the deaths of Dora and of Steerforth and the departure of Mr Peggotty and Em'ly: 'all that remained – a ruined blank and waste' (*DC*, 886). The 'ruined blank' is a world without sustaining associations or associates. In his European travels David's is a mind as incapable of acquiring new memories – 'I see myself passing on among the novelties of foreign towns . . . as a dreamer might; bearing my painful load through all, and hardly conscious of the objects as they fade before me' (*DC*, 886) – as it is of contemplating his old ones, which have wrought such havoc among those he has associated with one another, both in experience and in memory. Passing through many places and many languages, he becomes as truly isolated from the conversible world as Micawber imagines himself to be in his letters. The 'blank', however, is an intensification of a previous blank period, when he first moved into rooms of his own in London – 'I missed Agnes. I found a tremendous blank, in the place of that smiling repository of my confidence' (*DC*, 416). The 'ruined blank' can only be overcome if David's mind can acquire alternative associative possibilities, a process which begins when a letter from Agnes is conjoined with an experience of the sublimity of the Swiss landscape:

> Dotted here and there on the mountain's-side, each tiny dot a home, were lonely wooden cottages, so dwarfed by the towering heights that they appeared too small for toys. So did even the clustered village in the valley, with its wooden bridge across the stream, where the stream tumbled over broken rocks, and roared away among the trees. In the quiet air, there was a sound of distant singing – shepherd voices; but, as one bright evening cloud floated midway along the mountain's-side, I could almost have believed it came from there, and was not earthly music. All at once, in this serenity, great Nature spoke to me; and soothed me to lay down my weary head upon the grass, and weep as I had not wept yet, since Dora died! (*DC*, 887)

'Nature' here seems to be the 'cause' of David's release, but the following paragraph tells us that, 'I had found a packet of letters awaiting me but a few minutes before, and had strolled out of the village to read them', and then a further paragraph states, 'The packet was in my hand. I opened it, and read the writing of Agnes' (*DC*, 888). The time sequence of the events and the time sequence of the narrative are deeply ambiguous: the 'I had found . . . a few minutes before' directs us to a time before his encounter with 'great Nature' but nothing indicates when the narrative returns to the point after that encounter, so that the release of the 'sublime' and the reading of Agnes's letter appear to be simultaneous, a simultaneity which will then be confirmed by their having become newly associated in his mind: 'I resolved to remain away from home for some time longer; to settle myself for the present in Switzerland, which was growing dear to me in the remembrance of that evening', a new association which allows him 'to resume my pen; to work' (*DC*, 889).

This new foundation for David's associational framework is also the beginning of a reorganisation of his old associations (and his old associates): 'I cannot so completely penetrate the mystery of my own heart, as to know when I began to think that I might have set its earliest and brightest hopes on Agnes. I cannot say at what stage of my grief it first became associated with the reflection, that, in my wayward boyhood, I had thrown away the treasure of her love' (*DC*, 889–90). The reorganisation of the past around Agnes suggests the possibility that he can 'cancel the mistaken past' (*DC*, 890), but the desire to cancel the past would simply make permanent the 'blank' by which his memories have been erased. To actually reach Agnes, to recover 'the treasure' he has lost, he will actually have to traverse again the ground he has already travelled and to re-engage both with the associates and the associations that he wishes could be cancelled. On his return to London, therefore, real time begins to mimic the timelessness with which associational connections can be repeated in the mind, taking David back to re-encounter his very earliest associates. Sitting before a fire he thinks as 'the live coals . . . broke and changed' of 'the principal vicissitudes and separations that had marked my life' when, suddenly, 'I found my eyes resting on a countenance that might have arisen out of the fire, in its association with my early remembrances' (*DC*, 902–3). The person who steps from thought into reality is the very practitioner who attended David's birth, taking him back to the time when his own associations were originally a 'blank', yet to be written upon. Surprisingly at a realistic level but unsurprisingly in a narrative in which 'the efficacy of causes lie in the determination of the mind', Mr Chillip is still a medical practitioner, one who happens to have the Murdstones as a neighbour, and is able to tell David that Murdstone's new wife is undergoing exactly what David's mother suffered at his hands. Real time consists, like psychological time, of the repetition of past associations: 'Does he gloomily profess to be', David asks '(I am ashamed to use the word in such association) religious still?' (DC, 906). The associations which Chillip recalls are then carried by David on a repeat of his childhood journey to Dover and to his aunt, who directs him to visit Agnes, who, in another defiance of the progress of time, has re-established her father's house 'as it used to be', so that reality and David's associative recall of his childhood – 'the well-remembered ground' (DC, 911) – remain identical with one another.

This collusion of past and present is prelude to Agnes's transformation of the 'blank' into its opposite, the rich vein of recollection which we, as readers, have actually been experiencing in reading David's account of his life: 'With the unerring instinct of her noble heart, she touched the chords of memory so softly and harmoniously, that no one jarred within me; I could listen to the sorrowful, distant music, and desire to shrink from nothing it awoke'. The recovery of the past through his old associate marks his return to the conversible world, the world in which Agnes has been, throughout, his most initimate and enduring association. Through Agnes the past can be reshaped and all its associations subsumed to a new emotional tenor which will transform the nature of David's associations: 'blended with it all, was her dear self, the better angel of my life' (DC, 912). Memory and reality being thus harmoniously retuned, the destructive elements of David's past associations can be allowed to be recollected because they are now locked into new chains – quite literally in the case of Uriah Heep and Steerforth's servant, Littimer, whom he encounters in a model prison run by his old headmaster Creakle, and almost as finally in the case of Em'ly and Micawber, who are emigrants in Australia.

In the final pages of *David Copperfield*, Dickens thus has David re-trace his steps from birth and exclusion – in his meeting with Chillip and the conversation about the Murdstones, through his journey to Dover and to school (Aunt Betsey and Agnes), to his dealings with Heep and Steerforth – not as recollected associations but as re-encountered realities, realities which can now be understood differently because he has recovered, through Agnes, the associative path from which his life since adolescence had been one long digression. His new home thus becomes a nexus of past associations, past associations which continue to transpose themselves from the psyche into reality: so Peggotty's 'rough forefinger, which I once associated with a pocket nutmeg-grater, is just the same, and when I see my least child catching it as it totters from my aunt to her, I think of our little parlour at home, when I could scarcely walk. My aunt's old disappointment is set right, now. She is godmother to a real living Betsey Trotwood; and Dora (the next in order) says she spoils her' (*DC*, 947). In *David Copperfield* the order of a psychological reality triumphs over the destructive effects of time by allowing the phantoms of the past to be, quite literally, called back into a new existence, emerging from old into new associations.

IV

In George Eliot's *Middlemarch*, associationist psychology forms the backdrop of the characters' experiences:

> Scenes which make vital changes in our neighbours' lot are but the background of our own, yet, like a particular aspect of the fields and trees, they become associated for us with the epochs of our own history, and make a part of that unity which lies in the selections of our keenest consciousnesses.
>
> The dream-like association of something alien and ill-understood with the deepest secrets of experience seemed to mirror that sense of loneliness which was due to the very ardour of Dorothea's nature.[42]

The language of association had come to be, by the mid-nineteenth century, a common resource on which authors could draw for the delineation of character, in the knowledge that their readers would understand the psychological processes involved. It represented an accepted scientific truth about the nature of the workings of the mind. In *Tristram Shandy* and in *David Copperfield*, on the other hand, association is not simply a means of describing the inner life of the characters: it has invaded the very nature of the writing. The act of writing, like the act of reading, is an associational act, dependent on the contingent associational patterns of both writer and reader. The innovative narrative structure of these novels depends upon their making the theory and consequences of association the shaping principle of their narration: their form is the outcome of their exploration of the associative interactions not only of mind and world, but of novelist and reader:

---

[42] George Eliot, *Middlemarch*, 360.

I am this month one whole year older than I was this time twelve-month; and having got, as you perceive, almost into the middle of my fourth volume — and no farther than to my first day's life — 'tis demonstrative that I have three hundred and sixty-four days more life to write just now, than when I first set out: so that instead of advancing, as a common writer, in my work with that I have been doing at it – on the contrary, I am just thrown so many volumes back . . . (*TS*, 286)

Trsitram's crisis is a comic parody of all associationist art – it can advance only by returning to the past, just as David Copperfield can only recover himself by seeing the boy he was through Agnes's eyes:

We stood together in the same old-fashioned window at night, when the moon was shining: Agnes with her quiet eyes raised up to it; I following her glance. Long miles of road then opened out before my mind; and, toiling on, I saw a ragged way-worn boy, forsaken and neglected, who should come to call even the heart now beating against mine, his own. (*DC*, 937)

The significance of the present can only be known through eyes to which the past is ever present. Agnes reassociates David with his past as a still living present just as Tristram resurrects his old associates as still living realities: associationism resists the unidirectionality of time as expressed in the unidirectionality of causation. By using associationist psychology 'to reverse the order of nature, and make that secondary, which is really primary', by making the external world dependent for its structure on the inner workings of the mind, both novels seek to defy that fall by which our past is lost to us, fading back into the blank from which it originally emerged.

Nicholas Dames has suggested that there is a particular texture to the fiction of the mid-nineteenth century that comes from the fact that in Georgian and earlier Victorian culture memory exists only to consolidate a usable past: the characters who enact this form of memory he describes as 'amnesiac selves', and what they share is 'a nostalgic goal: to eliminate the possibility, in psychological terms, of traumatic fixation, and in narratological terms, of eruption of desultory, chaotic reminiscences'.[43] This kind of memory he sees

---

[43] Nicholas Dames, *Amnesiac Selves: Nostalgia, Forgetting and British Fiction, 1810– 1870* (Oxford: Oxford University Press, 2001), 7.

as resulting from the fact that the writers of this period lie 'between the associationism of Locke, Hume, Hartley, and the hysteria theories of Freud and
Breuer, between Rouseauistic reveries and Proustian *mémoire involontaire*'.[44]
Though *David Copperfield* undoubtedly uses memory towards towards a sense
of closure whose virtue is the recovery of practical life, it does not so much
stand between 'Lock, Hume, Hartley' on the one side and 'Freud and Breuer'
on the other as enact the process by which the former were incorporated
into the latter. And far from suppressing 'desultory, chaotic reminiscences'
David Copperfield makes reality itself operate precisely as though its guiding
principle *were* such 'desultory, chaotic reminiscences'. The potential chaos
of association, like the potential for chaos in David's disordered movement
between different conversational groups, emerges into an order by the recovery of a shared memory – the memory that David shares with Agnes – that
allows the writer, like the Humean philosopher, to escape the agonistic isolation of his mode of understanding the world and return to a common world
of conversation. And if this is a memory which recovers the past as it is
'enacted only in the light of an end, of death; a memory that is always only
the necessary prehistory of the present',[45] nonetheless that prehistory of the
present is a world of strange and traumatic attractors. David, indeed, points
forward to his own death at the novel's conclusion as though it is the end in
the light of which his previous experience has to be understood:

> O Agnes, O my soul, so may thy face be by me when I close my life
> indeed; so may I, when realities are melting from me, like the shadows
> which I now dismiss, still find thee near me, pointing upward! (*DC*,
> 950)

David's address to Agnes not only reinforces the novel's conversational
structure, his description of what will happen at the point of death – 'realities
are melting from me' – describes punningly but only too accurately what has
been the structure of the novel he and we have just completed: the self melts
reality to the order of its own associations. Dickens's novel, unlike Sterne's,
may seem to have a conventional structure, and may be read as an example of
autobiographical realism, but it is reality as defined by the British associationist
tradition in its exploitation of the consequences of Hume's suggestion that

---

[44] Ibid., 11.
[45] Ibid., 4.

'the efficacy of causes lie in the determination of the mind': it dissolves realism and lays the ground not only for the anti-realist elements in Dickens's later fiction but for ways in which the associationist novel was to develop in the modernist period.

Indeed, in its recovery of the past through the unpredictable processes of association, it prefugures Proust's *A la Recherche du Temps Perdu* in which, as A. E. Pilkington suggests, it is integral to Proust's conception of memory that

> its laws are subordinated to those of habit. The power of something inherently trivial to resurrect the past – a power which important things or *familiar* sensations do not possess – springs from the fact that such a sensation (the taste of the madeleine, the clink of a spoon) or expression . . . is able to retain all its force precisely because it does not 'fade' through becoming habitual. . . The past is restored through what had been forgotten as unimportant and that consequently has not been devitalised by 'habitual memory'.[46]

Mill's 'law of obliviscence' is turned inside out: that which has apparently been fogotten, which has never been returned to in the sequence of associations, retains the capacity for a recovery of the past far more intense than any associational train which has been regularly revisited. Dickens's novel enacts the total recovery of the past under the order of a new and dominant emotional context, which determines the order and structure of the writer's associations; Proust's represents a similar resurrection of the past but one based on the recovery of forgotten and apparently disconnected sensations whose associative power is such that they allow the return of the past as an immediately available part of the present.

The past as a living present which is celebrated in Proust's work is already implicit in Dickens's, but whereas for Proust the moment of associative recovery allows the reconstitution of the totality of the past, in Dickens the similar recovery of the past is a revelation of just how malleable that past world is, of how its recollection is also a reshaping. It may be the recovery of the past as *'temps perdu'*, but it is also the recognition of the past as a world continually reorganised by an associative power that is governed from the

---

[46] A. E. Pilkington, *Bergson and his Influence: A Reassessment* (Cambridge: Cambridge University Press 1976), 167.

present. In Proust, the recovery of the past is the recovery of a *real* past, however much it may be founded on a purely accidental association: in Dickens, it is the recovery of an *unreal* past always subject to associative connections of which the *real* past could never have been aware. Kafka, who was so deeply influenced by *David Copperfield*, is the inheritor of this aspect of Dickens's novelistic procedures, underlining the extent to which developments in nineteenth-century associationism stimulated some of the most significant narrative experiments of modernism.

4 The Mythic Method and the Foundations of Modern Literary Criticism

In his 'Introduction' to the Ninth Edition of the *Encyclopaedia Britannica* (which was to become an intellectual landmark of Victorian culture), Professor T. S. Baynes of St Andrews University suggested that its aim was to assemble 'the available facts of human history, collected over the widest areas' and to present them, 'carefully co-ordinated and grouped together, in the hope of ulti-mately evolving the laws of progress, moral and material, which underlie them, and which, when evolved, will help to connect and interpret the whole onward movement of the race'.[1] The Ninth Edition saw its territory not as a series of separate branches of knowledge but as an as yet unrealised totality in which all disciplines would be contributors to an evolutionary account of human his-tory. To this endeavour, the new science of anthropology was central:

> Many branches of mental philosophy, again, such as Ethics, Psychology and Aesthetics, while supplying important elements to the new science [of Anthropology] are at the same time largely interested in its results and all may be regarded as subservient to the wider problems raised by the philosophy of history.[2]

Anthropology, as the study of how human beings evolved from the savage to the civilised, represents the foundation on which all other disciplines are built

---

[1] *Encyclopaedia Britannica* (Edinburgh: A. & C. Black, 1875), Vol. I, vii.
[2] Ibid.

and the location to which they return. One of the most striking applications of this hypothesis in the early volumes of the Ninth Edition was William Robertson Smith's discussion of the anthropological evidence of the Old Testament. His article on the 'Bible', analysing it as a document in the evolution of primitive peoples, was sufficiently radical that it resulted in a heresy inquiry and his ultimate dismissal from the chair of divinity which he held at the University of Aberdeen.

When, after Baynes's death, Robertson Smith took over the editorship of the Ninth Edition, he was committed to carrying through a reassessment of all knowledge in the light of the theory of evolution and assembled a group of contributors who were, or were to become, leading figures in what amounted to a revolution in the understanding of the history of humankind as well as of the world which it inhabited. James Clerk Maxwell, whose *Treatise on Electricity and Magnetism* (1873) was to prepare the way for Einstein's theory of relativity, contributed articles on physics, and J. G. Frazer, subsequently author of *The Golden Bough* (1890), provided articles on 'Mythology', as well as on 'Totem' and 'Taboo', topics which would later become key terms in the title of one of Freud's major texts. Another of the younger contributors was James Sully, whose *Outlines of Psychology* (1884) marked a significant development in empirical psychology. For the Ninth Edition, however, Sully provided the entry on 'Aesthetics', which surveyed aesthetic thinking from the ancients through to post-Kantian and post-Hegelian German thought, as well as considering in some detail the various national traditions of European thought. It concluded, however, with 'English Writers', of whom the most prominent were those in the associationist tradition from Hutcheson to Herbert Spencer.

Sully's view that associationist aesthetics represents the most scientific – because most psychological, as opposed to metaphysical – theory of art is hardly surprising, given that his own psychological work relies heavily on associationist theory, but his combination of associationism with an evolutionary perspective was not only typical of the emphasis of the Ninth Edition as a whole but led to a striking reformulation of the relationship between associationism and its *a priori* opponents. In addressing the issue which the associationist tradition throws most forcefully into relief, 'the question of the relativity of aesthetic impressions', Sully suggests that 'the true method of resolving this difficulty would be to look on aesthetic impressions more as a growth, rising, with the advance of intellectual culture, from the crude enjoyments of sensation to the more refined and subtle delights of the cultivated mind'.[3] The relativity of aesthetic experience is not to be understood as simple differences of taste but as developments in the nature of the experiences which are possible at different periods in human history and at different levels of cultural advancement. 'Beauty' is not a fixed but an evolving category, and its understanding depends both on our knowledge of the workings of the human mind and of the mind's development over the vast timescale of evolutionary history. Sully's article concludes, therefore, by noting the importance of Herbert Spencer's account of beauty in his *Psychology* (1855), one which 'offers a new theory of the genesis of the pleasures of beauty and art, based on his doctrine of evolution':[4]

> The first, and lowest class of pleasures, are those of simple sensation, as tone and colour, which are partly organic and partly the results of association . . . The highest order of pleasures are those of the aesthetic sentiments proper, consisting of the multitudinous emotions ideally excited by aesthetic objects, natural and artistic. Among these vaguely and partially revived emotions Mr Spencer reckons not only those of the individual, but also many of the constant feelings of the race. Thus he would attribute the vagueness and apparent depth of musical emotion to associations with vocal tones, built up during the course of vast ages.[5]

Our aesthetic experiences are not immediate, nor are they based on associations acquired simply in the course of our own experience; they are mediated by associational connections accumulated over the whole course of human history, both biological and civilisational. Our lack of understanding of this, according to Sully, is owing to the fact that 'comparatively little has been done in a purely scientific manner to determine the nature and functions of Art',[6] because comparatively little has been done yet to understand the workings of the mind in a purely scientific manner. Aesthetics could only be properly founded on the development of a scientific Psychology which was only beginning to be established.

Significantly, then, one of the entries in the Ninth Edition which made the biggest impact on late nineteenth-century culture was that on 'Psychology' itself, written by the then almost unknown James Ward, who was a colleague

---

[3] Ibid., 'Aesthetics', 213–14.
[4] Ibid., 224.
[5] Ibid., 224.
[6] Ibid., 214.

of Robertson Smith's at Cambridge. Such was the perceived importance of his article that he was awarded honorary doctorates by a variety of universities on the strength of it, and the discipline of psychology itself, as an area of intellectual enquiry distinct from philosophy, is often dated to the publication of Ward's article. Like many others in the 1880s, Ward was attempting to find a way out of the apparent deadlock between the empiricism of Mill and Bain on the one hand – there is nothing in the mind that has not developed from its sensations – and the idealism that had been derived by philosophers such as T. H. Green and Edward Caird from their study of Kant and Hegel, in which the mind functioned through *a priori* categories that structure all experience even before it engages with its sensations.[7] Ward's response was to treat the mind as a historical and evolutionary phenomenon, whose content in its contemporary manifestation began neither as a Lockean *tabula rasa* nor as the product of transcendental categories. In *Heredity and Memory*, a lecture delivered in 1912, he argued that psychology had to take account of the influence of heredity, because 'provided we look at the world from what I would call a spiritualistic and not from the usual naturalistic standpoint, psychology may shew us that the secret of heredity is to be found in the facts of memory'.[8] Memory, Ward suggested, was not merely personal, because humanity's spiritual evolution can only be understood if we accept 'the inheritance of the permanent achievements of one generation by the next' (*HM*, 12). By the workings of what Ward calls the 'law of habit' – that is, the gradual mechanization of action by repetition until it becomes a skill which needs no conscious reflection – a

---

[7] For an account of Ward as part of the 'English' tradition, see G. Dawes Hicks, 'The Philosophy of James Ward', *Mind*, New Series, Vol. 34, No. 135 (July 1925), 280–99: '... he approached the discussion of philosophical problems, as the leaders of the English empirical school had always approached them, from the basis of a psychological analysis of the individual mind. Not that he ever committed their mistake of regarding the critical investigation of knowledge as a psychological problem; he had learnt too thoroughly the lesson of Kant for that. But he realised, early, I think, in his career, that the two ways of dealing with the nature of experience, essentially distinct though they are, must necessarily throw light on one another, and that for a complete treatment of human knowledge we need to employ both. And, so far as psychology itself is concerned, the standpoint of Locke, Berkeley and Hume seemed to him to be the proper standpoint' (281).

[8] James Ward, *Heredity and Memory, being the Henry Sidgwick Memorial Lecture delivered at Newnham College, 9 November 1912* (Cambridge: Cambridge University Press, 1913), 6; hereafter cited in the text as *HM*.

single individual who lived as long as humanity had existed would become increasingly more proficient at tasks he or she had done before. Equally, evolution works by transforming the acquired skills of one generation into bodily and mental capacities that are passed on to succeeding generations. As Ward explains it in his article in the *Encyclopaedia Britannica*,

> What was experienced in the past has become instinct in the present. The descendant has not consciousness of his ancestors' failures when performing by 'an untaught ability' what they slowly and painfully found out. But if we are to attempt to follow the genesis of mind from its earliest dawn it is the primary experience rather than the eventual instinct that we have first of all to keep in view. To this end, then, it is proposed to assume that we are dealing with one individual which continuously advanced from the beginning of psychical life, and not with a series of individuals of which all save the first have inherited certain capacities from its progenitors. The life-history of such an imaginary individual, that is to say, would correspond with all that was new, all that could be called evolution or development, in a certain typical series of individuals each of whom advanced a certain stage in mental differentiation.[9]

Ward envisaged humanity as a whole starting like a Lockean individual, its mind a *tabula rasa*, but through genetic inheritance acquiring the 'innate ideas' that the empiricist tradition had begun by denying. Thus Kantians would be correct in believing that the mind is structured by categories which have never been part of the (modern) individual's experience; they are wrong in thinking, however, that these are universal and transcendental categories to which the human mind is necessarily subject: they are, rather, the historical and contingent categories produced by the 'engrams'[10] – memories written into the body – laid down by the 'sensational' experiences of our distant ancestors. Ward points to the fact that the embryos of modern species recapitulate in brief the whole history of the development of that species, and though 'it took thousands of

---

[9] James Ward, 'Psychology', *Encyclopaedia Britannica*, Vol. XX (Edinburgh: A. & C. Black, 1886), 44–5.

[10] Ward attributes the term 'engram' to Professor R. Semon of Munich in *Die Mneme als erhaltendes Prinzip im Wechsel des organischen Gechehens* (1908), though the notion of 'organic memory' he attributes to 'Professor Ewald Hering in a lecture, *Concerning Memory as a general function of Organized Matter*, delivered at Vienna in 1870' (*HM*, 27).

years, say, to produce the first chicken, . . . the hen's egg reaches the same level in three weeks' (*HM*, 17). The 'doctrine of the inheritance of acquired characters' is, Ward insists, not only Aristotle's and Lamarck's theory, but Darwin's as well (*HM*, 20), and Ward accuses evolutionary theorists of having neglected this fact: 'Imagine then,' he suggests, 'what would happen if now from this time forth every new generation had to begin where the old *began* and not where it left off; if no single human product from now onwards outlasted the individual who produced it; if in short all tradition and inheritance were from henceforth no more' (*HM*, 35). This is the condition to which we would be reduced if we accepted the neo-darwinian assertion that it is impossible for offspring to inherit the acquired characteristics of their parents. For Ward, however, the slate is not wiped clean with each new birth: each generation acquires some portion of the mental habits of its predecessor which have just as much a structuring effect on our consciousness as the Kantian categories. This 'psychological or mnemic theory of heredity' (*HM*, 42–3) underpins the notion of an 'organic memory' (*HM*, 43) inherent in the body – 'in short, what habit is for individual life that is heredity for racial life' (*HM*, 52). We are born not as a *tabula rasa* but as already written over by the 'engrams' of 'pre-natal, so to say, prehistoric life' (*HM*, 51). We are, quite literally, the 'mnemic' residue of our forebears, and our memories, like our bodies, cannot help but recapitulate the whole history – and indeed the 'prehistory' – of humanity.

Even although Ward claimed to be going beyond the associationism of the Mills and Bain – 'great as are the advances that psychology owes to the doctrine of association, the time has come to question its finality and to circumscribe its range'[11] – the 'Lockean' basis of his theory, as with so many of the psychologies of the late nineteenth century, discarded the 'atomism' of the associationists only by reincorporating association itself into a more complex framework. Ward challenges 'atomism' by insisting that we never 'experience a mere sensation of colour, sound, touch, and the like; and what the young student mistakes for such is really a perception, a sensory presentation combined with various sensory and motor presentations and with representations – and having thus a definiteness and completeness only possible to complex presentations' (*PP*, 46). Even the simplest sensation is part of a 'presentational continuum', and the simplest connection within this continuum is not 'association' but what Ward calls, after Herbert Spencer,

---

[11] James Ward, *Psychological Principles* (Cambridge: Cambridge University Press, 1918), 191; hereafter cited in the text as *PP*.

'assimilation', 'a process much simpler and more fundamental than association' (*PP*, 82–83) and 'which – so far from being the form of true association – is presupposed in all association properly so called' (*PP*, 83). Significantly, however, Spencer's own definition of 'assimilation' is 'automatic association' (*PP*, 83), so that no sooner is association cast out as the fundamental element in the workings of the mind than it is reincorporated under a new rubric. Equally, at the level of the mind's most complex operation, the presentational continuum continues to operate *as if* by the power of association, though in this case the connections between experiences are actually being shaped by *dissociation*. Thus, when we recall events from the past we prevent their evanescence, but as a consequence 'the reduplicated portions of the train are strengthened' (*PP*, 62) and become connected together in ways which did not exist in the original experience: the end result is, 'by partial and more or less frequent reduplications of the train upon itself to convert it into a partially new continuum' which Ward describes as the 'ideational continuum' (*PP*, 62). This set of 'ideal' connections between elements in our memory is produced not *by* association but by the *decay* of the original associations which held the elements together:

> Thus as the joint effect of obliviscence and reduplication we are provided with a flow of ideas distinct from the memory-train and thereby with the material, already more or less organized, for volitional and intellectual manipulation. We do not experience this flow – save very momentarily and occasionally – altogether undisturbed; even in dreams and reverie it is continually interrupted and diverted. Nevertheless it is not difficult to ascertain that, so far as it is left to itself, it takes a very different course from that which we should have to retrace if bent on reminiscence and able to recollect perfectly. (*PP*, 62)

The unpredictable connections produced by *association* are matched by the equally unpredictable connections generated by the *dissociation* of the original memory train, and it is this associated-and-dissociated 'flow' of past experience, continually changing with each return of its elements, through which each of us responds to the events of our immediate experience. 'Association', in other words, remains fundamental to the workings of the human mind even when association*ism* – defined as atomistic psychology – is under challenge.

This is particularly so in the case of aesthetic experience, and Ward's account of it is thoroughly associationist:

Perhaps of all aesthetical principles the most wide-reaching, as well as practically the most important, is that which explains aesthetic effects by association. Thus, to take one example where so many are possible, the croaking of frogs and the monotonous ditty of the cuckoo owe their pleasantness, not directly to what they are in themselves, but entirely to their intimate association with spring-time and gladness. At first it might seem, therefore, that there is nothing fresh in this principle . . . But this is not altogether true: aesthetic effects call up not merely ideas but ideals. A great work of art improves upon the real in two respects: it intensifies and it transfigures. It is for art to gather, into one focus, cleared from dross and commonplace, the genial memories of a lifetime, the instinctive memories of a race . . . (PP, 70)

In art the 'ideational continuum' becomes a continuum of ideals in which are fused not only the key memories of individual experience but the 'instinctive memories of a race' – 'a wider range and flow of pleasing ideas than we can ordinarily command' (PP, 70). Art depends upon the activation of a memory which can call on those engrams and operates in the same fashion as heredity: each work of art recapitulates in the moment of its creation – like the embryo of the chicken – the whole history of the evolution which made it possible. The canon of art, too, is an 'ideal continuum' in a communal memory which is structured only by its most significant moments, relegating to obliviscence all that has not been returned to with regularity, and constructing relations between the significant moments which have no reality in any original experience but which operate as an 'ideal' chain of associations reconfigured when the individual links in the actual chain have been forgotten.

II

Ward's article on 'Psychology' was being written almost contemporaneously with those on 'Taboo' and on 'Totemism' commissioned from his close friend, James Frazer. It was on a walking tour of Spain in 1883 that Ward encouraged Frazer to take up the study of primitive mythology, a study which was to dominate Frazer's life and to lead to the many versions of The Golden Bough Frazer composed between 1890 and 1922. Frazer's account of the primitive mind drew on one side from the work of Robertson Smith on the evolution of religion and, on the other, from Ward's psychology. For Frazer, the history of the human mind in its progress from magic, to religion, and on to science could be explained entirely on the basis of association. Indeed, Ward's description of the process of association and dissociation in the memory chain underlies Frazer's explanation of the evolution of totemism into polytheism:

> . . . the tribal totem tends to pass into an anthropomorphic god. And as he rises more and more into human form, so the subordinate totems sink from the dignity of incarnations into the humbler character of favourites and clients; until, at a later age, the links which bound them to the god having wholly faded from memory, a generation of mythologists arises who seek to patch up the broken chain by the cheap method of symbolism. But symbolism is only the decorous though transparent veil which a refined age loves to throw over its own ignorance of the past.[12]

The 'links' of the 'broken chain' having 'faded from memory', in exactly the process of obliviscence and dissociation which Ward describes, a new set of connecting links – of possible associations – between the remaining elements have to be *forged* by mythologists. Mythology is the retrospective reconstruction of a substitute set of associations to replace those which once formed an orderly (if not a rational) chain of connections in the mind of the savage. The business of the anthropologist is to get behind the work of the mythologists and to reconstruct the actual associations by which the savage mind apprehended the world. It is a business fraught with difficulty but underpinned by those 'engrams' through which the experience of each generation is written into the body of its successors:

> Thus from an examination, first, of savagery and, second, of its survivals in civilisation, the study of Social Anthropology attempts to trace the early history of human thought and institutions. The history can never be complete, unless indeed science should discover some mode of reading the faded record of the past of which we in this generation can hardly dream. We know indeed that every event, however insignificant, implies a change, however slight, in the material constitution of the universe, so that the whole history of the world is, in a sense, engraved upon its face, though our eyes are too dim to read the scroll.[13]

---

[12] J. G. Frazer, *The Golden Bough* (Edinburgh: Canongate, 2004; 1890), 787.
[13] Ibid., 861.

The past of humanity, 'engraved upon its face', makes the savage 'a human document',[14] but one whose meanings we can barely discern. What remains is the 'Comparative Method', by which 'we can to a certain extent, by comparing [savages] with each other, construct a scale of social progression and mark out roughly some of the stages on the long road that leads from savagery to civilisation': thus, 'in the kingdom of mind such a scale of mental evolution answers to the scale of morphological evolution in the animal kingdom'.[15]

To trace that 'mental evolution' the analyst required an understanding of the universal principles of the psyche and these, for Frazer, were provided by associationism.[16] Primitive magic was nothing more than a confusion of the fundamental forms of association originally described by Hume – association by similarity, association by contiguity and the association which we treat as causal. In the savage mind associations of similarity and of contiguity are assumed to be the same as causal connections, so that it is possible to explain, and, therefore to intervene in, the world by recognising or replicating similarities (wax figures representing one's enemies) or by the repetition of contiguities (fertility is increased or blighted by contact with certain people or animals). 'The fatal flaw of magic lies not in its general assumption of a sequence of events determined by law', Frazer insists, but in mistakenly applying 'one or other of two great fundamental laws of thought, namely, the association ideas by similarity and the association of ideas by contiguity in time and space':

A mistaken association of similar ideas produces homeopathic or imitative magic: a mistaken association of contiguous ideas produces contagious magic. The principles of association are excellent in themselves, and indeed absolutely essential to the working of the human mind. Legitimately applied they yield science; illegitimately applied they yield magic, the bastard sister of science.[17]

---

[14] Ibid., 862.

[15] Ibid.

[16] Frazer's debt to associationism has been noted, for instance, by Gillian Beer; see 'Speaking for the Others: Relativism and Authority in Victorian Anthropological Literature', in Robert Fraser (ed.), *Sir James Frazer and the Literary Imagination: Essays in Affinity and Influence* (London: Macmillan, 1990), 41ff.

[17] J. G. Frazer, *The Golden Bough* (one-volume edition; London: Macmillan, 1922), 49–50.

Mistaking the 'subjective' associations produced by similarity and contiguity for the 'objective' associations of causality; recreating past associations through the lens of 'mythology' in order to account for the dissociations produced by evanescence; reiterating and elaborating associations in the hope of making their connections more universal – all trap the savage mind in a chaos of error. Indeed, it is precisely to this 'chaos' that Frazer's critics pointed as the disabling weakness of his theory: as Evans-Pritchard puts it, 'if primitive man really mistook an ideal connection for a real one and confused subjective with objective experience, his life would be a chaos. He could not exist . . .' Coleridge's 'phantasmal chaos' returns as the unacceptable condition from which 'mind' as we know it could never have emerged: 'in a world so conceived almost everything would all the time be affecting almost everything else, and all would be chaos'.[18] Since progress from such chaos would have been impossible the fact that progress *has* been possible proves that chaos cannot have been the truth of that earlier phase of the human mind.

Frazer's critics, however, fail to take account of the depth of his Humean scepticism, for Frazer accepts that progress may itself be only an illusion and that our 'science', based on supposedly 'objective' causality, may be no more than an effect of association, no less illusory than the primitive connections to which we feel ourselves so superior. Modern science may appear to be the recovery of the power of magic, so potent is its ability to transform reality but, as Frazer sceptically predicts at the conclusion of the 1922 edition of *The Golden Bough*, science itself may be discovered to be simply another error, and an error which we will be happy to dispense with, since the world that science offers us is a bleak and painful one compared to the riches of the magical world:

> The dreams of magic may one day be the waking realities of science. But a dark shadow lies athwart the far end of this fair prospect. For however vast the increase in knowledge and of power which the future may have in store for man, he can scarcely hope to stay the sweep of those great forces which seem to be making silently but relentlessly for the destruction of

---

18 Both quotations are cited by David Richards, 'A Tour of Babel', in Robert Fraser (ed.), *Sir James Frazer and the Literary Imagination*; Edward Evans-Pritchard, *A History of Anthropological Thought* (London: Faber and Faber, 1981), 150; John Skorupski, *Symbol and Theory: A Philosophical Study of Theories of Religion in Social Anthropology* (Cambridge: Cambridge University Press, 1976), 138.

all this starry universe in which our earth swims as a speck or mote . . .
Yet the philosopher who trembles at the idea of such distant catastrophes
may console himself by reflecting that these gloomy apprehensions, like
the earth and sun themselves, are only parts of that unsubstantial world
which thought has conjured up out of the void, and that the phantoms
which the subtle enchantress has evoked to-day she may ban to-morrow.
They too, like so much that to common eyes seems solid, may melt into
air, into thin air.[19]

The 'chaos' of magic may, in fact, be preferable to the 'truths' of science;
and the 'truths' of science may be based merely on the false premise that
'causality' is something quite different from 'association'. Frazer, like Hume,
discovers that the 'reason' by which he banishes superstition turns itself into
a superstition: the world of science is not only an evolutionary development from the world of magic, it is still, like magic, 'conjured up out of
the void'. The associational mistakes that characterise savage magic may, in
fact, be continued in those associations which modern science believes itself
to have established as properly 'causes': 'I am too familiar with the hydra
of error', Frazer wrote in his 'Preface', 'to expect that by lopping off one of
the monster's heads I can prevent another, or even the same, from sprouting
again'.[20] He was referring to his critics' errors but the power of association
to produce false connections continually threatened to undermine the discoveries made possible by the 'science' of the 'comparative method' – what,
after all, were his comparisons based on but associations by similarity drawn
from the memory of J. G. Frazer, associations which were themselves only
too like 'that large class of myths which are made up to explain the origin of
a religious ritual and have no other foundation than the resemblance, real or
imaginary, which may be traced between it and some foreign ritual'?[21] Take,
for instance, Frazer's original account of the Druid fire festivals in which,
every five years, living victims were sacrificed:

besides these quinquennial festivals, celebrated on so grand a scale and
with, apparently, so large an expenditure of human life, it seems reasonable to suppose that festivals of the same sort, only on a lesser scale, were

[19] Frazer, *The Golden Bough* (1922), 713.
[20] Ibid., vii.
[21] Ibid., 5.

held annually, and that from these annual festivals are lineally descended some at least of the fire-festivals which, with their traces of human sacrifices, are still celebrated year by year in many parts of Europe. The gigantic images constructed of osiers or covered with grass in which the Druids enclosed their victims remind us of the leafy framework in which the human representative of the tree-spirit is still so often encased. Considering, therefore, that the fertility of the land was apparently supposed to depend upon the due performance of these sacrifices, Mannhardt is probably right in viewing the Celtic victims, cased in osiers and grass, as representatives of the tree-spirit or spirit of vegetation.[22]

We move from 'apparently' through 'it seems reasonable to suppose' to the assertion that *some* of the modern fire festivals *must* be descended from these Druidic performances – a fragile chain of connections which will reach its tentative conclusion – 'Mannhardt is *probably* right' – only by way of a personal association: – 'the gigantic images . . . *remind* us of the leafy framework'. The apparent impersonality of 'us' cannot conceal that Frazer's reconstruction of the associations by which the primitive mind connected together the elements of its world is itself an associative structure, drawn from the vast personal storehouse of myth in Frazer's own memory, and yet appealing to his readers to trace in themselves those same associations, those same engrams written into their 'organic memory'. As Robert Fraser puts it, 'the book's strength seems to be this: that, as the pages unfurl, each of its readers out of his very individual experience, evinces the distinct impression that he is remembering something'.[23]

What *The Golden Bough* provided for its readers was a model of the human mind bound together by associations rooted in prehistory, and a demonstration of how the fragmentary remains of ancient rites and myths could be reconstructed by retracing their (possible) associative interconnections. And what it suggested, was the power of those ancient associations – the 'engrams' of prehistory – to resist the progressive development of civilisation: on the *tabula* of the mind later writing does not obscure or obliterate earlier texts – rather, it is the later writing that fades rapidly to leave only the outlines of an almost forgotten script:

---

[22] Frazer, *The Golden Bough* (2004), 592–3.

[23] Robert Fraser, 'The Face Beneath the Text', in Robert Fraser (ed.), *Sir James Frazer and the Literary Imagination*, 13.

The reason why the higher forms of superstition or religion (for the religion of one generation is apt to become the superstition of the next) are less permanent than the lower is simply that the higher beliefs, being a creation of superior intelligence, have little hold on the minds of the vulgar, who nominally profess them for a time in conformity with the will of their betters, but readily shed them and forget them as soon as these beliefs have gone out of fashion with the educated classes. But while they dismiss without a pang or an effort articles of faith which were only superficially imprinted on their minds by the weight of cultured opinion, the ignorant and foolish multitude cling with a sullen determination to far grosser beliefs which really answer to the coarser texture of their undeveloped intellect. Thus while the avowed creed of the enlightened minority is constantly changing under the influence of reflection and enquiry, the real, though unavowed, creed of the mass of mankind appears to be almost stationary, and the reason why it alters so little is that in the majority of men, whether they are savages or outwardly civilised beings, intellectual progress is so slow as to be hardly perceptible.[24]

Progress is largely an illusion: the mass of humanity are not only engraved with a psychological 'prehistory' but continue actually and actively to live in that prehistory:

When we survey the existing races of mankind from Greenland to Tierra del Fuego, or from Scotland to Singapore, we observe that they are distinguished one from the other by a great variety of religions, and that these distinctions are not, so to speak, merely coterminous with the broad distinctions of race, but descend into the minuter subdivisions of states and commonwealths, nay, they honeycomb the town, the village, and even the family, so that the surface of society all over the world is cracked and seamed, sapped and mined with rents and fissures and yawning crevasses opened up by the disintegrating influence of religious dissensions. Yet when we have penetrated through these differences, which affect mainly the intelligent and thoughtful part of the community, we shall find underlying them all a solid stratum of intellectual agreement among the dull, the weak, the ignorant, and the superstitious, who constitute, unfortunately, the vast majority of mankind . . . It is beneath our feet – and not very far

---

[24] Frazer, *The Golden Bough* (1922), 861.

beneath them – here in Europe at the present day, and it crops up on the surface in the heart of the Australian wilderness and wherever the advent of a higher civilisation has not crushed it underground. This universal faith, this truly Catholic creed, is a belief in the efficacy of magic.[25]

For Frazer, the analysis of the savage mind was increasingly *not* the reconstruction of a conjectural history of humanity's progress towards civilisation: its achievement, rather, is 'to run shafts down into this low mental stratum' and 'to discover its substantial identity everywhere'.[26] 'It is not our business here', he comments, 'to consider what bearing the permanent existence of such a solid layer of savagery beneath the surface of society, and unaffected by the superficial changes of religion and culture, has upon the future of humanity', but,

> The dispassionate observer, whose studies have led him to plumb its depths, can hardly regard it otherwise than as a standing menace to civilisation. We seem to move on a thin crust which may at any moment be rent by the subterranean forces slumbering below. From time to time a hollow murmur underground or a sudden spirt of flame into the air tells of what is going on beneath our feet.[27]

The 'Age of Religion' may have been everywhere 'preceded by an Age of Magic', but magic remains more potent: 'systematic enquiries carried on among the less educated classes, and especially among the peasantry, of Europe have revealed the astonishing, nay, alarming truth that a mass, if not the majority, of people in every civilised country is still living in a state of intellectual savagery'.[28] And magic retains its potency because it has its 'roots deep down in the mental framework and constitution of the great majority of mankind'[29] – deep down, in other words, in the psychological activity of association.

It is entirely appropriate then, that when, W. B. Yeats, one of Frazer's most purposeful readers in the 1890s, writes about his belief in magic he combines it with a conception of an engramic memory that is structured on associationist

---

[25] Ibid., 55–6.
[26] Ibid.
[27] Ibid., 56.
[28] Frazer, 'The Scope of Social Anthropology', *The Golden Bough* (2004), 860.
[29] Frazer, *The Golden Bough* (1922), 59.

principles. He offers 'three doctrines, which have, as I think, been handed down from early times, and been the foundations of nearly all magical practices':

(1) That the borders of our mind are ever shifting and that many minds can flow into one another, as it were, and create or reveal a single mind, a single energy.

(2) That the borders of our memories are as shifting, and that our memories are a part of one great memory, the memory of Nature herself.

(3) That this great mind and great memory can be evoked by symbols.[30]

The power of symbols derives from the fact that 'the Great Memory associates them with certain events and moods and persons', and such symbols are 'of all kinds, for everything in heaven or earth has its association, momentous or trivial, in the Great Memory'.[31] Such beliefs have led generations of critics to see Yeats as an eccentric or eclectic thinker, constructing theories in defiance of contemporary science, and indeed Yeats dramatises himself as in opposition to all modern thought: ' . . . if some philosophic idea interested me, I tried to trace it back to its earliest use, believing that there must be a tradition of belief older than any European Church, and founded upon the experience of the world before the modern bias'.[32] Yeats's theories of the mind, however, share a great deal with Ward's psychology: that 'memory of Nature the visionaries claim for the foundation of their knowledge'[33] is very little different from Ward's 'psychological or mnemic theory of heredity' (HM 42–3), and, if we substitute 'engram' for 'Anima Mundi', Ward would have entirely agreed with Yeats's belief that a 'bird's instinct proved the existence of the Anima Mundi, with its ideas and memories'.[34] Equally, Yeats's view of myth is closely aligned with Frazer's associationist account, since both Frazer and Yeats were engaged in constantly translating back and forth between the language of empirical psychology and the language of magic: 'All sounds, all colours, all forms,' Yeats declared in 1900, 'either because of their pre-ordained energies or because of long association, evoke indefinable and yet precise emotions, or, as I prefer to think, call down among us certain disembodied powers, whose footsteps

---

[30] W. B. Yeats, 'Magic', *Essays and Introductions* (London: Macmillan, 1961), 28.

[31] Ibid., 50.

[32] Yeats, 'Hodos Chameliontos', *Autobiographies*, 265.

[33] Yeats, 'The Philosophy of Shelley's Poetry', *Essays and Introductions*, 74.

[34] Ibid., 265.

over our hearts we call emotions'.[35] 'Long association' becomes a 'disembodied power' just as, for Frazer, the two principles of the magician's power – homeopathic magic and contagious magic – are nothing else but 'different misapplications of the association of ideas'.[36] The similarities intensify when one considers that Frazer, like Yeats, was disposed to set his theories within a philosophy of history which was cyclical – 'human affairs, like the courses of the heaven, seem to run in cycles: the social pendulum swings to and fro from one extremity of the scale to the other: in the political sphere it has swung from democracy to despotism, and back again from despotism to democracy'[37] – and maintained a theory of society much closer to a Nietzschean 'will to power' than to a democratic liberalism: 'the community', he insists, is everywhere 'dominated by the will of an enlightened minority even in countries where the ruling power is nominally vested in the hands of the numerical majority' because, 'disguise it as we may, the government of mankind is always and everywhere essentially aristocratic'.[38]

Their associationism also united them in a profound fear of the breakdown of memory and of the loss of those associations that can connect our passing, individual experiences with the contents of the 'Great Memory' and the significance of the 'engram'. Thus Yeats believed that the conflict in which he was engaged in Ireland was between those who valued memory and those who had lost it: 'we had opposing us from the first, though not strongly from the first, a type of mind which had been without influence in the generation of Grattan, and almost without influence in that of Davis, and which has made a new nation of Ireland, that was once old and full of memories'.[39] An Ireland 'full of memories' is an Ireland in which poetry connects with ancient religion because poets, like 'the makers of religions' have 'gathered into their ceremonies the ceremonies of more ancient faiths, for fear a grain of the dust turned into crystal in some past fire, a passion that had mingled with the religious idea, might perish if the ancient ceremony perished'.[40] The urgency of such recollection has a far more pragmatic interest for Frazer, whose concern was the loss of the evidence – 'fragmentary and dubious as it is' – which allows us to peer into the 'measureless past of human life on

---

[35] Yeats, 'The Symbolism of Poetry', *Essays and Introductions*, 156–7.

[36] Frazer, *The Golden Bough* (1922), 12.

[37] Frazer, 'The Scope of Social Anthropology', *The Golden Bough* (2004), 855.

[38] Ibid.

[39] Yeats, 'Poetry and Tradition', *Essays and Introductions*, 250.

[40] Yeats, 'Ireland the Arts', *Essays and Introductions*, 203.

earth'. [41] For Frazer, the 'organic memory' of the savage – no matter how appalling in its content – was 'a record of man's efforts to raise himself above the level of the beast', and the very fragility of those records has established them, in the late nineteenth century, as 'among the most precious archives of humanity': 'They were neglected and despised when they might have been obtained complete; and now wise men would give more than a king's ransom for their miserably mutilated and imperfect remains'.[42] It was for such 'mutilated and imperfect remains' that Yeats and Lady Gregory went in search in the West of Ireland, remnants of an alternative way of experiencing the world to that of 'the mechanical logic and commonplace eloquence'[43] of the modern nation:

> I lived amid mystery. It seemed as if these people possessed an ancient knowledge. Ah, if we could but speak face to face with those they spoke to. 'That old man,' Lady Gregory said to me of an old man who passed us in the wood, 'may have the mystery of the ages.'[44]

Yeats desired *contact* with 'the mystery of the ages' in order to acquire the secret of the primitive; Frazer wanted to unravel that mystery and so reveal the superiority of enlightened humanity. Just, however, as Frazer's account of the survival of magic among the modern masses undermined the security of progressive history, so his conception of science undermined the certainty of the march away from savagery. According to his Gifford lectures, intellectual progress is achieved when 'the mind, in obedience to a fundamental law, seeks to form a conception which will simplify, and if possible unify, the multitudinous and seemingly heterogeneous phenomena of nature';[45] but the possibility of such 'progress' is continually put in doubt by his scepticism:

> Thus alike in regard to the organic and inorganic world the science of today has attained to that unity and simplicity of conception which the human intellect imperiously demands if it is to comprehend in some measure the infinite complexity of the universe, or rather of its shadows reflected on the illumined screen of the mind. Yet, as that complexity is

---

[41] Frazer, 'The Scope of Anthropology', *The Golden Bough* (2004), 862.
[42] Ibid., 863.
[43] Yeats, *Memoirs*, 178.
[44] Ibid., 126.
[45] Frazer, 'The Worship of Nature', *The Golden Bough* (2004), 871.

infinite, so the search for the ultimate unity is probably endless also. For we may suspect that the finality, which seems to crown the vast generalisations of science, is after all only illusory, and that the tempting unity and simplicity which they offer to the weary mind are not the goal but only halting-places in the unending march.[46]

Simplicity may not be an end be but may be only a route back towards complexity: in the case, for instance, of atoms, 'may it not be that each of these tiny suns comprises within itself a still tinier sun, or rather an incalculable number of such suns in the shape of atoms, and that in every one of these atoms of an atom a solar system, nay a whole starry universe, a miniature copy of ours, with all its wealth of vegetable and animal life, is, like our own, in a process of evolution and decay?'[47] And then, too, 'we must constantly bear in mind that the atoms and electrons into which modern science resolves the material world are as truly beyond the reach of our senses as are gnomes and fairies, and any other spiritual beings'.[48] If Frazer's scepticism drives him to deny simplicity in favour of an exfoliating complexity in which the supernatural may be ultimately no less real than the 'reality' of science, Yeats's belief in the supernatural was constantly challenged from the other direction, by a scepticism which exerted itself particularly on those – even those closest to him – whom he suspected of a too easy acceptance of the truths of a spiritual world:

> [George Russell] spoke of reincarnation, and Maud Gonne asked him, 'How soon a child was reborn, and if [reborn] where?' He said, 'It may be reborn in the same family.' I could see that Maud Gonne was deeply impressed, and I quieted my more sceptical intelligence, as I have so often done in her presence. I remember a pang of conscience. Ought I not to say, 'The whole doctrine of the reincarnation of the soul is hypothetical. It is the most plausible of the explanations of the world, but can we say more than that?' or some like sentence?[49]

Frazer's science, like Yeats's supernatural, rests equally on foundations that are no better than 'hypothetical': 'from their customs, beliefs, and traditions

---

[46] Ibid., 872.
[47] Ibid., 880.
[48] Ibid., 879.
[49] Yeats, *Memoirs*, 48.

as a solid basis of fact', Frazer declares, 'the anthropologist may work back a little way hypothetically through the obscurity of the past'[50] but 'we must be content with a very brief, imperfect, and in large measure conjectural account of man's mental and social development in prehistoric ages'.[51]

Warwick Gould has suggested that Frazer and Yeats 'faced each other across an enormous intellectual chasm', because Frazer was 'an associationist, a rationalist, with a Whig theory of history and evolutionary model of human development',[52] but as we have seen, Frazer's theory of history was far less optimistic than this suggests, and if Yeats, as Gould suggests, 'knew his apocalyptic was a critique of what to him was the Victorian "myth" of progress',[53] then Frazer's account of the survival of magic was no less decisive in undermining that myth. In *Aftermath*, a final supplementary compilation of yet more evidence about the pervasive delusions into which the human mind is drawn, he declared that he was 'led on, step by step, into surveying, as from some specular height, some Pisgah of the mind, a great part of the human race; I was beguiled, as by some subtle enchanter, into inditing what I cannot but regard as a dark, a tragic chronicle of human error and folly, of fruitless endeavour, wasted time, and blighted hopes'. The effort rationally to annotate all the irrationalisms of human history becomes itself a 'tragic chronicle' of 'fruitless endeavour, wasted time', however much Frazer might have hoped that his researches would 'serve as a warning, as a sort of Ariadne's thread, to help the forlorn wayfarer to shun some of the snares and pitfalls into which his fellows have fallen before him in the labyrinth of life'.[54] That the myth of the labyrinth becomes an explanation of the labyrinthine myths in which Frazer found himself enmeshed reveals the fundamental duality that made *The Golden Bough* so powerful: it sceptically unveiled the foundations of myths, legends and rituals to discover that it was only by means of the myths themselves that their falsehood could be comprehended. Far from being a rationalist believer in a 'linear, culminative model of history',[55] Frazer's associationism led him to see himself as a kind of magician, because all human – or, perhaps, we should say Humean – perception involved a kind of magic:

---

50 Frazer, 'The Scope of Social Anthropology', *The Golden Bough* (2004), 854.
51 Ibid., 861.
52 Warwick Gould, 'Frazer and Yeats', in Robert Fraser (ed.), *Sir James Frazer and the Literary Imagination* (London: Macmillan, 1990), 137.
53 Ibid.
54 J. G. Frazer, *Aftermath* (London: Macmillan, 1936), vi.
55 Gould, 'Frazer and Yeats', *Sir James Frazer and the Literary Imagination*, 137.

. . . every one of us is perpetually, every hour of the day, implicitly constructing a purely imaginary world behind the immediate sensations of light and colour, of touch, of sound, and of scent which are all that we truly apprehend; and oddly enough it is this visionary world, the creation of thought, which we dub the real world in contradistinction to the fleeting data of sense. Thus viewed, the mind of man may be likened to a wizard who, by the help of spirits or the waving of his magic wand, summons up scenes of enchantment which, deceived by the very perfection of his art, he mistakes for realities.[56]

What we take to be reality is only the 'ideal continuum' produced by the associations and dissociations of memory. The anthropologist and the poet both

> send imagination forth
> Under the day's declining beam, and call
> Images and memories
> From ruin or from ancient trees
> (W. B. Yeats, 'The Tower')[57]

because both are subject to the 'sudden conviction that our little memories are but a part of some great Memory that renews the world and men's thoughts age after age, and that our thoughts are not, as we suppose, the deep, but a little foam upon the deep'.[58] A classicist at heart, what remains for Frazer, as for Yeats, out of this wrack of time, is not scientific truth but poetic truth: 'Yes, the gods of Greece are gone', he writes, 'and only poets are left to mourn their departure', quoting Wordsworth as confirmation:

> 'Great God! I'd rather be
> A Pagan suckled in a creed outworn;
> So might I, standing on this pleasant lea,
> Have glimpses that would make me less forlorn;
> Have sight of Proteus rising from the sea;
> Or hear old Triton blow his wreathed horn.'[59]

---

[56] J. G. Frazer, *Aftermath*, vi.

[57] Yeats, *Collected Poems*, 219.

[58] Yeats, 'The Philosophy of Shelley's Poetry', *Essays and Introductions*, 79.

[59] Frazer, 'The Worship of Nature', *The Golden Bough* (2004), 877; *WW*, 270, 'The world is too much with us'.

Such nostalgia, however, reflects a profound sense that only art defies time and history:

> There are monuments, airy monuments, monuments of words, which seem so fleeting and evanescent, that will yet last when your cannons have crumbled and your flags have mouldered into dust. When the Roman poet wished to present an image of perpetuity, he said that he would be remembered so long as the Roman Empire endured . . . The Roman Empire itself has long passed away, like the empire of Alexander, like the empire of Charlemagne, like the empire of Spain, yet still amid the wreck of kingdoms the poet's monument stands firm, for still his verses are read and remembered.[60]

And such 'poetic truth' is founded on precisely the same workings as dominated the 'savage mind' for, as he quotes from a passage of W. Ellis's *Polynesian Researches*,

> By their rude mythology, each lovely island was made a sort of fairyland, and the spells of enchantment were thrown over its varied scenes. The sentiment of the poet that –
>> "Millions of spiritual creatures walk the earth,
>> Unseen, both when we wake and when we sleep,"
> was one familiar to their minds; and it is impossible not to feel interest in a people who were accustomed to consider themselves surrounded by invisible intelligences . . .[61]

While the progress of science is a 'process of despiritualising the universe',[62] by which both animism and poetry are evacuated of their significance, the 'idealism' of romantic poetry recuperates the 'animism' of the savage mind.

Thus it is that the form of Frazer's writing defies his scientific and progressive ideology: what he provides is, quite literally, the re-collection – and the recollection – of what modernity is trying to transcend and, in that transcendence, to erase from memory. Frazer's work declares the modern world to be necessarily amnesiac in its erasure of the savage past and yet defies

---

[60] Frazer, 'The Scope of Social Anthropology', *The Golden Bough* (2004), 866.
[61] Frazer, 'The Worship of Nature', *The Golden Bough* (2004), 873.
[62] Ibid., 877.

that amnesia by the sheer quantity of his evidence, the vast, 'multitudinous and seemingly heterogeneous phenomena'[63] which he tries to simplify into the unity of a science. Frazer might have aimed at providing 'that unity and simplicity of conception which the human intellect imperiously demands if it is to comprehend in some measure the infinite complexity of the universe',[64] since the theory of association allowed him to reduce the vast complexity of his mythic material to two simple principles – association by similarity and by contiguity – but rather than restraining associational activity and correcting its mistakes, Frazer's mythic material offered itself as a further stimulus to the associative activity of the modern poet and the modern reader: what he actually provided was fodder for 'poetry and imagination, always the children of far-off multitudinous things';[65] what he provided was a stream of new 'symbols that set the mind wandering from idea to idea, emotion to emotion'[66] – a vast new compendium of material available to the associating mind, and, in defiance of progressive theories of history, re-infusing modernity with the deepest deposits of the past. For Yeats, the problem with a poet like Shelley was that though 'he seems in his speculations to have lit on that memory of Nature the visionaries claim for the foundation of their knowledge', his 'ignorance of their more traditional forms, give some of his poetry an air of rootless fantasy'[67] because,

> It is only by ancient symbols, by symbols that have numberless meanings besides the one or two that the writer lays emphasis on, or the half-score he knows of, that any highly subjective artist can escape from the barrenness and shallowness of a too conscious arrangements, into the abundance and depth of Nature.[68]

Those 'numberless meanings' produce what Yeats describes as the 'emotion of multitude' and the 'emotion of multitude' is the highest achievement of art. It is, quite literally, an emotion which invokes or provokes a multitude of associations, and the more multitudinous it is, the more profound the aesthetic experience which accompanies it. Reading, for Yeats, is precisely the freeing of

---

[63] Frazer, 'The Worship of Nature', *The Golden Bough* (2004), 871.

[64] Ibid., 872.

[65] Yeats, 'Emotion of Multitude', *Essays and Introductions*, 215.

[66] Ibid., 216.

[67] Yeats, 'The Philosophy of Shelley's Poetry', *Essays and Introductions*, 74.

[68] Ibid., 87.

the associative process in order that we can allow it to escape from the confines of our knowledge and our will:

> One must allow the images to form with all their associations before one criticises. If you suspend the critical faculty, I have discovered, either as a result of training, or, if you have the gift, by passing into a slight trance, images pass rapidly before you. If you suspend also desire, and let them form of their own will, your absorption becomes complete and they are more clear in colour, more precise in articulation. But the images pass before you linked by certain associations, and indeed in the first instance you have called them up by their association with traditional forms and sounds.[69]

The technique of all great art is to stimulate that 'emotion of multitude'; the business of the reader is to have mind which can respond with a multitude of associations that pass beyond the limits of the personal into the 'pre-natal, so to say, prehistoric life' of Ward's 'engram'. Thus Shelley's poetry could become real to Yeats only when he was able to situate it within his own associational nexus and find connections that linked it to what he believed to be his own national traditions:

> I have re-read his *Prometheus Unbound* for the first time for many years, in the woods of Drim-na-Rod, among the Echtge hills, and sometimes I have looked towards Slieve ná nOg where the country people say the last battle of the world shall be fought till the third day, when a priest shall lift a chalice, and the thousand years of peace begin. And I think this mysterious song utters a faith as simple and as ancient as the faith of those country people, in a form suited to a new age . . .[70]

Becoming 'ancient' despite belonging to 'a new age', becoming Irish despite being English, becoming associated in Yeats's memory with his people's memories, Shelley's poem becomes effective art, capable of inducing, in an appropriate mind, the conjunction of the 'simple' and the 'multitudinous', of the modern with the ancient, of the mysterious with the lucid, that is the characteristic of all great art.

---

[69]   Yeats, 'Anima Mundi', *Mythologies*, 344.
[70]   Yeats, 'The Philosophy of Shelley's Poetry', *Essays and Introductions*, 77–8.

III

'The mythic method', T. S. Eliot declared in his review of Joyce's *Ulysses*, has 'the importance of a scientific discovery. No one else has built a novel upon such a foundation before'.[71] Eliot's summary of Joyce's achievement in combining elements of Homer's epic with a story of modern urban life – 'it is simply a way of controlling, of ordering, of giving a shape and a significance to the immense panorama of futility and anarchy which is contemporary history'[72] – has often been quoted, but its qualifications are less often noted. First, the mythic method is one 'already adumbrated by Mr Yeats, and of the need for which I believe Mr Yeats to have been the first contemporary to be conscious'; second, 'Psychology (such as it is, and whether our reaction be comic or serious), ethnology, and *The Golden Bough* have concurred to make possible what was impossible even a few years ago'.[73] For Eliot, Joyce's 'mythic method' stands on the shoulders of Yeats, Psychology, and Frazer, a triumvirate that might equally define the foundations of his own *The Waste Land*, published in 1922, with its famous footnote declaring that

> to another work of anthropology I am indebted in general, one which has influenced our generation profoundly; I mean *The Golden Bough*; I have used especially the two volumes *Adonis, Attis, Osiris*. Anyone who is acquainted with these works will immediately recognise in the poem certain references to vegetation ceremonies.[74]

And the associationist conception of the workings of the mind which Frazer's work implies is equally present in Eliot's note to line 46 of *The Waste Land*:

> I am not familiar with the exact constitution of the Tarot pack of cards, from which I have obviously departed to suit my own convenience. The Hanged Man, a member of the traditional pack, fits my purpose in two ways; because he is associated in my mind with the Hanged God of Frazer, and because I associate him with the hooded figure in the passage of the disciples to Emmaus in Part V . . . The Man with Three Staves (an

---

[71] T. S. Eliot, 'Ulysses, Order and Myth', *The Dial*, November 1923, LXXV, 5, 482.

[72] Ibid., 483.

[73] Ibid.

[74] T. S. Eliot, *Collected Poems 1909–1962* (London: Faber, 1963), 80.

authentic member of the Tarot pack) I associate, quite arbitrarily, with the Fisher King himself.[75]

The word 'associate' in this passage is not used casually by Eliot, for his early critical writings reveal his intimacy with the associationist tradition. In 1933, for instance, while trying to define the power of a certain kind of imagery, he pointed to 'its saturation – I will not say with "associations" for I do not want to revert to Hartley – but with feelings too obscure for the authors even to know what they were'.[76] Hartley is set aside in a gesture which effectively reinscribes associationism into Eliot's language of 'feelings', and in an essay from the 1940s, 'The Music of Poetry', Eliot is less hesitant about recuperating the associationist context: the 'music of poetry' he defines as 'a point of intersection: it arises from its relation first to the words immediately preceding and following it, and indefinitely to the rest of its context; and from another relation, that of its immediate meaning in that context to all the other meanings which it has had in other contexts, to its greater or less wealth of association'.[77] The music of poetry depends, in other words, on a version of Yeats's 'emotion of multitude' – on the wealth of associational recollection which the words of the poem are able to release in the reader.

Eliot's detailed knowledge of associationist psychology is also clear from his account of the achievement of F. H. Bradley, the English idealist philosopher on whom he wrote a dissertation at Oxford from 1911 to 1914.[78] In illustration of the power of Bradley's style, he chose a passage in which Bradley is attacking Alexander Bain's account of the workings of association with the aim of revealing the frailties of Mill's psychology; Eliot, however, does not let Bradley's criticisms stand unqualified but turns his discussion to a defence of Mill and Bain:

> People are inclined to believe that what Bradley did was demolish the logic of Mill and the psychology of Bain. If he had done that, it would have been a lesser service than what he has done; and if he had done that it would have been less of a service than people think, for there is

---

[75] Ibid., 80–1.

[76] T. S. Eliot, *The Use of Poetry and the Use of Criticism* (London: Faber, 1933), 147.

[77] T. S. Eliot, *On Poetry and Poets* (London: Faber, 1957), 32.

[78] Later published as *Knowledge and Experience in the Philosophy of F. H. Bradley* (London: Faber, 1964).

much that is good in the logic of Mill and the psychology of Bain. But Bradley did not attempt to destroy Mill's logic. Anyone who reads his own *Principles* will see that his force is directed not against Mill's logic as a whole but only against certain limitations, imperfections and abuses. He left the structure of Mill's logic standing, and never meant to do anything else.[79]

Mill's associationist logic and Bain's associationist psychology remain 'standing' even after Bradley's critique, and Eliot's support of them was made necessary precisely because his own criticism was so deeply dependent on the implications of associationist theory. In the influential essay on 'The Metaphysical Poets' (1920), for instance, it is in the language of association that Eliot seeks to account for the effects of the imagery of the Metaphysicals: 'we find, instead of the mere explication of the content of a comparison, a development by rapid association of thought which requires considerable agility on the part of the reader'.[80] The rapidity of the process of association is made even more demanding for the reader by the fact that the imagery entwines two different and conflicting trains of associations in a single image:

> some of Donne's most successful and characteristic effects are secured by brief words and sudden contrasts:
>> A bracelet of bright hair about the bone
> where the most powerful effect is produced by the sudden contrast of associations of 'bright hair' and of 'bone'. This telescoping of images and multiplied associations is characteristic . . .[81]

'Sudden contrasts of associations' produce precisely that multiplication of associational material that is required by Yeats's 'emotion of multitude', directly echoed in Eliot's 'multiplied associations'. And when, in 1917, Eliot chose his model of 'the perfect critic', he chose a French critic who had insisted on a return to the founding sources of British empiricism:

> La sensation est la base du tout, de la vie intellectuelle et morale aussi bien que de la vie physique. Deux cent cinquante ans après Hobbes, deux cent

---

[79] Eliot, 'Francis Herbert Bradley', *Selected Essays*, 448.
[80] Eliot, *Selected Essays*, 282.
[81] Ibid., 283.

ans après Locke, telle a été la puissance déstructive du kantisme réligieux, qu'on est réduit à insister sur d'aussi élémentaires aphorismes . . .[82]

The return to the empiricist sources of the mind in sensation was also a return to the associationist principles that explained how those sensations were combined into new and, in literary terms, surprising configurations. Modern poetry, for de Gourmont, was the product of 'association' and 'dissociation', the interweaving of the multitude of sensations associated in complex layers in the modern mind:

> Il nous est impossible de dissocier les images doubles ou triples qui naissent simultanément, a l'idée d'un fait, en nos cervaux troublés par des sensations tumultueuses; comme il était impossible à Homère d'opérer une association qui maintenant se fait toute seule et malgré nous.[83]

The importance of the 'image' – an importance that Eliot and Pound were to promote as the core of the poetic process – derived from the fact that it was the point of interaction between 'sensation' and 'emotion':

> Une idée n'est pas une chose immatérielle, il n'y a pas de choses immatérielles; c'est une image, mais usée et des lors sans force; elle n'est utilisable qu'associée à un sentiment, que 'devenue sentiment'.[84]

It is only by its associations that an image can become a sentiment and it is only by concentrating on the power of association that poetry can be

---

[82] Rémy de Gourmont, *Le Problème du Style* (Paris, 1902) 69; see Eliot, *The Sacred Wood* (London: Faber, 1920), 13: 'Sensation is at the base of everything, intellectual and moral life as well as physical. Two hundred and fifty years after Hobbes, two hundred years after Locke, such has been the destructive power of religious Kantianism, that one is reduced to insisting on such elementary aphorisms'.

[83] Rémy de Gourmont, *Le Problème du Style*, 89–90: 'It is impossible for us to dissociate those double or triple images which are born simultaneously, at the idea of a thing, in brains which are disturbed by a tumult of sensations; just as it was impossible for Homer to construct an association which now happens entirely by itself and without our intervention'.

[84] Ibid., 45. 'An idea is not an immaterial thing, there are no immaterial things; it is an image, but so well used that it is without impact; it cannot be used except by associating it with a feeling, so that it has "become feeling"'.

fully effective. Thus in 'Reflections on Contemporary Poetry' in 1917, Eliot suggests that 'it is unmistakably human to attach the strongest emotions to definite tokens' and distinguishes between poets according to their treatment of such attachments:

> [With Donne] the feeling and the material symbol preserve exactly their proper proportions. A poet of morbidly keen sensibilities but weak will might become absorbed in the hair to the exclusion of the original association which made it significant; the poet of imaginative and reflective power more than emotional power would endow the hair with ghostly or moralistic meaning. Donne sees the thing as it is . . .[85]

The 'thing as it is' is the thing in its associations, what Eliot described in his essay on 'Andrew Marvell' as 'the suggestiveness of true poetry', 'the aura around a bright clear centre',[86] phrases which echo Yeats's declaration that 'there cannot be great art without the little limited life of the fable, which is always better the simpler it is, and the rich, far-wandering, many-imaged life of the half-seen world beyond it'.[87]

If we return to Eliot's notes to *The Waste Land*, however, what is striking is his insistence on the *arbitrariness* of his associations with the figures from *The Golden Bough*. Yeats had read Shelley by a 'mythic method' which sought to establish common ground between Shelley's mythology, Yeats's knowledge of the occult tradition, and the traditions of Irish mythology. By revealing such interconnections, Shelley's poetry 'loses something of its appearance of idle fantasy',[88] and poet, poem and reader are united 'by ancient symbols, by symbols that have numberless meanings besides the one or two the writer lays emphasis on'.[89] Eliot's insistence that 'The Man with Three Staves (an authentic member of the Tarot pack) I associate, quite arbitrarily, with the Fisher King himself' reverses the technique of Yeats's 'mythic method' by insisting on the *privacy* of the ways in which myth is being exploited in *The Waste Land*. Far from providing the basis of a *common* mythology, the elements of Frazer's mythic narrative are being co-opted to a purely private set of associations. Unlike almost all associationist theorists from Hallam or Mill to Yeats, Eliot refuses to

---

[85] Eliot, 'Reflections on Contemporary Poetry', *The Egoist*, iv, 8 (1917), 118.

[86] Eliot, 'Andrew Marvell', *Selected Essays*, 300.

[87] Yeats, 'The Emotion of Multitude', *Essays and Introductions*, 216.

[88] Yeats, 'The Philosophy of Shelley's Poetry', *Essays and Introductions*, 87.

[89] Ibid., 87.

accept that the understanding of a poem rests on retracing the psychology of the poet. Even Yeats's reading of Shelley offers what he believed Shelley *would* have thought, had he properly studied the sources of his imagery in ancient mythology. What Eliot does share with Hallam, however, is the belief that the poet's mind is intrinsically different from 'ordinary' minds:

> When a poet's mind is perfectly equipped for its work, it is constantly amalgamating disparate experience; the ordinary man's experience is chaotic, irregular, fragmentary. The latter falls in love, or reads Spinoza, and these two experiences have nothing to do with each other, or with the noise of the typewriter or the smell of cooking; in the mind of the poet these experiences are always forming new wholes.[90]

In the poet's mind, everything is associated with everything else, creating (exactly as the Mills suggested, with their images of the wheel of colours producing the image of white or the fusion of chemicals to produce a new substance) 'new wholes'. Ordinary human beings, however, are just as remote from the proper *reading* of poetry as they are from the creation of it: in the reading of 'the ordinary emotional person', what takes place is simply 'the accidents of personal association',[91] whereas in the mind of the critic association takes an entirely different course:

> these suggestions made by a work of art, which are merely personal, become fused with a multitude of other suggestions from multitudinous experience, and result in a new object which is no longer purely personal, because it is a work of art itself.[92]

Just as the poet is someone capable of 'multitudinous' association, so the critic brings to the work of art a 'multitude of other suggestions from multitudinous experience' that are used not to empathise with the associative process of the poet but to make something which will 'result in a new object which is no longer purely personal'. In other words, the effective reading of a poem is *not* the effective understanding of the poet's associative processes: it is the construction of an original – indeed, even an 'arbitrary' – set of associations

---

[90] Ibid.
[91] Eliot, 'The Perfect Critic', *The Sacred Wood*, 7.
[92] Ibid., 7.

which form a new whole and constitute a new object. Ezra Pound's refrain, 'make it new' is, in Eliot's theorising, something that occurs with every successful reading of a poem: the linguistic elements of the work enter into a completely unforeseeable associational context to create a new object that is 'a work of art itself'.

What connects these two entirely different associational contexts is Eliot's conception of 'tradition', as laid out in that founding statement of Anglophone literary theory, 'Tradition and the Individual Talent' from 1919. It is an essay which recapitulates Eliot's associationist account of the poetic mind as 'a receptacle for seizing and storing up numberless feelings, phrases, images, which remain there until the particles which can unite to form a new compound are present together'.[93] Even down to the word 'compound' this would have sat comfortably in John Stuart Mill's, or even James Mill's, account of the way in which ideas 'run into one another, to coalesce as it were, and out of many form one idea; which idea, however in reality complex, appears to be no less simple, than any one of those of which it is compounded'.[94] What is different, however, from the Mills' conception of the psyche, is that Eliot invokes a transpersonal mind of the kind that Ward had posited in his 'Psychology' article in the *Encyclopaedia Britannica*:

> [The poet] must be aware that the mind of Europe – the mind of his own country – a mind which he learns to be much more important than his own private mind – is a mind which changes, and that change is a development which abandons nothing *en route*, which does not superannuate either Shakespeare, or Homer, or the rock drawing of the Magdalenian draughtsmen.[95]

Just as Ward's engrams connect the present back to the deepest sources of the emergence of humanity in prehistory, so tradition links the poet back to the earliest of prehistoric artistic achievements; and just as, for Ward, the 'mnemic theory of heredity' ensures the survival of 'all tradition and inheritance', so, for Eliot, the 'mind of Europe' is a mind which 'abandons nothing'. What is held in that European mind is 'the existing monuments' of the tradition which

---

[93] Eliot, 'Tradition and the Individual Talent', *Selected Essays*, 19.

[94] James Mill, *Analysis of the Phenomena of the Human Mind* (London, 1829), I, 90; quoted John Stuart Mill, *Examination of Sir William Hamilton's Philosophy*, 254.

[95] Eliot, 'Tradition and the Individual Talent', *Selected Essays*, 16.

form 'an ideal order among themselves, which is modified by the introduction of the new (the really new) work of art among them'.[96] Both the ideality of the tradition and process by which it is changed echo Ward's psychology: for each of us, the past is an ideal structure produced 'by partial and more or less frequent reduplications of the train upon itself' which leave us with an 'ideational continuum'[97] quite different from our actual past experience; equally, the 'presentational continuum' of immediate experience means that at 'any given moment we have a certain whole of presentations, a "field of consciousness" psychologically one and continuous; at the next we have not an entirely new field but a partial change within this field'.[98] The closeness of Eliot's conception to these developments in British psychology can be traced, for instance, in the work of G. F. Stout, a student of Ward's and the author of several influential works on psychology in the late 1890s and early 1900s. Following Ward in envisaging a mind as a 'whole' which develops through evolution, Stout describes the structures which are produced and inherited over time as 'ideal constructions', the outcomes of the 'ideational process' which turns mere sensation into meaning through processes of association. It is these 'ideal constructions' which become the constitutive context for new experiences and with which the experiences of the individual have to cohere:

> The ideal combinations which arise in the individual mind can only become permanent parts of the ideal structure representing the real world if they are entertained by other minds also, and so become current in the society to which the individual belongs . . . ideal combinations which are generally current in society tend to maintain themselves in the mind of the individual, even though he has never himself verified them, and even though his own personal experience is unfavourable to them . . . [The 'crank'] is maintaining his own individual ideas against the vast work of ideal construction which has been built up by the co-operative thinking of many generations. It is true that this ideal structure is in process of constant development; and that, as it grows, it rectifies itself, excluding ideal combinations which had previously formed integral parts of it, and receiving into itself others which it had previously rejected.[99]

---

96 Ibid., 15.
97 Ibid., 62.
98 Ward, 'Psychology', *Encyclopaedia Britannica*, Vol. XX, 45.
99 G. F. Stout, *Manual of Psychology* (London, W. B. Clive, 1913), Book I, Ch. III, 644–5.

'The vast work of ideal construction' unites the 'ideal combinations which arise in the individual mind' with a structure which 'has been built up by the co-operative thinking of many generations' in precisely the same way that Eliot's 'individual talent' is bound into the 'ideal' order of the 'tradition'. Eliot's 'tradition' is, in effect, a 'mnemic heredity', a chain of transpersonal associations whose 'ideal' structure has been produced by the twin forces of obliviscence – memories disappearing from consciousness – and the reformation of new associations between the remaining memories. The 'individual talent' will only be remembered within this structure by submitting to the fact that 'he shall conform, that he shall cohere' while, at the same time, he knows that the 'ideal' order is in continual reconstruction as associations between its elements are remade by the addition of a each new experience. The multitudinous recollections of poet and critic will, in the end, be recovered and reshaped in the ideal relations of the 'great monuments' of art, monuments which can exist only in the process of being associated together in the 'mind of Europe'.

Joyce's 'mythic method' has the importance of a 'scientific discovery' because it exemplifies an art that has become self-conscious of the relationship that Eliot draws between contemporary writing and the literature of the past. Joyce's method is the literary acknowledgment of an engramic memory that links his text to the oldest texts of the European tradition. The 'mythic method' provides the horizon towards which arbitrary personal associations can be directed in order that they can find an 'objectivity' and an 'impersonality' that will return as a multitudinous increase in the associative potential of the individual work – a multitudinousness which, like the embryo, repeats in brief the totality of human experience. As Eliot put it, in 1919,

> The maxim, return to the sources, is a good one. More intelligibly put it is that the great poet should know everything that has been accomplished in poetry (accomplished, not merely produced) since its beginnings – in order to know what he is doing himself. He should be aware of all the metamorphoses of poetry that illustrate the stratifications of history that cover savagery. For the artist is, in an impersonal sense, the most self-conscious of men; he is therefore the most and the least civilized and civilizable; he is the most competent to understand both the civilized and the primitive.[100]

---

[100] T. S. Eliot, 'War Paint and Feathers', *The Athenaeum*, 4668 (17 October 1919), 1036.

For 'poet' read 'poem' or 'novel': the great work of literature should 'illustrate the stratifications of history that cover savagery'; it should 'understand both the civilized and the primitive'; it should have learned from Yeats, Psychology and Frazer that literature, like the mind, is nothing but a much overwritten *tabula*, and that a literature which seeks to represent the modern mind must represent it through the history of writing – by a method that links modernity to myth.

IV

In *The New Criticism*, originally published in 1941, John Crowe Ransom identified I. A. Richards as the first of the 'new critics': 'discussion of the new criticism must start with Mr. Richards' because what Richards offers 'amounts to a complete aesthetic of poetry'.[101] That aesthetic, in the years between Richards's book written in collaboration with C. K. Ogden, *The Meaning of Meaning* (1923), and his *The Philosophy of Rhetoric* (1936), was to have a profound effect on the development of modern literary criticism and on the teaching of literature: Richards's analysis of his students' responses to poetry in *Practical Criticism* (1929) provided both the concept – 'practical criticism' – and the methodology by which subsequent generations of students were taught how to read literature, and technical terminology invented by Richards – for instance, his distinction between 'tenor' and 'vehicle' in metaphor – was widely adopted by other critics. And through the work of Richards's student, William Empson, in *Seven Types of Ambiguity* (1930), the notion of 'ambiguity' as a primary characteristic of literary language became widely accepted: as Richards, himself, put it in *The Philosophy of Rhetoric*, 'when the old Rhetoric treated ambiguity as a fault in language, and hoped to confine or eliminate it, the new Rhetoric sees it as an inevitable consequence of the powers of language and as the indispensable means of most of our most important utterances – especially in Poetry and Religion'.[102] Richards's work underpinned the development of a decisively modern – indeed, a *modernist* – criticism, which provided the tools for a new kind of reading to match the new kinds of poetry being written in the period before 1939 – 'in depth and precision at once it is beyond all earlier criticism

---

[101] John Crowe Ransom, *The New Criticism* (Westport: Greenwood Press, 1979; 1941), 3.

[102] I. A. Richards, *The Philosophy of Rhetoric* (Oxford: Oxford University Press, 1936) 40; hereafter cited in the text as *PR*.

in our language', as Ransom put it.[103] And yet, in *The Philosophy of Rhetoric*, Richards still takes as his representative of the kind of criticism he is trying to overcome the eighteenth-century Scottish theorist, Lord Kames, whose *Elements of Criticism* dates from 1761; and what, according to Richards, distorts Kames's analyses are 'his theories about trains of ideas and images [which] are typical 18th Century Associationism – the Associationism of which David Hartley is the great prophet – and the applications of these theories in the detail of the Rhetoric are their own refutation' (*PR*, 17). That the 'new criticism' still takes associationism as the mainstream against which it has to define itself is underlines just how powerful the associationist tradition had been: indeed, Richards believes that 'it is impossible to read Hartley, for example, without deep sympathy if we realize what a task he was attempting' (*PR*, 18), and that what he himself offers as a 'new' rhetoric 'has associationism among its obvious ancestors' (*PR*, 15), because associationism represented the 'beginnings, first steps in a great and novel venture, the attempt to explain in detail how language works and with it to improve communication' (*PR*, 17).

Richards's closeness to the associationist tradition is clear throughout *Principles of Literary Criticism* (1924). The echo of William James's *Principles of Psychology* is far from accidental, for Richards's aim is to construct nothing less than a science of reading on the foundations of empirical psychology, a psychology that acknowledges its co-workers to be 'students of Stout or Ward'.[104] Richards was in fact a student of Stout's but his materialist approach to mental events – 'we are our bodies, more especially our nervous systems, more especially still the higher or more central co-ordinating parts of it'[105] – looks back to Bain, the Mills and, indeed, Hartley. The primordial units of Richards's 'mental events', are 'impulses', whose role is a modernised version of the 'impressions' and 'ideas' of the earlier empiricists; as in Mill or Bain, 'impulses' may be analysed into atomic units but are rarely to be met with in isolation: 'It is often convenient to speak as though simple impulses were in question, as when we speak of an impulse of hunger, or an impulse to laugh, but we must not forget how intricate all our activities are' (*PLC*, 66). These

---

103 Ransom, *The New Criticism*, x: he is describing the work of R. P. Blackmur, whom he sees as typical of the outcomes of the New Criticism that Richards inaugurates.

104 I. A. Richards, *Practical Criticism* (London: Kegan Paul, Trench, Trubner, 1929), 322; hereafter cited in the text as *PC*.

105 I. A. Richards, *Principles of Literary Criticism* (London: Routledge, 1967; 1924), 64; hereafter cited in the text as *PLC*.

'impulses' consist, according to *The Meaning of Meaning*, not only of immediate sensations and individual recollections but of past meanings which 'have left, in our organisation, engrams, residual traces which help to determine what the mental process will be',[106] and in those engrams subsist the 'relics' which J. G. Frazer had revealed to be 'still in harmony with the thoughts and feelings of others, who, though they are drilled by their betters into an appearance of civilisation, remain barbarians or savages at heart'.[107] Modern people 'are hardly aware of the extent to which these relics survive at their doors, still less do they realise how their own behaviour is moulded by the unseen hand of the past'.[108] Richards's account of memory seeks to bypass the 'the crude assumption that the only way in which what is past can be repeated is by records being kept' – the view of older associationists – and he sketches an alternative conception of the mind as consisting of 'energy systems of prodigious complexity and extreme delicacy of organization' which are capable of an 'indefinitely large number of stable poises'. The achievement, or re-achievement, of one of these 'poises' is the equivalent to the revival of memory traces: 'its state on the later occasion would appear to be the *revival* of its state on the former, but this would not be the case any more than a cumulus cloud this evening is a revival of those that decorated the heavens last year' (*PLC*, 80). Such a system, in other words, produces the same outcome as the 'old associationist' account of the mind by *appearing* to perform those revivals from memory traces which modern neurology has proved unlikely. And it is to these apparent revivals that we owe our aesthetic experiences, because,

> the states of aesthetic contemplation owe their fullness and richness to the action of memory; not memory narrowed down and specialised as is required in reference, but memory operating in a freer fashion to widen and amplify sensitiveness. In such conditions we are open to more diffused and more heterogeneous stimulation, because the inhibitions which normally canalise our responses are removed. (*PLC*, 267–8)

Richards charts the operation of this freer form of memory as 'a stream

---

[106]   C. K. Ogden and I. A. Richards, *The Meaning of Meaning* (London: Kegan, Paul, Trench, Trubner, 1923), 138.

[107]   Ibid., 33; quotation from J. G. Frazer, *Psyche's Task* (London: Macmillan, 1909), 169.

[108]   Ibid., 33.

of reaction in which six distinct kinds of events may be distinguished':

I   The visual sensations of the printed words
II Images very closely associated with these sensations
III Images relatively free
IV References to, or 'thinkings of', various things
V   Emotions
VI Affective-volitional attitudes (*PLC*, 90)

These he presents in diagrammatic form as a series of mutually interacting fibres of 'stimulation' which, in its combination of various kinds of associations with emotions, is clearly an elaboration of a traditional associationist account of how meaning is generated from individual words:

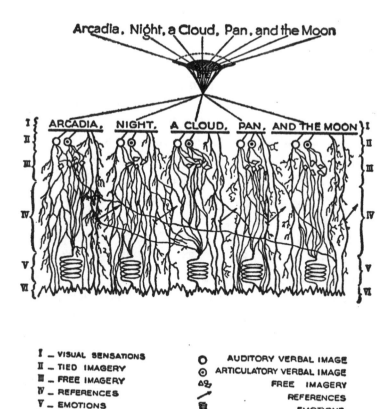

For Richards, art is fundamentally based on the reactivation of associated memories – the 'revival' of impulses which 'run' and 'develop' in ways that are dependent 'upon the condition of the mind, and this depends upon the impulses which have previously been active in it' (*PLC*, 95). From an initial impulse spreads out an accumulating chain of effects:

> The thin trickle of stimulation which comes in through the eye finds an immense hierarchy of systems of tendencies poised in the most delicate stability. It is strong enough and rightly enough directed to disturb some of these without assistance. The literal sense of a word can be grasped on the prompting of the mere sight of it, . . . But the effects of this stimulation are immensely increased and widened when it is reinforced by fresh stimulation from tied images, and it is through these that most of the emotional effects are produced. As the agitation proceeds new reinforcement comes with every fresh system which is excited. Thus, the paradoxical fact that so trifling an irritation as the sight of marks on paper is able to arouse whole energies of the mind becomes explicable. (*PLC*, 95–6)

Richards does not shy away from the implication which had always been the clear consequence of associationist theories of art: 'It is unquestionable that the actual experiences, which even good critics undergo when reading, as we say, the *same poem*, differ very widely. In spite of certain conventions, which endeavour to conceal these inevitable discrepancies for social purposes, there can be no doubt that the experiences of readers in connection with particular poems are rarely similar' (*PLC*, 88). The consequence is, in terms of imagery, that 'fifty different readers will experience not one common picture but fifty different pictures' (*PLC*, 93).

Precisely because it stimulates such richness of memory, poetry will produce in magnified form what, according to *The Meaning of Meaning*, is true of all language: 'The first necessity is to remember that since the past histories of individuals differ except in certain very simple respects, it is probable that their reactions to and employment of any general word will vary', so that even for those 'for whom every word used symbolises a definite and completely articulated reference' no matter how clear 'their ideas may be, they will probably not be ideas of the same things'.[109] So problematic, indeed, is this failure of coincidence between people's ideas that 'we ought to regard communication as

---

[109] Ogden and Richards, *The Meaning of Meaning*, 231.

a difficult matter, and close correspondence of reference for different thinkers as a comparatively rare event'.[110] The complexities of trying to align two minds that have been shaped by very different experiences and that have developed different literary specialisms – because modern readers have 'far more varied elements than has ever been the case before' – means that even 'under the most favourable circumstances' communication is a hazardous enterprise: individual memory plays such a decisive role that meaning is constantly deflected by discrepancies arising from personal associations:

> the communication in difficult cases depends upon the extent to which past similarities in experience can be made use of. Without such similar-ities communication is impossible. Difficult cases are those in which the speaker must himself supply and control a large part of the causes of the listener's experience; in which correspondingly the listener has to struggle against the intrusions of elements from his own past experience which are irrelevant. (*PLC*, 137)

The intrusion of such arbitrary associations makes it is almost impossible for the receiver of a communication *not* to transform it into some personal mean-ing irrelevant to the poet's purpose. The demands on the readers of poetry are enormous: 'Discrimination, suggestibility, free and clear resuscitation of ele-ments of past experience *disentangled from one another*, and control of irrelevant personal details and accidents, make up the recipient's gift' (*PLC*, 139). Readers, in other words, have to ensure a state of mind in which memory is released ('suggestible') to provide images that are not 'dated and placed' but are in a state of 'free reproduction', while at the same time ensuring that the suggestions thus generated are purged of 'irrelevant personal details and accidents' (*PLC*, 139–40). Such a state of mind, however, is precisely the most difficult for the ordinary person, who is 'under the necessity on most occasions of suppressing the greater part of the impulses which the situation might arouse', in order 'to keep any steadiness and clarity in his attitudes' (*PLC*, 134). The poetic mind, on the other hand, is 'pre-eminently accessible to external influences and discrimi-nating with regard to them', and 'distinguished further by the freedom in which all these impressions are held in suspension and by the ease with which they form new relations between themselves' (*PLC*, 139–40). The extreme discrep-ancy between these two forms of consciousness is revealed in the images of

---

[110] Ibid., 225–6.

isolation and madness which haunt Chapter Twenty-Two of *Principles* entitled, somewhat ironically, 'The Availability of the Poet's Experience'. On the one hand the poet is recognised as having a 'superficial resemblance to persons who are merely mental chaoses, unorganized, without selective ability and of weak and diffused attention', despite the fact of being 'essentially . . . the opposite of these' (*PLC*, 143). On the other hand, the banal mind of the reader, with its lack of associative flexibility, is threatened with a different kind of madness, that in which the past returns only as it was, with no new combinations or connections of experience, a condition close to mental illness:

> The patient in the asylum occupied in reliving the same piece of experience indefinitely does so (if he does) because he is limited very strictly in the range of his possible impulses, other impulses not being allowed to intervene. Hence the completeness with which he is said to reconstruct the past. Most revival is distorted because only some of the original impulses are repeated, new impulses being involved and a compromise resulting. (*PLC*, 140–1)

Poetic communication has to take place somewhere between the complete errancy of unfollowable associations in 'free reproduction' and the complete determinism of a mind which can only recover fixed memories in their original structure.

Principles of Literary Criticism is thus dominated not by the fulfilment of communication but by its failure. For Richards, however, this is not an *impasse* because poetry, unlike science, has no reference: images which it provokes in readers are neither true nor false; they do not describe the world but, as *The Meaning of Meaning* insisted, produce emotion and inculcate attitudes:

> As science frees itself from the emotional outlook, and modern physics is becoming something in connection with which attitudes seem rather *de trop*, so poetry seems about to return to the condition of its greatness, by abandoning the obsession of knowledge and symbolic truth. It is not necessary to know what things are in order to take up fitting attitudes towards them, and the peculiarity of the greatest attitudes which art can evoke is their extraordinary width. The description and ordering of such attitudes is the business of aesthetics.[111]

---

[111] Ibid., 271

Although as in previous associationist accounts poetry works 'by reaching some system in the brain in which effects take place not due merely to this present stimulus, but also to past occasions on which it has been combined with other stimulations' (*PLC*, 100), it does so only to produce emotions, and what makes discussion of art possible, despite the privacy of these 'revivals' and the lack of congruity between different people's senses of the meaning of words, is that 'provided the ends, in which the value of the poem lies, are attained, differences in the means need not prevent critics from agreement or from mutual service' (*PLC*, 88). Despite the emphasis on 'value', the 'ends' of poetry are, nonetheless, fundamentally quantitative:

> The people who are most keenly and variously interested, that is to say, the people whose lives are most valuable on our theory of value, the people for whom the poet writes and by his appeal to whom he is judged, inevitably build up their minds with far more varied elements than has ever been the case before. And the poet, in so far as he is equal to his opportunities, does the same. It is hard, and, in fact, impossible, to deny him his natural and necessary resources on the ground that a majority of his readers will not understand. (*PLC*, 171)

Challenged by Conrad Aiken about this quantitative implication of his theory, Richards did not attempt to ameliorate it: 'The purpose of the theory is just to enable us to compare different experiences in respect of their value; and their value, I suggest, is a quantitative matter', because 'the best life is that in which as much as possible of our possible personality is engaged' (*PLC*, 'Appendix A', 229). The state of aesthetic excitement which a poem produces, in other words, is directly related to the quantity of material which the reader's mind is capable of producing under the stimulus of the poem's language.

It was a theory of poetry which F. R. Leavis described as being 'curiously contemporary with Bentham'.[112] His cue for doing so was the strange historical loop that Richards's work took as he tried to reinforce the theories of *Principles of Literary Criticism* – a historical loop that involved re-enacting Coleridge's argument with Hartley. In *Coleridge on the Imagination* (1934), 'writing here as a Benthamite',[113] Richards sought to incorporate into his own theories

---

[112] Leavis, *Mill on Bentham and Coleridge*, 30.

[113] I. A. Richards, *Coleridge on Imagination* (London: Kegan, Paul, Trench, Trubner, 1934), 18; hereafter cited in the text as *CI*.

Coleridge's insights into the nature of the imagination while, at the same time, co-opting Coleridge to his own materialistic psychology:

> There can be little doubt, in the light of subsequent developments, that Coleridge as against Associationism of the Hartley-Condillac type was right all along the line. But, and here he exemplified a frequent pattern of philosophic advance, what has proved him right has been constructive developments on the part of the very materialistic-mechanistic doctrines that he was attacking – developments of a kind that he did not foresee. . . . Were Coleridge alive now, he would, I hope, be applauding and improving doctrines of the type he, as a metaphysician, thought least promising in his own day. For when he kept to psychology, he often showed a very curious prescience of developments to come. (*CI*, 67)

To Leavis, the 'effort to restate Coleridge in terms of Bentham' appeared to be more an effort 'to *replace* Coleridge by Bentham'.[114] The Benthamite emphasis is clear – and clearly admitted – in Richards's transformation of Coleridge's distinction of Fancy from Imagination:

> Anyone who is well acquainted with Coleridge's ways of discussing Fancy and Imagination will notice that I have, at several places above, translated them in terms which might sometimes have been repugnant, as suggesting mechanical treatment, to Coleridge himself. In place of 'the power by which one image or feeling is made to modify many others and by a sort of *fusion to force many into one*', I have used phrases which suggest that it is the number of connexions between the many, and the relations between these connexions, that give the unity – in brief, that the co-adunation is the inter-relationship of the parts' (*CI*, 85–6).

Richards's *translation* reverses those tactics by which we have seen associationists claim to have equivalent chemical or mechanical means of matching Coleridge's 'fusion', and reincorporates into Coleridge's version of the Imagination the *quantitative* production of associated material by which associationism had always defined the nature of aesthetic experiences. The power of poetry is not in an act of transcendence but in an act of *extension* on the part of the reader:

---

[114] Leavis, *Mill on Bentham and Coleridge*, 28–9.

. . . these very movements – untrackable as they perhaps are, and unin-
ducible as they almost certainly are by other words – are the very life of
the poem. In these searchings for meaning of a certain sort its being consists. The poem is a quest, and its virtue is not in anything said by it, or in
the way in which it is said, or in a meaning which is found, or even what is
passed by in the search. (*CI*, 216–17)

The poem is *in* the mental processes by which, to revert to Alison, 'our
imagination is seized, and our fancy busied in pursuit of all those trains of
thought, which are allied to this character or expression' (*AET*, 2). What
Richards takes from Coleridge, however, is the notion that 'in Imagination
the parts of the meaning – both as regards the ways in which they are
apprehended and the modes of combination of their effects in the mind
– mutually modify one another' (*CI*, 86). In this process of 'mutual modification' the mind of the reader is not moving away from the poem into a
train of personal associations: rather, the associations work back and forth
between different elements of the poem, continually enriching and intensifying the apparent connectedness of those elements. Instead of veering away
from the poem the associations cluster and combine within it. Coleridge
had used Shakespeare's description of Adonis's flight – 'Look! How a bright
star shooteth from the sky/So glides he in the night from Venus's eye' – as
an instance of Imagination because of 'how many images and feelings are
here brought together without effort and without discord – the beauty of
Adonis—the rapidity of his flight—the yearning yet helplessness of the
enamoured gazer—and a shadowy ideal character thrown over the whole'
(*CI*, 83); Richards's account of why these two lines are an instance of the
imagination at work has a very different, and quantitative, stress:

the more the image is followed up, the more links of relevance between
the units are discovered. As Adonis to Venus, so these lines to the reader
seem to linger in the eye like the after-images that make the trail of the
meteor . . . The separable meanings of each word . . . are here brought
into one. And as they come together, as the reader's mind finds cross-
connexion after cross-connexion between them, he seems, in becoming
more aware of them, to be discovering not only Shakespeare's meaning,
but something which he, the reader is himself making. His understanding
of Shakespeare is sanctioned by his own activity in it. (*CI*, 83).

The associative activity of the mind, linking together the possibilities of 'cross-connexion', produce an intensifying 'mutual modification' in which there is no phrase of the passage 'which does not carry, at first unnoticed, secondary and tertiary co-implications among their possibilities of interpretation' (*CI*, 94). The quality of the poetry lies in the possibility it offers for this seemingly unending play between the possibilities of reference, suggestion, tone and rhythm, this seemingly unending process of 'making' which appears to replicate in the experience of the reader the creative activity of the author. The poetry is in the process, which is why 'with the best poetry there is nowhere to arrive' (*CI*, 213). The associative interconnections which earlier theorists saw as a product of the reading mind delving into its own past history now become associative interconnections contained within the boundaries of the poem – but they are there, still, only because the reading mind has offered them up, was capable of offering them up, and their being there means that we only 'seem' to be discovering Shakespeare's meaning as we produce our own.

Two years later, in *The Philosophy of Rhetoric*, Richards was able to use this revised version of Coleridge in his challenge to the leftovers of eighteenth-century associationism:

> When we see the simplest-seeming concrete object, its concreteness comes to it from the way in which we are bringing it simultaneously into a number of sorts. The sorts grow together in it to form that meaning . . . If we forget this and suppose that we start with discrete impressions of particulars ('fixities and definites' as Coleridge called them) and then build these up into congeries, the theorem I am recommending collapses at once into contradications and absurdities. That was the fault of the old Hartleian Associationism . . . A particular impression is already a product of concrescence. Behind it, or in it, there has been a coming together of *sortings*. When we take a number of particular impressions – of a number of different white things, say – and abstract from them an idea of whiteness, we are explicitly reversing a process which has already been implicitly at work in our perception of them as all white. (*PR*, 36)

The Coleridgean allusion cannot conceal, however, that Richards is misconstruing, if not misrepresenting Hartleian Associationism. As an empiricist, Hartley accepts that all mental activity is *derived* from sensation, but that does not mean that we are ever conscious of 'discrete impressions of particulars'.

Indeed, the whole point of Hartley's theory is to allow us to reach back from complex experiences to their possible particulars:

> One may hope, therefore, that, by pursuing and perfecting the doctrine of associations, we may some time or other be enabled to analyse all that vast variety of complex ideas, which pass under the name of ideas of reflection, and intellectual ideas, into their simple compounding parts, *i.e.* into the simple ideas of sensation, of which they consist. This would be greatly analogous to the arts of writing, and resolving the colours of the sun's light, or natural bodies, into their primary constituent ones. (*O*, 75–6)

The aim of this decomposition of complex ideas is, for Hartley, that 'it would afford great light and clearness to the art of logic, thus to determine the precise nature and composition of the ideas affixed to those words which have complex ideas, in a proper Sense, *i.e.* which excite any combinations of simple ideas united intimately by association; also to explain, upon this foundation, the proper use of those words, which have no ideas' (*O*, 76). It is an aim which runs in parallel with Richards's own – the hope that 'psychology might be able to tell us so much about our minds that we would at last become able to discover with some certainty what we mean by our words and how we mean it', or, that through rhetoric we 'may in time learn so much about words that they will tell us how our minds work' (*PR*, 136). And Richards could not have opposed his own account of '*sortings*' to traditional associationism had he recalled John Stuart Mill's account of the formation of concepts: 'We neither conceive them, nor think them, nor cognise them in any way, as a thing apart, but solely as forming, in combination with numerous other attributes, the idea of an individual object. But, though thinking them only as part of a larger agglomeration, we have the power of fixing our attention on them, to the neglect of the other attributes with which we think them combined'.[115] Hartley and Mill, however, would have immediately recognised Richards's account of metaphor as one that still conformed to the principles of their associationist model:

> Let us consider more closely what happens in the mind when we put together – in a sudden and striking fashion – two things belonging to

---

[115] Mill, *Collected Works*, Vol. 9, *Examination of Sir William Hamilton's Philosophy*, 309.

> very different orders of experience. The most important happenings
> – in addition to a general confused reverberation and strain – are the
> mind's efforts to connect them. The mind is a connecting organ, it works
> only by connecting and it can connect two things in an indefinitely large
> number of different ways . . . In all interpretation we are filling in con-
> nections. . . (PR, 125)

'Connecting' may now be doing the business that 'associating' formerly did,
but the model of the mind's activity in aesthetic experience is the same: 'The
reader, I would say, will try out various connections, and this experimentation
– with the simplest and most complex, the most obvious and the most
recondite collocations alike – is the movement which gives meaning to all fluid
language' (PR, 125), because it is of the very nature of poetry that it maximises
'our freedom to fill in', because 'the absence of explicitly stated intermediate
steps . . . is the main source of its powers' (PR, 125).

What salvages such associational activity from mere subjectivism, however, is a theory of 'myth' which Richards constructs in *Coleridge on Imagination*.
Literature and criticism are both engaged in the 'mythic method' because the
world we inhabit is itself essentially a product of the imagination. What the
imagination discloses in poetry is at one with what it discloses about Nature
– not the Nature that we engage in for practical purposes (technology) or
understanding (science) but 'a Nature in which our hopes and fears and
desires, by projection, can come to terms with one another', a Nature such
as 'the religions in the past have attempted to provide for man' (CI, 169–70).
Such 'projected' forms of Nature are not 'make-belief' [*sic*], which 'is an
enervating exercise of fancy not to be confused with imaginative growth';
neither are they an 'amusement or diversion to be sought as a relaxation
and escape from the hard realities of life', because 'they are these hard realities in projection, their symbolic recognition, co-ordination and acceptance'
(CI, 171). In a mythical structure, as in a poem, 'the divergent strivings of
our being are brought into "balance and reconciliation"', and without those
mythologies 'man is only a cruel animal without a soul – for a soul is a central
part of his governing mythology – he is a congeries of possibilities without
order and without aim' (CI, 172). But that this poetic mythology should not
still be subject to defamation as inadequate by comparison with the 'truths'
of science, science too has to be declared a 'mythic method': 'knowledge in
all its varieties – scientific, moral, religious – has come to seem a vast mythology' (CI, 227):

If we grant that all is myth, poetry, as the myth-making which most brings 'the whole soul of man into activity', and as working with words, 'parts and germinations of the plant', and, through them, in 'the medium by which spirits communicated with one another becomes the necessary channel for the reconstitution of order. (*CI*, 228)

The poetic imagination becomes central again to the totality of human life, and Coleridge's valuation of it accepted – but only in the context of a scepticism which turns everything into myth and knows that no myth ever gives us access to the Absolute: 'if every myth is a projection of some human situation, of some co-ordination of human feelings, needs and desires, the scope of its relevance and therefore of its proper influence upon action must be limited' (*CI*, 174). Poetry and criticism, harnessed in this sceptical service of myth, turn chaos into order by transforming the merely subjective into the objectivity of the very world we inhabit – even though we know that that world – like Hume's and like Frazer's – is a fiction.

V

The first type of ambiguity which is analysed in William Empson's *Seven Types of Ambiguity* (1930) is that in which 'a word, a syntax, or a grammatical structure, while making only one statement, is effective in several ways at once'.[116] As an example, Empson offers Shakespeare's line 'Bare ruined choirs, where late the sweet birds sang', with the following analysis:

> The comparison is sound, because ruined monastery choirs are places in which to sing, because they involve sitting in a row, because they are made of wood, are carved into knots and so forth, because they used to be surrounded by a sheltering building crystallised out of the likeness of a forest, and coloured with stained glass and painting like flowers and leaves, because they are now abandoned by all but the gray walls coloured like the skies of winter, because the cold and Narcissistic charm suggested by choir-boys suits well with Shakespeare's feeling for the object of the Sonnets, and for various sociological and historical reason ('for oh,

---

[116] William Empson, *Seven Types of Ambiguity* (London: Chatto and Windus, 1930), 3.

the hobby-horse is forgot,' and the Puritans have cut down the Maypoles), which it would be hard now to trace out in their proportions; these reasons, and many more relating the simile to its place in the Sonnet, must all combine to give the line its beauty, and there is a sort of ambiguity in not knowing which of them to hold most clearly in mind. Clearly this is involved in all such richness and heightening of effect, and the machinations of ambiguity are among the very roots of poetry.[117]

The 'very roots of poetry' are a set of associations which no other reader than Empson himself would have been able to produce; certainly, John Crowe Ransom, while acknowledging that the analysis is 'so fascinating and so knowing that his sophisticated readers will be rather ashamed to hold back and disavow them', nonetheless feels that even for 'ideal' readers 'there is really no consciousness of so great a wealth of meanings to choose from'.[118] Ransom offers an alternative in which the birdsong refers to Shakespeare's own verses: what the image provokes in the reader is the question 'what is the matter with Shakespeare's verses, which have turned so slight, or so dull and sour'.[119] But Ransom also acknowledges that after reading Empson's analysis 'reading will never again be able to be as dull and unimaginative as it must have been before Empson showed its possibilities'.[120] Indeed, Empson's associations have become part of the memory which the poem evokes and the reader who has read Empson cannot escape the recollection of Empson's recollections: 'I have not yet – at least until Empson came into my view – dared to go as far as I liked in exploring it',[121] Ransom confesses. Ransom's difficulty underlines the associationist structure of Richards's and Empson's theory of both creativity and reading:

> What we usually describe as thinking is a much more attractive mental exercise: it consists in following out a train of ideas, a process which affords us most of the pleasures of thinking, in the stricter sense, without its pains and bewilderments. Such trains of associations may, and in the minds of men of genius often do, lead to new and valuable ideas. But – accidents apart – the condition for this happy result is a wide available

---

[117] Ibid.
[118] Ransom, *The New Criticism*, 122–3.
[119] Ibid., 126.
[120] Ibid., 131.
[121] Ibid., 129.

background of relevant experience. The valuable idea is, in fact, the meet-ing-point, the link between separate parts of this field of experience. It unites aspects of existence that ordinarily remain unconnected, and in this lies its value. The secret of genius is perhaps nothing else than this greater availability of all experience coupled with larger stores of experi-ence to draw upon. (*PC*, 249–50)

Which reader, though, can match that 'wide available background of relevant experience'? It is a question which Richards addressed in *Practical Criticism* in considering the 'irrelevant associations and stock responses' of his students (referred to by number in the following passage):

> Slightly more complicated are these instances where it is a train of thought, not a memory, that intrudes. The home-sickness of 10.1, the opinions on the musical quality of hymns (8.2) and on the proper use of music (8.12, 8.32), the historical background of 9.111 and the politics of 9.15, betray themselves as having nothing to do with the matter, but it is not so easy to decide about the War Memorial (7.43) or Joanna Southcott's Gladstone-bag (13.5). The associated train of ideas may be merely an *ignis fatuus*, or a flash of inspiration. Everything depends upon how essential the bond of thought or feeling may be that links it with the poem. We have to ask whether it really springs from the meaning or whether it is an accidental by-product of a reading which does not realise the meaning; whether the train of association has at least started right and is rooted in something essential, and whether or not accidents of the individual reader's mood or history or temperament have twisted it. (*PC*, 237–8)

The language of associationism – 'train', 'link', 'accidents of the individual reader's mood or history' – helps define what is *inappropriate* in a reader's response: we might be back with Locke and association as the explanation of *failed* understanding. At the same time, only associations can produce an *appropriate* outcome: how, though, is it possible to distinguish those associations that are 'rooted in something essential' from those which are 'accidents' and have 'nothing to do with the matter'? Defining the boundary between the 'merely personal' and the relevant recollection proves to be extraordinarily difficult: 'memories, whether of emotional crises or of scenes visited or incidents observed, are not to be hastily excluded as mere personal intrusions. That they are personal is nothing against them – all experience is personal

– the only conditions are that they must be genuine and relevant, and must respect the liberty and autonomy of the poem' (*PC*, 240). On the one side is the 'autonomy of the poem'; on the other the fact that we cannot ever shut out our personal associations in our reading experience – 'all experience is personal'.

The boundary line between relevant and irrelevant personal associations was to be the crucial backdrop for the development of the 'new criticism' and would dominate, if sometimes in concealed form, issues in Anglophone literary criticism through to the 1960s. The word 'connotation' – originally invented by James Mill, and used by John Stuart Mill in his *Logic* – came to be used for the associative potential of words as though by its very scientificity it could restrict associational potential. Thus in Cleanth Brooks's *The Well Wrought Urn* (1949), the development of connotation is both the artist's and the critic's distinctive task. In an extension of Empson's 'ambiguity' to the structural level of the poem, Brooks describes all literature as necessarily 'paradoxical', because,

> The paradoxes spring from the very nature of the poet's language: it is a language in which the connotations play as great a part as the denotations. And I do not mean that the connotations are important as supplying some sort of frill or trimming, something external to the real matter in hand. I mean that the poet does not use a notation at all – as the scientist may properly be said to do so. The poet, within limits, has to make up his language as he goes.[122]

The poet's use of language is 'disruptive' because 'the terms are continually modifying each other, and thus violating their dictionary meanings'[123] and the critic's job is to help the reader towards a grasp of the connotations as defined by the whole context of the poem, and, beyond that, the whole context of the literary tradition of which the poem is a part. As he puts it in a rejoinder to Yvor Winters, 'in the poems with which we have been concerned the words *are* used skilfully and the given context is of immense importance. Under such conditions not only "the feelings communicated by the word" are modified, but . . . the meaning of the complex of words'.[124] The power of such shifts, however, derive from the fact, as Brooks says of an image in

---

[122] Cleanth Brooks, *The Well Wrought Urn* (London: Dennis Dobson, 1949), 8.
[123] Ibid.
[124] Ibid., 217.

Donne, that they seem 'to come in a natural stream of association'.[125] For Brooks, context – both the context of the individual poem and the context of the literary tradition – form the limits of connotation and define the appropriate limits of association, and Richards's co-option of Coleridge's conception of the '*modifying* power of imagination'[126] takes a central place in the elaboration of a criticism for which poetry is 'inherently ambiguous and polysemous' while, at the same time, achieving, through the balance of its elements, a sense of order and stability. As W. K. Wimsatt formulated it in *The Verbal Icon* (1954):

> The multiple meaning of words when realized through appropriate contexts is the technical side of a quality in poetry which we may call something like 'complexity' – provided, however, that we mean by that not the negative complexity of disorder or mere obscurity or mere multiplicity, but a positive and structural complexity, the varied fabric of organic unity. (*VI*, 270)

The lengthy completion of Wimsatt's sentence rules out the critic's or reader's associations as constituting appropriate elements in the aesthetic experience simply because they contribute to its quantitative impact – we have to achieve a 'multiplicity' of meaning which is not 'disorder', which supports 'the axis of order or being against chaos' (*VI*, 271). By means of the 'intentional fallacy' – which rules out 'author psychology' as 'private and idiosyncratic' (*VI*, 10) – and the 'affective fallacy' – which rules out the reader's response as a 'confusion between the poem and its results' (*VI*, 21) – Wimsatt sought a criticism which could acknowledge in poetry 'a way of fixing emotions or making them more permanently perceptible' (*VI*, 38); the nature of that fixing, however, reveals the associationist foundations of the 'new criticism', since

> it is a well known but nonetheless important truth that there are two kinds of real objects which have emotive quality, the objects which are the reasons for human emotion, and those which by some kind of association suggest either the reasons or the resulting emotion: the thief, the enemy or the insult that makes us angry, and the hornet that sounds and stings

---

[125] Ibid., 14–15.

[126] W. K. Wimsatt, *The Verbal Icon: Studies in the Meaning of Poetry* (London: Methuen, 1970; 1954), 115; hereafter cited in the text as *VI*.

somewhat like ourselves when angry; the murderer or felon, and the crow that kills small birds and animals or feeds on carrion and is black like the night when crimes are committed by men. (*VI*, 36)

Wimsatt's example of the murderer and the crow is itself an unacknowledged association that takes us back to Empson, and his analysis of a speech in *Macbeth*: 'Light thickens, and the Crow/Makes Wing to th' Rookie Wood'.[127] Empson's analysis charts the possible relationships between crows and rooks, and the 'suggestion' invoked by specific words: 'there is a suggestion of witches' broth, or curdling blood, about *thickens*'.[128] Wimsatt's confidence in the critic's ability to trace a poem's 'clear and nicely interrelated meanings, its completeness, balance, and tension' (*VI*, 39) is itself founded on an example of which Empson declares:

> Personally I am pleased and given faith by this analysis, because it has made something which seemed to me magical into something that seems to me sensible. But those readers who think the line ineffective, and those to whom it has always been an overt dramatic irony, will alike be unimpressed.[129]

'Completeness, balance, and tension' falls back into personal association. Wimsatt insists that 'if objects are ever connected by "emotional congruity", as in the association psychology which J. S. Mill inherited from the eighteenth century, this can only mean that similar emotions attach to various objects because of similarity in the objects or in their relations' (*VI*, 27), but his insistence does not mean that 'the objective critic' can ever escape those 'merely personal' associations which disrupt the 'subjective' readings of those whom he is trying to lead towards 'an intuitive and full realization of poems themselves' (*VI*, 83). Indeed, by the very restriction of his associative range, one might say, Wimsatt is preventing the poem from achieving its real aim, because he is producing a poem which represents only a limited version of its total potential meaning – a smooth, balanced poem of contained academic connections stands in the place of the poem which interacts with and disrupts the living flow of the reader's associational responses.

---

[127] Empson, *Seven Types of Ambiguity*, 23.
[128] Ibid., 24.
[129] Ibid., 25.

A poetry not so contained and restricted would, for Wimsatt, be a poetry striving to return to its earlier status as myth, and a 'new myth is something which Yeats and Melville have apparently just fallen short of giving us'. In the modern world, however, such new myths have a problematic status: 'they want a new myth when the main thing alleged against the old myth is that it *was* a myth' (*VI*, 278). Within four years of the publication of *The Verbal Icon*, however, Northrop Frye's *An Anatomy of Criticism* proposed that literature was, precisely, a myth: '*mythos*' is the 'structural organizing principle of literary form',[130] both in terms of individual works and in terms of the totality of literature. The archetypal themes of myth – as analysed by Frazer, whose work, Frye notes, 'purports to be a work of anthropology, but it has had more influence on literary criticism than in its own alleged field, and it may yet prove to be really a work of literary criticism' (*AC*, 109) – provide, together with the Bible and Classical mythology, 'a grammar of literary archetypes' to which all individual works of literature can be related, and by which their formal structure can be identified. And what this structure provides is precisely the kind of 'objective' criticism that allows critics to escape from their own idiosyncratic associations, by establishing what constitute publicly identifiable and therefore shared patterns of association:

> The critic has a subjective background of experience formed by his temperament and by every contact with words he has made, including newspapers, advertisements, conversations, movies, and whatever he read at the age of nine. He has a specific skill in responding to literature which is no more like this subjective background, with all its private memories, associations, and arbitrary prejudices, than reading a thermometer is like shivering. (*AC*, 28)

For Frye, the symbolic structures of myth represent a set of public and traditional 'associations', such as 'the association of a god's death with autumn or sunset' (*AC*, 36), and these associations are transferred from myths proper into the generic structures of literary works:

> In a myth we can have a sun-god or a tree-god; in a romance we may have a person who is significantly associated with the sun or trees. In more

---

[130] Northrop Frye, *Anatomy of Criticism: Four Essays* (Princeton: Princeton University Press, 1957), 341; hereafter cited in the text as *AC*.

realistic modes the association becomes less significant and more a matter of incidental, even coincidental or accidental, imagery. (*AC*, 137)

Where association is most intense, however, is in the lyric because the creation of a lyric involves 'an associative rhetorical process, most of it below the threshold of consciousness, a chaos of paranomasia, sound-links, ambiguous sense-links and memory-links' (*AC*, 271–2). Significantly, in Frye's schema of literary history it is this lyrical mode which dominates the modern period (which Frye dates from Edgar Allan Poe), a period in which 'the object is to liberate the distinctive rhythm of lyric' (*AC*, 272). It is precisely this model of the literary that is, for Frye, the basis of 'the rhetorical analysis founded on ambiguity' (*AC*, 273) characteristic of the New Criticism. Indeed, Frye anticipates all the arguments I have given above for the associationist basis of the New Criticism when he notes that such 'lyric-centred criticism' is based on the genre which is closest to the 'chaos' of association 'below the threshold of consciousness'. But Frye's own mythic method depends no less on the workings of association: 'verbal creation begins in associative babble' but such 'verbal association is still a factor of importance even in rational thought' (*AC*, 334), and 'as soon as one starts to think of the role of association and diagram in argument, one begins to realize how extraordinarily pervasive they are' (*AC*, 336). Myths are such 'associative diagrams': 'Whether or not one is etymologically justified in associating Prometheus with forethought or Odysseus with wrath, the poets have accepted such associations and they are data for the critic' (*AC*, 334).

Frye's theory is to criticism, we might say, as Joyce's 'mythic method' is to literature: it provides a boundary and a teleology for the process of association. Indeed, Frye's account of the 'mythic method' of *Ulysses* summarises its associational significance: 'The romantic archetypes of Hamlet and Ulysses are like remote stars in a literary heaven looking down quizzically on the shabby creatures of Dublin obediently intertwining themselves in the patterns set by their influences' (*AC*, 314) – for 'patterns set by their influences' read 'associations', associations whose apparently local chaos clusters into order only under the gravitational pull of the more powerful but more distant associations that both Eliot and Frye call 'myth'. In Frye, as in Eliot and Joyce, the 'mythic method' is a method designed to uncover – or recover – a fundamental engram, and to reveal the ways in which, as a 'strange attractor', it can turn the apparent chaos of our subjective associations into an order that recalls, recounts and recapitulates the whole of human history.

VI

In *The Symbolist Movement in Literature,* dedicated to Yeats and read by Eliot, Arthur Symons describes the working methods by which the poetry of Mallarmé is produced:

> Imagine the poem already written down, at least composed. In its very imperfection, it is clear, it shows the links in the process by which it has been riveted together; the whole process of its construction can be studied. Now most writers would be content; but with Mallarmé the work has only begun. In the final result there must be no sign of the making, there must be only the thing made. He works it over, word by word . . . By the time the poem has reached, as it seems to him, a flawless unity, the steps in the process have been only too effectually effaced; and while the poet, who has seen the thing from the beginning, still sees the relation of point to point, the reader, who comes to it only in its final stages, finds himself in a not unnatural bewilderment.[131]

Mallarmé *eliminates* everything which can provide a 'relation of point to point', everything which can reveal the associations from which his imagery derives: his principle, according to Symons, is 'that to name is to destroy, to suggest is to create',[132] but the act of creation is passed from poet to reader since it is in the reader that those suggestions take shape.

The elimination of the author's associations creates a text which is both deliberately opaque and, at the same time, an effective stimulus to the associational activity of the reader – or, rather, to the associational activity of the critic who provides readers with a set of associational connections that makes sense of what is *lacking* in the poem. It is in this interaction between the poem which has been deliberately denuded of its author's associational connections and the critic whose associational memory provides the missing links of the chain that modern poetry and modern literary criticism were formed. Each of the major movements of 'high' modernist poetry – from Ezra Pound's Imagism to the Surrealism of the 1930s – were variants on Symons's description of Mallarmé's theories, and the logic of it is clear in I. A. Richards's account of how readers should approach T. S. Eliot's *The Waste*

---

[131] Symons, *The Symbolist Movement in Literature,* 72.
[132] Ibid., 71.

Land. Given the acknowledged obscurity of the poem, the reader, according to Richards, has to decide,

> Whether the poem is worth the trouble it entails. For 'The Waste Land' this is considerable. There is Miss Weston's *From Ritual to Romance* to read, and its 'astral' trimmings to be discarded – they have nothing to do with Mr. Eliot's poem. There is Canto Twenty-Six of the *Purgatorio* to be studied – the relevance of the close of that canto to the whole of Mr. Eliot's work must be insisted on . . . There is the central position of Tiresias in the poem to be puzzled out . . . When all this has been done by the reader, when the materials with which the words are to clothe themselves have been collected, the poem still remains to be read. And it is easy to fail in this undertaking. (*PLC*, 233)

The critic *directs* the reader to the appropriate – because publicly available – associational contexts that are required for the reading of the poem, since although Eliot's earlier poetry has 'the air of monologue, of a stream of associations' (*PLC*, 234), in his later poetry 'the pretence of a continuous thread of associations is dropped' (*PLC*, 234). The power of the poetry will depend on the depth and significance of the memories which it is able to evoke in the reader: to achieve this, it will itself have to be saturated in memory. As Eliot put it in 'Tradition and the Individual Talent', 'not only the best but the most individual parts of [the poet's] work may be those in which the dead poets, his ancestors, assert their immortality most vigorously';[133] or as Yeats put it:

> Communication with the *Anima Mundi* is through association of thoughts or images or objects: the famous dead and those of whom but a faint memory lingers, can still – and it is to no other end, that all unknowing, we value posthumous fame – tread the corridor and take the empty chair.[134]

Poetry evokes ghosts, who come as harbingers of those depths of memory that connect the present with the engrams of a savage past, that allow us to recapitulate the whole history of human development since its primitive beginnings, that recollect and recover the myths by which the modern mind is

---

[133] T. S. Eliot, 'Tradition and the Individual Talent', *Selected Essays* (London: Faber and Faber, 1951), 14.

[134] Yeats, *Explorations*, 527.

still shaped. The poetry and criticism of the modernist movement is a haunted literature, restlessly sifting memory for a significant revelation, for the arrival of, the survival of, a myth: or, as Eliot put it in *Four Quartets*, for the moment when the poet catches 'the sudden look of some dead master/Whom I had known, forgotten, half recalled', for the moment when he recognises 'in the brown baked features/The eyes of a familiar compound ghost/Both intimate and unidentifiable'[135] – an associate, the recovery of ancient association, which is not merely subjective because it has survived obliviscence to become part of the ideal continuum and, therefore, remains written on the *tabula* of human history.

---

[135] T. S. Eliot, 'Little Gidding', *Collected Poems 1909–1962*, 217.

5 Chaos and Conversation: Pater, Joyce, Woolf

There is a passage in the 'Aeolus' chapter of James Joyce's *Ulysses* in which a conversation about rhetoric – 'One of the most polished periods I think I ever listened to in my life fell from the lips of Seymour Bushe', J. J. O'Molloy opines to Stephen[1] – is suddenly interrupted by a passage which appears to belong to Stephen Dedalus's stream of consciousness but which many critics agree is an allusion to, or a parody of, Dickens's style in *David Copperfield*:

> –A few wellchosen words, Lenehan prefaced. Silence!
> Pause. J. J. O'Molloy took out his cigarettecase.
> False lull. Something quite ordinary.
> Messenger took out his matchbox thoughtfully and lit his cigar.
> I have often thought since on looking back over that strange time that it was that small act, trivial in itself, that striking of that match, that determined the whole aftercourse of both our lives. (*U*, 115; 7: 759–640)

It has been argued that the beginning of the final sentence imitates the tone of Victorian autobiographical narration and is probably based on David Copperfield's reflections on the wedding of Peggotty and Barkis[2] – 'I have often thought, since, what an odd, innocent, out-of-the-way kind of wedding

---

[1] James Joyce, *Ulysses*, ed. Hans Walter Gabler (London: Penguin, 1986), 114; 7:747; hereafter cited in the text as *U*, with page number followed by chapter and line number.

[2] Don Gifford with Robert J. Seidman, *Ulysses Annotated* (Berkeley: University of California Press, 1988), 146.

it must have been . . .' (*DC*, 201) – but critics have disagreed on how we are to read it: is it Stephen's mind, replete with literary matter, which finds its thought by repeating phrases from his reading? Or is it a Joycean voice which intrudes to comment, from a more knowing perspective than Stephen's, on events whose significance Stephen cannot yet understand? Indeed, did Joyce note in Dickens's phrasing an echo of Tristram's comment on Toby and the fly – 'I often think that I owe one half of my philanthropy to that one accidental impression' (*TS*, 131; II, 12) – so that we are to hear *Tristram Shandy* through *David Copperfield*, together forming a tradition in which we are to read Joyce's text?

We know that Joyce had to write an essay on Dickens in 1912 (Dickens's centenary year) in his attempt to become a licensed schoolteacher in Italy,[3] and that *David Copperfield* is parodied in 'Oxen of the Sun' in Mrs Purefoy's reference to her husband by Dora's pet name for David – 'And as her loving eyes behold her babe she wishes only one blessing more, to have her dear Doady there with her to share her joy' (*U*, 342; 14: 1320) – but is this particular Dickens novel invoked both here and in 'Aeolus' because Joyce's relationship to Stephen Dedalus is similar to Dickens's relationship to David Copperfield, each a partly autobiographical representation of a younger self struggling towards becoming the writer who can retrace his earlier experience? Did Joyce see in David's flight to the continent after the death of Dora a reversed image of his own flight to the continent with Nora, and in David's recovery of memory by his return to England a challenge to his own recuperation of memory by his refusal to return to Ireland? Is that why he reverses Dora's recollection of her unfulfilled life by retracing Dickens's phrase about her on her deathbed – 'with the old shake of her curls' – in the context of Mrs Purefoy's 'happy *accouchement*' and plentiful children: 'With the old shake of her pretty head she recalls those days' (*U*, 343; 14: 1326)?

Once set running, the possible associations between the two works multiply: for instance, when David decides to use Traddles's office as his business address, Dickens describes the event in a strangely suggestive way: 'The girls had gone, when my name burst into bloom on Traddles's door' (*DC*, 918). Richard Ellmann insists that 'Bloom' is a realistic name in *Ulysses*, and that in one chapter Joyce 'deliberately confuses' the fictional Leopold Bloom with a real Joseph Bloom, a dentist, 'and in another he lists as one of Leopold's old

---

[3] Richard Ellmann, *James Joyce* (Oxford: Oxford University Press, 1982), 320–1.

addresses 38 Lombard Street, which was actually Joseph Bloom's address',[4] but as David's name 'blooms' in Dickens's novel, it sets off a train of related imagery: Dora is recollected as 'the Blossom that had withered in its bloom' (*DC*, 936); Peggoty describes David's children as 'these heer flowers' (*DC*, 940) – Bloom, of course, is also Henry Flower – and addresses David as 'your own sweet blooming self' (*DC*, 940). Is Stephen's search for a 'blooming self' through his encounter with Bloom based on David's encounters with Micawber who, like Bloom, is 'a sort of town traveller for a number of miscellaneous houses' (*DC*, 213)? Would Bloom, in later times, be able to write of his Dedalean friend as Micawber wrote to David: 'though estranged (by the force of circumstances over which I have had no control) from the personal society of the friend and companion of my youth, I have not been unmindful of his soaring flight' (*DC*, 945)? Is Stephen's 'soaring' Dedalean flight a recapitulation of David's?

Returning to the original passage in 'Aeolus', we may note something odd not only about the intervention of Dickens's phraseology in the stream of consciousness but about the detailed working of the language:

> Messenger took out his matchbox thoughtfully and lit his cigar.
>
> I have often thought since on looking back over that strange time that it was that small act, trivial in itself, that striking of that match, that determined the whole aftercourse of both our lives.

What makes this passage stand out is its insistent use of 'that': it is, as Thomas Jackson Rice puts it, 'a portentous narrative cliché, its banality reinforced by its awkward style',[5] a portentousness that has alerted some readers to the fact that '*that match*' in Stephen's consciousness is not necessarily identical with the 'match' that comes out of the 'matchbox'. The very repetition of 'that's undermines the confidence with which we can point to '*that* match', and opens up the alternative meanings that 'match' might have. Thus the 'match' to which the sentence refers may be the kind that occurs in a sporting contest – Stephen, after all, is about to 'match' himself against the rhetorical traditions of Dublin with his own 'wellchosen words' – or the kind of 'match' that David makes with Dora or Joyce with Nora – or even, as Robert Spoo has

---

[4] Ibid., 375.

[5] Thomas Jackson Rice, *Joyce, Chaos and Complexity* (Urbana: University of Illinois Press, 1997), 82.

suggested, that Stephen makes with Bloom.[6] The shift to a different stylistic context undermines the causal relation in which 'that match' stands *between* 'took out his matchbox and lit his cigar', and detaches the sentence from its environment, both linguistic and referential, to open up a space into which alternative meanings can flow. The sentence, in other words, defeats its own content, since what it asserts – 'that determined the whole aftercourse of both our lives' – is posited on an absence, an indeterminacy in the language itself, one whose 'aftercourse' is the very opposite of 'determined' since it leaves the actual reference of the word 'both' entirely indeterminate. For the re-reader of this chapter, J. J. O'Molloy's words some eight pages earlier take on a new significance: 'Who has the most matches?' (107; 7, 463).

The allusion to Dickens, which seems so strangely inserted into the novel, occurs in a chapter – the seventh – which is full of other strange insertions in the form of the newspaper headlines which interrupt and comment upon the events of the chapter. As Richard Ellmann has suggested, 'by whomever composed, the headlines serve as a warning that the view of reality so far presented may not suffice indefinitely'.[7] That 'view of reality so far presented' was shaped by what Ellman describes as the 'initial style' of the first six chapters of the novel, the style that has come, loosely, to be described as a 'stream of consciousness' technique, in which events are rendered through the detailed reproduction of the flow of associations in a character's mind:

> He crossed to the bright side, avoiding the loose cellarflap of number seventyfive. The sun was nearing the steeple of George's church. Be a warm day I fancy. Specially in these black clothes feel it more. Black conducts, reflects, (refracts is it?), the heat. But I could not go in that light suit. Make a picnic of it. His eyelids sank quietly often as he walked in happy warmth. Boland's breadvan delivering with trays our daily but she prefers yesterday's loaves turnovers crisp crowns hot. Makes you feel young. Somewhere in the east: early morning: set off at dawn. Travel round in front of the sun, steal a day's march on him. Keep it up for ever never grow a day older technically. Walk along a strand, strange land, come to a city gate, sentry there, old ranker too, old Tweedy's big moustaches, leaning on a long kind of spear. (*U*, 47; 4, 77–87)

---

[6] Robert Spoo, 'Teleology, Monocausality, and Marriage in Ulysses', *ELH*, Vol. 56, No. 2 (Summer 1989), 439–62, 452.

[7] Richard Ellmann, *Ulysses on the Liffey* (London: Faber, 1974), 73.

The associations which govern the transitions in Bloom's thought – the uncertain scientific knowledge, the constant return to Molly, the imaginary travel in the East – provide the reader with an implicit map of the uniqueness of this particular mind, a uniqueness that depends on its stock of memories and the ways in which they interact. The development of such 'stream of consciousness' techniques are often traced to William James's discussion, in Chapter IX of *Principles of Psychology* (1890), of 'The Stream of Thought'. James wished to challenge the discrete nature of the elements in traditional associationism, and, in particular, Bain's view that 'the stream of thought is not a continuous current, but a series of distinct ideas, more or less rapid their succession; the rapidity being measurable by the number that pass through the mind in a given time'.[8] Thought, James insisted, 'is nothing jointed; it flows. A "river" or a "stream" are the metaphors by which it is most naturally described. *In talking of it hereafter, let us call it the stream of thought, of consciousness, or of subjective life*'.[9] Ironically, James himself, in the subsequent development of his 'radical empiricism' in the first decade of the twentieth century, was to reject his own notion of the continuous stream and to return to a conception of states of mind as consisting of smaller psychic units, claiming Bergson as support for his reversion to the fundamental proposition of the British empiricist tradition.[10] But though James might have provided the terminology by which critics have defined the 'stream of consciousness' technique, earlier British psychologists were no less aware of both the complexity and the *flowing* nature of the associating mind. Indeed, James commended Bain's discussion of 'compound association' as one to which he had nothing to add, and in that discussion Bain points out that although 'we have assumed the links of association to be single or individual; we must now consider the very frequent case of the union of several bonds of contiguity or similarity', bonds which include emotions and volitions as well as 'purely intellectual' ones.[11] Associations linked by an emotion will seem to be portions of a continuous state rather than singular 'events'. Following in Bain's footsteps, James Sully,[12] in his *Outlines of Psychology* (1884), provides the following description of 'complex association':

---

[8] Quoted, Gerald E. Myers, 'Introduction', *The Principles of Psychology*, xxvii.

[9] James, *Principles of Psychology*, Vol. 1, 233.

[10] See Myers, 'Introduction', *The Principles of Psychology*, xxxiii ff.

[11] Bain, *Mental and Moral Science*, 151.

[12] See James Sully, *My Life and Friends: A Psychologist's Memories* (London: T. Fisher Unwin, 1918), for an account of his relations with Bain, particularly 182ff.

One element may enter as a member into a number of distinct combinations. Thus the image of the Colisseum at Rome is associated with that of events in my personal history, of pleasant days passed at Rome, of historical events, such as the gladiatorial combats of the Empire, its conquests and luxury &c. The threads of association are not distinct and parallel, like the strings of a harp, but intersect one another, forming an intricate network.[13]

The 'intricate network' suggests a multidimensional conception of association, rather than the 'train' of individual, atomic units, and one in which association shades off into what Sully describes as the 'wide obscure region of the subconscious' that consists of a 'whole aggregate or complex of mental phenomena, sensations, impressions, thoughts, etc. most of which are obscure, transitory, and not distinguished'.[14] The resources for the fictional presentation of character through complex 'threads of association' were thus well-developed in late-nineteenth-century British psychology – long before the development of the Freudian psychology to which 'stream of consciousness' is regularly related.[15] For many, Freudian psychology represents the absolute antithesis of the 'passivity' so often imputed to associationism but if we are to judge by Freud's usual instruction to his patients about how to proceed when entering into analysis, the distinction may not be so significant:

Your talk with me must differ in one respect from an ordinary conversation. Whereas usually you rightly try to keep the threads of your story together and to exclude all intruding associations and side issues, so as not to wander too far from the point, here you must proceed differently. You will notice that as you relate things various ideas will occur to you which you feel inclined to put aside with certain criticisms and objections. You will be tempted to say to yourself: 'This or that has no

---

[13] James Sully, *Outlines of Psychology* (London: Longmans, Green, 1884), 272.

[14] Ibid., 74.

[15] See, for instance, C. Hugh Holman, Addison Hibbard and William Flint Thrall (eds), 'The Stream-of-Consciousness Novel', *A Handbook to Literature* (New York: Odyssey Press, 1960), which both claims a Freudian provenance and undermines it at the same time: 'In a major sense, the present-day stream-of-consciousness novel is a product of Freudian psychology with its structure of psychological levels although it first appeared in *Les Lauriers sont coupés*, by Eduard Dujardin, in 1887' (471–2).

connection here, or it is quite unimportant, or it is nonsensical, so it cannot be necessary to mention it.' Never give in to these objections, but mention it even if you feel a disinclination against it, or indeed just because of this . . . Act as if you were sitting at the window of a railway train and describing to someone behind you the changing views you see outside.[16]

The patient travels in a train, passively, through 'changing views' as trains of associations pass through the mind. Freud's not quite 'ordinary conversation' into which the free associations emerge suggests that the techniques of psychoanalysis are an elaboration of Hume's conception of association as conversation, and conversation as association – to such an extent, indeed, that Robert M. Young may be correct in his view that Freud's basic assumptions 'were elaborated in his early and rather orthodox associationist works'.[17]

Joyce's knowledge of the associationist tradition, as John S. Rickard has pointed out, had a much more local source in Father Michael Maher's defence of a Christian conception of the self in his book on *Psychology*, of which Joyce owned a copy and which he seems to have used in constructing Stephen's musings on the self in 'Proteus'.[18] Maher's main antagonists are those of the 'sensationalist' tradition – like Hume and Mill – who do not recognise either the reality of the soul or the rationality of the mind, and he contextualises his arguments against them by a detailed examination of the theories of memory and association within the British tradition, drawing particularly on the work of Sir William Hamilton and James Sully. Given Joyce's ambivalence towards the oppressiveness of Catholic theology, Maher's discussion probably encouraged rather than deflected Joyce's interest in Hume and Humean scepticism – sufficiently, at any rate, for Richard Ellman to claim that Aristotle and Hume stand opposed to each other in the structure of *Ulysses*, and that 'the dominant mood from the *Wandering Rocks* through *Circe* is scepticism, Bloom's Day but also, for the nine hours from three to midnight, Hume's day'.[19] Like many others born in the latter part of the nineteenth century, however, Hume's

[16] Quoted in Clark, *Freud: the Man and the Cause*, 122.
[17] Robert M. Young, 'Association of Ideas', in Philip P. Wiener (ed.), *Dictionary of the History of Ideas* (New York: Scribner's, 1968), Vol. 1, 111–18; also available at http://human-nature.com/rmyoung/papers/paper58.html.
[18] John S. Rickard, *Joyce's Book of Memory: The Mnemotechnics of Ulysses* (Durham, SC: Duke University Press, 1999), 24.
[19] Richard Ellmann, *Ulysses on the Liffey*, 96.

conception of the self as 'nothing but a bundle or collection of different perceptions, which succeed each other with an inconceivable rapidity, and are in
a perpetual flux and movement' (*T*, 252) was familiar to Joyce from that most
influential of early modernist texts, Walter Pater's *The Renaissance* (1873).[20]
Indeed, Joyce wrote his early essay on Clarence Mangan in an imitation of
Pater's style, and parodied it in *Ulysses* in 'Oxen of the Sun', and the connection
was still sufficiently evident for T. S. Eliot to comment to Virginia Woolf that
Joyce was 'founded upon Walter Pater with a dash of Newman'.[21] As David
Masson pointed out as early as 1865, in his study of *Recent British Philosophy*,
Hume's scepticism – indeed, his nihilism – had developed a renewed relevance
as a result of the impact of scientific developments since the mid-century.[22]
Modern science predicts 'the collapse or winding-down of the whole solar
system', so 'that a period will come when all the energy locked up in the solar
system and sustaining whatever of motion or life there is it, will be exhausted',
leaving only 'a defunct and featureless community of rest and death',[23] and
this, according to Masson, is entirely compatible with the 'simple ruthlessness'
of Hume's philosophy which shows that,

> on the principles of philosophical reason, even this reality must vanish
> from the universe, and not a rack be left to float in the void. This succes-
> sion of ideas, which is called Mind, and which is all that is really known,
> has *it*, when you investigate sufficiently, any substratum of continuous
> being? Is not Mind, too, if you come to that, a hypothesis beyond the
> facts? Is there any certainty, any substantiality at all, anything but an
> illusive series of phantasms flitting in a vague nothingness of Time and
> Space?[24]

It is from a position of Humean scepticism that Pater, in an early essay,
attacks Coleridge's 'struggle against the relative spirit'[25] as a struggle against

---

[20] Richard Ellmann, *James Joyce*, 94–5.

[21] Leonard Woolf (ed.), *A Writer's Diary: Being Extracts from the Diary of Virginia Woolf* (London: Hogarth Press, 1953), 49.

[22] David Masson, *Recent British Philosophy: A Review with Criticisms* (London: Macmillan, 1865), 154.

[23] Ibid., 151–2.

[24] Ibid., 32.

[25] Walter Pater, 'Coleridge', *Appreciations: With an Essay on Style* (London: Macmillan, 1889), 67.

modernity itself, since 'modern thought is distinguished from ancient by its cultivation of the "relative" spirit in place of the "absolute"',[26] with the consequence that to 'the modern spirit nothing is, or can be rightly known, except relatively and under conditions'.[27] Pater's account of scepticism, and the importance to it of the essay form, might equally be an account of Hume's transition from philosopher to essay writer: 'the form of the essay . . . [is] the literary form necessary to a mind for which truth itself is but a possibility, realisable not as a general conclusion, but rather as the elusive effect of a particular personal experience'.[28] Hume's insistence that 'when I enter most intimately into what I call *myself*, I always stumble on some particular perception or other, of heat or cold, light or shade, love or hatred, pain or pleasure', and that, as a consequence, 'I never can catch *myself* at any time without a perception, and never can observe any thing but the perception' (*T*, 252), forms the basis of Pater's famous account of the self in the 'Conclusion' to *The Renaissance*:

> But when reflexion begins to play upon those objects they are dissipated under its influence; the cohesive force seems suspended like some trick of magic; each object is loosed into a group of impressions – colour, odour, texture – in the mind of the observer. And if we continue to dwell in thought on this world, not of objects in the solidity with which language invests them, but of impressions, unstable, flickering, inconsistent, which burn and are extinguished with our consciousness of them, it contracts still further: the whole scope of observation is dwarfed into the narrow chamber of the individual mind . . . Analysis goes a step further still, and assures us that those impressions of the individual mind to which, for each one of us, experience dwindles down, are in perpetual flight . . . To such a tremulous wisp constantly reforming itself on the stream, to a single sharp impression, with a sense in it, a relic more or less fleeting, of such moments gone by, what is real in our life fines itself down.[29]

Pater's critical technique, like his scepticism, is an elaboration of Humean associationism, exploiting what Wolfgang Iser describes as 'the randomness

---

[26] Ibid., 65.

[27] Ibid.

[28] Walter Pater, *Plato and Platonism* (London: Library Edition, 1910), 175–6.

[29] Walter Pater, *The Renaissance*, ed. Kenneth Clark (London: Fontana/Collins, 1961; 1873), 221–2.

of experience and the subjectivity of perception'[30] in order to increase 'the diversified chain of impressions, the fashioning of which takes us further and further away from the picture itself, and deeper and deeper into Pater's own imagination', into 'an unbounded realm of associations'.[31] Pater's insistence on 'for ever curiously testing new opinions and courting new impressions, never acquiescing in a facile orthodoxy',[32] became the hinterland of modernism's search for new narrative techniques based on the exploration of those momentary impressions and that 'unbounded realm of associations' that were the only reality of the self.

Indeed, Pater's criticism repeats, in the aesthetic sphere, the paradox that underlies Hume's philosophy: the rational search for order in the mind is undone by the discovery of its profound irrationalism. Pater's 'aesthetic critic' is in search of a communicable truth: his function 'is to distinguish, to analyse, and separate from its adjuncts, the virtue by which a picture, a landscape, a fair personality in life or in a book, produces this special impression of beauty or pleasure, to indicate what the source of the impression is, and under what conditions it is experienced'.[33] The apparent objectivity of 'to distinguish, to analyse, and separate', or the scientific search for effective causes in 'the source of the impression' or determining contexts in 'under what conditions', dissolves, however, into an actual procedure of intense subjectivity, one which makes his perceptions, if communicable, no more than the connections of an intensely personal and private process of association:

> She is older than the rocks among which she sits; like the vampire, she has been dead many times, and learned the secrets of the grave; and has been a diver in deep seas, and keeps their fallen day about her; and trafficked for strange webs with Eastern merchants; and as Leda, was the mother of Helen of Troy, and, as Saint Anne, the mother of Mary; and all this has been to her but as the sound of lyres and flutes . . .[34]

What other observer of Leonardo's painting could have connected these images and characters in this train of recollection? How are we to replicate

---

[30] Wolfgang Iser, *Walter Pater: The Aesthetic Moment*, trans. David Henry Wilson (Cambridge: Cambridge University Press, 1987; 1960), 7.

[31] Ibid., 43–4.

[32] Pater, *The Renaissance*, 222–3.

[33] Ibid., 28.

[34] Ibid., 123.

this process in order to discover 'what the source of the impression is, and under what conditions it is experienced'? The attempt to establish a *scientific* and *objective* explanation of the workings of the mind – or of the workings of art – produces an outcome which is profoundly private and deeply subjective – a chaos of strange attractors.

In Pater's essay the displacement of the work of art by the observer's associations that was always implied by the associationist tradition is taken to a level of intensity in which the *style* of the criticism becomes itself the defining work of art, one which assiduously imposes itself upon its original object. The apparent paradox that Pater's theories and critical practice left to his successors was that no matter how accurate their work, no matter with what fidelity they rendered their characters' experiences and the flow of their minds in the processes of association, those carefully constructed portraits would be displaced and supplanted by readerly associations that the writer could not foresee or control. Since the success of art depends on its capacity for generating associations, no work of literature can avoid the displacement of the writer's associative connections by the reader's: and yet, if the work of art is to have many readers the writer must find a technique by which the chaos of those associating minds can be bent to some kind of sustainable order.

Whether or not T. S. Eliot's account of Joyce's 'mythic method' was accurate to Joyce's intent, it effectively predicted one of the major roles for Joyce criticism in the rest of the century – the search for the order that underlies the chaotic surface of *Ulysses*. Indeed, recent studies of Joyce in relation to chaos theory – Thomas Jackson Rice's *Joyce, Chaos and Complexity* (1997) and Peter Francis Mackey's *Chaos Theory and James Joyce's Everyman* (1999) – have sought to use chaos theory itself to explain and justify the 'complexity' of *Ulysses* as a literary enactment of the ontological truths revealed by chaos theory: 'the entire novel explores how trivial things and chance shape meaning and life, the contingent nature of experience, our faith that order persists beneath the chaos of life, our participation in aboriginality, and the opportunities for change always before us'.[35] Chaos, in effect, becomes a new principle of order, and the Joycean text, by destroying traditional realism, becomes a mimesis of the world which realism could not recognise but which Joyce, like Poincaré, anticipates. But criticism's search for the order which the mythic method constructs out of chaos has in fact had exactly the opposite effect: in searching

---

[35] Peter Francis Mackey, *Chaos Theory and James Joyce's Everyman* (Gainesville: University of Florida Press, 1999), 63.

for all the clues and all the connections that will reduce chaos to order, each piece of literary detection only increases the potential for chaos by adding yet another set of possible connections, yet another layer of memories to be recalled in the mind of the ideal reader.

Take, for example, the previously cited analysis by Robert Spoo of the Dickens interpolation in 'Aeolus': having suggested that the 'match' in the passage is the match between Stephen and Bloom, he goes on to suggest that 'matches in this period frequently went by the trade name of "Vestas", and Vesta was the Roman goddess of the hearth, that is of domestic life'. This 'pun buried' in the passage, he suggests, is to be picked up when 'Stephen will presently refer to "Dublin vestals" in his Parable'.[36] In order to grasp the passage properly, the reader must associate 'match' with vesta – a not impossible expectation for the re-reader, since (though Spoo does not note it) a vesta match actually appears in 'Wandering Rocks' (*U*, 189; 10, 403) – and know its classical meaning in order to understand the irony of Stephen's attribution of it to the two old Dublin women. It is entirely possible that Joyce manufactured such intricacy of detail but what puts them into circulation in Joyce criticism is, again and again, the language of 'association'. Without tracing fugitive associations much Joycean criticism would be bereft of any rationale. Even though it does not recognise itself – or, indeed, Joyce – as working in an associationist tradition, Joycean criticism is, to a large extent, an account of the associations generated in well-informed readers – or of the associations which critics think that readers ought to have as they progress through the text.

Thus, according to Richard Ellmann, the difficulty Joyce faced in writing *Ulysses*, was that 'much of the imagery' of Stephen's previous fictional life 'had derived from the name of Dedalus and its association with the legendary maker of mazes and wings';[37] 'this whole chain of associations', Udaya Kumar explains of Molly's reading, 'is evoked through verbal similarity';[38] 'Ithaca', according to Richard E. Madtes, 'is constructed largely on this associational pattern – again and again one question will trigger another';[39] by the end of the same chapter, according to Karen Lawrence, 'the respondent sinks

---

[36] Robert Spoo, 'Teleology, Monocausality, and Marriage in Ulysses', *ELH*, Vol. 56, No. 2 (Summer 1989), 439–62, 453.

[37] Ellmann, *Ulysses on the Liffey*, 4.

[38] Udaya Kumar, *The Joycean Labyrinth: Repetition, Time and Tradition in Ulysses* (Oxford: Clarendon Press, 1991), 22.

[39] Richard E. Madtes, *The 'Ithaca' Chapter of Joyce's Ulysses* (Ann Arbor: UMI Research Press, 1983), 77.

into a spasm of verbal associations, in a realm of imagination that fuses the child's world with the mythic';[40] and according to Alan Roughley, Derrida's deconstructive reading of Ulysses is 'an operation which is performed upon the terms of binary opposition and the network, or "chain" of terms associated with each of the units in the binary pair'.[41] What else is Gifford and Seidman's *Ulysses Annotated* but a guide to the possible associational contexts that any reader needs in order to make sense of the text? Take, for instance, the following passage from 'Hades':

> As they turned into Berkeley street a streetorgan near the Basin sent over and after them a rollicking rattling song of the halls. Has anybody here seen Kelly? Kay ee double ell wy. Dead march from *Saul*. He's as bad as old Antonio. He left me on my ownio. (*U*, 80; 6, 372ff)

Of this passage we are told where Berkeley Street is (but not why it is so named or why 'street' is uncapitalised, or if we should recall how Bloom reacted, in 'Calypso', when 'Quick warm sunlight came running from Berkeley road, swiftly' (*U*, 50; 4, 240); that the Basin is the 'City Basin, a rectangular reservoir just west of Berkeley Street' – is its rectangularity significant? – should we be preparing to contrast it with the 'vast circumterrestrial ahorizontal curve' of water celebrated in 'Ithaca' (*U* 549; 17, 208)?; that 'Kelly' is an 'American adaptation (1909) by William J. Mckenna . . . from the English song "Kelly of the Isle of Man" (1908) by C. W. Murphy and Will Letters' (adept readers will, of course, see the association with the Murphy of 'Eumaeus' and the relationship between the second composer's name and the alphabetization of Kelly's name, as well as the connection with the sandwichboardmen bearing the name HELY around the city); 'Handel's Dead March', we are informed, 'is traditionally played in British military funerals' (– an ironic counterpoint to Dignam's non-military, perhaps even non-British funeral?) ; and Antonio is 'an Italian ice-cream merchant who treats his benefactors much as Kelly from the Isle of Man treated his', appearing in a song which, we are told, 'was a forerunner of all the Kelly songs' (though why is not explained).[42] The build-up of associational contexts around each word and phrase generates an excess of

---

[40] Karen Lawrence, *The Odyssey of Style in Ulysses* (Princeton: Princeton University Press, 1981), 197.

[41] Alan Roughley, *James Joyce and Critical Theory: An Introduction* (Hemel Hempstead: Harvester Wheatsheaf, 1991), 276.

[42] Gifford and Seidman, *Ulysses Annotated*, 112–13.

information to be brought into play in the reading these four lines of Joyce's text, and yet that information (as my parenthetical questions suggest) in no way exhausts the innumerable associative links that might possibly relate them to the rest of the text. By providing sources for the allusions and references, Gifford and Seidman offer the illusion of mastering the text, when, in fact, they are simply providing more material to help make it unmasterable, as each fragment in the already substantial body of the text multiplies the 'associated' material which the 'educated' – if not the 'ideal' – reader might possibly bring into play.

Criticism of Joyce's work is haunted by the word 'association' – the similarity between the Jews and the Irish, Ellmann tells us, was one on which Joyce insisted, because both were 'impulsive, given to fantasy, addicted to associative thinking' (395) – and yet the associationist aesthetics from which Joyce's work emerges – the aesthetics of Pater and of Yeats – are rarely acknowledged in accounts of the historical context in which Joyce was working. As a consequence, the paradox of Joycean criticism's endless production of possible associations was 'solved' by making Joyce a precursor of poststructuralist theories of language. As Derek Attridge and Daniel Ferrer put it in their introduction to *Post-structuralist Joyce* (1984),

> The academic machinery that once turned out useful information to guide the ordinary reader through the Joycean maze has become an uncheckable generator of endlessly proliferating secondary literature, revealing *in toto* something about Joyce's texts (and about all literary texts?) to which each individual contribution, in its attempt to arrive at final answers, is oblivious, the infinite productivity of interpretative activity, the impossibility of closing off the processes of signification, the incessant shifting and opening-out of meaning in the act or reading and re-reading.[43]

The switch of focus – from the search for meaning to the processes by which meaning is generated – was to have enormous consequences for Joyce studies: Joyce became the writer 'ahead of his time' who had to wait for his interpreters to catch up; an exemplary deconstructionist before deconstruction; a writer who had discovered that we could never uncover the full 'presence' of a text

---

[43] Derek Attridge and Daniel Ferrer, *Post-structuralist Joyce: Essays from the French* (Cambridge: Cambridge University Press, 1984), 7–8.

and therefore the necessary 'unreadability' of all texts: 'the aim', Attridge and Ferrer, explain, 'is not to produce a *reading* of this intractable text, to make it more familiar and exorcise its strangeness, but on the contrary to confront its unreadability'.[44]

This moment of intersection between continental theory and Irish-English literature was celebrated in Colin McCabe's *James Joyce and the Revolution of the Word* (1979). Like many later readings, McCabe represented Joyce's writing as a fulfilment of the theoretical linguistics of Ferdinand de Saussure, and, in particular, of his analysis of the 'sign' as consisting of two components, the 'signifier' and the 'signified', the latter quite distinct from a word's referent in the world. For structuralist and poststructuralist critics, analysis of the literary text was not conducted in the hope of discovering its original or fundamental meaning – its relationship to some real world to which it referred – but rather, in McCabe's words, in the recognition that 'the separation between signifier and signified must be accentuated so that the spectator is aware of the constant production of meaning in which he or she is implicated'.[45] This 'revolutionary' conception of literary language is set in direct contrast to the 'realist' text, with its 'empiricist' presuppositions about the transparency of language:

> The conviction that the real can be displayed and examined through a perfectly transparent language is evident in George Eliot's Prelude to *Middlemarch*. In that Prelude she talks of those who care 'to know the history of man, and how the mysterious mixture behaves under the varying experiments of Time' and the language of empiricism runs through the text. . .[46]

What the reading of such realist texts involves 'for us is passive consumption', whereas in Joyce's work, McCabe insists, reading 'becomes an active metamorphosis, a constant displacement of language'.[47] The failure of criticism in relation to Joyce's texts is that texts which defy such 'passive consumption', such 'transparent language' are not amenable literary interpretation: 'literary criticism itself cannot cope with Joyce's texts because those texts refuse to

---

[44] Ibid., 10.

[45] Colin McCabe, *James Joyce and the Revolution of the Word* (London: Macmillan, 1979), 75.

[46] Ibid., 18.

[47] Ibid., 2.

reproduce the relation between reader and text on which literary criticism is predicated'.[48]

The presumption that empiricism demands the naturalization of language and the transparency by which we see through language to the real is a common theme of this 'continental turn' in British criticism: a typical and influential text of the period is Catherine Belsey's *Critical Practice* (1980), which conflates 'common sense', 'empiricism' and 'realism' in a shared suppression of the awareness that language *intervenes* between ourselves and the world: 'the transparency of language is an illusion';[49] in the realist text, 'the world evoked in the fiction, its patterns of cause and effect, of social relationships and moral values, largely confirm the patterns of the world we seem to know'; 'Realism offers itself as transparent'; it is an 'empiricist assumption that the text reflects the world'.[50] This is to be countered by a 'post-Saussurean theory [which] starts from an analysis of language, proposing that language is not transparent', and from which 'it becomes possible . . . to liberate the plurality of the text'.[51] The irony of this contextualisation of the value of 'poststructuralism' is that it profoundly misunderstands the nature of 'empiricism' in the British tradition and of the 'common-sense' to which it is allied. Belsey uses the difference between colours in different languages to illustrate the fact that, according to Saussure, 'if words stood for pre-existing concepts, they would all have exact equivalents in meaning from one language to the next; but this is not true'.[52] But it was precisely the founding assertion of British empiricism that, in the words of John Locke, though 'words, by long and familiar use . . . come to excite in men certain ideas so constantly and readily, that they are apt to suppose a natural connexion between them', nonetheless 'they *signify* only men's peculiar ideas, and that *by a perfectly arbitrary Imposition*'.[53] Because languages are 'gradually establish'd by human conventions without any promise' (*T*, 490), and conventions are different in different societies, it is inevitable that, as Locke insists, there may be a 'great store of words in one language *which have not any that answer them*

---

[48] Ibid., 3.

[49] Catherine Belsey, *Critical Practice* (London: Routledge, 1980), 4.

[50] Ibid., 51.

[51] Ibid., 55.

[52] Quoted ibid., 39; Ferdinand de Saussure, *Course in General Linguistics*, trans. Wade Biskin (London: Fontana, 1974; 1916), 116.

[53] John Locke, *An Essay Concerning Human Understanding*, Bk III, Ch. ii, 8, 408.

in another.[54] Hume and Hartley's associationism only underlined the contingency from which languages are constructed:

> It will easily appear from the observations here made upon words, and the associations which adhere to them, that the languages of different ages and nations must bear a great general resemblance to each other, and yet have considerable particular differences; whence any one may be translated into any other, so as to convey the same ideas in general, and yet not with perfect precision and exactness. They must resemble one another, because the phaenomena of nature, which they are all intended to express, and the uses and exigencies of human life, to which they minister, have a general resemblance. But then, as the bodily make and genius of each people, the air, soil, and climate, commerce, and sciences, religion, &c. make considerable differences in different ages and nations, it is natural to expect, that the languages should have proportionable differences in respect of each other. (O, 281–2)

To Thomas Reid it is precisely part of our 'common sense' that 'there is often neither similitude between the sign and thing signified, nor any connection that arises necessarily from the nature of the things . . . The word *gold* has no similitude to the substance signified by it; nor is it in its own nature more fit to signify this than any other substance; yet, by habit and custom, it suggests this and no other'.[55] Indeed, for Reid, what is the 'common sense' of humanity in general is revealed not in individual words and their referents but by 'what is common in the structure of languages, ancient and modern, polished and barbarous'.[56]

The kind of *transparent* language that Belsey attributes to empiricism and to 'common sense' is in fact, for Hartley, the prelapsarian language from which our fallen condition entirely excludes us:

> If we suppose mankind possessed of such a language, as that they could at pleasure denote all their conceptions adequately, *i.e.* without any deficiency, superfluity, or equivocation; if, moreover, this language depended upon a

---

[54] Ibid., Book III, Ch. v, 8, 432.

[55] Ronald E. Beanblossom and Keith Lehrer (eds), *Thomas Reid, Inquiry and Essay* (Indianapolis: Hackett Publishing, 1983), 'An Inquiry into the Human Mind on the Principles of Common Sense', 41.

[56] Ibid., 'Essays on the Intellectual Powers of Man', 157.

few principles assumed, not arbitrarily, but because they were the shortest and best possible, and grew on from the same principles indefinitely, so as to correspond to every advancement in the knowledge of things, this language might be termed a philosophical one, and would as much exceed any of the present languages, as a paradisiacal state does the mixture of happiness and misery, which has been our portion ever since the fall. And it is no improbable supposition, that the language given by God to *Adam* and *Eve*, before the fall, was of this kind; and, though it might be narrow, answered all their exigencies perfectly well. (*O*, 315–16)

Associationist empiricism, in other words, could not, without self-contradiction (or the arrival at a paradisal state) maintain any other theory of language than one founded on the arbitrariness of meaning and on the *non-transparency* and *non-translatability* of languages. And given that language functions on the basis of such fundamentally arbitrary associations, it is inevitable that it will generate a *plurality* of meanings from the distinctiveness of the associational patterns laid down in the minds of different hearers and readers: 'every man has so inviolable a liberty to make words stand for what ideas he pleases, that no one hath the power to make others have the same ideas in their minds that he has, when they use the same words that he does', Locke tells us,[57] and it can be no less so in relation to the constructions of literary language, when their prime purpose is the excitation of associations which will not only necessarily be different in each reader but will differ in each reader at different times.

The poststructuralist effort 'to liberate the plurality of the text'[58] and to 'produce' rather than 'consume' meaning from the differential potentialities of the signifier thus ironically recapitulates the theories of an empiricism to which it believes it is radically opposed. 'As we read a text,' McCabe tells us, 'we are convinced that the meanings we consume are present in the text and originate in the author. But just as the interaction of the shell and ear produce the roar that the drinkers hear [in 'Sirens'], so it is the interaction between the discourses of the reader and the discourses of the text which produces the meanings that we extract'.[59] Replace 'discourse' with 'association' and the sentence might have been uttered by Francis Jeffrey, who declares on behalf of Archibald Alison that aesthetic experience is 'occasioned, not by any inherent

---

[57] Locke, *Essay Concerning the Human Understanding*, Book III, Ch. ii, 8, 408
[58] Belsey, *Critical Practice*, 55.
[59] McCabe, *James Joyce and the Revolution of the Word*, 85.

virtue in the objects before us, but by the accidents, if we may so express ourselves, by which these may have been enabled to suggest or recal to us our own past sensations and sympathies'.[60] The associationist reader *produces* the text in the interaction between the associational implications of the words and his or her own associational activity, and since much of that activity derives its potency from the experience of other works of literature – 'the images and recollections which have been associated with such objects, in the enchanting strains of the poets, are perpetually recalled'[61] – the experience is one of an expansive intertextuality which would not be inappropriately characterised by these words of Roland Barthes:

> The logic that governs the Text is not comprehensive (seeking to define 'what the work means') but metonymic; and the activity of associations, contiguities, and cross-references coincides with a liberation of symbolic energy . . . The Text is plural. This does not mean just that it has several meanings, but rather that it achieves plurality of meaning, an *irreducible* plurality. The Text is not a coexistence of meanings but a passage, transversal; thus it answers not to an interpretation, liberal though it may be, but to an explosion, a dissemination.[62]

Poststructuralism is, in effect, a rediscovery (by a different route/root) of the readerly energy posited in associationist theories of art. However, lacking any acknowledgment of the Joyce who was the inheritor of the associationist implications of the theories of Pater and Yeats, poststructuralist criticism has presented *Ulysses* as a new kind of *writing* which invokes a new kind of reader rather than the outcome of a theory *reading* which provokes a new kind of writing. Far from bringing order to chaos, the 'mythic method' stimulates rather than restrains the disorderly multiplication of associative connections and intersections, weaving that 'intricate network' of public and private associations by which the work of art – or art as *work* – is produced. In *Ulysses*, Joyce's own memories – 'See this. Remember' (*U*, 158; 9, 294) – will be woven together by the self he will in future become, so that 'in the future, the sister

---

[60] Francis Jeffrey, *The Edinburgh Review*, Vol. XVIII, No. XXXV (May 1811), 8.

[61] Ibid., 20.

[62] Roland Barthes, 'From Work to Text', in Josué V. Harari (ed.), *Textual Strategies: Perspectives in Post-Structuralist Criticism* (London: Methuen, 1980), 76–7. In a different translation in Stephen Heath (ed.), *Image—Music—Text* (London: Fontana, 1977; originally published 1971), 158.

of the past, I may see myself as I sit here now but by reflection from that which then I shall be' (*U*, 160; 9, 383–6). That weaving of past and present undertaken by the artist will be repeated, however, by a reader who brings a different past to bear on this present; the artist survives transformation, like Stephen's version of Shakespeare, only by accepting the offspring his work engenders: 'He is a ghost, a shadow now, the wind by Elsinore's rocks or what you will, the sea's voice, a voice heard only in the heart of him who is the substance of his shadow, the son consubstantial with the father' (*U*, 162; 9, 478–82). Art is a ghostly conversation between two trains of association, each weaving and unweaving the other. Joyce's recognition that his readers' associations will inevitably displace or transform the author's is imaged, perhaps, in Stephen's eviction from the Martello Tower, so that the final word of the first chapter, apparently in Stephen's consciousness but isolated in a paragraph by itself, is directed at the reader as much as it is at Mulligan: 'Usurper'.

Joyce's response to this inevitable usurpation explains what has been, since its first publication, a major problem about the structure of *Ulysses*: the stylistic shifts which, from 'Aeolus' onward, overlay the 'initial style' – as established in the first six chapters – with increasingly problematic narrative voices. We can understand these shifts by recognising that Stephen's two moments of achieved creativity in *Ulysses* – the story of the 'Dublin vestals' in 'Aeolus' and his account of Shakespeare in 'Scylla and Charybdis' – are both narrated against and in response to conversational interruptions, as though modelling the ways in which, just as Stephen must rise above the interventions of his associates, Joyce's own narrative art must survive others' associative reinvention of his text:

> Dubliners
> – Two Dublin vestals, Stephen said, elderly and pious, have lived fifty and fiftythree years in Fumbally's lane.
> – Where is that? the professor asked.
> – Off Blackpitts, Stephen said.
> Damp night reeking of hungry dough. Against the wall. Face glistening tallow under her fustian shawl. Frantic hearts. Akasic records. Quicker darlint!
> On now. Dare it. Let there be life.
> – They want to see the views of Dublin from the top of Nelson's pillar.
>   (*U*, 119; 7, 922–31)

The professor's intervention produces a flow of associational recollection in Stephen which interrupts his own narrative just as, in the following pages, it will be interrupted by comments from Professor McHugh, by the narrative following Bloom's departure from the newspaper office, and by those ironically intrusive headlines. Since 'Aeolus' is the first chapter in which we access the minds of both Bloom and Stephen, it is as though, in recognition of the dispersal of associative contexts within the narrative, Joyce allows the environment of the action – the newspaper office – to develop its own associative potential, one which both mimics and apparently pre-empts the associative workings in the mind of the reader by inserting, between the reader and the action, an alternative flow of associations shaped by a mind whose only concern is to turn story into headline. As associationist theorists had always stressed, 'the diversity of tastes corresponds to the diversity of occupations . . . the inferior station of life, by contracting the knowledge and affections of men within very narrow limits produces insensibly a similar contraction in their notions of the beautiful and the sublime' (*AET*, 62–3). Associations are rarely sufficiently free-flowing for the fulfilment of aesthetic effects but are limited by the habitual associative contexts into which the mind has been constrained. This was the fundamental issue in Hume's 'Of the Standard of Taste': 'those finer emotions of the mind are of a very tender and delicate nature, and require the concurrence of many favourable circumstances to make them play with facility and exactness, according to their general and established principles. The least exterior hindrance to such small springs, or the least internal disorder, disturbs their motion, and confounds the operation of the whole machine' (*E*, 232). What 'Aeolus' initiates is the introduction of hypothetical readers into the text, each with their own limited but dominating associational contexts, each, as it were, re-reading the text from a point beyond the end of the action, and thereby allowing Joyce to parody in advance the 'exterior hindrance' by which such limited associational contexts can have 'determined the whole aftercourse' of his text.

When 'Aeolus' was first published in serial form, as Hugh Kenner noted in *Joyce's Voices*,[63] there were no headlines: the headlines were introduced for the book publication and therefore represent, quite literally, a later perspective on the text – a response to it over and above its original form. In a chapter which is *a stream of speech and speeches* rather than a *stream of consciousness*, the headlines disrupt the forward flow of the talk not only by its textual interruption on the

---

[63] Hugh Kenner, *Joyce's Voices* (London: Faber and Faber, 1978).

page but by the fact that, like all headlines, they can only be written when the story is already known:

WHAT? – AND LIKEWISE – WHERE?

> – But what do you call it? Myles Crawford asked. Where did they get the plums? (*U*, 122; 7, 1050–1)

By their knowledge of the future, the headlines reveal that the apparently free-flowing speech in the newspaper office is as fixed and predictable as the rigid lines of type of the newspaper itself – '*Rose of Castille*. See the wheeze? Rows of cast steel. Gee!' (*U*, 111; 7, 591). The flow of voices moving forward turns into voices recollected; the present voices mould themselves to repeat past voices – 'Noble words coming' (*U*, 117; 7, 836) – and while the headlines appear to intercept in advance the free flow of conversation what they actually reveal is that those 'noble words' are no longer 'coming': each is not only fixed in *type*, and learned by rote, but is incapable of stimulating anything but a predictable response – a train of associations that runs on 'rows of cast steel'.

From 'Aeolus' onwards, it is as though we are confronted by a text that is already a *re*-reading of an ur-text to which have we have no direct access. In each case an associational context has forced itself upon and weaves its way through the text to supplant the events of the narrative in a process that mirrors (or 'matches') associationist theories of how the reader's mind operates when engaged in an aesthetic experience:

> –Well, says the citizen, what's the latest from the scene of the action? What did those tinkers in the city hall at their caucus meeting decide about the Irish language?
> O'Nolan, clad in shining armour, low bending made obeisance to the puissant and high and mighty chief of all Erin and did him to wit of that which had befallen, how the grave elders of the most obedient city, second of the realm, had met with them in the tholsel, and there, after due prayers to the gods who dwell in ether supernal, had taken solemn counsel whereby they might, if so be it might be, bring once more into honour among mortal men the winged speech of the seadivided Gael.
> – It's on the march, says the citizen. To hell with the bloody brutal Sassenachs and their *patois*. (*U*, 266; 12, 1180–91)

The flow of re-readerly associations – deriving in this case from Irish epic material inflected by nineteenth-century medievalism – superimposes itself upon and transforms the presentation of the action. Whether it is the translation of language into music in 'Sirens', or the adoption of the prose of romantic fiction in the first half of 'Nausicaa', or the successive stylistic parodies of 'Oxen of the Sun', the stream of consciousness of a potential *reader* of the novel envelopes the events in the limitations of a particular associational structure and does so with increasing intensity until – in 'Eumaus' and 'Ithaca' – it is almost impossible for us to see what is happening through the density of the hypothetical re-reader's interventions. We are placed in the position of the cab driver at the end of 'Eumaus':

> The driver never said a word, good, bad or indifferent, but merely watched the two figures, *as he sat in his lowbacked car*, both black, one full, one lean, walk towards the railway bridge, *to be married by Father Maher*. As they walked they at times stopped and walked again continuing their *tête à tête* (which, of course, he was utterly out of) about sirens, enemies of man's reason, mingled with a number of other topics of the same category, usurpers, historical cases of that kind while the man in the sweeper car or you might as well call it in the sleeper car who in any case couldn't possibly hear because they were too far simply sat in his seat near the end of lower Gardiner street *and looked after their lowbacked car*.
>
> (U, 543; 16, 1885–94)

The characters are 'too far' from us to be audible; lost behind the workings of a narrative voice that merges events (the silent driver) and associations (the lines from the song 'The Low-Backed Car' in italics) which appear to share the same ontological status in the world, Joyce effectively opens up a gulf *between* the narrative voice and the events being described, a gulf already filled with a hypothetical reader's associations which will, in turn, tease and tease out the real reader's own associational activity. The disjunction between narrative method and narrative content, the conflict between the associative context of the narrative voice and the conversations it is describing, force the reader into acknowledging the significance of his or her own associational response to the text. The parody of readerly association becomes, in effect, the stimulus to the real fulfilment of the associational imperative: we are forced to fill the gap between narrative method and narrative events with our own associational content.

That is why, perhaps, lurking in the song which is woven through the final paragraph of 'Eumaeus' is the name *Father Maher*, as though, like one of those moments in 'Wandering Rocks', a fictional and a real person are mistaken for one another. Stephen and Bloom are 'to be married by Father Maher' – is this the same Father Maher whose handbook of psychology Joyce annotated? The purpose of Michael Maher's book was to marry modern psychology – and especially associationist psychology – with Catholic doctrine, and he does so by claiming (in an echo of Coleridge's discussion of Hume's association-ism) that modern associationist theory is entirely anticipated in the work of St Thomas Aquinas, and true only insofar as it is in conformity with Aquinas's teachings:

> We have this co-identity in *nature* and in *time*, or what Hamilton calls the laws of *direct* and of *indirect* remembrance, laid down by St Thomas as the two general principles of association. Accordingly, notwithstanding the contempt with which writers of the Associationist school have invari-ably exhibited towards the schoolmen, we find in these terse remarks of St Thomas, now over six hundred years old, a statement and analysis of the Laws of Association virtually as complete and exhaustive as that given by any psychologist from Hobbes to Mr Herbert Spencer.[64]

The scholasticism of Stephen and the scientism of Bloom are married in a psychology which, according to Maher, can unite both the medieval and the modern. As associations are shared between them, they become associates, and the solipsism with which both Stephen and Bloom have been threatened in the earlier part of the novel is overthrown in the recognition of their potentially shared identities:

> Did they find their educational careers similar?
> Substituting Stephen for Bloom Stoom would have passed successively through a dame's school and high school. Substituting Bloom for Stephen Blephen would have passed successively through the preparatory, junior, middle and senior grades of the intermediate and through the matriculation, first arts, second arts, and arts degree courses of the royal university. (*U*, 558; 17, 549–54)

---

[64] Michael Maher, *Psychology* (London: Longmans, Green & Co., 1890), 210–11.

The exchange of pasts parodically enacts the marriage of their minds in a conversation which progresses 'as if both their minds were travelling, so to speak, in the one train of thought' (U, 536; 16, 1580–1).

The 'mathematical catechism' of 'Ithaca' seeks to impose on the world a rigid structure in which a 'conversation' between two people is turned into the rehearsal of a fixed set of truths; but such a method is incapable of describing or re-presenting the free flow of a conversation where question and answer are not preprogrammed, and where characters are actually engaged in a process of self-discovery. As with the headlines in 'Aeolus', the questioning of the catechism assumes both that the future is already known – 'What statement was made, under correction, by Bloom concerning a fourth seeker of pure truth, by name Aristotle, mentioned, with permission, by Stephen?' (U, 563; 17, 715–16) – and that everything can be fitted into fixed and rigid patterns of explanation. Conversation, however, defies such rigidities, and just as in *Tristram Shandy* – 'Only I am trying to build many planes of narrative with a single esthetic purpose. Did you ever read Laurence Sterne?', Joyce wrote to Eugene Jolas[65] – or in *David Copperfield*, the novel committed to the process of association is also a novel committed to the freedom of conversation. Which is why, in *Ulysses*, the climax of Bloom's and Stephen's day is a conversation that takes place in a narrative style designed to negate the openness both of association and of conversation The hypothetical re-reader in 'Ithaca' is a voice trying to subdue chaos to a fixed formula in which a question can never provoke an answer it has not foreseen. Its linguistic determinism, however, is the context in which, through the associational medium of conversation, Joyce reasserts the freedom to associate (in both the psychological and social senses) that its dogmatism would deny.

II

In *The Oxford Book of Modern Verse*, W. B. Yeats declared Walter Pater the first modern poet and his description of the Mona Lisa to be of 'revolutionary importance',[66] an importance which Yeats underlined by reshaping Pater's prose as *vers libre*:

---

[65] Eugene Jolas, 'My Friend James Joyce', in S. Givens (ed.), *James Joyce: Two Decades of Criticism* (New York: Vanguard Press, 1948), 11–12.

[66] W. B. Yeats, *The Oxford Book of Modern Verse* 1892–1935 (Oxford: Clarendon Press, 1936), viii.

She is older than the rocks among which she sits;
Like the Vampire,
She has been dead many times,
And learned the secrets of the grave;
And has been a diver in deep seas,
And keeps their fallen day about her;
And trafficked for strange webs with Eastern merchants;
And, as Leda,
Was the mother of Helen of Troy,
And, as St Anne,
Was the mother of Mary;
And all this has been to her but as the sound of lyres and flutes,
And lives
Only in the delicacy
With which it has moulded the changing lineaments,
And tinged the eyelids and the hands.

Pater's Mona Lisa becomes an endless string of memories, as though she is already aware of every association which might be made with her. In choosing this passage Yeats was strikingly situating the beginning of modern poetry in an associationist context, for Pater's early essays looked back to Wordsworth 'as the true forerunner of the deepest and most passionate poetry of our own day'[67] precisely because, for Wordsworth, 'Human life . . . is for him at first only an additional, accidental grace on an expressive landscape. When he thought of man, it was of man in the presence and under the influence of these effective natural objects, and linked to them by many associations'.[68] For Pater, Wordsworth's poetry exemplifies, 'the close connexion of man with natural objects, the habitual association of his thoughts and feelings with a particular spot of earth'.[69] In Pater's account of the power of association in Wordsworth's poetry, Yeats must also have seen a prediction of his own art, since Pater describes Wordsworth's poetry at its most intense as one in which the poet 'appeared to himself as but the passive recipient of external influences, . . . attracted by the thought of a spirit of life in outward things, a single, all-pervading mind in them of which man, and even the poet's imaginative energy,

---

[67] Walter Pater, 'Wordsworth', *Appreciations*, 63.
[68] Ibid., 47.
[69] Ibid.

are but moments – that old dream of the *anima mundi*'.[70] In Pater's version of the Mona Lisa, the art object seems to acquire that universal memory which he presents Wordsworth as aspiring towards, with the result that the character herself seems to be presciently aware of the endless memories the artwork will provoke in its readers.

Joyce's revolution of the novel concludes with a similar transformation: the novel which, chapter by chapter, has been imposing increasingly insistent and limited associational contexts on the action is suddenly transposed into the consciousness of a woman whose memories seem as limitless and as time-defying as Pater's Mona Lisa. Indeed, in 'Oxen of the Sun' Molly appears as 'Our Lady of the Cherries', embedded in a Paterian style which is also a studied associationism: 'A scene disengages itself in the observer's memory, evoked, it would seem, by a word of so natural a homeliness as if those days were really present there (as some thought) with their immediate pleasures' (*U*, 344; 14, 1359–62).[71] Molly, whose day began by reading a novel and being stuck at the meaning of 'metempsychosis' (*U*, 52; 4, 339), becomes, by its end, like the Mona Lisa, one of those who can 'remember their past lives' (*U*, 53; 4, 365) as though it 'were really present there'. Molly is the embodiment of an aesthetic devoted to the recollection of the past and if her many-manned past makes her a parodic version of Pater's many-womaned Mona Lisa, her freeflowing recollections of her various associates conclude Joyce's novel with a version of the very process which literature, in the associationist tradition, is designed to provoke in its readers. Having absorbed into herself all the readerly energies that have been expended in the previous chapters, she becomes the reservoir of associations from which all future readings – Bloom's, Stephen's, and the reader's – will recommence, quite literally forcing us back to the beginning of the novel to reread it in the light of her memories.

If, however, we do to Molly's associative flow what Yeats did to Pater's prose, what becomes clear is that Molly's 'monologue' is, in fact, more like a dialogue of the many-selved person that Molly is:

now what could you make of a man like that Id rather die 20 times over than marry another of their sex of course hed never find another woman

---

[70] Ibid., 55.

[71] See F. C. McGrath, 'Pater Speaking Bloom Speaking Joyce', in Laurel Brake and Ian Small (eds), *Pater in the 1990s* (Greensboro: ELT Press, 1991), 95–105 for a detailed analysis of Joyce's transcriptions from Pater and his construction of a Paterian style in this passage.

like me to put up with him the way I do know me come sleep with me yes
and he knows that too at the bottom of his heart take that Mrs Maybrick
that poisoned her husband for what I wonder in love with some other
man yes it was found out on her wasn't she the downright villain to go
and do a thing like that of course some men can be dreadfully aggravating
drive you mad and always the worst word in the world what do they ask
us to marry them for if were so bad as all that comes to yes because they
cant get on without us (U, 613; 19, 231–40)

The continuous typography conceals the (many possible) structures that are
unveiled when the passage is read aloud:

Now what could you make of a man like that?
Id rather die 20 times over than marry another of their sex!
of course hed never find another woman like me to put up with him the
way I do.
know me come sleep with me!
yes and he knows that too at the bottom of his heart!
take that Mrs Maybrick that poisoned her husband
for what I wonder? in love with some other man?
yes it was found out on her
wasn't she the downright villain to go and do a thing like that?
of course some men can be dreadfully aggravating, drive you mad.
and always the worst word in the world!
what do they ask us to marry them for if were so bad as all that comes
to?
yes because they cant get on without us

Molly's 'monologue' is a multi-vocal dialogue between her past selves whose
climax, like the climax of the associationism which her 'monologue' represents,
is a return to the world of conversation. Molly, like the women of the 'conversible world' to whom Hume addressed himself, is one of 'the Sovereigns of the
Empire of Conversation' (E, 535) and it is by way of a gesture towards Hume's
argument about the uncertainty of all future causes and effects – 'That the sun
will not rise to-morrow is no less intelligible a proposition, and implies no more
contradiction than the affirmation, that it will rise' (EHU, 25–6) – that Molly's
memory returns to that empire of conversation:

so there you are they might as well try to stop the sun from rising tomor-
row the sun shines for you he said the day we were lying among the
rhododendrons on Howth head in the grey tweed suit and his straw
hat the day I got him to propose to me yes first I gave him the bit of
seedcake out of my mouth and it was a leapyear like now yes 16 years
ago my God after that long kiss I near lost my breath yes he said I was a
flower of the mountain yes so we are flowers all a womans body yes that
was one true thing he said in his life and the sun shines for you today
yes that was why I liked him because I saw he understood or felt what
a woman is and I knew I could always get round him and I gave him all
the pleasure I could leading him on till he asked me to say yes (*U*, 643;
19, 1572–1580)

In the pause before replying to the proposal, however, Molly's mind traces a
series of associations that carry her back to Gibraltar – 'and the Spanish girls
laughing in their shawls and their tall combs and the auctions in the morning
the Greeks and the jews and the Arabs and the devil knows who else from
all the ends of Europe' (*U,* 643; 19, 1585–9) – to the first time that a man
asked her to say 'yes', and it is from the reconnection of past with present,
of association with conversation, that she is able to respond: 'and I thought
as well him as another and then I asked him with my eyes to ask again yes
and then he asked me would I yes to say yes my mountain flower and first I
put my arms around him yes and drew him down to me so he could feel my
breasts all perfume yes and his heart was going like made and yes I said yes I
will Yes' (*U*, 643–4; 18, 1604–9).

Association turns into conversation, conversation into a new kind of
association, reaffirming that our associations are parts of the 'conversible
world'. Which is why Jerry Fodor is wrong to see in Molly's 'soliloquy' in
'Penelope' an inadvertent *parody* of the associationist version of the mind
as an unorganisable chaos. Through the flow of apparently accidental associations the past is winnowed for significance and returns to revitalise the
present and reshape the future: 'and yes I said yes I will Yes' (*U*, 644; 18,
1608–9). 'Will', and therefore order and organisation, emerges from association through conversation, but in doing so it does not displace chaos: rather
it returns to it, renews itself from it, just as the structure of a work of art
emerges out of, returns to and gains meaning only in its interaction with the
apparently chaotic contingencies of our individual associations.

III

To recreate her father, Leslie Stephen, as the Mr Ramsay of *To the Lighthouse*, Virginia Woolf read David Hume, because Stephen, author of the *History of English Thought in the Eighteenth Century*, was committed to rescuing 'the English empiricists, Locke, Berkeley, Hume, from Taine's contention that they were insignificant',[72] and, especially, to re-establishing Hume's significance:

> From [Hume's] writings we may date the definite abandonment of the philosophical conceptions of the preceding century, leading in some cases to an abandonment of the great questions as insoluble, and, in others, to an attempt to solve them by a new method. Hume did not destroy ontology or theology, but he destroyed the old ontology; and all later thinkers who have not been content with the mere dead bones of extinct philosophy, have built up their systems upon entirely new lines.[73]

As Beer suggests, it is because of Hume's importance to Stephen that his philosophy is so central in *To the Lighthouse*, dominating its reflections on 'the survival of the object without a perceiver, the nature of identity and non-entity, the scepticism about substance'.[74] Beer, like Anne Banfield in *The Phantom Table*,[75] is concerned with the relation of subject and object as it is transmitted from Hume through Leslie Stephen to Woolf's contemporaries, Bertrand Russell and G. E. Moore, and Stephen's account of Hume's theory of perception – 'That table, which just now appears to me, is only a perception and all its qualities are qualities of perception' (*ETEC*, 46–7) – she finds echoed directly in *To the Lighthouse* – ' "Think of a kitchen table then," he told her, "when you're not there" '[76] – and provides the shaping influence on its narrative technique: 'Table, house, tree, and stone: those four objects . . . are crucial to the narra-

---

[72] Noel Annan, *Leslie Stephen: The Godless Victorian* (London: Weidenfeld and Nicolson, 1984), 223.

[73] Leslie Stephen, *English Thought in the Eighteenth Century*, 2 Vols (London: Smith, Elder and Co., 1902; 1876), Vol. 1, 43; hereafter cited in the text as *ETEC*.

[74] Gillian Beer, *Virginia Woolf: The Common Ground* (Edinburgh: Edinburgh University Press, 1996), 32.

[75] Ann Banfield, *The Phantom Table: Woolf, Fry, Russell and the Epistemology of Modernism* (Cambridge: Cambridge University Press, 2000).

[76] Virginia Woolf, *To the Lighthouse* (Harmondsworth: Penguin, 1964; 1927), 28; hereafter cited in the text as *TL*.

tive and the play of associations in *To the Lighthouse*.[77] Despite her own use of the language of association, however – 'The repertoire of associations is richly at work here'[78] – Beer does not locate Woolf in relation to what was the most important aspect of her father's inheritance from Hume, his acceptance of its foundation in associationist psychology:

> Association is in the mental what gravitation is in the natural world. The name signifies the inexplicable tendency of previously connected ideas and impressions to connect themselves again. We can only explain mental processes of any kind by resolving them into such cases of association. Thus reality is to be found only in the ever-varying stream of our feelings, bound together by custom, regarded by a 'fiction' or set of fictions as implying some permanent set of external or internal relations, and becoming beliefs only as they acquire liveliness. Chance, instead of order, must, it would seem, be the ultimate objective fact, as custom, instead of reason, is the ultimate subjective fact. (*ETEC*, 44)

Stephen's account of Hume's psychology underlines how inherent the notion of 'stream of consciousness' is in the associationist tradition: 'We are conscious only of an unceasing stream of more or less vivid feelings' (*ETEC*, 44). And what is important about this foundation is not its philosophical trenchancy but its validation in contemporary empirical psychology: 'We may, perhaps, admit that Hume's account of the process by which a belief in the external world is actually suggested is fairly accurate, or coincides, as far as the contemporary state of psychology would allow, with the explanations given by later thinkers' (*ETEC*, 40). As a consequence, there would be no escape from Humean scepticism and the fact that 'the world is a chaos, not an organised whole' (*ETEC*, 58), were it not that the object of philosophical psychology has changed since Hume wrote: the self can no longer be regarded as merely personal – and, therefore, subject to dissolution when it has been emptied of 'its supposed innate ideas and *a priori* truths' – because the 'organism remains, though the laws of its operation are only revealed to us by the experience upon which it operates' (*ETEC*, 54). Consciousness can no longer be considered mere *self*-consciousness because – post-Darwin – the 'self' has to be envisaged in a new historical and biological depth.

---

[77] Beer, *Virginia Woolf: The Common Ground*, 38.
[78] Ibid., 40.

Even by 1865 Pater had already been conscious of a profound change in the way that psychology had to view the nature of the human mind and in his essay on Coleridge had challenged Coleridge's desire to 'apprehend the absolute'[79] by insisting on the physical sources of humanity's highest achievements:

> Always, as an organism increases in perfection, the conditions of its life become more complex. Man is the most complex of the products of nature. Character merges into temperament: the nervous system refines itself into intellect. Man's physical organism is played upon not only by the physical conditions about it, but by remote laws of inheritance, the vibration of long-past acts reaching him in the midst of the new order of things in which he lives.[80]

The insistence on inheritance is what, for Stephen, allows contemporary followers of Hume to escape the 'unmitigated' scepticism that commentators had seen in Hume's philosophy:

> Modern thinkers of Hume's school meet the difficulty [of the mind imposing its own forms upon experience] by distinguishing between the *a priori* element in the individual mind and in the mind of the race. Each man brings with him certain inherited faculties, if not inherited knowledge; but the faculties have been themselves built up out of the experience of the race. Such a conception, however, was beyond Hume's sphere of thought. . . (*ETEC*, 56)

Such a notion might have produced a conception of human beings as inevitably uniform products of an implacable evolutionary development. But what Pater insisted on was that though 'the mind of the race, the character of the age, sway him this way or that through the medium of language and current ideas', individual human beings are so uniquely responsive to their environment that the distant effects of 'the mind of the race' are transformed in each individual experience: 'he is so receptive, all the influences of nature and society ceaselessly playing upon him, so that every hour in his life is unique'.[81]

---

[79] Pater, *Appreciations*, 68.
[80] Ibid., 66.
[81] Ibid., 66–7.

If James Ward's 'engrams' allowed Humeans like Stephen to turn aside the severity of Hume's demolition of the subject, because they make the subject transtemporal and transindividual, at the same time, the accidental and contingent nature of association means that for each of us our experience of the world is always uniquely individual. As a consequence, the relation between the objective and the subjective undergoes a radical realignment, because the objective is not that which is truly 'out there' in the real, but that portion of our subjective experiences which overlaps with and is in accord with what we learn of others' subjective experiences: 'The faculties of the individual have been built up by the past experiences of the race. The primary distinction between object and subject is only intelligible as distinguishing between the perceptions peculiar to the individual and those common to the race' (*ETEC*, 60). What is 'objective' is not what is undeniably existent in the world: it is what belongs to our common inheritance and to our common sense of the world. It is the world we share – even though it may be, from another point of view, mere illusion. It is what Mrs Ramsay discovers over the dinner table in *To the Lighthouse:* 'there is a coherence in things, a stability; something, she meant, is immune from change, and shines out (she glanced at the window with its ripple of reflected lights) in the face of the flowing, the fleeting, the spectral, like a ruby' (*TL*, 121). Mr Ramsay is not a direct portrait of Leslie Stephen or his philosophy: rather, Woolf has divided Stephen's philosophy between Mr and Mrs Ramsay, giving him the scepticism, the individualistic inability to escape from the Humean dilemma, and her the sense of what is 'common to the race', what survives the 'flowing, the fleeting, the spectral', what is passed on from generation to generation: 'Of such moments, she thought, the thing is made that remains for ever after. This would remain' (*TL* 60).

Among those most closely connected with Stephen's work was James Sully – Stephen, as editor of the *Cornhill Magazine*, was responsible for encouraging his career as a writer and reviewer – and Sully, as we have seen, is one of those late nineteenth-century psychologists who conceive of association as flowing from the 'wide obscure region of the subconscious', a subconscious consisting of the 'influences which can be seen to have acted on the whole species, man included' and which 'have left behind them a yet deeper impress in the innate mental structure of the nineteenth century boy or girl'.[82] Sully's version of associationism was used by and praised by Fr Michael Maher, who

---

[82] James Sully, *Sensation and Intuition: Studies in Psychology and Aesthetics* (London: C. Kegan Paul, 1880), 6.

believed that in his 'exposition of the Associationist system' he had actually overthrown the 'old doctrine of a purely passive mind, wherein sensations through a process of agglutination coalesce into all kinds of intellectual products'. According to Maher, Sully's psychology offered a mind of 'active powers of attention, comparison and judgment' which meant that 'the best part of Mr Sully's description of mental operations belongs to an alien conception of the mind', one closer to the Thomist tradition.[83] Sully, however, was building on the active conception of the mind proposed by Bain – for whom the mind's activity flowed from the body's excess of physical energy – a derivation that Bain recognised by inviting Sully to apply for his chair at the University of Aberdeen when he retired. Sully had not only been a close friend of Stephen's but was a visitor to the St Ives summer residence on which the house in *To the Lighthouse* is based,[84] and his major works emphasise that aesthetic experience depends on 'numerous vague associations',[85] both those 'which can be seen to have acted on the whole species' and those which derive from personal or civilizational refinement. The source of aesthetic intensity lies in the 'retentive power of the mind',[86] and in its ability to recall and distinguish 'different impressions and ideas, and of clearly noting their points of resemblance'.[87] The more capacious the memory the more effective the associative resonance of the work of art: 'In all the higher aesthetic enjoyments, notably those of poetry, this rapid and extended emotional inference is very conspicuous. For example, the pleasures flowing from a sympathetic reading of another's feelings involve a high degree of this emotional inference, being the results of numerous and rapid revivals of pleasurable idea[s] corresponding to our own past experiences, and possibly to those of our progenitors'.[88] The level of development of civilisation also contributes to the extension of those associative connections upon which aesthetic experience depends:

> Culture by multiplying our recollections, increases our conceptive power, and enables us to imagine unbounded regions of possible existence and experience, where only a slender thread of certainty is attainable.

---

[83] Maher, *Psychology*, 212.

[84] In *My Life and Friends: A Psychologist's Memories*, Sully describes his visit as 'one of the memorable experiences of my life' (312).

[85] Sully, *Sensation and Intuition*, 359.

[86] Ibid., 357.

[87] Ibid.

[88] Sully, *Sensation and Intuition*, 359.

Accordingly, the accumulation of ideas vastly enlarges the region of pleasurable imaginative activity. Out of its numerous emotional experiences a
cultivated mind is able to fill up the most vaguely suggested regions with
multitudes of grateful ideas; and this effect, like that of emotional com-
prehension, is one chief element in the pleasures of all the higher forms
of art.[89]

Aesthetic pleasure is a function of the memory both of the individual and of
the society of which he or she is a part because the increase in associational
material allows almost everything to become aesthetically interesting.

The dim and vast, the hidden and remote, whether suggested in visible
space or in the invisible regions of another's mind, have a peculiar value
for a mind well stored with pleasurable conceptions. In this manner, a
high degree of mental development, by producing a vast increase of
imaginative activity, serves to widen the area of aesthetic delight, surrounding every mode of clear, pleasurable perception with an additional
semi-luminous zone of pleasurable fancy.[90]

The last sentence points forward to Woolf's famous statement in 'Modern
Fiction' that 'life is not a series of gig lamps symmetrically arranged; life is a
luminous halo, a semi-transparent envelope surrounding us from the beginning of consciousness to the end',[91] just as Woolf's equally famous assertion
in the same essay that the 'mind receives a myriad impressions', that 'from
all sides they come, an incessant shower of innumerable atoms'[92] looks back
to Pater's 'world, not of objects in the solidity with which language invests
them, but of impressions, unstable, flickering, inconsistent, which burn and
are extinguished'.

Woolf inherited from her father and from his intellectual circle not just an
awareness of the importance of Hume to modern metaphysics but of Hume
as psychologist, and association as the foundation of that psychology. The
associationist basis of Woolf's account of art is clear from her description of
Dostoevsky's technique in 1917:

---

[89] Ibid., 360.

[90] Ibid., 360.

[91] Andrew McNeillie (ed.), *The Essays of Virginia Woolf, Vol. IV, 1925–1928*
    (London: Hogarth Press, 1994), 'Modern Fiction', 160.

[92] Ibid.

From the crowd of objects pressing upon our attention we select now this one, now that one, weaving them inconsequently into our thought; the associations of a word perhaps make another loop in the line, from which we spring back again to a different section of our main thought, and whole process seems both inevitable and perfectly lucid. But if we try to construct our mental processes later, we find that the links between one thought and another are submerged. The chain is sunk out of sight and only the leading points emerge to mark the course. Alone among writers Dostoevsky had the power of reconstructing those most swift and complicated states of mind, of rethinking the whole train of thought in all its speed, now as it flashes into light, now as it lapses into darkness; for he is able to follow not only the vivid streak of achieved thought, but to suggest the dim and populous underworld of the mind's consciousness where desires and impulses are moving blindly beneath the sod. [93]

Dostoevsky's achievement is a paradoxical one since it rests on the precision with which he represents processes of association so rapid that they are lost even to immediate retrospection: his power lies in his ability make visible the associations which are apparently invisible even to the most careful introspection. Dostoevsky's work thus goes beyond the realism of self-observation to what we might call a reconstructive realism that reveals what, even to psychology, can only be hypothetical since it describes events in consciousness that are subject to immediate obliviscence or take place below the threshold of individual awareness.

Woolf's account of Joyce's method in *Ulysses* emphasizes its ability to uncover psychological processes similar to those presented in Dostoevsky's fiction: 'he is concerned at all costs to reveal the flickerings of that innermost flame which flashes its messages through the brain, and in order to preserve it he disregards with complete courage whatever seems to him adventitious, whether it be probability, or coherence, or any other of these signposts which for generations have served to support the imagination of a reader when called upon to imagine what he can neither touch nor see'.[94] At the time when she first wrote this (under the title 'Modern Novels' in the *Times Literary Supplement*,

---

[93] Andrew McNeillie (ed.), *The Essays of Virginia Woolf, Vol. II, 1912–1918*, (London: Hogarth Press, 1987), 'More Dostoevsky', 85.

[94] Andrew McNeillie (ed.), *The Essays of Virginia Woolf, Vol. IV, 1925–1928*, 'Modern Fiction', 161.

10 April 1919),[95] Woolf had read only the sections of *Ulysses* published in the *The Egoist*. What she was describing was the 'initial style' – the interior monologue – and she makes clear her concerns about the limitations of the Joyce's technique: 'Is it due to the method that we feel neither jovial nor magnanimous, but centred in a self which in spite of its tremor of susceptibility never reaches out or embraces or comprehends what is outside and beyond?'.[96] Later, she was to describe *Ulysses* as 'a memorable catastrophe – immense in daring, terrific in disaster'.[97] This, she suggests in 1919, may be an inadequacy of Joyce's imagination – 'Does the emphasis laid perhaps didactically upon indecency contribute to this effect of the angular and the isolated?' – rather than the method, in which 'case we need not attribute too much importance to the method' because what the method reveals is simply 'how much of life is excluded and ignored' in most modern fiction, so much so that it is a revelation to return to earlier, more inclusive methods – 'did it not come with a shock to open *Tristram Shandy* and even *Pendennis*, and be by them convinced that there are other aspects of life, and larger ones into the bargain?'. It is not method that is crucial, because 'any method is right, every method is right, that expresses what we wish to express';[98] what is crucial is what demands expression and, after reading *Ulysses*, Woolf is brought back to the fact that whatever this is 'lies very likely in the dark places of psychology',[99] dark places which have been most effectively revealed not by any writer in English but by the Russians.

This juxtaposition of the limitations of *Ulysses* with the achievements of Russian fiction – in the light of which 'one runs the risk of feeling that to write any fiction save theirs is a waste of time'[100] – reinforces John Mepham's argument that Woolf refused to follow Joyce in the matter of method: although she experiments with 'first person stream-of-consciousness technique of her early stories' it proved such 'a definitive failure' that 'she rejected it once and for all'.[101] Equally, however, she needed to reject the Russians and the terms in

[95] See McNeillie, fn.1, *The Essays of Virginia Woolf, Vol. IV, 1925–1928*, 'Modern Fiction', 164.

[96] Andrew McNeillie (ed.), *The Essays of Virginia Woolf, Vol. III, 1919–1924* (London: Hogarth Press, 1988), 'Modern Novels', 34.

[97] *The Essays of Virgina Woolf, Vol. IV, 1925–1928*, 'How it strikes a contemporary', 237.

[98] *The Essays of Virginia Woolf, Vol. III, 1919–1924*, 'Modern Novels', 34.

[99] *The Essays of Virginia Woolf, Vol. IV, 1925–1928*, 'Modern Fiction', 162.

[100] Ibid., 163.

[101] John Mepham, *Virginia Woolf: A Literary Life* (Basingstoke: Macmillan, 1991), 69.

which she does so are significant: the Russians may have a 'natural reverence for the human spirit' but it is a human spirit enfolded in 'the utmost sadness' by a 'hopeless interrogation that fills us with a deep, and finally it may be with a resentful, despair'.[102] If, however, as her father had argued, 'the primary distinction between object and subject is only intelligible as distinguishing between the perceptions peculiar to the individual and those common to the race' (*ETEC*, 60), then both the nature of the boundary line between subject and object and the contents of the 'dark places of psychology' will be different for different races:

> But perhaps we see something that escapes them, or why should this voice of protest mix itself with our gloom? The voice of protest is the voice of another and an ancient civilisation which seems to have bred in us the instinct to enjoy and fight rather than to suffer and understand. English fiction from Sterne to Meredith bears witness to our natural delight in humour and comedy, in the beauty of the earth, in the activities of the intellect, and in the splendour of the body.[103]

The 'dark places of psychology' have to be uncovered in this cultural context, in this 'ancient civilisation', and by refusing to lock itself into the 'perceptions peculiar to the individual' – as the Joycean method does – it will uncover precisely what is 'common to the race': 'Whether he wishes to or not, there is a constant pressure on an English novelist to recognise these barriers, and, in consequence, order is imposed on him and some kind of form; he is inclined to satire rather than to compassion, to scrutiny of society rather than understanding of individuals themselves'.[104] The object of analysis, in other words, for the English novelist, will not be the isolated self of the interior monologue: it will be a self in which there is an ancient inheritance, both the genetic inheritance that is ages deep and the inheritance that comes from being part of a highly developed civilisation, in which barely conscious associations surround 'every mode of clear, pleasurable perception with an additional semi-luminous zone of pleasurable fancy'.[105] The exploration of the interiority of such a self will discover not its isolation and its peculiarity but its commonality and its communality. If, as James Sully suggests, 'it is a highly plausible supposi-

---

[102] *The Essays of Virginia Woolf, Vol. IV, 1925–1928*, 'Modern Fiction', 163.

[103] Ibid., 163.

[104] Ibid., 187, 'The Russian Point of View'.

[105] Sully, *Sensation and Intuition*, 360.

tion that in by far the greater number of our emotional activities there is a considerable amount of natural capacity which is a development of ancestral experience',[106] then the individual mind can only be understood as a portion of that larger experience. There is no 'I' that not founded on a 'we': our shared associations are with our closest and our most distant associates: 'In the midst of chaos there was shape; this eternal passing and flowing (she looked at the clouds going and the leaves shaking) was struck into stability' (*TL*, 183).

That is why, when Mrs Ramsay's 'ghost' first appears at the climactic moment of *To the Lighthouse*, Lily is looking at the world through the eyes of someone else's recollections:

> She looked now at the drawing-room step. She saw, through William's eyes, the shape of a woman, peaceful and silent, with downcast eyes. She sat musing, pondering (she was in grey that day, Lily thought). Her eyes were bent. She would never lift them. Yes, thought Lily, looking intently, I must have seen her look like that, but not in grey; nor so still, nor so young, nor so peaceful. (*TL*, 201)

Mrs Ramsay appears as the compound recollection of both Lily's and William's memories, a recollection 'organic' rather than personal – 'It was one's body feeling, not one's mind' (*TL*, 203) – which will embed itself as one of those memories that goes beyond the personal, as mind and reality become one and the same: 'For the whole world seemed to have dissolved in this early morning hour into a pool of thought, a deep basin of reality' (*TL*, 203). A memory of something which never occurred ('not in grey'), constructed through the separate associations of two minds which have become themselves associated – 'That was typical of their relationship. Many things were left unsaid' (201) – can recover life out of death because it is through such associations that the passage from the subjectivity of the individual mind to the communality of 'the thing [that] is made that remains for ever after' (*TL*, 60) is achieved. Mrs Ramsay returns as though in fulfilment of the belief among the later psychologists of the British empiricist tradition that there is, however minimally in individual instances, a hereditary dimension to memory and that memory does not simply perish with the perishing of our impressions and ideas.

The transpersonal memory that allows Mrs Ramsay's return emerges through a narrative structure which is, in turn, based on conversations

---

[106] Ibid., 109

which take place – or seem to take place – beyond the boundaries of normal experience: 'A curious notion came to her that he did after all hear the things she could not say' (*TL*, 203). Unuttered and unheard conversations form the medium through which transpersonal associations are encountered: 'She addressed old Mr Carmichael again. What was it then? What did it mean?' (*TL*, 204); 'He is a sarcastic brute, James would say' (*TL*, 206), 'There! Cam thought, addressing herself silently to James' (234), 'They had been thinking the same things and he had answered her without her asking him anything' (237). The silence in which such conversations between the living take place, replicate the communication which exists between the living and the dead, and both are the result of associations which, being shared between apparently separate minds, gesture towards a level of the psyche which is not only common to all but in its commonality resists the destructive effects of time: 'The space would fill; if they shouted loud enough Mrs Ramsay would return' (*TL*, 205).

Through those unspoken conversations Woolf dramatises the remaking of associations, both in the recollections of individuals and in the relations between persons, to the point where the recollected can become the (apparently) real: 'Mrs Ramsay – it was part of her perfect goodness to Lily – sat there quite simply in the chair . . . cast her shadow on the step' (*TL*, 230). Lily's perception of her as actually sitting there is possible only because the memory of her sitting there has been established as a shared memory that has become a part of the very fabric of reality for the community of which she is a part. Since 'the real' consists of our common and shared associations, our common and shared associations transform memory into 'reality', and the process of the novel itself is the construction of such transpersonal associations – we, as readers, acquire the associative connections of many individual minds and, in doing so, become the living repositories of that larger and more extensive psyche in which all of the characters participate. The novel forces us to enact, as we link image to image, impression to impression, the process by which associations themselves are linked together in a pattern that goes beyond the experience of any particular mind, allowing us to escape from the solipsism of our private consciousness into the aobjectivity of a common world.

It is the need to find a narrative method which can combine the specifically English 'natural delight in humour and comedy, in the beauty of the earth, in the activities of the intellect, and in the splendour of the body' with the subtleties of the Russians as analysts of the psyche that drives the development of Woolf's novelistic experiments. The 'silent' conversations of the last section of *To the Lighthouse* point forward to the narrative style of *The Waves*,[107] in which conversation takes place not at a realistic or social level but between the psyches of the characters at their moments of most intense self-reflection, moments which also reveal how much each of their minds is constituted by the experience of those with whom, from childhood, they have associated, and whose inner lives reach down to ancient and hereditary deposits:

> My roots go down to the depths of the world, through earth dry with brick, and damp earth, through veins of lead and silver. I am all fibre. All tremors shake me, and the weight of the earth is pressed to my ribs. Up here my eyes are green leaves, unseeing. I am a boy in grey flannels with a belt fastened by a brass snake up here. Down there my eyes are the lidless eyes of a stone figure in a desert by the Nile. (*TW*, 7)

These sentences are posited on 'said Louis', a saying which is as little available to public inspection as are the archaeological depths which he can recover from beyond the bounds of his personal memories. The characters 'communicate' with each other from these depths of the psyche, but communication is possible precisely because, at such depths, what they uncover is not personal but what is shared between them. If Louis seems to himself 'already to have lived many thousand years' (*TW*, 52), to be one whose 'destiny' has been 'to plait into one cable the many threads, the thin, the thick, the broken, the enduring of our long history' (*TW*, 168), then Bernard, equally, is in search of the oneness that unifies the many – 'I do not believe in separation. We are not single' (*TW*, 53) – and the multiplicity that accumulates in the self: 'I am Bernard; I am Byron; I am this, that and the other . . . For I am more selves than Neville thinks' (*TW*, 72). The self may contain the residues of the past – 'I shall be like my mother, silent in a blue apron locking up the cupboards', Susan thinks (*TW*, 80) – or it may extend to include 'the other' within itself, 'I think I am the field, I am the barn, I am the trees: mine are the flocks of birds' (*TW*, 78). The subjective and the objective, the personal and the impersonal are compounded in a flow of associations that passes from mind to mind as though they were all parts of one mind, and that passes from mind

---

[107] Virginia Woolf, *The Waves*, ed. Gillian Beer (Oxford: Oxford University Press, 1992); hereafter cited in the text as *TW*.

to body as though all the characters were, like the chorus of sports players whom Neville observes, parts of single body: 'On they roll; on they gallop; after hounds, after footballs; they pump up and down attached to oars like sacks of flour. All divisions are merged – they act like one man' (*TW*, 73). The social world that Woolf identifies as the pressing context of English life – 'time is limited; space crowded; the influence of other points of view, of other books, even of other ages, makes itself felt'[108] – contains and limits the apparently passive subjectivism of Pater's 'impressions, unstable, flickering, inconsistent, which burn and are extinguished', and of Woolf's own 'incessant shower of innumerable atoms': those showering impressions accumulate from and return to a shared substratum of common memory formed in the activities of a shared social world, a social world in which many are called to 'act like one man'. And such action is not gender-specific: as Jinny notes, 'These broad thoroughfares – Piccadilly South, Piccadilly North, Regent Street and the Haymarket – are sanded paths of victory driven through the jungle. I too, with my little patent-leather shoes, my handkerchief that is but a film of gauze, my reddened lips and my finely pencilled eyebrows, march to victory with the band' (*TW*, 162).

It is in action, rather than in passive perception or recollection, that our associations are forged, associations that establish the boundaries between the objective and the subjective. Thus in his long final conversation with a silent guest over dinner, Bernard discovers that, 'I am not one person: I am many people; I do not altogether know who I am – Jinny, Susan, Neville, Rhoda, or Louis; or how to distinguish my life from theirs' (*TW*, 230), because 'life withers when there are things we cannot share' (*TW*, 221). And although we may be conscious of 'a rushing stream of broken dreams, nursery rhymes, street cries, half-finished sentences and sights – the elm trees, willow trees, gardeners sweeping, women writing – that rise and sink even as we hand a lady down to dinner' (*TW*, 213), that internal flux is matched by our ability to take action in the world: 'I remarked with what magnificent vitality the atoms of my attention dispersed, swarmed round the interruption, assimilated the message, adapted themselves to a new state of affairs and had created by the time I put back the receiver, a richer, stronger, a more complicated world in which I was called upon to act my part and had no doubt whatever that I could do it' (*TW*, 218). 'To act my part' hovers between two possible meanings of

---

[108] *The Essays of Virginia Woolf, Vol. IV, 1925–1928*, 187, 'The Russian Point of View'.

'act' – to do, to mimic doing; to perform, to put on a performance – whose apparent opposition *The Waves* will reveal to be false: Bernard can only *act* as Bernard because the part of Bernard is defined for him in part by his relations with the others with whom he shares his life. We are surrounded by 'shadows of people one might have been; unborn selves' (*TW*, 241) but the self that one acquires is a product not only of one's own private experiences but of the actions and of the thoughts of those in whose lives one has been a participant:

> Am I all of them? Am I one and distinct? I do not know. We sat here together. But now Percival is dead, and Rhoda is dead; we are divided; we are not here. Yet I cannot find any obstacle separating us. There is no division between me and them. As I talked I felt, 'I am you'. This difference we make so much of, this identity we so feverishly cherish, was overcome . . . Here on my brow is the blow I got when Percival fell. Here on the nape of my neck is the kiss Jinny gave Louis. My eyes fill with Susan's tears. (*TW*, 241)

Our experiences are the consequences of others' actions; their actions are, quite literally, inscribed in the body of our memory.

There is considerable irony, therefore, that in his *Philosophy of David Hume* Norman Kemp Smith takes Leslie Stephen to task for promulgating a nineteenth-century misreading of Hume's associationism as 'the fullest expression of scepticism', one in which 'reality is to be found only in the ever-varying stream of feelings, bound together by custom, regarded by a "fiction"' (*ETEC*, 44). It is an attack that Virgina Woolf would not have read, since it was not part of Kemp Smith's original article on Hume's realism, published in *Mind* in 1905, but in emphasising Hume's debt to Francis Hutcheson, and insisting on Hume's theory of 'natural belief' about certain aspects of the world – ''tis in vain to ask, *Whether there be body or not?* This is a point, which we must take for granted in all our reasonings' (*T*, 187) – Kemp Smith was actually reading back into Hume the argument that Leslie Stephen himself had made the basis of his proposed escape from Hume's scepticism. 'Whilst Hume', Stephen suggests, 'was right in limiting the mind to experience, and in declaring the existing distinction of object and subject to involve an error, he was wrong in not observing that the possibility of making the distinction implied an operative mind, and in not seeing that the process by which the distinction works itself into corresponding with the facts is legitimate, though not, in his sense, reasoning'.[109] Stephen's emphasis on the fact that 'the organism remains'[110] underlines that we can only understand the workings of the mind 'when we introduce the social element'.[111] Stephen's emphasis on the importance of the 'social element' actually provides the ground for Kemp Smith's insistence that we should read Hume first as a moral philosopher, concerned with the relations of individuals in society, and only later as a metaphysician concerned with the relation of subject and object; as Kemp Smith puts it, 'the determining influence in human, as in other forms of animal life, is feeling, not reason or understanding'.[112] That is why Hume can say in the *Enquiry*: 'My practice, you say, refutes my doubts. But you mistake the purport of my question. As an agent, I am quite satisfied in the point' (*EHU*, 38). Stephen's account of Hume may emphasise its sceptical passivity but only in order to insist that contemporary associationism has progressed beyond Hume precisely by its emphasis both on transpersonal memory and on agency. James Sully, for instance, after tracing the effects of association on belief, indicates that,

> So far we have been examining the laws of belief with respect simply to the passive mind, by supposing, that is to say, a consciousness wholly made up of sensation, thought, and feeling. It is easy to see that this is a very incomplete solution to the problem. The human mind does not pass a quiescent existence of pure feeling and idea. As action and active impulse run all through human life, so they enter more or less into all forms of consciousness.[113]

Associations are created by 'action and active impulse' as much as by 'sensation, thought and feeling', since it is, originally, in the child, by virtue of 'vigorous activity' that 'a number of muscular movements' will gradually achieve 'the approach of [an] anticipated enjoyment'[114] with which they will be thereafter associated:

> 'I was running,' said Jinny, 'after breakfast. I saw leaves moving in a hole in the hedge . . . I was frightened. I ran past Susan, past Rhoda, and

---

[109] Ibid., 50.

[110] Ibid., 54.

[111] Ibid., 60.

[112] Kemp Smith, *Philosophy of David Hume*, 11.

[113] Sully, *Sensation and Intuition*, 111.

[114] Ibid.

Neville and Bernard in the tool-house talking. I cried as I ran faster and faster. What moved the leaves? What moves my heart, my legs? And I dashed in here, seeing you green as a bush, like a branch, very still, Louis, with your eyes fixed. 'Is he dead?' I thought, and kissed you . . . (*TW*, 8)

For Louis, Jinny's action creates an inescapable association – 'Jinny broke the thread when she kissed me in the garden years ago' (*TW*, 182) – and it is such associations 'beyond and outside our own predicament' which Bernard realises become 'symbolic, and thus perhaps permanent, if there is any permanence in our sleeping, eating, breathing, so animal, so spiritual and tumultuous lives' (*TW*, 208).

This is why such 'plot' as *The Waves* has is focused on the loss of Percival, the man of action, whose death in the service of empire threatens to unravel the associations of the other characters: 'Barns and summer days in the country, rooms where we sat – all now lie in the unreal world which is gone', Neville says, 'My past is cut from me' (*TW*, 124). Percival's life represents for the others the possibility of imposing order on the world – 'By applying the standards of the West, by using the violent language that is natural to him, the bullock-cart is righted in less than five minutes. The Oriental problem is solved' (*TW*, 111) – but as the underlying mockery of Bernard's imagining implies, it is not easy to keep chaos at bay. Bernard may arm himself with the consciousness that they 'stride not into chaos' because they participate in 'a world that our own force can subjugate and make part of the illumined and everlasting road' (*TW*, 120); Neville may insist that we 'Oppose ourselves to this illimitable chaos . . . this formless imbecility' (*TW*, 188); Louis may take comfort in being part of a greater whole in which their apparently trivial actions accumulate into something significant: 'My shoulder is to the wheel; I roll the dark before me, spreading commerce where there was chaos in the far parts of the world' (*TW*, 139). But at the same time, they know that 'the earth is only a pebble flicked off accidentally from the face of the sun and that there is no life anywhere in the abysses of space' (*TW*, 187), so that the making of history, too, is an illusion: 'the lighted strip of history is past and our Kings and Queens; we are gone; our civilization; the Nile; and our life. Our separate drops are dissolved; we are extinct, lost in the abysses of time, in the darkness' (*TW*, 188). Chaos emerges into order as reflection changes into action; action decomposes into chaos as it returns to reflection and recollection: 'Yes', Bernard says, 'this is the eternal renewal, the incessant rise and fall and fall and rise again' (*TW*, 247).

In *To the Lighthouse*, Woolf dramatised the return of agency through the recovery of community and communality. Mr Ramsay's recollections of the story of David Hume 'grown enormously fat' and 'stuck in a bog' (*TL*, 79), and having to be rescued by an old woman 'on condition he said the Lord's Prayer' (*TL*, 85), are an ironic reflection on Ramsay himself – who is stuck in a metaphysical bog and in search of female sympathy – and on the scepticism which discovers that it is dependent, after all, on the agency of other human beings. This recovery of agency is celebrated both in the completion of Lily's painting and in the arrival of the family party at the lighthouse: 'and they both rose to follow him as he sprang, lightly like a young man, holding his parcel, on to the rock' (236). In *The Waves*, on the other hand, the agency that creates order is constantly threatened by the entropic decay into which energy dissipates itself – 'Life is not susceptible perhaps to the treatment we give it when we try to tell it . . . It is strange how force ebbs away and away into some dry creek' (*TW*, 223) – and just as constantly rouses itself again to action; 'we rise, we toss back a mane of white spray; we pound on the shore; we are not to be confined' (*TW*, 223). The associations which Bernard has accumulated from his childhood associates and which begin to dissipate in his final conversation, accumulate again in the mind of each reader: just as the characters' 'conversations' are more like a rereading of their own past, so our reading of them is more like a conversation producing a new pattern to the associative connections of which they are constructed. The novel itself is as life is to Louis:

> To read this poem one must have myriad eyes, like one of those lamps that turn on slabs of racing water at midnight in the Atlantic, when perhaps only a spray of seaweed pricks the surface, or suddenly the waves gape and up shoulders a monster . . . The poet who has written this page (what I read with people talking) has withdrawn . . . And so (while they talk) let down one's net deeper and deeper and deeper and gently draw in and bring to the surface what he said and she said and make poetry. (*TW*, 165)

In each of us the novel is a net for drawing to the surface the depths of our own associational energy, without which the novel itself would be merely a one-sided conversation. We do so, however, 'while they talk': reading – for both reader and character – takes place within and alongside conversation. And to discover the order which emerges from conversation one must be prepared, like Woolf's characters, to be conversant with chaos.

6 The Lyrical Epic and the Singularity of Literature

One of the major innovations of twentieth-century modernist writing is the non-narrative long poem – what I have previously described as the 'lyrical epic'.[1] Its emergence can be traced in Yeats's efforts to shape all of his poetry as a single epic totality in which each poem will stand as a contributing lyrical moment, a macrocosmic ambition which is then reflected in the microcosm of individual poems which consist, like 'Nineteen Hundred and Nineteen' or 'The Tower', of a sequence of lyrics not obviously continuous with one another either in content or verse form. The possibilities of the lyrical epic begin to be explored in Ezra Pound's draft *Cantos* published in *Poetry* (Chicago) in 1917, partly under the influence of Joyce's *Ulysses,* with which both Pound and Eliot were familiar from an early date because of their involvement in its serial publication. It then achieves its most influential (if accidental) form in Pound's editing of T. S. Eliot's *The Waste Land* in 1922, whose tactics and techniques are developed in the following forty years by poets from widely different cultural backgrounds: Hugh MacDiarmid's *A Drunk Man Looks at the Thistle* (1926), David Jones's *In Parenthesis* (1937), William Carlos Williams's *Paterson* (1948–52), H. D.'s *Helen in Egypt* (1961), not to mention Eliot's own *Four Quartets* (1935–42) and the 108 completed poems of Pound's *Cantos*. All are attempts to maintain over the course of a long poem the requirements of a modernist aesthetic that refuses to allow to poetry any of those narrative resources of character and plot which had become degraded by their dominance in novels intended for the mass reading public that modernists had come to regard as

---

[1] See my *Yeats, Eliot, Pound and the Politics of Poetry* (London: Croom Helm, 1982).

the enemy of art. In his essay on 'The Symbolism of Poetry', published in 1900, W. B. Yeats offered an explanation of how a lyric can be transformed into an epic:

> A little lyric evokes an emotion, and this emotion gathers others about it and melts into their being in the making of some great epic; and at last, needing an always less delicate body, or symbol, as it grows more powerful, it flows out, with all it has gathered, among the blind instincts of daily life, where it moves a power within powers, as one sees ring within ring in the stem of an old tree.[2]

Yeats's account derives from the associationist context of his early criticism: the apparently non-narrative form of the lyric gathers around it a series of associations which, in their links, begin to take on a narrative shape, and can thereby be merged into the form of an epic. That epic, in turn, will provoke associations – 'all it has gathered' – that become a force in the world by reshaping a people's consciousness and thereby transforming its history. A lyrical emotion, apparently self-contained and distant from the narrative of the world's events, is in fact the origin and end of its historical narrative: 'I am certainly never sure, when I hear of some war, or of some religious excitement, or of some new manufacture, or of anything else that fills the ear of the world, that it has not all happened because of something that a boy piped in Thessaly'.[3] It is in this dialogue between the non-narrative lyric and the associational narrative which it provokes that the form of the lyrical epic becomes possible: the non-narrative lyrical moments which alone constitute *poetry* in the modern age (all other writing being simply prose) finds narrative completion in the associational connections by which the reader constructs those moments into an order, elaborating the successive structure of (one) possible narrative which will unify the poem's elements.

The associationist foundations of such lyrical epics are clear in T. S. Eliot's introduction to his translation of St-John Perse's *Anabase* in which, he suggests, 'any obscurity of the poem, on first reading, is due to the suppression of "links in the chain", of explanatory and connecting matter, and not just to incoherence or to love of cryptogram'.[4] The lack of narrative connection in

---

[2] W. B. Yeats, 'The Symbolism of Poetry', *Essays and Introductions*, 157–8.

[3] Ibid., 158.

[4] St-John Perse, *Anabase*, trans. T. S. Eliot (London: Faber and Faber, 1959), 'Introduction', 9.

the poem is a consequence of the erasure of the 'links in the chain' of associations by which they had been connected in the poet's mind; the reading of the poems reverses that process by allowing new links to be established in the associative activity of the reader: 'the reader', as Eliot put it, 'has to allow the images to fall into his memory without questioning the reasonableness of each at the moment; so that, at the end, a total effect is produced. Such selection of a sequence of images and ideas has nothing chaotic about it. There is a logic of the imagination as well as a logic of concepts'.[5] The final sentence may emphasise the role of 'imagination', but the crucial element in the actual process of producing the poetry is 'memory'. It is only from the connections that develop in the reader's memory that the 'total effect' will be generated: the 'logic of the imagination', which allows us to see the fragments as a new whole, is only possible when those fragments are enveloped by the associative connections that the sequence acquires in the memory of the reader, associative connections which provide at least the outlines of a narrative order.

It is a form, as I. A. Richards noted in his discussion of *The Waste Land* in the Appendix to *Principles of Literary Criticism*, beset with 'an unusual amount of irritated or enthusiastic bewilderment', a bewilderment that Richards attributed to 'the unobtrusiveness, in some cases the absence, of any intellectual thread upon which the items of the poem are strung' (*PLC*, 231). For Richards, Eliot's poem has to be read as a 'music of ideas', one in which ideas 'of all kinds, abstract and concrete, general and particular . . . are arranged, not that they may tell us something, but that their effects in us may combine into a coherent whole of feeling and attitude' (*PLC*, 233), and if we fail to find this 'coherent whole' it can only be because 'we have been trying to put the fragments together on a wrong principle' (*PLC*, 235). Poems which are trying *not* to 'tell us something' are bound to be inherently difficult for those who read in the expectation of narrative or thematic order but the difficulty which readers encounter in these poems is more demanding than the mere lack of narrative sequence. It as though, having entered upon an *aesthetics of difficulty*, each of the poems mentioned above deliberately adds to that difficulty by the particular poetic tactics it employs: in Yeats's private symbolism, in Pound's arcane use of history, in Eliot's deployment of apparently arbitrary allusions, in MacDiarmid's creation of 'synthetic Scots', in David Jones's Celtic mythology, in H.D.'s play with alternative versions of Greek mythology, in Williams's 'found poetry' of newspaper and letter, it seems that the poetry deliberately

---

[5] Ibid., 9–10.

builds barriers against the reader seeking to find 'the logic of the imagination' that binds the fragmentary elements of the poem into some kind of whole. The resources of a common body of knowledge (such as Wordsworth expected of his readers) are simply inadequate to the understanding of these poems. As Richards pointed out, the reader has to do some preliminary work to acquire the materials necessary for making any aesthetic experience possible. Ordinary knowledge and ordinary experience are inadequate to the task. As T. S. Eliot put it in 'Reflections on Contemporary Poetry' in 1917, referring to the work of Jean de Bosschère,

> M. de Bosschère is an intellectual by his obstinate refusal to adulterate his poetic emotions with human emotions. Instead of refining ordinary human emotion . . . he aims direct at the emotions of art. He thereby limits the number of his readers, and leaves the majority groping for a clue that does not exist. The effect is sometimes an intense frigidity which I find altogether admirable.[6]

Eliot's gleeful delight in the discomfiture of those in search of 'ordinary human emotion' (that is, 'the majority') underlines the extent to which these poems challenge their readers not just at one but at all the levels of difficulty that George Steiner identified, in his essay 'On Difficulty', as standing between readers and modern literary texts. Those readers, according to Steiner, are confronted not only by the contingent difficulties of the language, the references, the allusions which need to be 'looked up' and acquired if the poetry is to make basic verbal sense, they also have to overcome the modal difficulties of entering into a cultural context which, to most modern readers, 'is either a closed book or the terrain of academic research'[7] rather than one of real empathy (that is, involving recognisably 'human emotions' of the kind Eliot dismisses). In addition, however, they have to overcome the 'tactical' difficulty of writers who refuse 'the banal and constricting determinations of ordinary, public syntax' (*OD*, 35). For Steiner, the problems posed by these various obstacles to understanding are increasing because modern readers are already cut off from the kinds of literary culture, and the kinds of training in rhetoric, which were familiar to readers in the past. Even if, however, some or

---

[6] T. S. Eliot, 'Reflections on Contermporary Poetry; *The Egoist*, iv, 9 (October 1917), 133.

[7] George Steiner, *On Difficulty and Other Essays* (Oxford: Oxford University Press, 1972), 33; hereafter cited in the text as *OD*.

all of these levels of difficulty might be encountered in past poetry, readers of modernist poetry are confronted with an additional and more demanding level of difficulty, one which Steiner describes as 'ontological', and which involves a breach in the 'contract of ultimate or preponderant intelligibility between poet and reader, between text and meaning' (*OD*, 40). This 'ontological' difficulty Steiner traces to 'Mallarmé's dictum of 1894 that poetry has "gone wrong" since the magisterial, but ultimately erroneous, achievement of Homer. By becoming linear, narrative, realistic, publicly-focused, the art of Homer and his successors – this is to say of the near totality of Western literature – had lost or betrayed the primal mystery of magic' (*OD*, 43). It is a crisis that Steiner sees as reflected in the philosophy of Heidegger, with its desire to return to the pre-Socratics, and Steiner's essay, written in 1978, correctly judged what would become the predominant context for understanding the 'difficulty' of modernist texts in the following decades: 'difficulty' arises in modernism from the poets' recognition that they had to recover language as 'the house of Being and the home of human beings', but to do so had to resist the language which 'becomes a mere container for their sundry preoccupations'.[8] A criticism shaped by the concerns of Heidegger's philosophy would insist that these are poems in which the poet performs what the metaphysician can only strive towards, because 'thinking does not overcome metaphysics by climbing still higher, surmounting it, transcending it somehow or other; thinking overcomes metaphysics by climbing back down into the nearness of the nearest'.[9] Poetry, which to Arnold and the Victorians had to take on the burden of religion, has to take on the burden of philosophy, has to become the medium in which language recovers itself from philosophy and from the wrong turn that Western culture took with Plato and Aristotle; the 'true poet' has, in Steiner's words, 'to force his way upstream to the Orphic sources of his art', and to recover 'the illuminations of authentic existence reflected in the pre-Socratics' (*OD*, 43).

This way of understanding the difficulty of modernist poetry, whether in its positive Heideggerian sense of the poet's ability to recover the forsaken 'house of Being' or its negative Derridean sense of the unending struggle to escape the metaphysics of Being and the power of logocentrism, undoubtedly

---

[8] Martin Heidegger, 'Letter on Humanism', David Farrell Krell (ed.), *Martin Heidegger: Basic Writings*, trans. Frank A. Capuzzi (New York: Harper and Row, 1977), 193–242; in Lawrence Cahoone (ed.), *From Modernism to Postmodernism: An Anthology* (Oxford: Blackwell, 1996), 304.

[9] Ibid., 300.

speaks to modernist poetry's sense of crisis, and to the crisis of language in which the poetry is implicated. But a Heideggerian 'return of Being' or a Derridean plurality in which one finds only 'traces, foretellings, recallings, fore-blows and after-blows which no present will have preceded or followed',[10] can account historically for the emergence of the non-narrative long poem in the Anglophone world only if that poetry was presciently engaged with the issues defined by a later philosophy. Thus the non-narrative long poem in English might be seen to be based on the example of those French poets – Mallarmé in particular – whose work is read as initiating a new self-consciousness about language's relation to the world: 'The reference is lifted, but reference remains: what is left is only the writing of dreams, a fiction that is not imaginary, mimicry without imitation, without verisimilitude, without truth or falsity, a miming of appearance without concealed reality, without any world behind it'.[11] One tradition of criticism, initiated very early by Edmund Wilson's *Axel's Castle* (1931), would argue that Anglophone modernist poetry does indeed stem directly from those developments in French poetry, and therefore must also reflect its underlying assumptions about the nature of language. A later elaboration of this view in Marjorie Perloff's *The Poetics of Indeterminacy: Rimbaud to Cage* (1981) argues for two lines of development from French poetry: one, stemming from Mallarmé, leading to the 'high modernism' of Yeats, Eliot, Stevens, and the other, stemming from Rimbaud, leading to the 'postmodern' work of Pound, Stein and Williams. It is in this second tradition that the stylistic consequences of the kinds of linguistic indeterminacy later elaborated by Derridean deconstruction are most fully revealed. In either case, poets in English are to be seen developing the very issues which Derrida's form of deconstructive criticism finds already articulated in Mallarmé: insofar as they – or their texts – follow their French exemplars they are already engaged with the metaphysics of Being and the deconstruction of that logocentrism which releases the text into 'the undecidable'.[12]

These issues, however, as we have seen in relation to Joyce, were ones with which the Anglophone tradition had already had to engage as it worked through the consequences of associationist conceptions of art. Associationism had none of the 'thetic' intent that assumed that language could ever stand in

---

[10] Jacques Derrida, 'The Double Session', *A Derrida Reader: Between the Blinds*, ed. Peggy Kamuf (Hemel Hempstead: Harvester Wheatsheaf, 1991), 184.

[11] Ibid.

[12] Ibid., 185.

a direct relation with a transcendent 'truth'. When Derrida asserts that 'literary writing has, almost always and almost everywhere, in accordance with diverse fashions and across diverse ages, lent itself to that *transcendent* reading, that search for the signified which we here put in question',[13] the 'almost and everywhere' excludes the whole associationist tradition, which never inclined itself to a search for a 'transcendental' mode of reading. And when Derrida insists on the importance of the 'trace' he recapitulates the very terminology of Hartley's conception of how associations are imprinted on the fabric of the brain, a terminology which equally (if differently) insists that 'signification is *a priori* written'[14] since, for Hartley, it is the writing on the brain that provides the materials of signification, and that *arche-writing* takes place (as we have seen) in a fallen world in which we have no access 'to the full presence of the logos'.[15] And as developers and critics of associationism alike insisted, the trace could never be returned in its original purity: each trace was necessarily a re-trace which changed the very thing it traced, so that meaning could never be identical with itself, from past to present, from sentence to sentence. If Locke's introduction of the notion of association was designed to protect the clarity of meaning by providing an explanation for those minds in which it had become obscured, the extension of association to the totality of human experience radically undermined all such fixity and made of meaning a continual retracing which necessarily destabilised and deformed the original from which it derived. Even more importantly, it means that where there is no retracing the trace fades under the force of obliviscence and the very associations of which our words are formed are decomposed into new collocations. If, as John Stuart Mill, following Hume, insists, the objects of our perception are nothing but bundles 'of simultaneous possibilities of sensation',[16] then words too are nothing but 'possibilities of association', only some of which will be retraced on any particular encounter with the word and, as with all other groups of associations, will change as the traces of which they are composed decay or are revitalised. Derrida's 'différance', insofar as it is the necessary deferral of the full and immediate presence of meaning, had always been implicit in associationist accounts of language – or, rather, associationism never assumed

---

[13] Jacques Derrida, '...That Dangerous Supplement...', *Acts of Literature*, ed. Derek Attridge (London: Routledge, 1992), 104.

[14] Jacues Derrida, 'Of Grammatology', *A Derrida Reader*, 42.

[15] Ibid., 43.

[16] John Stuart Mill, *Collected Works*, IX, *Examination of Sir William Hamilton's Philosophy*, 200.

the possibility of 'presence', since the sign was meaningful precisely because it inspired the recollection of a moment (probably forgotten in terms of its original occurrence and certainly complicated by its later situations of use) in which signifier and signified came to be associated. As such, all signs were based on initially contingent and arbitrary conjunctions, conjunctions which were both reinforced and reshaped by later associational contexts. Association cannot help but be, in Derridean terms, 'dissemination' – forever 'escaping the horizon of the unity of meaning'.[17] This is why, perhaps, Derrida's description of the nature of the work of literature repeats Hume's account of the paradox of the self that we can never discover separate from the flow of particular impressions and ideas – 'if you proceed to analyze all the elements of a literary work', Derrida says, 'you will never come across literature itself, only some traits which it shares or borrows'.[18] 'Literature itself', like the Humean self, is a fugitive entity which we can never isolate from the particular impressions and ideas that we observe as they come into consciousness.

The possibility of this parallel between Derrida's deconstructive notion of literature and Hume's philosophy arises from the fact that Hume's associationism is not integral to what Derrida describes as the 'the logocentric epoch,'[19] an epoch which he takes to be figured in the writings of Rousseau and to be central to the whole of the Western tradition of philosophy from Plato's 'pharmakon' to Mallarmé's poetics.[20] If such logocentrism has indeed been the dominant tradition of Western philosophy then the moment of its overthrow, the moment when 'difference' replaces the 'same' as the basis of metaphysics, is, as Gilles Deleuze suggests, the moment of Hume's analysis of repetition, his account of how 'repetition changes nothing in the object repeated, but does change something in the mind which contemplates it'.[21] For Deleuze, 'associationism possesses an irreplaceable subtlety' (DR, 92) in its ability to show how 'habit *draws* something new from repetition – namely difference' (DR, 94). The power of Hume's account of the psyche lies in its 'having founded a whole theory of artificial signs on these relations of association' (DR, 102), because in the Humean perspective 'there is no continuity

---

[17] Jacques Derrida, 'Signature, Event, Context', *A Derrida Reader*, 99.

[18] 'An Interview with Jacques Derrida', *Acts of Literature*, 73.

[19] Jacques Derrida, ' ...That Dangerous Supplement ...', *Acts of Literature*, 107.

[20] See 'The Double Session', *A Derrida Reader*, 169–99.

[21] Gilles Deleuze, *Difference and Repetition*, trans. Paul Patton (London: Continuum, 2004; 1968), 90; hereafter cited in the text as *DR*.

apart from that of habit, and . . . we have no continuities apart from those of our thousands of component habits' (*DR*, 95) which arise from association. Thus 'the role of the imagination, or the mind which contemplates in its multiple and fragmented states is to draw something new from repetition, to draw difference from it' (*DR*, 97), a difference in which 'the succession of present presents is only the manifestation of something more profound – namely, the manner in which each continues the whole life' (*DR*, 105). There is no 'whole', however, which can be identified separate from the series of presents of which we are immediately conscious, but that series of presents already contains, in its awareness of its repetition of and difference from the past, an awareness of the extent to which 'the past is presupposed by every representation' (*DR*, 103). Any moment of present awareness is always also a moment of past awareness: 'The present and former presents are not, therefore, like two successive instants on the line of time; rather, the present one necessarily contains an extra dimension in which it represents the former and also represents itself' (*DR*, 102). As John Stuart Mill had explained, if 'we speak of the Mind as a series of feelings, we are obliged to complete the statement by calling it a series of feelings which is aware of itself as past and future', in which case, since the 'Mind or Ego' cannot be 'something different from any series of feelings' we have to accept 'the paradox, that something which *ex hypothesi* is but a series of feelings, can be aware of itself as a series'.[22] It is a paradox which also characerises the lyrical epic, a form which is constructed as 'a series of feelings' inhering in various images which are yet (somehow) more than mere series.

For the lyrical epic, as for the associationist tradition in general, the crucial issue is not the metaphysics of Being; the crucial issue is, in Deleuze's terms, the fact that mind is possible only as the 'difference' that 'lies between two repetitions' (*DR*, 97), a 'difference' which allows us to apprehend 'time as a living present, and the past and the future as dimensions of this present' (*DR*, 97). It is an account of the mind that makes memory central, but not a memory in which a present moment recalls a past moment as its successor, the past moment returning in its isolated purity; it is one in which every moment can only be experienced insofar as it differentiates itself from or repeats to some degree a moment of the past. The present is only knowable through its pastness: the past is only recoverable in its presentness. It is by such a structure that the lyrical epic is informed: it is a poem which cannot simply be 'read',

---

[22] Mill, *Collected Works*, IX, *Examination of Sir William Hamilton's Philosophy*, 194.

it can only be *re*-read, both in the sense that its series will only make sense as series when we return to each of its elements in the awareness of the whole series, but also in the sense that the lyrical epic is also a *rereading* of previous literature, the making new and present what was past and (nearly) forgotten. Just as readers, in returning to the beginning of a lyrical epic read each of its lyrical moments as suffused with the memory of the rest of series – suffused, as it were, with a past which is also the future of the poem that they are beginning to reread – so the poem itself is also a return to and recollection of the literature which constitutes the series in which this particular poem takes its place – as well, of course, as a prophecy of the rest of the series still to come. As we transform chaos into order by recovering the 'links in the chain' that have been erased from the poem, so the poem too is bringing into a new order the past from which it emerges, which it recalls into the present and which it projects into the future. The poem requires the reader to re-establish the 'links in the chain' on the same basis that the poem itself re-establishes the links in a lost chain of literary tradition. 'Back to Dunbar' was the paradoxical war-cry of MacDiarmid's Scottish modernism, making explicit that the 'it' in Pound's 'Make it new' was the past.

The lyrical epic, it has sometimes been argued, is a poem which needs to be read as if it represented the contents of a particular mind, as a development of the dramatic monologue in which each element reflects back upon and points to the nature of an unstated consciousness in which we will discover both the interconnection and the unity of its various elements. As C. K. Stead put it, 'it is an image of human life consistent with the state of feeling which governs the poem'.[23] But this is simply to dramatise as an *individual* experience the potential which the lyrical epic has for calling forth many different possible unifications as a result of different states of feeling coming to govern the poem: the poem, in other words, does not direct us towards a particular 'state of feeling' but requires us to enact – and then to re-enact – different ways in which its elements could be connected together as they call forth alternative patterns of associations. The poem will always be, therefore, necessarily *different*, both in itself for the same reader at different moments in time and for different readers in the same time. The lyrical epic is the form which exploits to the maximum the associationist tradition's conception of a work of art which exists only in the stimulation of the reader's associations: there is no poem as a single, unitary object, only a potentiality for unification when the poem is

---

[23] C.K. Stead, *The New Poetic* (Harmondsworth: Penguin, 1967), 220.

experienced in a mind which can call on an adequate associational reservoir. The poem is so structured that its remaking with each rereading is not simply a fact of the reading process, one which takes place in relation to any work of literature, but one which is enforced by its very form: fragmentation forces the reader to acknowledge the reading process by which (according to the associationist tradition) all works of literature are governed but which most ignore or conceal. As the reading mind finds the links which connect what is apparently mere series, the poem becomes an involution of the past in the present and the present with the past; the lyrical epic engages the reader in the process by which the human mind, through its associational capacity, can discover an order and a coherence in a world apparently dominated by chaos, and can do so without recourse to anything but that associational activity itself.

To some readers, of course, the task will prove impossible: the poem will remain a blank. Others, by dint of effort and continual rereading or by the acquisition of specialised knowledge, will finally be able to make the poem 'work'. It is precisely because the lyrical epic so forcefully embodies the associationist model of the mind and of art that it can produce such deeply opposed critical judgments. The classic example, perhaps, is Pound's *Cantos*: to some Pound's work is the great achievement of twentieth-century poetry; to others, it is a chaotic failure. John Harwood, for instance, suggests that the evaluation of the *Cantos* has been bedevilled by the fact that,

> Within the 'Pound cult', the problem has been defined out of existence by the critical equivalent of moving the goalposts; Hugh Kenner, for instance, once claimed that 'Pound's principal achievement' was to 'dispense with' subject, plot, and 'line of philosophic development'. Along with this we have the various forms of special pleading derived from Pound himself, centred on the 'ideogrammic method', the 'new method of scholarship' and the 'luminous detail'. Here the strategy is to claim that these techniques work in opposition to, or on a higher plane than, normal logical or narrative structures, whereas the chaos of the *Cantos* is itself a compelling demonstration of the fact that they only work in conjunction with more mundane forms of organisation and understanding.[24]

---

[24] John Harwood: 'These fragments you have shelved (shored)': Pound, Eliot and *The Waste Land*', in Andrew Gibson (ed.), *Pound in Multiple Perspective: A Collection of Critical Essays* (Basingstoke: Macmillan, 1993), 188–215, 207.

The various poetic methods to which Harwood alludes are, however, all variants on the associationist foundations from which Pound's poetry developed in the 'Imagist' movement in London before the First World War: Pound's conception of the 'Image' involved the secularisation of Yeats's conception of the symbol as an occult power, a secularisation that led to Pound's conception of the 'image' as being that 'which presents an intellectual and emotional complex in an instant of time'.[25] Pound's 'image' is a modernised version of the 'fusion' by which associationists had described the creation of complex ideas and their accompanying emotion: the 'image' is, therefore, more than 'an idea', because it is 'a vortex or cluster of fused ideas and is endowed with energy'[26] – the energy to provoke ideas and emotions (that is, associations) in its readers.

Whatever his theory, however, Pound's actual technique is based not so much on 'fusion' as on that other pole of associationist aesthetics – *dissociation*. Setting side by side two images which have no obvious connection with each other forces the reader to try to find associative links between them. Since aesthetic experience is nothing other than the activity of associative connection, the effort that this search for associations produces will, in theory at least, intensify the aesthetic experience. It is a procedure that William H. Gass has attributed to Pound's 'habit of emotional dissociation':

> he was incapable of the consecutive steps of thought, or of the painstaking definition or systematic and orderly development of any idea . . . Disjunction is Pound's principal method of design. If he saw the world in fragments, it was because he needed fragments, and because his psyche hated wholes. In a whole, the various parts might get in touch with one another. In a whole, the grounds for their meeting might be discovered and explored; but Pound preferred luminous juxtapositions, ignitions which would take place without the need of connection, as if powder and flint would fire without a strike.[27]

Whether Gass was aware of it or not, his terminology points back to a key element in the critical vocabulary of the period of emergent modernism

---

[25] Ezra Pound, *Literary Essays of Ezra Pound*, ed. T. S. Eliot (London: Faber and Faber, 1960), 4.

[26] Ezra Pound, *The New Age*, XVI, 28 January 1915, 349.

[27] William H. Gass, 'Unoriginal Sins', *The Times Literary Supplement*, 13–19 January 1989, 27–8, 28

around the First World War. 'Dissociation' is a concept brought into play by associationist theory, and, in the work of Rémy de Gourmont,[28] is used to describe the process by which a writer can deliberately seek to uncouple habitual associations in order to produce new and original combinations. Eliot uses it in this way of Virginia Woolf:

> A good deal of the charm of Mrs. Woolf's shorter pieces consists in the immense disparity between the object and the train of feeling which it has set in motion. Mrs. Woolf gives you the minutest datum, and leads on to explore, quite consciously, the sequence of images and feelings which float away from it ... The book is one of the most curious and interesting examples of the process of dissociation which in that direction, it would seem, cannot be exceeded.[29]

The term 'dissociation' was, of course, to become famous through Eliot's development of the notion of the 'dissociation of sensibility': in this, 'dissociation' represents the historical breakdown of 'association' rather than deliberate breakage of habitual associations. In his essay on 'The Metaphysical Poets', Eliot uses dissociation initially in the first sense: Johnson, he tells us 'has hit by accident, on one of their peculiarities, when he observes that "their attempts were always analytic"; he would not agree that, after the dissociation, they put the material together again in a new unity'.[30] 'Dissociation' breaks up habitual patterns of association, leaving the poet free to then create new and unexpected kinds of connections. That ability to dissociate and recombine associations, however, is something that Eliot believed had been lost to English poetry:

> We may express the difference by the following theory: The poets of the seventeenth century, the successors of the dramatists of the sixteenth, possessed a mechanism of sensibility which could devour any kind of experience. They are simple, artificial, difficult, or fantastic, as their predecessors were . . . In the seventeenth century dissociation of sensibility set in, from which we have never recovered; and this dissociation, as is natural, was aggravated by the influence of the two most powerful poets

---

[28] See Rémy de Gourmont, *La Culture des Idées* (Paris, 1900).
[29] T. S. Eliot, 'London Letter', *The Dial*, 71 (August 1921), 216–17.
[30] T. S. Eliot, *Selected Essays*, 'The Metaphysical Poets', 286.

of the century, Milton and Dryden . . . while the language became more refined, the feeling became more crude.[31]

'Dissociation' in this historical context implies an inability to associate freely across 'any kind of experience'; it reduces the poetic mind towards the 'ordinary man's experience', which is 'chaotic, irregular, fragmentary', as compared with the mind of the poet in which the most diverse are being associated so that 'these experiences are always forming new wholes'.[32] The dissociation of sensibility is a historical break which limits and encompasses the associative energy of the poet and prevents him from invoking 'the whole literature of Europe and within it the whole of the literature of his own country'.[33]

The question posed by Gass's account of Pound's technique is how, if the poet is committed to a process of 'dissociation', can the elements of the poem become re-associated? And the answer is, only in a mind which has access to the sense of cultural continuity that Eliot proposes, one which can bring to the poem cultural resources that allow the poem to become its own memory-bank, thereby generating associative connections between its individual elements and between the cultural histories that it invokes; as Michael Alexander puts it in an entirely untechnical but appropriate way, 'the elements of the composition, unfathomable as some of them appear at first, mingle with a freedom and naturalness which makes all credible and acceptable'.[34] To some the poem is a blank; to others an ultimate richness: both are possible and, indeed, inevitable outcomes of the associationist method of the poetry. The debate between those who find it blank and those who find it endlessly fruitful is pointless until both sides have identified the fundamental requirements involved in the poem's aesthetic, for the poem may be found as blank by a reader who simply refuses to acknowledge its associationist intent as it is by a reader who finds that it raises no effective associational connections in his or her own memory: the basis of their judgment that the poem is a failure will, however, be quite different.

The important issue, then, is to identify the structural principle of the lyrical epic, whose driving force lies in the effort to connect the personal associations of the poet, arising out of a limited local memory, with a transpersonal system

---

[31] Ibid., 287–8.

[32] Ibid., 287.

[33] T. S. Eliot, *Selected Essays*, 'Tradition and the Individual Talent', 14.

[34] Michael Alexander, *The Poetic Achievement of Ezra Pound* (Edinburgh: Edinburgh University Press, 1998; 1979), 205.

of associations which will justify the 'objectivity' of those personal associations by revealing their integration in unbroken sequence that is rooted in some form of communal past. It is the effort to reveal through an apparently present series that not only is the past 'presupposed by every representation' (*DR*, 103) but that the totality of the past is always recoverable because it is implicated in the series of our immediate experiences: as T. S. Eliot put it in his study of F. H. Bradley, 'in order to know what a particular event is you must know the soul to which it occurs, and the soul exists only in the events which occur to it; so that the soul is, in fact, the whole past insofar as that past enters into the present, and it is the past as implied in the present'.[35] Shorn of its Bradleian metaphysic, this becomes the aesthetic of 'Tradition and the Individual Talent' in which 'the historical sense involves a perception, not only of the pastness of the past, but of its presence' because 'not only the best, but the most individual parts' of a poet's work will be 'those in which the dead poets, his ancestors, assert their immortality most vigorously'.[36] Poetry is where the dead associate themselves with the living, where the living find their associations with the dead, and it is the purpose of the lyrical epic to bring back into association as much of the past as possible. Without that continuity, without that link to the deepest strata of the mind and of history, art itself would be put in jeopardy: 'is it possible for art', Eliot asked in 1924, 'the creation of beautiful objects, and of literature to persist indefinitely without its primitive purposes: is it possible for the aesthetic object to be a direct object of attention?'[37] Yeats had put the same issue three decades earlier:

> Have not poetry and music arisen, as it seems, out of the sounds the enchanters made to help their imagination to enchant, to charm, to bind with a spell themselves and the passers-by? These very words, a chief part of all praises of music or poetry, still cry to us of their origin. And just as the musician or the poet enchants and charms and binds us with a spell of his own mind when he would enchant the mind of others, so did the enchanter create or reveal for himself as well as for others the supernatural artist or genius, the seeming transitory mind made out of many minds.[38]

---

[35] T. S. Eliot, *Knowledge and Experience in the Philosophy of F. H. Bradley* (London: Faber and Faber, 1964), 79.

[36] T. S. Eliot, *Selected Essays*, 14.

[37] T. S. Eliot, *Criterion*, II (July 1924), 490.

[38] W. B. Yeats, 'Magic', *Essays and Introductions*, 43.

In the lyrical epic a 'seeming transitory mind' is made out of many minds by including within its own body the many voices of the past, allowing the past to suffuse the present with their associations. The poem is not a communication of a traditional kind: its dissociations are provocations to association, to that activity of the mind in search of fugitive connections which will create order out of apparent chaos, and will do so by linking our individual memories into a transpersonal memory capable of recalling all of the history – or, at least, its 'ideal continuum' – that connects us to those original associations laid down in the darkness of savagery. The poem, therefore, must dramatise the loss and return of memory, symbolically represented in patterns of exile and homecoming, but such drama is enacted not only in the 'events' of the poem but in the mind of the reader: the poem provides us with a memory system which, once mastered, is capable of generating – or, rather, re-generating – association on a scale that will allow the reading mind to discover the depths of its own inner resources, which are, potentially, the depths of the totality of the human mind in history. Or, if it fails to do so, is diagnostic of a reading mind still cut off from its own deepest resources. The lyrical epic is a mnemophone which calls and recalls until the voice of the past can speak again in the mouth of the present, until the present can resound with all the voices of the past.

In its ambition and its achievement, in its challenge to the forms of traditional epic, in its ability to engage the modern and the ancient, the lyrical epic stands as testimony to the radical potential of the associationist account of both the conception and reception of poetry; in the troubled history of its evaluation, in its despairing sense of the impossibility of ever achieving finality, in the resistance of critics who cannot accept its presuppositions, the lyrical epic also confirms the profound challenge which associationist theories pose to common conceptions of meaning and of reading. Eliot's *The Waste Land* stands, perhaps, as a possible *reductio ad absurdum* of the associationist aesthetic: its accidental structure created by the interventions of Ezra Pound, its allusive style endlessly open to the discovery of new possible connections between this text and many another, its invocation of myth either a hermeneutic 'red herring' or the discovery of some ultimate truth of the foundations of literature, its autobiographical elements always tempting the possibility of the discovery of some binding, personal set of associations in the mind of the poet. Or, it may be, it stands as its fulfilment: a poem which defies narrative emplotment and character development, that invokes a multitudinous hinterland of allusive intertextualities, that negotiates a relationship between the modern and the barbaric, that *works* – or allows readers to work in productive ways with whatever they can bring to the poem.

The lyrical epic was made possible by the readerly dynamics of association-ism and its critical reception – as in the case of Joyce's *Ulysses* – has depended, implicitly, on the same associationist foundations. Acknowledgment of that context both explains the apparent 'obscurity' of such poetry and justifies what has been, for most readers, their actual mode of reading – following and developing the patterns which emerge as the poem inspires, intensifies and interacts with the networks of their own associational recollections. The outcome is – necessarily – a unique remaking of the poem on every reading, a remaking to which previous readings of the poem, and readings of interpreta-tions of the poem, continually add. In associationist theory this is, of course, true of all literary experience, but in the lyrical epic that awareness is brought to bear on the very form and structure of the poem: the poem knows that it is inhabited by, is haunted by, endless memories; the poem knows that by seeking the sources of our communal memory it invokes those memories and reactivates them, sending them back into the community as enrichments to all future aesthetic experience. This awareness that they exist to generate a unique act of re-creation, that they can succeed only through *working* with the reader's associations, that they are incomplete and dependent structures, represents their radical challenge to the notion that there is some ultimate and communi-cable experience inherent in each individual work of literature.

As we have seen, I. A. Richards attempted to protect the communicability of the effect of a literary work not in terms of its content but in terms of its structure, its achievement of a 'feeling of revealed significance, this attitude of readiness, acceptance and understanding, which has led to so many "Revelation Doctrines" but which is in fact not a form of knowledge but a 'successful adjustment to life' (*PLC*, 224). But this effort to ground associationism in an effect whose structure is identical in all readers, even if its content is entirely different, fails to come to terms with the radicalism of the associationist aesthetic: the fact that the poem is inevitably different for different readers, the fact that when we attempt to discuss 'the poem' what we are actually discussing are the differences between our deeply personal constructions of what the poet has provided; the fact that the work is transformed as interpretations accumulate and elaborate further associational potential – these are the reasons why the lyrical epic has been the focus of such profound critical debate and such widely differing evaluations. The lyrical epic radically challenges the institutional requirement that there be a publicly accessible object which can be, if not 'objectively', then 'impersonally' analysed. Within an associationist aesthetic the 'impersonal' would be no more than a matter of tactical agreement within a particular community of readers sharing the same memories: even so, however, every act of reading would be a recreation as unique to its reader as it is usually assumed, within romantic theories, that the work's creation is unique to its author.

These issues have been foregrounded in recent criticism in debates about the 'New Aestheticism', a position from which critics have sought to re-establish the relevance of Kant's conception of the aesthetic and to redeem it from those interpretive perspectives that insist on reading all versions of the aesthetic as concealments of ideology. For the 'New Aestheticism', the power of art depends on its ability to resist all the categories by which we ordinarily structure our experience of the world: 'Although not telling the truth or being just in itself, art opens a space to question and challenge the "first order" formulations of epistemology and ethics that hold sway in the lifeworld'.[39] New Aestheticism's effort to reconstruct the notion of the aesthetic as that which stands outside and beyond all the determinations of social life, that which provides a ground for a critique of the utilitarian requirements of practical life, invokes notions not only of a specially privileged mode of understanding but of the absolute uniqueness of each aesthetic object: the aesthetic is by definition that which defeats and defies any system of rules by which we might try to understand it or reduce it to order – it is, quite literally, incomparable. This is an argument that Derek Attridge has pursued in *The Singularity of Literature*, in which he argues the need for us to acknowledge the uniqueness of each response to a literary work:

> In an inventive response the reader attempts to answer to the work's shaping of language by a new shaping of his or her own (which will in turn invite further responses) – whether it be in the form of a literal act of writing, an inward composition, a speech or intervention in a discussion, a change in behaviour. What this means, of course, is that it will in turn partake of the literary to some degree, and demand of its readers a response of the same inventive kind. The prospect of an endless chain of responses may sound alarming, but it only becomes

---

[39] John J. Joughin and Simon Malpas (eds), *The New Aestheticism* (Manchester: Manchester University Press, 2003), 'The New Aestheticism: an introduction', 11.

so if we conceive literature as possessing an extractable content which can finally be isolated – and hence possessing those qualities of self-presence, universality, historical transcendence, and absolute signification on which the Platonic tradition of aesthetics is based. But literature is characterized precisely by its lack of any such content – which, of course, is why we re-read, with no end in sight to our re-readings.[40]

The very terminology here – 'an endless chain of responses' – invokes the central metaphor of an associationist aesthetic, despite the fact that Attridge would see his own Kantian or deconstructive position as drawing on a very different tradition. As determinedly as Attridge, however, associationism insists on the 'singularity' of literature – every reading, every re-reading will necessarily invoke a different set of associations and therefore produce a different artwork. The associations provoked by particular readings will in turn pass into a publicly available memory-bank to reshape later readings. Associations thus form a kind of feedback loop which continually enlarges and intensifies the associational productivity of those works to which we regularly return.

Attridge insists that the significance of art derives from the fact that in each successful work of art we encounter 'the other', but that this encounter is not with 'the other as such (how could I?) but the remolding of the self that brings the other into being as, necessarily, no longer entirely other'.[41] It is an argument which is founded on a complex series of negotiations within contemporary philosophy about the nature of the 'other' and about how – epistemologically and ethically – it is possible to have a relation to the 'other'. Within this negotiation, literature is, for Attridge, a crucial resource because it is one of few ways in which we can be brought into contact with that 'other'. Each act of creation is a refusal of the categories which ordinarily govern our lives, so much so that 'the irruption of the other into the same does not, and cannot, sit comfortably within any of the explanatory frameworks by which we characterize the possible'.[42] Though almost 'impossible' to achieve, contact with this irreducible 'other' is both, for Attridge, the means and the justification of literature: each act of creation brings the 'other' into existence, as something previously unknown, while each act of reading reverses the process and attempts to assimilate that 'other' back into the world of the same:

---

[40] Derek Attridge, *The Singularity of Literature* (London: Routledge, 2004), 93.

[41] Ibid., 24.

[42] Ibid., 135.

The text that functions powerfully as literature (rather than as exhortation, description, mystification, and so on) uses the materials of the same – the culture which it and the reader inhabit and within which they are constituted – in such a way as to open onto that which cannot be accounted for by those materials (though they have in fact made possible its emergence). And the response to such a work – the responsible response, the one that attempts to apprehend the other as other – is a performance of it that, while it inevitably strives to convert the other to the same, strives also to allow the same to be modified by the other.[43]

This is an argument founded on a binary opposition between the 'same' and the 'other' as mutually exclusive categories: the self must reach out towards what is beyond itself, to an ancounter with the 'other', despite the fact that it can never actually reach beyond the boundaries its selfhood, beyond the 'self-same'. From an associationist perspective, however, the encounter with the other has a very different origin and structure: what we encounter in the reading of a work of literature is the flow of our own associations, associations which are both 'ours' – whether arising from our own past experience or from some form of hereditary deposit – and yet have a structure which we have never before encountered, since they are the product of the unique interaction of this work of literature with memories which, as reshaped by obliviscence, return in a form which we have never before experienced. Our associations will correspond neither to previous sensations (since what we recall are those sensations as reconstructed in an associative process to which some actual memories are always lost) nor to any previously encountered associations (because any repeated association will always be changed by entering into a new context of recollections): as a result we discover ourselves to be 'other', or recover ourselves as 'other', to anything we had ever previously envisaged or encountered. The 'other' is not something to be engaged with as external to me: it is already within me. What returns in my associational reverie is both my own memories reconstituted into a pattern I have never before experienced and those others who, like Tristram Shandy's relatives, have shaped my most intimate associations.

Attridge's 'other' emerges from the complexities of Kantian and Hegelian philosophy as something alien that I have to come to terms with, something alienating with which I have to find a resonance. It is founded, still, on the

---

[43] Ibid., 124.

self-identity of a Cartesian 'ego' to which the associationist tradition never subscribed – or, rather, from which Hume's philosophy was designed to allow us to escape. As Kemp Smith's and Deleuze's account of the Humean self both emphasise, the self is not a given but emerges into existence through having already internalised the other, by having learned through its associations its intimacy with the other:

> Our affections depend more upon ourselves, and the internal operations of the mind, than any other impressions; for which reason they arise more naturally from the imagination, and from every lively idea we form of them. This is the nature and cause of sympathy; and 'tis after this manner we enter so deep into the opinions and affections of others, whenever we discover them. (*T*, 319)

That which is most internal to ourselves – our 'affections' which 'depend more upon ourselves, and the internal operations of the mind, than any other impression' – is also that which most intimately links us to 'the opinions and affections of others'. This necessarily relational interconnection of self and other is the reason why the same act of the sympathetic imagination is required to identify with our own past self (or selves), as to identify with the 'other'. It is precisely because we discover ourselves as other to ourselves that it is possible for us to be as much in sympathy with the 'other' as with ourself.

By invoking a Kantian discourse of categories in order to try to make sense of the singularity by which literature is able to invoke the other, Attridge must claim not only an absolute separation of self and 'other' but an absolute uniqueness for both art and persons: 'It is in the acknowledgment of the other person's uniqueness, and therefore of the impossibility of finding general rules or schemata to account fully for him or her, that one can be said to encounter the other as other'.[44] But this is a singularity which, from an associationist perspective, ignores the extent to which *we are our associates*, and fails to acknowledge that our uniqueness lies not in our separation from the rest of the world but in our relation to it – in our relatedness, in our associatedness. Similarly, the singularity that Attridge seeks for literature is one which requires the 'absolute' of something which defies all rules, whereas associationism requires only a repetition which is always different. Literature opens out towards the other not by forcing us to recognise the uniqueness of each

---

[44] Ibid., 33.

individual that we encounter – and so their absolute otherness to ourselves – but by allowing us to encounter through our own otherness – that otherness that we discover in our own past selves as they return in the process of association – the identity we hold in common with those with whom we associate. We are able to sympathise with the other not by reaching beyond the self but because it is only by the same act of identification that we can sympathise with what, most approrpiately, we call *our*self. The 'we' that is informed by our associates contains both self and other; it precedes any 'I' which might encounter the other as distinct and separate, and it is this 'we' to which our process of association continually returns us.

These recent efforts by the New Aestheticists to find in a revitalised Kantianism an explanation both of literature's uniqueness and its ability to allow us to reach out beyond ourselves to the 'other' returns us to the moment from which we began – Coleridge's desire to find a justification for art that ensures it is 'other' to our ordinary everyday existences, that it is marked as a repetition of the divine and as guarantor, therefore, of the spiritual significance of its creator. Such an effort to protect the significance of the aesthetic – even if, as in the work of Benjamin or Adorno, in secularised form – has dominated much of modern theory as it underlies the development of the New Aestheticism. Indeed, it is assumed that the nature of the 'aesthetic' as defined within this Kantian tradition represents the very nature of modernity itself. As Joughin and Malpas put it in their introduction to *The New Aestheticism*, 'Modernity's central concepts thus derive from cognitive rationality, moral autonomy and the power of social-political self-determination', all of which 'as a self-conscious discourse about the necessary interrelations of knowledge, morality, culture and history can be more reliably located at the end of the eighteenth century in the thought of German Idealism, and particularly in the philosophies of Kant and Hegel'. It is in this context that 'art comes to occupy its own semi-autonomous realm presided over for Kant by aesthetic judgment', and 'it is with Kant that aesthetics takes on its distinctly modern trappings'.[45] This historical framing of the issue of the aesthetic, however, assumes that the only alternative to a Kantian conception of the aesthetic is submission to some form of 'ideology critique' which reduces works of literature to being simply functions of their social origins. Such a construction of modernity and of the possibilities of art ignores both the historical fact of associationism's refusal of the Kantian

---

[45] 'Introduction', *The New Aestheticism*, 9, 11.

transcendental and its long-lasting influence on the aesthetic, both in practice and in theory.

It is symptomatic of the repression of this tradition of British aesthetic reflection in contemporary debates that one of the contributors to *The New Aestheticism*, Thomas Docherty, notes that the 'birth' of aesthetics can be dated to 'the texts of Hutcheson' (and therefore to the context of the emergence of Hume's associationism),[46] but his reference to Hutcheson is elided from the index to the book. It is an indicative act of cultural amnesia, because the loss of that intellectual context and of the alternatives which it can provide – both for our understanding of the emergence of the key concepts of modernity and of the ways in which these might be developed in contemporary theory – has not only warped our historical understanding of literature in Britain and Ireland over the past two hundred and fifty years, but, at the same time, has allowed so-called 'continental theory' to be presented as the only viable version of a theoretically informed response to literature and art. We need to reinstate in those debates the Hume to whom Kant was responding and whose philosophy continues to challenge modern forms of Kantianism; the Hume whom Bergson rediscovered and who, through Bergson, Deleuze reinstated as the very origin of the philosophy of difference. And alongside the recovery of these various Humes we need to acknowledge the developing association-ist accounts both of the mind and of art which resisted the consequences of the Kantian-Coleridgean model of the aesthetic. Associationism refuses to subscribe to the need for art's 'semi-autonomous realm' precisely because, in an associationist context, the aesthetic is not 'extra-ordinary' but is at one with our ordinary and everyday experience; indeed, it can be incited by any ordinary and mundane object in any ordinary mind. For associationism, the uniqueness of art does not require that 'semi-autonomous realm' in which it resides sepa-rate from the rest of our lives; nor does it require an escape from all the rules and categories which govern the rest of our experience. Since the aesthetic is nothing but the interaction of the work of art with the associative work of its reader or observer, each experience of art is as unique and singular and as unpredictable as a conversation, so that art and our responses to it do not take us into the realm of a rarely reachable 'sublime' but are simply portions of our common, and communal, 'conversible world'.

---

[46] Ibid., 25.

Bibliography

Abrams, M. H., *The Mirror and the Lamp: Romantic Theory and the Critical Tradition* (New York: W. W. Norton, 1958; 1953).

Alexander, Michael, *The Poetic Achievement of Ezra Pound* (Edinburgh: Edinburgh University Press, 1998; 1979).

Alison, Archibald, *Essays on the Nature and Principles of Taste* (Edinburgh: Bell and Bradfute, 1811; 1790).

Allen, Richard C., *David Hartley on Human Nature* (Albany: State University of New York Press, 1999).

Annan, Noel, *Leslie Stephen: The Godless Victorian* (London: Weidenfeld and Nicolson, 1984).

Armstrong, Isobel, *Victorian Poetry: Poetry, Poetics and Politics* (London: Routledge, 1993).

— (ed.), *Victorian Scrutinies* (London: Athlone Press, 1962).

Arnold, Matthew, *On the Study of Celtic Literature* (London: Smith, Elder and Co., 1867).

Attridge, Derek and Daniel Ferrer, *Post-structuralist Joyce: Essays from the French* (Cambridge: Cambridge University Press, 1984).

Bagehot, Walter, *The Collected Works of Walter Bagehot*, 7 Vols, ed. Norman St John-Stevas, Vol. I, The Literary Essays' (London: The Economist, 1965).

Baier, Annette C., *A Progress of Sentiments: Reflections on Hume's Treatise* (Cambridge, MA: Harvard University Press, 1991).

Bain, Alexander, *Mental and Moral Science* (London: Longmans, Green and Co., 1884).

— 'On "Association"- Controversies', *Mind*, Vol. 12, No. 46 (April, 1887).

Banfield, Ann, *The Phantom Table: Woolf, Fry, Russell and the Epistemology of Modernism* (Cambridge: Cambridge University Press, 2000).

Barthes, Roland 'From Work to Text', Josue V. Harari (ed.), *Textual Strategies: Perspectives in Post-Structuralist Criticism* (London: Methuen, 1980).

Bate, Walter Jackson, *From Classic to Romantic* (Cambridge MA: Harvard University Press, 1949).

Bechtel, William, 'Connectionism and the Philosophy of Mind: An Overview', Terence Horgan and John Tienson (eds), *Connectionism and the Philosophy of Mind* (Dordrecht: Kluwer, 1991), 30–59.

Beer, Gillian, *Virginia Woolf: The Common Ground* (Edinburgh: Edinburgh University Press, 1996).

Belsey, Catherine, *Critical Practice* (London: Routledge, 1980).

Bergson, Henri, *Matter and Memory*, 5th edn, trans. Nancy Margaret Paul and W. Scott Palmer (New York: Zone Books, 1991; 1911).

Berkeley, George, *The Works of George Berkeley*, ed. A. A. Luce and T. E. Jessop, 9 Vols (London: Nelson, 1948–57).

Brewer, William D., *The Mental Anatomies of William Godwin and Mary Shelley* (London: Associated University Presses, 2001).

Bristow, Joseph (ed.), *The Cambridge Companion to Victorian Poetry* (Cambridge: Cambridge University Press, 2000), 'Reforming Victorian Poetry: poetics after 1832', 1–24.

Bromwich, David, *Hazlitt: The Mind of a Critic* (Oxford: Oxford University Press, 1983).

Brooks, Cleanth , *The Well Wrought Urn* (London: Dennis Dobson, 1949).

Brown, Thomas, *Lectures on the Philosophy of the Human Mind*, 4 Vols (Edinburgh: Tait, 1820).

—— *Observations on the Nature and Tendency of the Doctrine of Mr Hume concerning the relation of Cause and Effect* (Edinburgh: Mundell and Son, 1806).

—— *Sketch of a System of the Philosophy of the Human Mind: Part First, comprehending the Physiology of the Mind* (Edinburgh: Bell & Bradfute, Manners and Miller and Waugh and Innes, 1820).

Burke, Edmund, *A Philosophical Enquiry into the Origins of our Ideas of the Sublime and the Beautiful, The Works of the Right Honourable Edmund Burke,* 16 Vols (London: C. and J. Rivington, 1826).

Caird, Edward, *Essays on Literature and Philosophy* (Glasgow: James Maclehose and Sons, 1892).

Carlyle, Thomas, *Sartor Resartus,* ed. Roger L. Tarr (Berkeley, CA: University of California Press, 2000; 1833).

—— 'Signs of the Times', *Works*, 30 Vols, Vol. 27, ed. H. D. Traill (London: Chapman and Hall, 1896–9).

Cash, Arthur H. and John M. Stedmond (eds), *The Winged Skull: Papers from the Laurence Sterne Bicentenary Conference* (London: Methuen, 1971).

Chappell, V. C., (ed.), *Hume* (London: Macmillan, 1968).

Chase, Cynthia (ed.), *Romanticism* (London: Routledge, 1993).

Clark, Ronald W., *Freud: the Man and the Cause* (London: Jonathan Cape and Weidenfeld and Nicolson, 1980).

Coleridge, Samuel Taylor, *Anima Poetae: From the Unpublished Notebooks of Samuel Taylor Coleridge,* ed. Ernest Hartley Coleridge (London: William Heinemann, 1845).

—— *Biographia Literaria or Biographical Sketches of My Literary Life and Opinions*, ed. James Engell and W. Jackson Bate, *Collected Works of Samuel Taylor Coleridge*, Vol. 7:1 (Princeton: Princeton University Press, 1983; 1817).

—— *Collected Letters of Samuel Taylor Coleridge,* ed. Earl Leslie Griggs, 6 Vols (Oxford: Clarendon

Press, 2000; 1956).

——The Friend, ed. Barbara E. Rooke, Collected Works, Vol. 4, 2 Vols (London: Routledge and Kegan Paul, 1969).

——The Notebooks of Samuel Taylor Coleridge, ed. Kathleen Coburn, 8 Vols (Princeton: Princeton University Press, 1957–62).

——Poetical Works, Collected Works of Samuel Taylor Coleridge, Vol. 16, ed. J. C. C. Mays (Princeton: Princeton University Press, 2001).

——Poetical Works, ed. E. H. Coleridge (Oxford: Clarendon Press, 1912).

——The Statesman's Manual, The Collected Works of Samuel Taylor Coleridge, Vol. VI, ed. R. J. White, Lay Sermons (Princeton: Princeton University Press, 1972).

Cross, Wilbur, The Life and Times of Laurence Sterne, 2 Vols (New Haven: Yale University Press, 1922).

Dames, Nicholas, Amnesiac Selves: nostalgia, forgetting, and British fiction, 1810–1870 (Oxford: Oxford University Press, 2001).

Deleuze, Gilles, Difference and Repetition, trans. Paul Patton (London: Continuum, 2004; 1968).

——Empiricism and Subjectivity: An Essay on Hume's Theory of Human Nature; trans. Constantin V. Boundas (New York: Columbia University Press, 1991; 1953).

Dickens, Charles, The Personal History of David Copperfield, ed. Trevor Blount (Harmondsworth: Penguin, 1966; 1849–50).

——Hard Times, ed. David Craig (Harmondsworth: Penguin, 1969; 1854).

Dickie, George, The Century of Taste: The Philosophical Odyssey of Taste in the Eighteenth Century (Oxford: Oxford University Press, 1996).

Doherty, Francis, 'Sterne and Hume: A Bicentenary Essay', Essays and Studies XII (1969), 71–88.

Eliot, George, Middlemarch, ed. W. J. Harvey (London: Penguin, 1965; 1871–2) Eliot, T. S., Collected Poems 1909–1962 (London: Faber, 1963).

——Knowledge and Experience in the Philosophy of F. H. Bradley (London: Faber, 1964).

——On Poetry and Poets (London: Faber, 1957).

——The Sacred Wood (London: Faber, 1920).

——Selected Essays (London: Faber and Faber, 1934).

——'Ulysses, Order and Myth', The Dial, November 1923, LXXV, 5, 482–3.

——The Use of Poetry and the Use of Criticism (London: Faber, 1933).

Ellmann, Richard, James Joyce (Oxford: Oxford University Press, 1982).

——Ulysses on the Liffey (London: Faber, 1974).

Engell, James, The Creative Imagination: Enlightenment to Romanticism (Cambridge, MA: Harvard University Press, 1981).

Evans-Pritchard, Edward, A History of Anthropological Thought (London: Faber and Faber, 1981).

Fodor, Jerry A., *Psychosemantics: The Problem of Meaning in the Philosophy of Mind* (Cambridge, MA: MIT Press, 1987).

Forster, John, *Life of Charles Dickens*, 2 Vols (London: Dent, 1927).

Fox, W. J., review of Ebenezer Elliott, *Monthly Repository*, N.S. vi (1832), 190. *Westminster Review*, XIV (January 1831), 210–24.

Fraser, Robert (ed.), *Sir James Frazer and the Literary Imagination: Essays in Affinity and Influence* (London: Macmillan, 1990).

Frazer, J. G., *The Golden Bough* (Edinburgh: Canongate, 2004; 1890).

— *The Golden Bough* (one-volume edition, London: Macmillan, 1922).

— *Psyche's Task* (London: Macmillan, 1909).

Freud, Sigmund, *New Introductory Lectures on Psychoanalysis*, trans. James Strachey, *The Pelican Freud Library*, Vol. 2 (Harmondsworth: Penguin, 1973).

Frye, Northrop, *Anatomy of Criticism: Four Essays* (Princeton: Princeton University Press, 1957).

Gass, William H., 'Unoriginal Sins', *The Times Literary Supplement*, 13–19 January 1989, 27–8.

Gerard, Alexander, *An Essay on Taste* (Menston, Yorkshire: Scolar Press, 1971; 1759).

Gibson, Andrew (ed.), *Pound in Multiple Perspective: A Collection of Critical Essays* (Basingstoke: Macmillan, 1993).

Gifford, Don with Robert J. Seidman, *Ulysses Annotated* (Berkeley: University of California Press, 1988).

Gould, Warwick, 'Frazer and Yeats', in Robert Fraser (ed.), *Sir James Frazer and the Literary Imagination* (London: Macmillan, 1990).

Gourmont, Rémy de, *Le Problème du Style* (Paris, 1902).

Hallam, A. H., 'On Some Characteristics of Modern Poetry', *Englishman's Magazine*, I (August 1831), 616–28.

— *Remains in Verse and Prose of Arthur Henry Hallam* (London: John Murray, 1863).

Hamilton, Sir William, *Lectures on Metaphysics and Logic*, ed. N. H. L. Mansell and John Veitch, 2 Vols (Edinburgh: William Blackwood & Sons, 1865).

Hardy, Florence Emily, *The Life of Thomas Hardy 1840–1928* (London: Macmillan, 1962).

Hardy, Thomas, *The Complete Poems of Thomas Hardy*, ed. James Gibson (London: Macmillan, 1976)

— *The Return of the Native* (London: Macmillan, 1974; 1878)

Hartley, David, *Observations on Man, his Frame, his Duty, and his Expectations* (London: S. Richardson for James Leake and Wm. Frederick, 1749).

— *Observations on Man*, ed. Joseph Priestley (London: J. Johnson, 1775).

Hayles, N. Katharine (ed.), *Chaos and Order: Complex Dynamics in Literature and Science* (Chicago: University of Chicago Press, 1991).

Hazlitt, William, *The Complete Works of William Hazlitt in Twenty-One Volumes*, ed. P. P. Howe (London and Toronto: Routledge, 1930–4).

Hedley, Douglas, *Coleridge, Philosophy and Religion: Aids to Reflection and the Mirror of the Spirit* (Cambridge: Cambridge University Press, 2000).

Hicks, G. Dawes, 'The Philosophy of James Ward', *Mind*, New Series, Vol. 34, No. 135 (July 1925), 280–99.

Hipple, Walter J., *The Beautiful, the Sublime and the Picturesque* (Carbondale: Southern Illinois University Press, 1957).

Holman, C. Hugh, Addison Hibbard and William Flint Thrall (eds), 'The Stream-of-Consciousness Novel', *A Handbook to Literature* (New York: Odyssey Press, 1960).

Holmes, Richard, *Coleridge: Early Visions* (London: Hodder and Stoughton, 1989).

— *Coleridge: Darker Visions* (London: HarperCollins, 1998).

Howes, Alan B., *Sterne: The Critical Heritage* (London: Routledge & Kegan Paul, 1974).

Hume, David, *Enquiries Concerning the Human Understanding and Concerning the Principles of Morals*, ed. L.A. Selby-Bigge (Oxford: Clarendon Press, 1962; 1777).

— *Essays Moral, Political and Literary*, ed. Eugene F. Miller (Indianapolis: Liberty Fund, 1985).

— *History of England from the Invasion of Julius Caesar to the Abdication of James the Second*, 8 Vols (London: A. Millar, 1763).

— *A Treatise of Human Nature*, ed. L. A. Selby-Bigge (Oxford: Clarendon Press, 1888).

— *Letters of David Hume*, ed. J. Y. T. Greig, 2 Vols (Oxford: Clarendon Press, 1932).

Hutcheson, Francis, *Philosophical Writings*, ed. R. S. Downie (London: Dent, 1994).

Iser, Wolfgang, *Walter Pate: The Aesthetic Moment*, trans. David Henry Wilson (Cambridge: Cambridge University Press, 1987; 1960).

James, William, *The Principles of Psychology*, 2 Vols (Cambridge, MA: Harvard University Press, 1981; 1890).

— *Talks to Teachers on Psychology* (Cambridge, MA: Harvard University Press, 1983; 1899).

Jeffrey, Francis, review of Alison's *Essays on Taste*, *Edinburgh Review*, Vol. XVIII, No. XXXV (May 1811), 1–45.

Jolas, Eugene, 'My Friend James Joyce', S. Givens (ed.), *James Joyce: Two Decades of Criticism* (New York: Vanguard Press, 1948).

Joyce, James, *Ulysses*, ed. Hans Walter Gabler (London: Penguin, 1986).

Kaiser, David Aram, *Romanticism, Aesthetics and Nationalism* (Cambridge: Cambridge University Press, 1999).

Kallich, Martin, *The Association of Ideas and Critical Theory in Eighteenth-century England* (The Hague: Mouton, 1970).

Kearns, Michael S., 'Associationism, the Heart, and the Life of the Mind in Dickens' Novels', *Dickens Studies*, 15 (1986), 111–44.

Kenner, Hugh, *Joyce's Voices* (London: Faber and Faber, 1978).

Kermode, Frank, *Romantic Image* (London: Routledge and Kegan Paul, 1957).

Kivy, Peter, *The Seventh Sense: A Study of Francis Hutcheson's Aesthetics and its Influence in Eighteenth-*

Century Britain (Oxford: Clarendon Press, 2003; 1976).

Kumar, Udaya, *The Joycean Labyrinth: Repetition, Time and Tradition in* Ulysses (Oxford: Clarendon Press, 1991).

Lamb, Jonathan, *Sterne's Fiction and the Double Principle* (Cambridge: Cambridge University Press, 1990).

Lawrence, Karen, *The Odyssey of Style in Ulysses* (Princeton: Princeton University Press, 1981).

Leavis, F. R. (ed.), *Mill on Bentham and Coleridge* (London: Chatto & Windus, 1950).

Livingston, Donald W., *Hume's Philosophy of Common Life* (Chicago: University of Chicago Press, 1984).

Locke, John, *An Essay Concerning Human Understanding*, ed. Peter H. Nidditch (Oxford: Clarendon Press, 1975).

Lockhart, J. G., *Memoirs of Sir Walter Scott*, 10 Vols (Edinburgh: Adam and Charles Black, 1869; 1836).

— 'Remarks on Godwin's New Novel, *Mandeville*', *Blackwood's Edinburgh Magazine*, 2 (December 1817): 26.

Lowes, John Livingston, *The Road to Xanadu: A Study in the Ways of the Imagination* (2nd edition, London: Constable, 1951; 1927).

Mackey, Peter Francis, *Chaos Theory and James Joyce's Everyman* (Gainesville: University of Florida Press, 1999).

Macpherson, James, *The Poems of Ossian and Related Works*, ed. Howard Gaskill (Edinburgh: Edinburgh University Press, 1996).

Madtes, Richard E., *The 'Ithaca' Chapter of Joyce's Ulysses* (Ann Arbor: UMI Research Press, 1983).

Maher, Michael, *Psychology* (London: Longmans, Green & Co., 1890).

Masson, David, *Recent British Philosophy: A Review with Criticisms* (London: Macmillan, 1865).

McCabe, Colin, *James Joyce and the Revolution of the Word* (London: Macmillan, 1979).

McGrath, F. C., 'Pater Speaking Bloom Speaking Joyce', Laurel Brake and Ian Small (eds), *Pater in the 1990s* (Greensboro: ELT Press, 1991), 95–105.

McNeice, Gerald, *The Knowledge that Endures: Coleridge, German Philosophy and the Logic of Romantic Thought* (Basingstoke: Macmillan, 1992).

Mepham, John, *Virginia Woolf: A Literary Life* (Basingstoke: Macmillan, 1991).

Mill, James, *Analysis of the Phenomena of the Human Mind, A new edition with notes illustrative and critical by Alexander Bain, Andrew Findlater, and George Grote*, edited with additional notes by John Stuart Mill, 2 Vols (London: Longman, Green, Reader and Dyer, 1869; 1829).

Mill, John Stuart, *Collected Works of John Stuart Mill*, ed. John M Robson and Jack Sillinger, 33 Vols (Toronto: University of Toronto Press, 1969–1991).

Miller, J. Hillis, *Charles Dickens: The World of his Novels* (Cambridge, MA: Harvard University Press, 1958).

— 'Tradition and Difference', *Diacritics* 2 (1972), 6–13, review of M. H. Abrams, *Natural Supernaturalism.*

Monk, Samuel, *The Sublime* (New York: Modern Language Association of America, 1935).

Morley, Henry, *English Writers: An Attempt towards a History of English Literature,* 11 Vols (London: Cassell, 1887).

Muirhead, J. H., *The Platonic Tradition in Anglo-Saxon Philosophy* (London: George Allen & Unwin, 1931).

Ogden, C. K. and I. A. Richards, *The Meaning of Meaning* (London: Kegan, Paul, Trench, Trubner, 1923).

Owenson, Sydney, Lady Morgan, *The Wild Irish Girl*, ed. Kathryn Kirkpatrick (Oxford: Oxford University Press, 1999).

Passmore, J. A, *Hume's Intentions* (Cambridge: Cambridge University Press).

Pater, Walter, *Appreciations: With an Essay on Style* (London: Macmillan, 1889).

— *Plato and Platonism* (London: Library Edition, 1910).

— *The Renaissance*, ed. Kenneth Clark (London: Fontana/Collins, 1961; 1873).

Paulin, Tom, *The Day-Star of Liberty: William Hazlitt's Radical Style* (London: Faber and Faber, 1998).

— *Thomas Hardy: The Poetry of Perception* (London: Macmillan, 1975).

Perse, St-John, *Anabase*, trans. T. S. Eliot (London: Faber and Faber, 1959).

Pope, Alexander, *The Poems of Alexander Pope,* ed. John Butt (London: Methuen, 1963).

Pound, Ezra, *Literary Essays of Ezra Pound*, ed. T. S. Eliot (London: Faber and Faber, 1960).

Priestley, Joseph, *A Course of Lectures on Oratory and Criticism* (Menston, Yorkshire: Scolar Press, 1970; 1777).

— *Institutes of Natural and Revealed Religion,* 2nd edn, 2 Vols (Birmingham, 1782; 1772).

Prigogine, Ilya and Isabelle Stengers, *Order out of Chaos: Man's New Dialogue with Nature* (London: Heinemann, 1984).

Ransom, John Crowe, *The New Criticism* (Westport: Greenwood Press, 1979; 1941).

Reed, Edward S., *From Soul to Mind: The Emergence of Psychology from Erasmus Darwin to William James* (New Haven and London: Yale University Press, 1997).

Reid, Thomas, *The Works of Thomas Reid, D. D.*, Preface, Notes and Supplementary Dissertations by Sir William Hamilton, Bart (Edinburgh: Maclachlan and Stewart, 1863).

— *Thomas Reid, Inquiry and Essay*, ed. Ronald E. Beanblossom and Keith Lehrer (Indianapolis: Hackett Publishing, 1983).

Rice, Thomas Jackson, *Joyce, Chaos and Complexity* (Urbana: University of Illinois Press, 1997).

Richards, David, 'A Tour of Babel', Robert Fraser (ed.), *Sir James Frazer and the Literary Imagination* (London: Macmillan, 1990), 81–101.

Richards, I. A., *Coleridge on Imagination* (London: Kegan, Paul, Trench, Trubner, 1934).

— *The Philosophy of Rhetoric* (Oxford: Oxford University Press, 1936).

— *Practical Criticism* (London: Kegan Paul, Trench, Trubner, 1929).

— *Principles of Literary Criticism* (London: Routledge, 1967; 1924).

Richardson, Alan, *British Romanticism and the Science of the Mind* (Cambridge: Cambridge University Press, 2001).

Richetti, John J. (ed.), *The Cambridge Companion to the Eighteenth-Century Novel* (Cambridge: Cambridge University Press).

— *Philosophical Writing: Locke, Berkeley, Hume* (Cambridge, MA: Harvard University Press, 1983).

Rickard, John S., *Joyce's Book of Memory: The Mnemotechnics of Ulysses* (Durham, SC: Duke University Press, 1999).

Roughley, Alan, *James Joyce and Critical Theory: An Introduction* (Hemel Hempstead: Harvester Wheatsheaf, 1991).

Rylance, Rick, *Victorian Psychology and British Culture, 1850–1880* (Oxford: Oxford University Press, 2000).

Saussure, Ferdinand de, *Course in General Linguistics*, trans. Wade Biskin (London: Fontana, 1974; 1916).

Scott, Walter, *Ivanhoe*, ed. Ian Duncan (Oxford: Oxford University Press, 1996).

— *Waverley*, ed. Andrew Hook (Harmondsworth: Penguin, 1972).

Serres, Michel, *Hermes: Literature, Science, Philosophy* , ed. Josué V. Harari and David F. Bell (Baltimore: Johns Hopkins University Press, 1982).

Sim, Stuart, 'Sterne. Chaos. Complexity', *Eighteenth Century Novel*, I (2001), 201–15.

Skorupski, John, *Symbol and Theory: A Philosophical Study of Theories of Religion in Social Anthropology* (Cambridge: Cambridge University Press, 1976).

Smith, Adam, *Essays on Philosophical Subjects*, ed. W. P. Wightman and J. C. Bryce (Indianapolis: Liberty Fund, 1982).

Smith, Crosbie and M. Norton Wise, *Energy and Empire: A Biographical Study of Lord Kelvin* (Cambridge: Cambridge University Press, 1989).

Smith, Norman Kemp, *The Philosophy of David Hume: A Critical Study of its Origins and Central Doctrines* (London: Macmillan, 1966; 1941).

Smollett, Tobias, *The Expedition of Humphry Clinker*, ed. Angus Ross (London: Penguin, 1965).

Snyder, Alice D., *Coleridge on Logic and Learning, with Selections from the Unpublished Manuscripts* (New Haven: Yale University Press, 1929).

Spencer, Herbert, *Pinciples of Psychology* (London: Longman, 1855).

Spoo, Robert, 'Teleology, Monocausality, and Marriage in Ulysses', *ELH*, Vol. 56, No. 2 (Summer 1989), 439–62.

Stafford, Fiona J., '"Dangerous Success": Ossian, Wordsworth, and English Romantic Literature', in Howard Gaskill (ed.), *Ossian Revisited* (Edinburgh: Edinburgh University Press, 1991).

Steinberg, Erwin R. (ed.), *The Stream-of-Consciousness Technique in the Modern Novel* (Port

Washington, New York: Kennikat Press, 1979).

Steiner, George, *On Difficulty and Other Essays* (Oxford: Oxford University Press, 1972).

Stephen, Leslie, *English Thought in the Eighteenth Century*, 2 Vols (London: Smith, Elder and Co.,
    1902; 1876).

Sterne, Laurence, *The Life and Opinions of Tristram Shandy*, ed. Graham Petrie (London: Penguin,
    1967; 1760).

Stewart, Dugald, *The Collected Works of Dugald Stewart, Volume 1, Dissertation: Exhibiting the Progress
    of Metaphysical, Ethical and Political Philosophy, since the Revival of Letters in Europe*, ed. Sir
    William Hamilton (Bristol: Thoemmes Press, 1994; 1854-60)

— *The Collected Works of Dugald Stewart, Volume II, Elements of the Philosophy of the Human Mind*, ed.
    Sir William Hamilton (Bristol: Thoemmes Press, 1994; 1854–60).

Stirling, J. Hutchison, 'Kant has not answered Hume', *Mind*, Vol. 9, Issue 36 (October 1884);
    Vol. 10; Issue 37 (January 1885).

Stout, G. F., *Manual of Psychology* (London: W. B. Clive, 1913; 1898).

Sully, James, *Outlines of Psychology* (London: Longmans, Green, 1884).

— *My Life and Friends: A Psychologist's Memories* (London: T. Fisher Unwin, 1918).

— *Sensation and Intuition: Studies in Psychology and Aesthetics* (London: C. Kegan Paul, 1880).

Sutton, John, *Philosophy and Memory Traces: Descartes to Connectionism* (Cambridge: Cambridge
    University Press, 1998).

Symons, Arthur, *The Symbolist Movement in Literature* (New York: E. P. Dutton and Co., 1958;
    1899, rev. edn, 1919).

Tennyson, Alfred, *The Poems of Tennyson*, ed. Christopher Ricks (London: Longmans, 1969)

Townsend, Dabney, 'The Aesthetics of Joseph Priestley', *The Journal of Aesthetics and Art Criticism*,
    Vol. 51, No. 4 (Autumn 1993), 561–71.

Traugott, John, *Tristram Shandy's World: Sterne's Philosophical Rhetoric* (Berkeley: University of
    California Press, 1954).

Turk, Christopher, *Coleridge and Mill: A Study of Influence* (Aldershot: Avebury, 1988).

Ward, A. W. and A. R. Waller (eds), *The Cambridge History of English Literature*, 15 Vols (Cambridge:
    Cambridge University Press, 1907).

Ward, James, *Heredity and Memory, being the Henry Sidgwick Memorial Lecture delivered at Newnham
    College, 9 November 1912* (Cambridge: Cambridge University Press, 1913).

— *Psychological Principles* (Cambridge: Cambridge University Press, 1918).

— 'Psychology', *Encyclopaedia Britannica*, 9th Edition, Vol. XX (Edinburgh: A&C Black, 1886).

Watson, J. R., *English Poetry of the Romantic Period 1789–1830* (London: Longman, 1992).

Watt, Ian, *The Rise of the Novel* (Berkeley: University of California Press, 1957).

Welsh, Alexander, *From Copyright to Copperfield: The Identity of Dickens* (Cambridge, MA: Harvard
    University Press, 1987).

Wilbanks, Jan, *Hume's Theory Of Imagination* (The Hague: Martinus Nijhoff, 1968).

Wimsatt, W. K., *The Verbal Icon: Studies in the Meaning of Poetry* (London: Methuen, 1970; 1954).

Woolf, Virginia, *A Writer's Diary: Being Extracts from the Diary of Virginia Woolf*, ed. Leonard Woolf (London: Hogarth Press, 1953).

—*The Essays of Virginia Woolf, Vol. II, 1912–1918*, ed. Andrew McNeillie (London: Hogarth Press, 1987).

—*The Essays of Virginia Woolf, Vol. III, 1919–1924*, ed. Andrew McNeillie (London: Hogarth Press, 1988).

—*The Essays of Virginia Woolf Vol. IV, 1925–1928,* ed. Andrew McNeillie (London: Hogarth Press, 1994).

—*The Waves*, ed. Gillian Beer (Oxford: Oxford University Press, 1992).

—*To the Lighthouse* (Harmondsworth: Penguin, 1964; 1927).

Wordsworth, William, *The Letters of William and Dorothy Wordsworth, Second Edition, Vol. I, The Early Years 1787–1805*, ed. Ernest de Selincourt (Oxford: Clarendon Press, 1967).

—*William Wordsworth*, ed. Stephen Gill (Oxford: Oxford University Press, 1984).

Work, James (ed.), *Tristram Shandy* (New York: Odyssey Press, 1940).

Yeats, W. B., *Autobiographies* (London: Macmillan, 1955).

—*Collected Poems of W. B. Yeats* (London: Macmillan, 1950).

—*Essays* (London: Macmillan, 1924).

—*Essays and Introductions* (London: Macmillan, 1961).

—*Explorations* (London: Macmillan, 1962).

—*Memoirs*, ed. Denis Donoghue (London: Macmillan, 1972).

—*The Oxford Book of Modern Verse 1892–1935* (Oxford: Clarendon Press, 1936).

—*Uncollected Prose, 1886–1896*, Vol. 1, ed. John P. Frayne (London: Macmillan, 1970).

—*Uncollected Prose, 1897–1939*, Vol. 2, ed. John P. Frayne and Colton Johnson (London: Macmillan, 1975).

Young, Robert M., 'The Association of Ideas', ed. Philip P. Wiener, *Dictionary of the History of Ideas* (New York: Scribner's, 1968), Vol. 1, 111–18.

Index